EDEXCEL INTERNATIONAL GCSE (9–1)
ENGLISH LANGUAGE A
Student Book

Roger Addison
Samantha Brunner
David Foster
Peter Inson
Robert O'Brien
Pam Taylor
Manjari Tennakoon

Published by Pearson Education Limited,
80 Strand, London, WC2R 0RL.

www.pearsonglobalschools.com

Copies of official specifications for all Pearson qualifications may be found on the website: https://qualifications.pearson.com

Text © Pearson Education Limited 2016
Edited by Lauren Bickley, Fleur Frederick and Andrew Lowe
Designed by Cobalt id
Typeset by Phoenix Photosetting, Chatham, Kent
Original illustrations © Pearson Education Limited 2016
Cover design by Pearson Education Limited
Picture research by Ann Thomson
Cover photo/illustration © Getty Images: Toby C

The rights of Roger Addison, Samantha Brunner, David Foster, Peter Inson, Robert O'Brien, Pam Taylor and Manjari Tennakoon to be identified as authors of this work have been asserted by them in accordance with the Copyright, Designs and Patents Act 1988.

First published 2016

21 20 19 18

11 10 9 8 7 6 5

British Library Cataloguing in Publication Data
A catalogue record for this book is available from the British Library

ISBN 978 0 435 18256 4

Copyright notice
All rights reserved. No part of this publication may be reproduced in any form or by any means (including photocopying or storing it in any medium by electronic means and whether or not transiently or incidentally to some other use of this publication) without the written permission of the copyright owner, except in accordance with the provisions of the Copyright, Designs and Patents Act 1988 or under the terms of a licence issued by the Copyright Licensing Agency, Barnard's Inn, 86 Fetter Lane, London EC4A 1EN (www.cla.co.uk). Applications for the copyright owner's written permission should be addressed to the publisher.

Printed in Slovakia by Neografia

Endorsement Statement
In order to ensure that this resource offers high-quality support for the associated Pearson qualification, it has been through a review process by the awarding body. This process confirms that this resource fully covers the teaching and learning content of the specification or part of a specification at which it is aimed. It also confirms that it demonstrates an appropriate balance between the development of subject skills, knowledge and understanding, in addition to preparation for assessment.

Endorsement does not cover any guidance on assessment activities or processes (e.g. practice questions or advice on how to answer assessment questions), included in the resource nor does it prescribe any particular approach to the teaching or delivery of a related course.

While the publishers have made every attempt to ensure that advice on the qualification and its assessment is accurate, the official specification and associated assessment guidance materials are the only authoritative source of information and should always be referred to for definitive guidance.

Pearson examiners have not contributed to any sections in this resource relevant to examination papers for which they have responsibility.

Examiners will not use endorsed resources as a source of material for any assessment set by Pearson. Endorsement of a resource does not mean that the resource is required to achieve this Pearson qualification, nor does it mean that it is the only suitable material available to support the qualification, and any resource lists produced by the awarding body shall include this and other appropriate resources.

INTRODUCTION TO THE COURSE	**VI**
ABOUT THIS BOOK	**VIII**
ASSESSMENT OVERVIEW	**X**
01 READING SKILLS	**2**
02 WRITING SKILLS	**24**
03 PAPER 1	**56**
04 PAPER 2	**208**
05 PAPER 3	**310**
EXAM PREPARATION	**326**
GLOSSARY	**330**
INDEX	**332**

COURSE STRUCTURE

2 READING SKILLS

4 TEXT ANALYSIS
- 4 SKIMMING AND SCANNING
- 6 EXPLICIT AND IMPLICIT MEANING
- 8 POINT – EVIDENCE – EXPLAIN
- 10 EVALUATING A TEXT

16 USE OF LANGUAGE
- 16 WORD CLASSES
- 18 CONNOTATIONS
- 20 DIFFERENT SENTENCE TYPES
- 22 SENTENCES FOR EFFECT

24 WRITING SKILLS

26 VOCABULARY
- 26 CHOOSING THE RIGHT VOCABULARY
- 28 VOCABULARY FOR EFFECT
- 30 LANGUAGE FOR DIFFERENT EFFECTS
- 32 WHY YOUR CHOICES MATTER

34 SENTENCES
- 34 SENTENCE TYPES
- 36 OPENING SENTENCES
- 38 SENTENCES FOR EFFECT
- 40 SENTENCE PURPOSE

42 STRUCTURE
- 42 PRINCIPLES OF STRUCTURE
- 44 PARAGRAPHING FOR EFFECT
- 46 LINKING IDEAS

48 PUNCTUATION AND SPELLING
- 48 ENDING A SENTENCE
- 49 COMMAS
- 50 APOSTROPHES
- 51 COLONS, SEMI-COLONS, DASHES, BRACKETS, ELLIPSES
- 52 COMMON SPELLING ERRORS
- 53 IMPROVE YOUR WRITING
- 54 PROOF-READING, CHECKING AND EDITING

56 PAPER 1

58 NON-FICTION TEXTS
- 58 TYPES OF TEXT
- 78 IDENTIFYING THE WRITER'S PERSPECTIVE
- 82 AUDIENCE AND PURPOSE
- 84 LANGUAGE FOR DIFFERENT EFFECTS
- 88 FACT, OPINION AND EXPERT ADVICE
- 90 THE STRUCTURE OF A TEXT
- 92 UNSEEN TEXTS
- 94 PUTTING IT INTO PRACTICE

96 TEXT ANTHOLOGY: NON-FICTION
- 96 *'THE DANGER OF A SINGLE STORY'* – CHIMAMANDA NGOZI ADICHIE
- 103 *A PASSAGE TO AFRICA* – GEORGE ALAGIAH
- 108 *THE EXPLORER'S DAUGHTER* – KARI HERBERT
- 113 *EXPLORERS, OR BOYS MESSING ABOUT* – STEVEN MORRIS
- 117 *BETWEEN A ROCK AND A HARD PLACE* – ARON RALSTON
- 122 *'YOUNG AND DYSLEXIC? YOU'VE GOT IT GOING ON'* – BENJAMIN ZEPHANIAH
- 129 *A GAME OF POLO WITH A HEADLESS GOAT* – EMMA LEVINE

134	*BEYOND THE SKY AND THE EARTH: A JOURNEY INTO BHUTAN* – JAMIE ZEPPA
141	*H IS FOR HAWK* – HELEN MACDONALD
147	*CHINESE CINDERELLA* – ADELINE YEN MAH

152 COMPARING TEXTS

152	IDENTIFYING KEY INFORMATION
154	ANALYSING THE TEXTS
162	COMPARISONS
168	SELECTING EVIDENCE
170	PUTTING IT INTO PRACTICE

174 TRANSACTIONAL WRITING

174	AN INTRODUCTION TO TRANSACTIONAL WRITING
176	WRITING FOR A PURPOSE: INFORM, EXPLAIN, REVIEW
180	WRITING FOR A PURPOSE: ARGUE, PERSUADE, ADVISE
184	WRITING FOR AN AUDIENCE
188	FORM
194	VOCABULARY FOR EFFECT
198	SENTENCES FOR EFFECT
200	OPENINGS AND CONCLUSIONS
202	IDEAS AND PLANNING
204	PUTTING IT INTO PRACTICE

208 PAPER 2

210 READING SKILLS: FICTION TEXTS

210	TYPES OF TEXT
212	FIGURATIVE LANGUAGE
216	CREATING CHARACTER, ATMOSPHERE AND EMOTION
220	NARRATIVE VOICE
222	STRUCTURE
226	PUTTING IT INTO PRACTICE

228 TEXT ANTHOLOGY: FICTION

228	'DISABLED' – WILFRED OWEN
232	'OUT, OUT—' – ROBERT FROST
236	'AN UNKNOWN GIRL' – MONIZA ALVI
241	'THE BRIGHT LIGHTS OF SARAJEVO' – TONY HARRISON
249	'STILL I RISE' – MAYA ANGELOU
256	'THE STORY OF AN HOUR' – KATE CHOPIN
260	'THE NECKLACE' – GUY DE MAUPASSANT
269	'SIGNIFICANT CIGARETTES' (FROM *THE ROAD HOME*) – ROSE TREMAIN
275	'WHISTLE AND I'LL COME TO YOU' (FROM *THE WOMAN IN BLACK*) – SUSAN HILL
283	'NIGHT' – ALICE MUNRO

288 IMAGINATIVE WRITING

288	OVERVIEW OF IMAGINATIVE WRITING
290	GENERATING IDEAS
292	PLOT
294	STRUCTURE
296	NARRATION
298	CHARACTERS
300	MONOLOGUES AND DIALOGUES
302	DESCRIPTIVE WRITING
304	VOCABULARY FOR EFFECT
306	SENTENCES FOR EFFECT
308	PUTTING IT INTO PRACTICE

310 PAPER 3

312	AN INTRODUCTION TO COURSEWORK
314	ASSIGNMENT A: POETRY AND PROSE TEXTS
319	ASSIGNMENT B: IMAGINATIVE WRITING

326 EXAM PREPARATION

330 GLOSSARY

332 INDEX

INTRODUCTION TO THE COURSE

This book has been written to help all students taking the Pearson Edexcel International GCSE English Language A (**4EA1**) (first examination June 2018). It is designed to enable them to achieve their full potential during the course and in the exam. It is written for both students and teachers. There are two specifications for the International GCSE course, English Language A (4EA1) and English Language B (4EB1).

This book is written to support specification A. Specification A of the International GCSE has two routes: one assessed entirely through exams and one that includes coursework. This book will prepare students for all aspects of the course.

STUDENTS

How will this book support you? We hope you will find it:

- useful in terms of developing your skills and techniques fully for the Pearson Edexcel International GCSE in English Language
- a helpful guide to your study of the selected texts from the Pearson Edexcel Anthology for the International GCSE
- a support in preparing for unseen passages.

This book will also assist you in writing your coursework and planning your revision.

STUDENTS AND TEACHERS

The book goes through the requirements for specification A, with explanations, suggestions and questions. It also includes a large number of practical activities and examples. These are for practice and will also help you to appreciate how really good answers are written and structured.

> **HINT**
> Remember to plan your work. The sooner you organise yourself and your ideas, the easier you will find your preparation for every section of the exam! This book aims to give you confidence by improving your skills and techniques.

KNOW YOUR TEXTS

It is very important to make sure that you have a really good grasp of the selected fiction and non-fiction passages and poems from Section A and Section B of the Anthology. Every year, examiners read International GCSE scripts in which the candidates write in a way that shows that they do not understand, or have not prepared carefully for, the texts that are set. Use the relevant sections from this book to strengthen your knowledge of the texts.

USE YOUR SOURCES

An important part of Paper 1 is the test of your ability to think quickly when confronted with unfamiliar (unseen) prose passages, to show that you have understood and responded to these passages, and that you can base your own writing on the ideas that you have met in these passages. Work through the 'Types of text' section in order to ensure that you are ready to read and analyse a variety of unseen passages in Paper 1.

KNOW AND APPLY YOUR TECHNICAL TERMS

Like other subjects, English has a number of technical terms which you may need to use. It is important that you know how to use the correct term and that you can spell it. Refer to the subject vocabulary within the margins of this book or the Glossary on pages 330–331 to help you. Even more importantly, you need to know how to explain why a particular device is used by looking at the writer's intentions. In your exams, you will always be given credit for explaining the effects of a word or phrase, whether or not you use the technical terms, but accurate use of the correct terms will make your writing more fluent and concise.

> **HINT**
> Make lists of technical terms and write out what you think they mean, then check your definitions against the glossary at the back of the book or the subject vocabulary in the margins.

IMPROVE THE STRUCTURE AND ORGANISATION OF YOUR ANSWERS
Look closely at the model answers that are given at various points throughout this book. This will help you to write detailed, successful responses.

PRESENT YOUR WORK EFFECTIVELY
The way in which you set out your own writing is important. You should practise producing writing that is:

- neat, regular and clear
- spelled accurately
- correctly punctuated
- set out in clear paragraphs.

Doing this will give you the following benefits.

- Examiners will form a positive impression of your work.
- Examiners will be able to read your answer easily; they will not be able to do so if your handwriting is poor or if it is not written in proper sentences.
- How you write, as well as what you write, will be considered when your work is marked.
- Good writing is useful for applications for jobs or college courses.
- Many jobs require the ability to write clearly, accurately and precisely.

KNOW YOUR OWN STRENGTHS AND WEAKNESSES
It is an excellent idea to keep a checklist of your most common errors in spelling, punctuation and grammar, since these are assessed in all specifications. When you receive a piece of work back from your teacher, read it through and make sure that you understand any comments or corrections.

- Keep a sheet of paper at the front or back of your folder, on which you can write out the correct spelling of words you have misspelled.
- Refer to this before handing in your work to make sure you have not made the same mistakes as before.
- Take some time to learn the spellings on your list.

▼ REMEMBER!
- Make the best use of lesson time.
- Make sure you know what you have to do in class.
- Be sure you understand what the homework is.
- If you are doing the coursework route, check what your coursework assignments are.

▼ MAKE NOTES!
- Write down key points from: teachers; books you read; class work; articles or worksheets.
- For International GCSE Specification A or the Certificate: annotate your copy of the Anthology carefully.
- Add points missed onto the end of your homework or practice questions when they are returned to you.

▼ SEEK HELP!
- Ask teachers to explain if you are unsure.
- Discuss with friends.
- Look things up using dictionaries, encyclopaedias and the internet.

▼ TAKE PART!
- Ask questions in class.
- Answer questions in class.
- Contribute to discussions.
- Be fully involved in group work. Don't let others do all the talking!

▼ KEEP UP!
- Hand in your work on time.
- Keep files or exercise books up to date.
- Make sure you do not get behind with your homework.
- Do not leave work unfinished. It is always difficult to remember what has been missed unless you amend it at the time.
- Check off completed work in your records.

▼ BE ORGANISED!
- Have a clear filing system for your work.
- Present your work neatly.
- Set yourself targets.
- Stick to deadlines.

HINT
Use a system such as different coloured cards or sticky notes to write down the **key points** on each text.

ABOUT THIS BOOK

This book is written for students following the Pearson Edexcel International GCSE (9–1) English Language A specification and covers both years of the course. The specification and sample assessment materials for English Language A can be found on the Pearson Qualifications website.

The course has been structured so that teaching and learning can take place in any order, both in the classroom and in any independent learning. The book contains five chapters: Reading Skills, Writing Skills, Paper 1, Paper 2 and Paper 3.

The Reading Skills and Writing Skills chapters cover fundamental areas of these two key areas of English Language.

Key points
Easy to understand, core points to be taken away from sections or texts.

Pearson Progression
Sample student answers have been given a **Pearson Step** from 1 to 12. This tells you how well the response has met the criteria in the **Pearson Progression Map**.

Exam-style questions
Questions tailored to the Pearson Edexcel specification to allow for practice and development of exam writing technique.

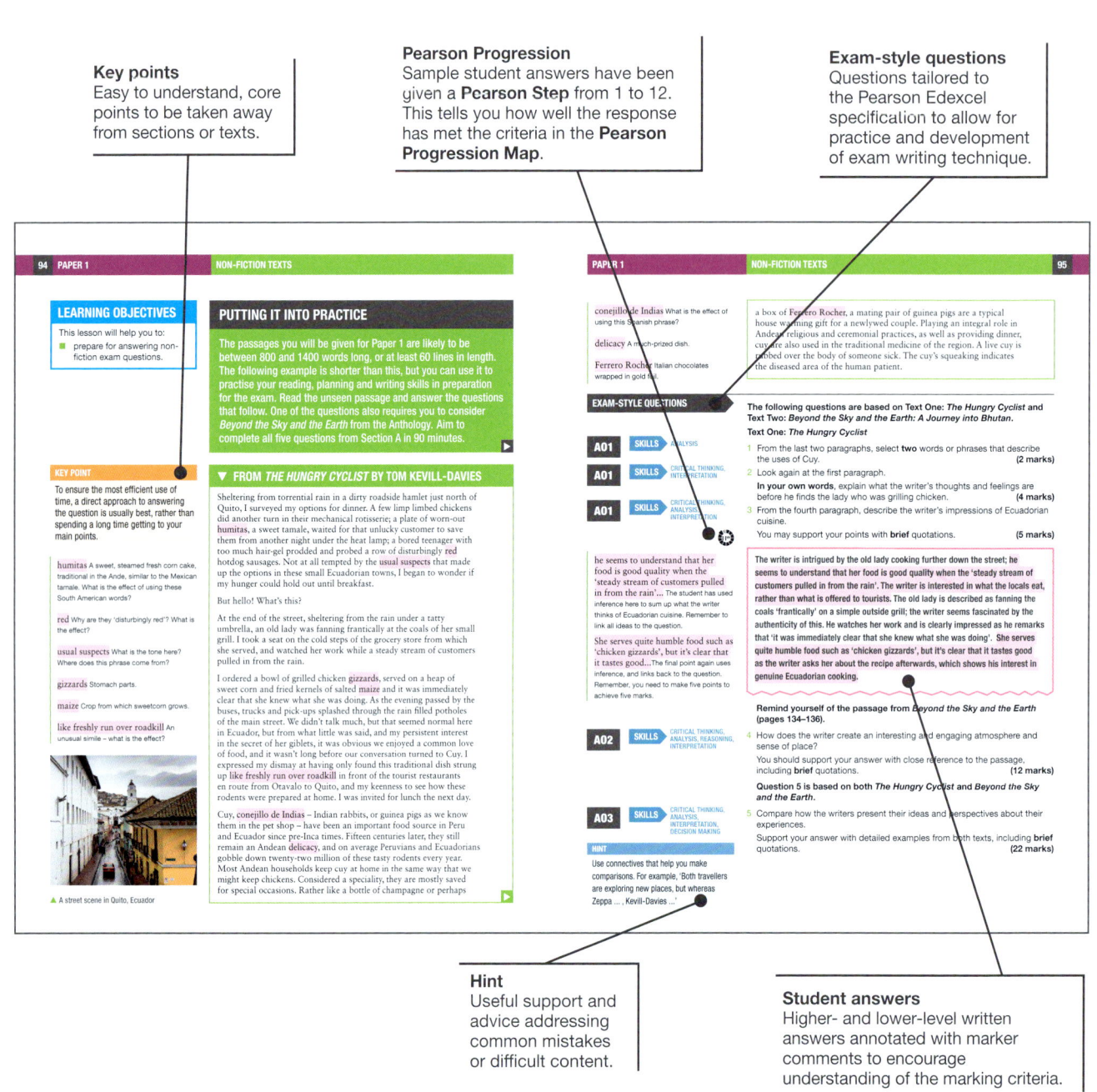

Hint
Useful support and advice addressing common mistakes or difficult content.

Student answers
Higher- and lower-level written answers annotated with marker comments to encourage understanding of the marking criteria.

ABOUT THIS BOOK

They build on and reinforce what students already know and develop essential skills that will allow them to succeed on this course. These chapters can be used to teach these reading and writing skills in blocks at the start of the course or integrated into relevant sections of the texts being studied.

The Paper 1 and Paper 2 chapters cover all of the content required by the course, mirroring the two exam papers for those taking this route. The information in the Paper 2 chapter will also help students taking the coursework route to prepare to complete their assignments. This is also supplemented by the Paper 3 chapter, which gives advice for those taking this coursework paper.

For each section or Anthology text, information is interspersed with activities in order to put learning into practice and exam-style questions to help you prepare and practise for the exam. Other features help to expand students' knowledge and reinforce their learning. All Anthology texts are reproduced in full, with detailed analysis and questions for each text.

You can find more information about the English Language A course, including the Specification and the Sample Assessment Materials, on the Pearson Edexcel website.

Learning objectives
Chapters and Units are carefully tailored to address key assessment objectives central to the course

Activities
A wide range of varied activities to encourage understanding and embed understanding as an individual, as well as in larger groups to establish cross-peer learning and communication.

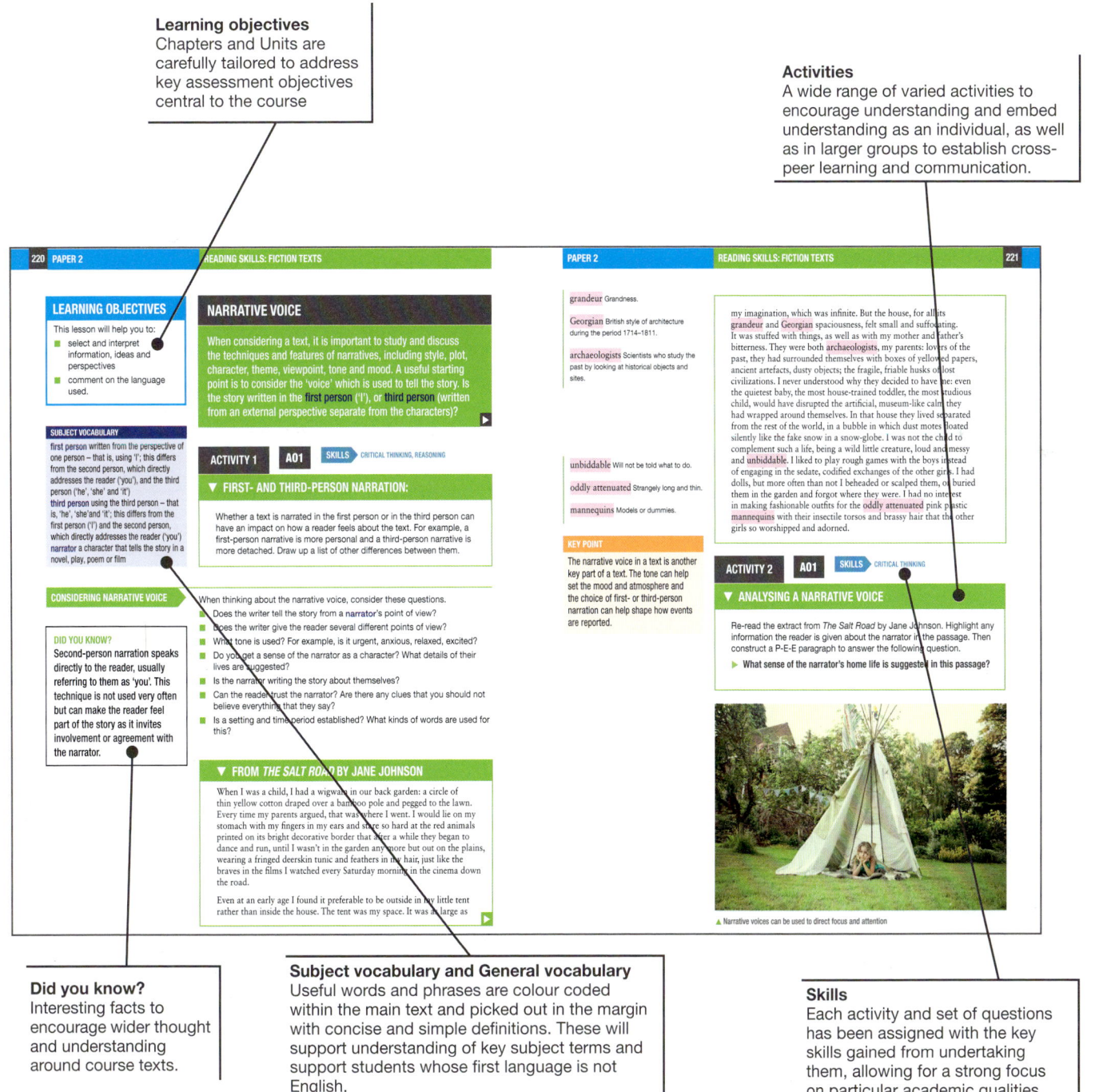

Did you know?
Interesting facts to encourage wider thought and understanding around course texts.

Subject vocabulary and General vocabulary
Useful words and phrases are colour coded within the main text and picked out in the margin with concise and simple definitions. These will support understanding of key subject terms and support students whose first language is not English.

Skills
Each activity and set of questions has been assigned with the key skills gained from undertaking them, allowing for a strong focus on particular academic qualities.

ASSESSMENT OVERVIEW

The following tables give an overview of the assessment for this course. You should study this information closely to help ensure that you are fully prepared for this course and know exactly what to expect in each part of the assessment.

There are two alternative routes that can be taken:

Route 1: 100% written exam papers (Paper 1 and Paper 2).

Route 2: 60% written examination paper and 40% internally assessed coursework (Paper 1 and Paper 3).

Paper 1 is the compulsory unit for all students taking International GCSE English Language A. Paper 2 is taken by those opting for the 100% exam route (Route 1). Those International GCSE students who opt for coursework take Paper 3 instead of Paper 2 (Route 2).

✈ ROUTE 1

▼ PAPER 1	▼ PERCENTAGE	▼ MARKS	▼ TIME	▼ AVAILABILITY
NON-FICTION TEXTS AND TRANSACTIONAL WRITING Written exam paper Paper code 4EA1/01 Externally set and assessed by Pearson Edexcel Single tier of entry	60%	90	2 hours 15 minutes	January and June exam series First assessment June 2018

▼ PAPER 2	▼ PERCENTAGE	▼ MARKS	▼ TIME	▼ AVAILABILITY
POETRY AND PROSE TEXTS AND IMAGINATIVE WRITING Written exam paper Paper code 4EA1/02 Externally set and assessed by Pearson Edexcel Single tier of entry	40%	60	1 hour 30 minutes	January and June exam series First assessment June 2018

ASSESSMENT OVERVIEW

ROUTE 2

▼ PAPER 1	▼ PERCENTAGE	▼ MARKS	▼ TIME	▼ AVAILABILITY
NON-FICTION AND TRANSACTIONAL WRITING Written exam paper Paper code 4EA1/01 Externally set and assessed by Pearson Edexcel Single tier of entry	60%	90	2 hours 15 minutes	January and June exam series First assessment June 2018

▼ PAPER 3	▼ PERCENTAGE	▼ MARKS	▼ TIME	▼ AVAILABILITY
POETRY AND PROSE TEXTS AND IMAGINATIVE WRITING Coursework Paper code 4EA1/03 Two teacher-devised assignments, internally set and assessed, and externally moderated by Pearson Edexcel	40%	60	n/a	January and June exam series First assessment June 2018

ASSESSMENT OBJECTIVES AND WEIGHTINGS

▼ SECTION	▼ ASSESSMENT OBJECTIVE	▼ DESCRIPTION	▼ % IN INTERNATIONAL GCSE
READING	AO1	Read and understand a variety of texts, selecting and interpreting information, ideas and perspectives	15%
	AO2	Understand and analyse how writers use linguistic and structural devices to achieve their effects	20%
	AO3	Explore links and connections between writers' ideas and perspectives, as well as how these are conveyed	15%
WRITING	AO4	Communicate effectively and imaginatively, adapting form, tone and register of writing for specific purposes and audiences	30%
	AO5	Write clearly, using a range of vocabulary and sentence structures, with appropriate paragraphing and accurate spelling, grammar and punctuation	20%

RELATIONSHIP OF ASSESSMENT OBJECTIVES TO UNITS

▼ UNIT NUMBER	▼ ASSESSMENT OBJECTIVE				
	AO1	AO2	AO3	AO4	AO5
PAPER 1	7%	8%	15%	18%	12%
PAPER 2 / PAPER 3	8%	12%	0%	12%	8%
TOTAL FOR INTERNATIONAL GCSE	15%	20%	15%	30%	20%

ASSESSMENT SUMMARY: ROUTE 1

▼ PAPER 1	▼ DESCRIPTION	▼ MARKS	▼ ASSESSMENT OBJECTIVES
NON-FICTION TEXTS AND TRANSACTIONAL WRITING PAPER CODE 4EA1/01	**Structure** Paper 1 assesses 60% of the total English Language A qualification. There will be two sections on the paper. Students must answer all questions in Section A and one question from a choice of two in Section B.		
	Section A: Non-fiction texts Students will study and analyse selections from a range of non-fiction. Students must: ■ develop skills to analyse how writers use linguistic and structural devices to achieve their effects ■ explore links and connections between writers' ideas and perspectives.	45	Questions will test the following Assessment Objectives: AO1 – 7% AO2 – 8% AO3 – 15%
	Section B: Transactional Writing Students will explore and develop transactional writing skills. Students must: ■ develop transactional writing skills for a variety of purposes and audiences ■ use spelling, punctuation and grammar accurately.	45	Questions will test the following Assessment Objectives: AO4 – 18% AO5 – 12%
	This is a single-tier exam paper and all questions cover the full ranges of grades from 9–1. The assessment duration is 2 hours 15 minutes. Closed book: texts are not allowed in the examination. However, students will be provided with any relevant extracts in the examination.	The total number of marks available is 90	

▼ PAPER 2	▼ DESCRIPTION	▼ MARKS	▼ ASSESSMENT OBJECTIVES
POETRY AND PROSE TEXTS AND IMAGINATIVE WRITING PAPER CODE 4EA1/02	**Structure** Paper 2 assesses 40% of the total English Language A qualification. There will be two sections on the paper. Students must answer the question in Section A and one question from a choice of three in Section B.		
	Section A: Poetry and Prose Texts from the *Pearson Edexcel International GCSE English Anthology* Students will study and analyse selections from a range of fictional poetry and prose texts. Students must: ■ develop skills to analyse how writers use linguistic and structural devices to achieve their effects.	30	Questions will test the following Assessment Objectives: AO1 – 8% AO2 – 12%
	Section B: Imaginative Writing Students will explore and develop imaginative writing skills. Students must: ■ develop imaginative writing skills to engage the reader ■ use spelling, punctuation and grammar accurately.	30	Questions will test the following Assessment Objectives: AO4 – 12% AO5 – 8%
	This is a single-tier exam paper and all questions cover the full ranges of grades from 9–1. The assessment duration is 1 hour 30 minutes. Closed book: texts are not allowed in the exam. However, students will be provided with any relevant extracts in the exam.	The total number of marks available is 60	

ASSESSMENT SUMMARY: ROUTE 2

▼ PAPER 1	▼ DESCRIPTION	▼ MARKS	▼ ASSESSMENT OBJECTIVES
NON-FICTION TEXTS AND TRANSACTIONAL WRITING PAPER CODE 4EA1/01	**Structure** Paper 1 assesses 60% of the total English Language A qualification. There will be two sections on the paper. Students must answer all questions in Section A and one question from a choice of two in Section B.		
	Section A: Non-fiction texts Students will study and analyse selections from a range of non-fiction. Students must: ■ develop skills to analyse how writers use linguistic and structural devices to achieve their effects ■ explore links and connections between writers' ideas and perspectives.	45	Questions will test the following Assessment Objectives: AO1 – 7% AO2 – 8% AO3 – 15%
	Section B: Transactional Writing Students will explore and develop transactional writing skills. Students must: ■ develop transactional writing skills for a variety of purposes and audiences ■ use spelling, punctuation and grammar accurately.	45	Questions will test the following Assessment Objectives: AO4 – 18% AO5 – 12%
	This is a single-tier exam paper and all questions cover the full ranges of grades from 9–1. The assessment duration is 2 hours 15 minutes. Closed book: texts are not allowed in the exam. However, students will be provided with any relevant extracts in the exam.	The total number of marks available is 90	

▼ PAPER 3	▼ DESCRIPTION	▼ MARKS	▼ ASSESSMENT OBJECTIVES
POETRY AND PROSE TEXTS AND IMAGINATIVE WRITING PAPER CODE 4EA1/03	**Structure** Paper 3 coursework assesses 40% of the total English Language A qualification. The assessment of the component is through two coursework assignments, internally set and assessed, and externally moderated by Pearson.		
	Section A: Poetry and Prose Texts from the *Pearson Edexcel International GCSE English Anthology* Students will study and analyse selections from a range of fictional poetry and prose texts. Students must: ■ develop skills to analyse how writers use linguistic and structural devices to achieve their effects.	30	Questions will test the following Assessment Objectives: AO1 – 8% AO2 – 12%
	Section B: Imaginative Writing Students will explore and develop imaginative writing skills. Students must: ■ develop imaginative writing skills to engage the reader ■ use spelling, punctuation and grammar accurately.	30	Questions will test the following Assessment Objectives: AO4 – 12% AO5 – 8%
	This is a single-tier coursework assignment and will cover the full ranges of grades from 9–1. There is no prescribed word length for the coursework paper. Typically the task may be up to 1000 words, but there are no penalties for exceeding this guidance.	The total number of marks available is 60	

READING SKILLS

Assessment Objective 1

Read and understand a variety of texts, selecting and interpreting information, ideas and perspectives

Assessment Objective 2

Understand and analyse how writers use linguistic and structural devices to achieve their effects

Assessment Objective 3

Explore links and connections between writers' ideas and perspectives, as well as how these are conveyed

This chapter focuses on some core reading skills that you can apply to all parts of the English Language A course. Working through these lessons and activities will help you to develop the reading skills that you will need for the exams and coursework assignments.

The chapter is split into the following sections:
- Text analysis
- Use of language.

In the reading sections of your exams you will need to be able to meet the Assessment Objectives AO1, AO2 and AO3.

LEARNING OBJECTIVES

This lesson will help you to:
- understand the main ideas that a writer is communicating
- summarise the key points of a text quickly
- build confidence in independent reading.

SKIMMING AND SCANNING

It can be difficult to know where to start when approaching a text for the first time. You need a methodical approach that allows you to understand the main ideas that are being communicated.

Skimming and scanning are two important reading techniques. They are often confused with one another, but they are very different skills. However, both help you to achieve the same aim: to read more quickly and effectively.

SKIMMING

Skimming is useful when you want to quickly get a general idea of what a text is about. When you skim, you read through the text three to four times faster than when you read each word in order to get a sense of the topic, ideas and information being conveyed.

WHEN SHOULD I SKIM?
- When you have a lot to read in a short space of time.
- When revising topics to identify key information.
- When locating a passage in a text.
- When finding relevant material when planning an essay.

SCANNING

Scanning refers to reading through material to find specific information. When you scan, you run your eyes over the information in a text and pull out specific words, phrases or pieces of information. You may not realise that you scan through different texts every day, from television guides to football results.

WHEN SHOULD I SCAN?
- When looking for specific pieces of information quickly.
- When locating a relevant quotation or section in a literature text.

KEY POINT

Skimming and scanning are important reading techniques. Skimming is reading quickly to get a general sense of a text. Scanning involves looking through a text for specific information.

HINT

To skim effectively, you don't read everything. What you read is more important than what you skip. Try to:
- highlight key points
- rephrase the main point of each paragraph in your own words
- underline any unfamiliar words.

ACTIVITY 1
SKILLS: DECISION MAKING

▼ **SKIMMING OR SCANNING?**

Read the following examples and identify which describes the process of skimming and which describes scanning.

1. You flick through a financial report to find a particular set of data.
2. You quickly go through a 20-page report in a few minutes to determine the overall subject, tone and a few key points.
3. You pick up a newspaper at a coffee shop, look over the first few pages and gather some general information about the events happening in the world.

READING SKILLS — TEXT ANALYSIS

SUBJECT VOCABULARY

topic sentence the first sentence in a paragraph, often used to explain the key idea

chronologically organised in linear time

flashback when the narrator of a story jumps out of the present in order to describe an event which happened in the past (often in the form of memories)

STRATEGIES FOR SKIMMING

- Read the **topic sentence**. This will give you a good sense of the ideas and structure of the whole text.
- Read the first and last paragraphs.
- Use chapter names, headings and subheadings as a guide.

STRATEGIES FOR SCANNING

- For scanning to be successful, be sure of your purpose. Think about what information you are looking for before you begin to scan the text.
- Consider how the text is structured. Is it arranged alphabetically, by category, **chronologically** or does it use other devices such as **flashback**?
- Use your index finger to help you, such as when scanning a timetable for a train time. Move your finger down the text at the same time as your eyes to help you to maintain focus.

ACTIVITY 2

SKILLS CREATIVITY, INNOVATION

▼ SKIMMING AND SCANNING RACE

► How fast are you at finding the information you need?

You need a dictionary, a pen, a piece of paper and a partner. Follow the instructions below carefully.

STEP 1 Open the dictionary at any page.

STEP 2 Write down the page number in the margin of the piece of paper.

STEP 3 Close your eyes and place your finger somewhere on the page of the dictionary.

STEP 4 See what word you have chosen. Write down its (first) definition, but NOT the word itself.

STEP 5 Repeat steps 1–4 until you have ten definitions on your page.

STEP 6 Now swap pieces of paper with your partner. See who can complete the written list with all the words first.

STEP 7 Now write a paragraph that is as short as possible and that uses all your partner's words.

ACTIVITY 3

SKILLS INITIATIVE

▼ SUMMARISING INFORMATION

Once you are confident that you understand the text, you need to be able to summarise the key points that the writer makes. A good summary phrases these points in a **concise** and **clear** style. Choose an extract and write a summary of it.

HINT

Use your own words in a summary wherever possible. Simply repeating sentences from the original text does not show that you have understood what the writer is communicating.

6 READING SKILLS — TEXT ANALYSIS

LEARNING OBJECTIVES

This lesson will help you to:
- interpret the information and ideas in a text
- read between the lines to work out what the text implies.

SUBJECT VOCABULARY

infer read between the lines

KEY POINT

Explicit meaning is where the writer **ex**plains their ideas.
Implicit meaning is where the writer **im**plies their ideas; you have to **in**fer and **im**agine based on what you know.

EXPLICIT AND IMPLICIT MEANING

To be a good reader, you need to understand both what a text tells you directly, or explicitly, and to **infer** based on what you think the writer indirectly, or implicitly, suggests in their text. This may be about the writer's views, character or theme.

▲ A couple on their wedding day.

EXPLICIT MEANING

The picture shows a woman in a dress holding flowers and standing close to a man in a suit.

IMPLICIT MEANING

You may be able to **infer** that this is a wedding photograph because you have experience of seeing this type of image being related to weddings.

▼ AN EXTRACT FROM *A WALK IN THE WOODS* BY BILL BRYSON

We hiked till five and camped beside a tranquil spring in a small, grassy clearing in the trees just off the trail. Because it was our first day back on the trail, we were flush for food, including perishables like cheese and bread that had to be eaten before they went off or were shaken to bits in our packs, so we rather gorged ourselves, then sat around smoking and chatting idly until persistent and numerous midgelike creatures (no-see-ums, as they are universally known along the trail) drove us into our tents. It was perfect sleeping weather, cool enough to need a bag but warm enough that you could sleep in your underwear, and I was looking forward to a long night's snooze – indeed was enjoying a long night's snooze – when, at some indeterminate dark hour, there was a sound nearby that made my eyes fly open. Normally, I slept through everything – through thunderstorms, through Katz's snoring and noisy midnight pees – so something big enough or distinctive enough to wake me was unusual. There was a sound of undergrowth being disturbed – a click of breaking branches, a weighty pushing through low foliage – and then a kind of large, vaguely irritable snuffling noise.

READING SKILLS — TEXT ANALYSIS

> Bear!
>
> I sat bolt upright. Instantly every neuron in my brain was awake and dashing around frantically, like ants when you disturb their nest. I reached instinctively for my knife, then realized I had left it in my pack, just outside the tent. Nocturnal defense had ceased to be a concern after many successive nights of tranquil woodland repose. There was another noise, quite near.
>
> "Stephen, you awake?" I whispered.
>
> "Yup," he replied in a weary but normal voice.
>
> "What was that?"
>
> "How the hell should I know?"
>
> "It sounded big."
>
> "Everything sounds big in the woods."
>
> This was true. Once a skunk had come plodding through our camp and it had sounded like a stegosaurus.

ACTIVITY 1

SKILLS: CRITICAL THINKING, ANALYSIS, INTERPRETATION

▼ INFERRING FROM A TEXT

Read the extract from *A Walk In the Woods* by Bill Bryson. In pairs, choose a paragraph each and consider the following questions.

▶ What does the narrator **tell** you about his thoughts and feelings?

▶ Which words and phrases allow you to **infer** his thoughts and feelings?

Draw a table with two columns, one for each question, and pick out the key words and phrases from your paragraph which convey explicit and implicit meaning.

KEY VOCABULARY

SUBJECT VOCABULARY

synonyms words that share the same meaning as other words; for example, 'quick' might be a synonym for 'fast'

connotations ideas linked to a word; ideas that have become associated with a word

Writers use a lot of similar phrases to convey meaning. Don't just use 'shows'; using some of these **synonyms** could improve your writing.

- highlights
- suggests
- is redolent of
- has **connotations** of
- exposes
- denotes
- illustrates
- conveys
- introduces
- portrays
- demonstrates
- emphasises
- signifies
- reflects
- implies
- represents
- reveals
- infers
- connotes.

READING SKILLS — TEXT ANALYSIS

LEARNING OBJECTIVES

This lesson will help you to:
- organise your ideas and structure your writing clearly and with direction.

POINT-EVIDENCE-EXPLAIN (P-E-E)

When writing, it is important to express points in a clear and structured way, so you should organise your writing into paragraphs. Each paragraph should be self-contained and make sense on its own. It should be constructed of a group of sentences which all link to the same idea, theme or topic.

MAKING THE PERFECT POINT

HINT

A quotation does not have to be **direct speech**: you can quote evidence from a science journal or a famous play in the same way.

SUBJECT VOCABULARY

quotations words from a text
quotation marks punctuation marks used to indicate where you have
direct speech words spoken by a character in a novel, play or poem
diction the writer's choice of words

The P-E-E chain stands for **Point-Evidence-Explain**. This is the order in which you should organise the information in each paragraph that you write.

1. State your basic **point** clearly and concisely. Your point should be relevant to the task or question that you have been set.
2. Demonstrate how you can support your opening statement with reference to a specific part of the text that you are writing about. **Quotations** can be used as **evidence** to support what you are saying and to help you to make your point. Try to select words or phrases from the text that precisely support your point and keep them as brief as possible. Use inverted commas, also known as **quotation marks**, to indicate where you have used words directly from another text.
3. Add an **explanation**. The first step is to explain how your quotation supports the point that you have made so that your reader knows why you have included it. In English Language, it is often useful to consider the use of language, going into some detail about the writer's choice of words (this is also known as **diction**) and considering any linguistic devices or techniques which have been used.

PERFECT PUNCTUATION

Short quotations of a single line or part of a line should be incorporated within quotation marks as part of the running text of your essay, 'just like this'. Quotations of two or more full lines should be indented from the main body of the text and introduced by a colon, like this:

> 'this is how you would quote a longer piece of text, but make sure that it is all relevant.'

PARAGRAPH SANDWICHES

You can think of your paragraph like a sandwich or burger, with three separate parts.

Top bun: opening topic sentence. Introduces the paragraph and your main idea.

Fillings: supporting sentences. This is the main part. Describe and explain your main point, using quotations and evidence to complement and support it.

Bottom bun: closing sentence. A concluding sentence to bring everything together

READING SKILLS — TEXT ANALYSIS

ACTIVITY 1

▼ SUMMARISING WITH P-E-E

Read this chain paragraph, summarising the novel *Of Mice and Men* by John Steinbeck. Copy the paragraph and colour code or label each part of the P-E-E chain. Each part of the chain may be more than one sentence.

> Set in the Great Depression of the 1930s, the novel tells of the close friendship between two farm workers, George and Lennie: 'I got you to look after me, and you got me to look after you'. The other men on the ranch are described as 'the loneliest guys in the world' and George and Lennie are proud of the fact that they have each other. The repetition of the second person pronoun 'you' here emphasises the close and reciprocal bond between the men. George and Lennie often repeat this line to one another when they are talking about their dreams for the future and Lennie is always excited when George reaffirms their friendship in this way. Their friendship gives them hope and joy in a desolate world.

KEY POINT

Follow these four rules for excellent writing:
1 Structure: ideas must be clearly expressed and logically sequenced.
2 Paragraphs: paragraphs should be well constructed and follow on from one another. Quotations should be correctly presented.
3 Vocabulary: use a wide range of key vocabulary with precision.
4 Spelling, punctuation and grammar: maintain accuracy throughout.

ACTIVITY 2

▼ P-E-E-RFECT LITERATURE PARAGRAPHS

Using a set text from your English Language studies, write your own question and P-E-E chain paragraph about a character or theme. The following questions are examples to help you to construct a question based on your own reading.

▶ How is the **protagonist** portrayed in the text?
▶ What is the main theme of the text?
▶ What is the author trying to convey through the text?
▶ How does the opening set the scene for the text?

Give your question and paragraph to a partner and check each other's work. Consider the following questions and clearly label examples of each within the paragraph.

Does the paragraph include the following?
■ A **point**?
■ Some **evidence**: a quotation or example?
■ an **Explanation**: an exploration of the quotation and what it shows? This may include:
　■ some comment on the **language or literary devices** used
　■ some understanding of the **writer's attitude**
　■ a **personal response** to the characters or themes of a text.

SUBJECT VOCABULARY

protagonist the main character

READING SKILLS — TEXT ANALYSIS

LEARNING OBJECTIVES

This lesson will help you to:
- approach a non-fiction text critically
- recognise fact and opinion and follow an argument
- build confidence in responding to a text
- understand how writers use language to influence their readers.

EVALUATING A TEXT

This section will help you to prepare for **Paper 1 Section A**, which will test your reading and critical skills. There will be questions on both a prepared and an unprepared non-fiction reading passage. This will be drawn from a range of contemporary non-fiction, including autobiography, travel writing, reportage, media articles, letters, diary entries and opinion pieces. You will find additional information on this section of the exam on pages 58-95.

EVALUATING A TEXT: A GUIDE

SUBJECT VOCABULARY

rhetorical device using language in a certain way to achieve an effect

When you read a text, you form an opinion. Understanding how writers present ideas is key to understanding how texts work. You need to be aware of a variety of ways in which writers use language to influence their readers.

The devices used tend to be linked to the purpose of the text. So a text that tries to persuade a reader of a particular opinion will use **rhetorical devices**, while a text that describes another country is likely to use a wide range of descriptive and figurative devices to establish a vivid sense of place.

When you read a new piece of non-fiction, you should first try to understand what points are being made.

▼ 'IT'S SO OVER: COOL CYBERKIDS ABANDON SOCIAL NETWORKING SITES' FROM *THE GUARDIAN*

From uncles wearing skinny jeans to mothers investing in ra-ra skirts and fathers nodding awkwardly along to the latest grime record, the older generation has long known that the surest way to kill a youth trend is to adopt it as its own. The cyberworld, it seems, is no exception.

The proliferation of parents and teachers trawling the pages of Facebook trying to poke old schoolfriends and lovers, and traversing the outer reaches of MySpace is causing an adolescent exodus from the social networking sites, according to research from the media regulator Ofcom.

The sites, once the virtual streetcorners, pubs and clubs for millions of 15- to 24-year-olds, have now been over-run by 25- to 34-year-olds whose presence is driving their younger peers away.

Although their love of being online shows no sign of abating, the percentage of 15- to 24-year-olds who have a profile on a social networking site has dropped for the first time – from 55% at the start of last year to 50% this year. In contrast, 46% of 25- to 34-year-olds are now regularly checking up on sites such as Facebook compared with 40% last year.

Overall, 30% of British adults have a social networking profile, against 21% in 2007 when Ofcom first did the research. Half the UK's online population have a Facebook profile and spend an average of nearly six hours a month on the site compared with four hours in May 2008.

"There is nothing to suggest overall usage of the internet among 15-to 24-year-olds is going down," said Peter Phillips, the regulator's head of strategy. "Data suggests they are spending less time on social networking sites."

James Thickett, director of market research at Ofcom, said that while older people seemed to be embracing social networking sites, Facebook and MySpace remained immensely popular with children under 16.

| READING SKILLS | TEXT ANALYSIS | 11 |

"Clearly take-up among under 16-year-olds is very high … so we cannot say for certain whether this is people in a certain age group who are not setting up social networking profiles or whether it's a population shift which is reflecting people getting older and having a social networking profile that they set up two years ago," he said. "The main point is the profile of social networking users is getting older."

The arrival of the 25- to 34-year-old age group, meanwhile, also appears to be behind the explosion in usage of Twitter.

ACTIVITY 1

SKILLS: CRITICAL THINKING, ANALYSIS, CREATIVITY, INNOVATION

▼ RECOGNISING FACT AND OPINION AND FOLLOWING AN ARGUMENT

Read the article taken from *The Guardian* newspaper. Complete two lists: one listing the facts used in this article and one listing the opinions. How do the use of the facts and opinions influence you?

Next, pull out the key arguments of this article and re-write each point in your own words. Summarise the article in five or six key points.

▼ 'SOCIAL WEBSITES HARM CHILDREN'S BRAINS' FROM *MAIL ONLINE*

Social networking websites are causing alarming changes in the brains of young users, an eminent scientist has warned.

Sites such as Facebook, Twitter and Bebo are said to shorten attention spans, encourage instant gratification and make young people more self-centred.

The claims from neuroscientist Susan Greenfield will make disturbing reading for the millions whose social lives depend on logging on to their favourite websites each day.

But they will strike a chord with parents and teachers who complain that many youngsters lack the ability to communicate or concentrate away from their screens.

More than 150 million use Facebook to keep in touch with friends, share photographs and videos and post regular updates of their movements and thoughts.

A further six million have signed up to Twitter, the 'micro-blogging' service that lets users circulate text messages about themselves.

But while the sites are popular – and extremely profitable – a growing number of psychologists and neuroscientists believe they may be doing more harm than good.

Baroness Greenfield, an Oxford University neuroscientist and director of the Royal Institution, believes repeated exposure could effectively 'rewire' the brain.

Computer games and fast-paced TV shows were also a factor, she said.

'We know how small babies need constant reassurance that they exist,' she told the Mail yesterday.

'My fear is that these technologies are infantilising the brain into the state of small children who are attracted by buzzing noises and bright lights, who have a small attention span and who live for the moment.'

Her comments echoed those she made during a House of Lords debate earlier this month. Then she argued that exposure to computer games, instant messaging, chat rooms and social networking sites could leave a generation with poor attention spans.

'I often wonder whether real conversation in real time may eventually give way to these sanitised and easier screen dialogues, in much the same way as killing, skinning and butchering an animal to eat has been replaced by the convenience of packages of meat on the supermarket shelf,' she said.

Lady Greenfield told the Lords a teacher of 30 years had told her she had noticed a sharp decline in the ability of her pupils to understand others.

'It is hard to see how living this way on a daily basis will not result in brains, or rather minds, different from those of previous generations,' she said.

She pointed out that autistic people, who usually find it hard to communicate, were particularly comfortable using computers.

'Of course, we do not know whether the current increase in autism is due more to increased awareness and diagnosis of autism, or whether it can – if there is a true increase – be in any way linked to an increased prevalence among people of spending time in screen relationships. Surely it is a point worth considering,' she added.

Psychologists have also argued that digital technology is changing the way we think. They point out that students no longer need to plan essays before starting to write – thanks to word processors they can edit as they go along. Satellite navigation systems have negated the need to decipher maps.

A study by the Broadcaster Audience Research Board found teenagers now spend seven-and-a-half hours a day in front of a screen.

Educational psychologist Jane Healy believes children should be kept away from computer games until they are seven. Most games only trigger the 'flight or fight' region of the brain, rather than the vital areas responsible for reasoning.

Sue Palmer, author of Toxic Childhood, said: 'We are seeing children's brain development damaged because they don't engage in the activity they have engaged in for millennia.

'I'm not against technology and computers. But before they start social networking, they need to learn to make real relationships with people.'

ACTIVITY 2

SKILLS REASONING, INTERPRETATION, DECISION MAKING

▼ DIFFERING WRITING SKILLS

Read the article 'Social websites harm children's brains', from *Mail Online*. Analyse it using the same steps as in Activity 1. What are the similarities and differences in the way that the two articles present ideas?

HOW WRITERS USE LANGUAGE TO INFLUENCE THEIR READERS

Once you have established the main ideas being communicated in a piece of non-fiction, you should consider whether the article is showing an opinion or bias. Look out for the following:

SUBJECT VOCABULARY

bias not fair; a particular point of view influenced by one's own or someone else's opinions
emotive language language that stirs emotion in the reader

- use of biased language
- use of emotive language
- stating of opinion as fact
- use of quotations or the reported views of others
- use of unsupported claims
- the given facts
- an argument.

ACTIVITY 3

SKILLS ANALYSIS, INTERPRETATION, COLLABORATION, INTERPERSONAL SKILLS

▼ PICKING OUT KEY INFORMATION AND RECOGNISING BIAS

Look back at the two articles from *The Guardian* and *Mail Online* again. In groups, answer the following questions, carefully considering how language has been used.

1. What view of teenagers are given and what are the main arguments raised in each article?
2. How are facts and opinions used in each article?
3. How is scientific research used to put across the main points of view in each article?
4. What linguistic devices have been used to present the point of view more powerfully in each article?

READING SKILLS   TEXT ANALYSIS   13

ACTIVITY 4
SKILLS ANALYSIS

▼ RHETORICAL DEVICES

Rhetorical devices are often used in texts that seek to present a particular point of view or opinion. Match the following rhetorical devices with the correct example sentence.

Emotive language	Kittens need a warm, dry, comfortable place for snoozing.
Personal pronouns	These vulnerable, weak kittens need our help.
Repetition	Over 100,000,000 cats need re-homing every week.
Rule of three	You can help us make a difference; all we need is £2 a month.
Hyperbole	Every year the number of cats on the streets increases, every year it is up to us to rescue them.

▲ They need 'a warm, dry, comfortable place for snoozing'.

ACTIVITY 5
SKILLS PROBLEM SOLVING, ADAPTIVE LEARNING, INNOVATION

▼ WRITING PERSUASIVELY

Write a letter to persuade an organisation to ban the use of animal fur in its products.
Include the following rhetorical devices in your letter:
- direct address
- rule of three
- emotive language
- imperative verbs
- repetition
- rhetorical questions.

Your letter must be at least three paragraphs long and should follow all the conventions of a normal letter.

SUBJECT VOCABULARY

emotive language language that produces an emotional reaction
personal pronoun a word used instead of a noun, such as 'I', 'you' or 'they'
repetition saying the same thing more than once to highlight its importance
rule of three where three things are linked or something is repeated three times in order to emphasise them and ensure they are memorable
hyperbole exaggerating for effect
direct address using second person pronouns 'you' or 'your'
imperative verbs verbs that give an instruction or command
rhetorical questions questions that are asked to make a point rather than to get an answer

ACTIVITY 6
SKILLS CRITICAL THINKING, ANALYSIS, REASONING, INTERPRETATION

▼ ANALYSING IDEAS

Read the following article, 'Myth of the Teenager' by Lucy Maddox, and answer the question.

▶ **How does Lucy Maddox present teenagers in this article?**

Your answer should:
- reflect on audience and purpose (that is, how and why language has been used for effect)
- show a detailed understanding of the article and the points that the writer is making
- identify a wide variety of devices used by the writer and analyse the effect in as much detail as possible
- use appropriate terminology throughout.

After answering the question, write a one-paragraph summary in which you say how your understanding of the topic has developed or changed as a result of reading this article. What impact has it had on you and why?

GENERAL VOCABULARY

ASBOs court orders used in the UK to restrict anti-social behaviour
hug a hoodie a slogan used to make fun of British politicians who attempt to engage with disaffected young people
stigmatised unfairly discriminated against or disapproved of
vilified discussed or described in a very negative way

SUBJECT VOCABULARY

stereotypes fixed and generalised ideas about particular types of people or groups
syntax the way in which words and phrases are arranged into sentences

'MYTH OF THE TEENAGER', BY LUCY MADDOX

Teenagers often get a bad press. There are easy stories to be mined here: ASBOs, underage drinking, "hug a hoodie," drug use–even, recently, the teenager who drugged her parents to access the internet.

These are not new stereotypes. As a shepherd in Shakespeare's *A Winter's Tale* puts it, "I would there were no age between 10 and three-and-20, or that youth would sleep out the rest; for there is nothing in the between but getting wenches with child, wronging the ancientry, stealing, fighting." Change the syntax, and this description could easily fit in many newspapers today.

Are the stereotypes fair? Is the idea of wild adolescence rooted in evidence? There are two sorts of arguments. On the one hand, neuroscientific evidence seems increasingly to suggest that this is a true developmental phase of its own—teenagers behave differently because their brains are different. On the other, some argue that teenagers behave differently because they are learning to handle so many new situations, and if we hold stereotypical ideas about their behaviour, we risk underestimating them.

Take the latter argument first. Philip Graham, a professor of psychiatry who has written extensively on what he perceives to be a misconception, believes that although hormonal and physical changes are occurring, most teenagers are not risky or moody. Graham sees teenagers as a stigmatised group, often highly competent yet treated as if they were not. He argues that teenagers need to be acknowledged as potentially productive members of society and that the more independence and respect they are given, the more they will rise to the challenge.

"Once young people reach the age of 14, their competence in cognitive tasks and their sexual maturity make it more helpful to think of them as young adults," says Graham. "Media coverage is almost uniformly negative. Adolescence is a word used to describe undesirable behaviour in older adults. Young people of 14, 15 or 16 are thought to be risk-takers… they are people who are experimenting. They are doing things for the first time and they make mistakes. Would you call a toddler who is learning to walk and who falls over all the time a risk-taker? These people are just beginning something."

Graham places less importance on the conclusions of research into risk-taking and on adolescent brain changes – "Not to say there are not a small minority who do take dangerous risks but I think the results have been over-generalised to justify the stereotype."

Instead, Graham argues that the way teenagers make decisions is related to encountering situations they haven't dealt with before. "If they are moving into new types of social situation they do need more help with that." He likens it to learning to drive, something you need expert help with at any age.

However, neuroscientific evidence suggests a basis for the teenage stereotype. Sarah-Jayne Blakemore, a professor at University College London, has specialised in researching the adolescent brain using a variety of techniques, including functional brain scanning. Although also concerned that teenagers can be vilified in the media, Blakemore rejects the idea that adolescence is entirely a social construct: "If you look throughout history at the descriptions of adolescence they are similar, and also in different cultures. Of course this is not to say that all adolescents are the same, but there is quite a lot of evidence that during this period of life there's an increase in risk-taking, peer influence

READING SKILLS — TEXT ANALYSIS

GENERAL VOCABULARY

inhibiting preventing or restraining someone or something
autonomy the ability to make independent decisions about yourself
bolshy British slang meaning argumentative or uncooperative
disincentive a factor that persuades someone not to do something

and self-consciousness." Blakemore's research suggests that during the teenage years the brain is still developing the capacity for certain sophisticated skills, including problem-solving, social skills and impulse control.

Blakemore and other researchers describe a gradual development of brain areas related to planning, inhibiting inappropriate behaviour and understanding other points of view. They also suggest a less linear development of the system in the brain that recognises and responds to rewards. "Teenagers tend to be more self-conscious," said Blakemore. "They show more risk-taking when their peers are present." Their social brain is changing and so is their ability to plan, inhibit impulses and make decisions.

"Research by Laurence Steinberg at Temple University in the US has shown that adolescents tend not to take into account future consequences of actions. For example, if you offer them a choice between having £10 now and £100 in six months, whilst adults tend to wait for the larger amount, most adolescents are more likely to go for the lower value now. Life in the future doesn't hold so much importance."

It might make sense, then, that a teenager trying to decide whether to tell a lie in order to go out, or to try an illegal drug, might be influenced more by the reward of the night out or the novel experience, or peer congratulation, than by longer-term negative consequences. "It's not that teenagers don't understand the risks," says Blakemore. "It's just that for some teenagers, in the moment, this understanding goes out of the window."

Despite their different views, both academics conclude that teenagers could benefit from being treated according to their development. Graham suggests friendly advice-giving. It is important to "recognise their desire for autonomy," he says. "They want to do more than they can. We should treat them differently because they are inexperienced… and first experiences are important. A bad experience can put you off something for a long time."

He does not advocate tolerating too much difficult behaviour, though: "Adolescents are influenced by the stereotype as well. If they expect to get away with being 'bolshy' for example… I don't think we should be particularly tolerant of bad behaviour in adolescence."

Blakemore thinks that we should adjust the way we try to motivate teenagers: "Anti-smoking campaigns, for example, might be more effective if they used short-term social negatives like bad breath as a disincentive, rather than longer-term health consequences. And we perhaps expect too much. "We expect them to act like adults but their brains aren't yet completely like an adult brain. Maybe we should be more understanding. Teaching adolescents about how their brains develop might be helpful."

Whether you attribute adolescent differences in decision-making to brain development or lack of experience, educational aims could include the handling of social dilemmas. Parents might be able to help by being explicit about the pros and cons of a situation, considering other people's views or negotiating in a transparent way. We should also bear in mind that teenagers are often uniquely affected by economic and political challenges such as high unemployment levels.

In my view, adolescence is a tricky time, where individuals often struggle to find their own identity in the face of a sometimes hostile outside world, whilst needing peer support. Both Blakemore and Graham are more phlegmatic. "Every time's a tricky time," says Graham. "You try being my age."

▲ Adolescents often struggle to find their own identity.

16 READING SKILLS — TEXT ANALYSIS

LEARNING OBJECTIVES

This lesson will help you to:
- identify the main parts of speech
- consolidate your understanding of the function of each.

WORD CLASSES

Words may be divided into groups called parts of speech. Words are classified as one of nine parts of speech:
- **verb**
- **noun**
- **pronoun**
- **adjective**
- **adverb**
- **preposition**
- **conjunction**
- **interjection**
- **determiners**.

PARTS OF SPEECH

SUBJECT VOCABULARY

verb a word that describes actions
noun a word that represents a person, place, object or quality
pronoun a word that is used instead of a noun
adjective a word that describes a noun or pronoun
adverb a word that describes a verb or an adjective
preposition a word that is used before a noun or pronoun to show time, place or direction
conjunction a word that joins parts of a sentence
interjection a word used to express a strong feeling
determiner a word used before a noun in order to show which thing is being referred to

Each part of speech signifies how the word is used, not what a word is. This means that the same word can be a noun in one sentence and a verb or adjective in the next. For example, the word 'book' in the following sentences.

- Books are made of ink, paper and glue.
  (In this case, 'books' is a noun and is the subject of the sentence.)
- Deborah waits patiently while Bridget books the tickets.
  (In this case, 'books' is a verb and the subject of the sentence is Bridget.)

If you were asked to describe the following photograph, you might say, 'The happy lady was laughing'.

▲ The sentence 'The happy lady was laughing' contains a noun, verb and adjective.

This sentence is made up of different parts of speech.

This is a **noun**. It is a **naming word**.

This is a **verb**. It is a word that describes **actions**.

The happy lady was laughing.

This is an **adjective**. It is a **describing word**. It tells you more about the **noun**.

READING SKILLS — TEXT ANALYSIS

ACTIVITY 1
SKILLS: ANALYSIS

▼ IDENTIFYING PARTS OF SPEECH

In the following sentences, circle the adjectives, tick the nouns and underline the verbs.
1. I tripped over the uneven floor.
2. The silly boy crashed his new bike.
3. When the old lady reached her house, she sat down.
4. We saw wild horses in the forest.
5. The large crowd cheered as the skilful player scored.
6. The giggling girls annoyed the teacher.
7. A prickly hedgehog snuffled in the dry leaves.
8. The lazy man was sleeping under the tall tree.

KEY POINT
All words are divided into nine classes, known as parts of speech.

PROPER NOUNS

Nouns that name particular things are called proper nouns and begin with capital letters. The names of people and places, days of the week, brand names, company names and titles of films are all proper nouns, e.g. Yara, France, Thursday, Google, Ford, *Avatar*.

PREPOSITIONS

A preposition tells you the position of one thing in relation to another.

> Altamash hid **behind** the tree.
>
> You cross **over** a bridge.

ACTIVITY 2
SKILLS: ANALYSIS

▼ USING PARTS OF SPEECH

Write a suitable word in the gap in each of the following sentences. In the brackets after each sentence, write down what part of speech it is.
1. Sam put the _____ suitcase on the floor. (_____)
2. Athens is the capital of _____. (_____)
3. The mountaineers _____ to the summit. (_____)
4. The children sang loudly at the _____. (_____)
5. The cat's _____ was soft and silky. (_____)
6. The helicopter _____ over the motorway. (_____)

HINT
Many verbs are 'doing' words and are used to describe actions, such as 'the boy **kicked** the ball'. Some verbs are 'being' words: 'The girl **is** muddy.'

READING SKILLS — TEXT ANALYSIS

LEARNING OBJECTIVES

This lesson will help you to:
- explore and develop your interpretations of language
- considering the associations that words hold and how they can be used to create meaning in a text.

SUBJECT VOCABULARY

denotation what something is

KEY POINT

Words and images can have a range of connotations that influence meaning and interpretation.

CONNOTATIONS

Connotations are the associations and ideas which a particular word or image suggests to a reader. It is important to consider the connotations implied by a text in order to explore its effects in detail.

ACTIVITY 1 — SKILLS: INTERPRETATION

▼ **CONNOTATIONS OF IMAGES**

Copy and complete the table, writing down the **denotation** and the connotation for each image. On a piece of paper, draw your own example of a sign or image. Ask a partner to look at your image and identify its denotation and connotation.

▼ IMAGE/SIGN	▼ DENOTATION	▼ CONNOTATION
(pirate flag)	Skull and crossbones	Pirates, poison, danger
(white dove)		
(sunflowers)		

READING SKILLS — TEXT ANALYSIS

ACTIVITY 2
SKILLS: ANALYSIS, INTERPRETATION

▼ CONNOTATIONS OF WORDS

> **KEY POINT**
>
> Connotations are how writers are able to convey their ideas to readers. Inferring information from a text is a critical skill in understanding what message and ideas the author wants to convey to readers.

Your local newspaper runs a weekly column called 'Why I love…', in which a guest writer is asked to write a short article to inform readers of a personal interest. Read the following extract, from a piece called 'Why I love reading', and consider the connotations of the highlighted words, and then answer the question.

> I love reading because I love getting to know *new characters. They become friends*: I inhabit their lives while I read and when I finish that book, I take a part of them with me. Reading gives me an escape from reality: *it's my magic carpet* that I can fly on whenever I choose, soaring off on adventures all over the world, from past to present, over the vast terrains of human history. I can see all of the colours of life as I go. They say you never read the same book twice: reading a new book makes me feel slightly new myself because I know something different; I've experienced something more. *Reading makes me a bigger, better, smarter version of myself.*

▶ **What ideas and attitudes to reading are suggested in the extract?**

Copy and complete the following table, considering the connotations of the highlighted words and phrases used in the extract. Then choose another quotation from the extract and consider its connotation.

▼ PHRASE	▼ CONNOTATION
'new characters… become friends'	By describing characters as 'friends', the writer demonstrates the emotional connection they feel with books and the companionship they get from reading.
'it's my magic carpet'	The metaphor describes reading as a 'magic carpet'. This has connotations of adventure and implies the fantastic experiences that the writer enjoys in reading books. The 'magic carpet' also has connotations of freedom and flight: books give this reader the wings to explore worlds which might otherwise be inaccessible to them.
'Reading makes me a bigger, better, smarter version of myself.'	

ACTIVITY 3
SKILLS: PROBLEM SOLVING, ADAPTIVE LEARNING

▼ CREATING YOUR OWN CONNOTATIONS

Using the extract 'Why I love reading' as a model, write two paragraphs of your own, entitled 'Why I love…' and 'Why I hate…'. Choose something that you will enjoy writing about: it can be anything from motorbikes to a particular website. Use bias, emotive language and connotations to create a positive or negative description of your chosen subjects. You may choose to use similes, metaphors and other figurative language to help you to do this.

LEARNING OBJECTIVES

This lesson will help you to:
- identify the main sentence types.

DIFFERENT SENTENCE TYPES

A sentence is a group of words that are put together in such a way as to mean something. It is a basic component of communication. Clumsy sentence structure leads to writing that is grammatically incorrect. Poor sentence structure will also prevent your ideas flowing in a coherent and logical way and make it much more difficult for the reader to understand what you are trying to convey. A writer's use of sentence structure often helps to convey meaning in a text. It is important to be able to identify and comment on this in the reading sections of the exam.

TYPES OF SENTENCES

'Friend, car, France holiday' is not a sentence as it doesn't make sense. 'I am driving my friend to France for a holiday' is a sentence. You can understand what it means as it makes sense on its own.
Sentences come in different forms.

- A **declarative** (or statement) **conveys** information.
  My car is red.
- An **interrogative** (or question) **asks** for information.
  Does it go fast?
- An **imperative** (or command) **tells** someone to do something.
  Get in.
- An **exclamation** shows that someone **feels strongly** about something.
  It's great!

HINT

Remember the conjunctions that you can use to create a compound sentence by using the acronym FANBOYS:
For, And, Nor, But, Or, Yet, So.

ACTIVITY 1   SKILLS   ANALYSIS

▼ SENTENCE TYPES

Match the sentences with the sentence types.
1. The door is open.   statement
2. Go and have a wash.   question
3. What a lovely surprise!   command
4. Have you seen my shorts?   exclamation

SIMPLE SENTENCES

SUBJECT VOCABULARY

clause a group of words that make up part of a sentence

A **simple sentence** contains a single subject, a verb and an object. This is also known as a **clause**.

The boy ate the chocolate.

Simple sentences may contain other elements or parts of a clause, but they only express one thing.

READING SKILLS — TEXT ANALYSIS

PARTS OF A CLAUSE

SUBJECT VOCABULARY

predicate the parts of a sentence that are not the subject, containing the verb and providing information about the subject

HINT

To determine the subject of a sentence, first isolate the verb and then make a question by placing 'who?' or 'what?' before it. The answer is the subject of the sentence.

A sentence must contain the following parts.

- The **subject** identifies the topic of a clause or, in other words, what it is about. Every complete sentence contains two parts: a subject and a predicate. The subject is what or whom the sentence is about, and the predicate tells you something about the subject. In the following sentence, the predicate is enclosed in brackets ( ), while the subject is **in bold**.

    My hockey teacher and his dog (go running every morning).

- The **verb** identifies the action of a clause or, in other words, what happens.

    Her boyfriend **gave** her a bunch of flowers.

- The **object** identifies who or what is directly affected by the action of the verb. This is always a noun or pronoun. Two kinds of objects follow verbs: direct and indirect objects. 'Her boyfriend gave her a bunch of flowers', contains a direct object ('Her boyfriend') and an indirect object: in this case the recipient of the direct object ('her').

Not all verbs are followed by objects:

    After work, David usually **walks** home.

Verbs that take objects are known as **transitive** verbs. Verbs not followed by objects are called **intransitive** verbs. Some verbs can be both.

A sentence may also contain the following components.

- The **complement** gives extra information about the subject or object.
- The **adverbial** gives additional information about a situation: when, where and how it happened.

ACTIVITY 2 — SKILLS ANALYSIS

▼ **PARTS OF A SENTENCE**

Find the subject, verb and object in the following sentences. Can you find any adverbials as well?
1 Last week, Peggy redecorated the kitchen.
2 Are you hungry yet?
3 Martin, be quiet.
4 Tuesday was very rainy and cold.

▲ 'Last week, Peggy redecorated the kitchen.'

COMPOUND SENTENCES

A compound sentence consists of two simple sentences (clauses) joined by a **conjunction**. A conjunction is a joining word. It may be used to join two sentences together.

    It was raining. I put up my umbrella. (two sentences)

    It was raining **so** I put up my umbrella. (one sentence with a conjunction)

SUBORDINATE CLAUSES

Subordinate clauses are often present in a sentence. They are called subordinate as they are second to the main action in the sentence; they are additional information that the sentence doesn't need to function.

    After his Dad gave him some pocket money, Andrew went to the cinema.

'After his Dad gave him some pocket money' is a subordinate clause. Anything between commas, dashes or brackets would be subordinate clauses too.

COMPLEX SENTENCES

A **complex sentence** contains a main sentence and one or more subordinate clauses that contribute to the meaning of the statement.

22 READING SKILLS — TEXT ANALYSIS

LEARNING OBJECTIVES

This lesson will help you to:
- use a full range of sentence structures
- control and vary sentence structure for effect in your writing.

SENTENCES FOR EFFECT

When sentence structure is repetitive and boring, writing is less interesting to read. Learning how to use sentence structure for effect will help you to engage your reader.

If writing contains little variety in sentence structure, it will be less interesting for the reader than if it contains a variety of sentence types that are handled well.

Little variety in sentence structure  Skilful control in the construction of varied sentence forms

EDINGLY OPENERS: VARYING SENTENCE STARTERS FOR IMPACT

EDINGLY openers consist of words ending in -ED (verbs), -ING (verbs) and -LY (adverbs). They can be an engaging way to begin sentences.

▶ **How could you change these sentences using this technique?**

1 I walked through the dark alley and suddenly a hand reached out and grabbed my shoulder.
2 I was breathing deeply as I crept through the deep, dark wood.
3 I was trapped and could not see a way out.

HINT

Use a comma or exclamation mark after the opener.

ACTIVITY 1

SKILLS: CRITICAL THINKING, ANALYSIS, INTERPRETATION

▼ **EXPLORING SENTENCE TYPES**

What is suspense? How do writers build suspense? Why do readers like a good mystery? What do you expect from a suspense story?
Read the following extract and see how many sentence types you can identify. Does it create a sense of suspense?

> The window shattered, sending glass cascading in all directions. Flames exploded into the room. I ducked, keeping my body as low as I could, desperately trying to avoid the smoke that was rapidly streaming across the ceiling. I scanned the room for other exits and was glad to see a small window on the far wall. The smoke was getting denser and started to expand, the cloud reaching down from the ceiling to the floor. My brain shouted, 'Move!' Frozen. Taking a deep breath of clean air, possibly my last, I pushed away from the wall to safety. As I struggled to open the window, I felt my heart pounding. My lungs screamed for air. The smoke descended and I worked blind, my eyes stinging. I pulled frantically at the catches, felt them give and tumbled out onto the ground below. I felt the heat escaping from the open window above and started to crawl slowly away.

READING SKILLS — TEXT ANALYSIS

▲ The sentence 'Grasping the handle, she turned it slowly' helps to build suspense.

KEY POINT

Sentence structure can be used for particular effect. For example, short, simple sentences can be used to build suspense or a sense of actions, whilst longer, complex sentences may be helpful in creating a layered character

ACTIVITY 2
SKILLS: ANALYSIS, INTERPRETATION, DECISION MAKING

▼ CREATING SUSPENSE

Compare the two extracts below and consider how effectively each has created a feeling of suspense. The first is written using short simple sentences and the second uses long complex sentences. Compare the two passages and then copy out and add to the table that follows, writing down the effects of using each type of sentence.

EXTRACT 1

Running. Faster. Faster. She grabbed the handle and turned it. Pushing the door open, she moved inside. No one was there. She turned and fled in the opposite direction.

EXTRACT 2

Jane stood in the doorway collecting her thoughts, delaying her decision until the last possible moment. As she plucked up her courage, she studied the door in front of her. It was crafted from an ancient-looking wood, the handle a simple metal ring. Jane glanced down at her shaking hand as she stretched out to turn the handle. She took two deep breaths, brushing her fringe from her pale face with nervous fingers. She stood a while, thoughts racing through her mind. Then, at last, she was ready. Grasping the handle, she turned it slowly; pushing the heavy door in front of her, she stepped into the hallway.

▼ SHORT, SIMPLE SENTENCES	▼ COMPLEX, LONGER SENTENCES
Develop tension	Give a detailed picture of the action

ACTIVITY 3
SKILLS: INTERPRETATION, ADAPTIVE LEARNING

▼ ADAPTING SENTENCE TYPES FOR EFFECT

Re-write the following extract as three sentences. What is the effect?

Ryan stood as still as stone, listening intently, but the faint rustling continued from inside the bedroom, so putting his good eye to the keyhole, he peered into the dimly lit room.

Re-write the following extract as five sentences. What is the effect?

He squinted through the gloom of the interior, which was quite deserted, with a single candle burning near the altar, thinking that it was sad to see an empty church on Christmas Eve, but, shrugging the thought away, he began a careful inspection of the places where the statue might have been concealed.

WRITING SKILLS

Assessment Objective 4

Communicate effectively and imaginatively, adapting form, tone and register of writing for specific purposes and audiences

Assessment Objective 5

Write clearly, using a range of vocabulary and sentence structures, with appropriate paragraphing and accurate spelling, grammar and punctuation

This chapter focuses on some core writing skills that you can apply to all parts of the English Language A course. Working through these lessons and activities will help you to develop the writing skills that you will need for the exams and coursework assignments.

The chapter is split into the following sections:
- Vocabulary
- Sentences
- Structure
- Punctuation and spelling.

In the writing sections of your exams you will need to be able to meet the Assessment Objectives AO4 and AO5.

WRITING SKILLS — VOCABULARY

LEARNING OBJECTIVES

This lesson will help you to:
- appreciate a writer's choice of words
- develop your own choice of words.

CHOOSING THE RIGHT VOCABULARY

Your words need to attract the attention of a reader and keep them engaged so that they will continue to read what you have written. Choosing the correct vocabulary is central to achieving this.

Words that engage the senses are particularly effective for this purpose. Look at the following opening sentences.

- It exploded in her face. (**sight**)
- Something was scratching under the door. (**sound**)
- From the kitchen came a reminder of the garlic that she loved. (**smell**)
- He pulled a face as if he had swallowed sour milk. (**taste**)
- The wind brushed his skin. (**touch**)

ACTIVITY 1   SKILLS: INNOVATION

▼ ENGAGING THE SENSES

Work with a partner and write two opening sentences using each of the senses: sight, sound, smell, taste and touch.

PRECISION

When you write or speak, your choice of words can be very important, especially when you write. When you speak, the person who is listening can ask you to explain yourself if anything you say is not clear. However, when you write, your reader will probably not be able to ask for an explanation so you have to get things right first time.

There are times when you need to be precise in your choice of words. Compare the following sentences, then answer the question.

> Some sort of animal could be seen approaching along the side of the road.

> A cat could be seen walking cautiously along the gutter.

▶ **Which of these two sentences is clearer and more precise? Which words and phrases bring about this effect?**

Next, compare the following sentences.

> Here at summer camp you will be under the supervision of a residential nurse and a medical practitioner who is available at any time.

> Welcome to summer camp where we hope you will enjoy being cared for.

You could read either of these sentences at the start of a stay at a summer camp and they would make sense. However, one immediately informs you of the medical precautions that have been taken and this suggests that

WRITING SKILLS — VOCABULARY

there might be a need for medical supervision. The second sentence simply provides a more appropriate, warmer welcome that expresses a hope that things go well.

Finally, compare the following sentences.

> Put dirty cutlery into the basket on the left and leave dirty crockery next to the sink on the right, taking care that no uneaten food is dropped carelessly onto the floor.

> Please leave your dirty cutlery and crockery in the places indicated; your keeping this area clean and tidy will help our staff who will appreciate your cooperation. Thank you.

The first sentence simply instructs you what to do and anticipates that you will be careless. The second example contains three very important words, 'please' and 'thank you'. This shows that the writer is addressing the reader with respect and consideration by showing why the reader's taking care will be appreciated by other people.

▶ Which of these two sentences will encourage better cooperation?

These examples show the impact that individual words can have and their significance in how a sentence is read.

ACTIVITY 2
SKILLS: CRITICAL THINKING, ANALYSIS, INTERPRETATION

▼ PRECISION IN ACTION

This extract is from an account of the sinking of the *Titanic*. The *Titanic* had been described as unsinkable, and so its sinking caused widespread shock in 1912. Read the following extract carefully, noticing the choice of language used to convey the witness's shock and horror. Then copy and complete the table, selecting key words and phrases that the writer uses to convey what they can see.

> In a couple of hours, though, she [the *Titanic*] began to go down more rapidly. Then the fearful sight began. The people in the ship were just beginning to realise how great their danger was. When the forward part of the ship dropped suddenly at a faster rate, so that the upward slope became marked, there was a sudden rush of passengers on all the decks towards the stern. It was like a wave. We could see the great black mass of people in the steerage sweeping to the rear part of the boat and breaking through into the upper decks. At the distance of about a mile we could distinguish everything through the night, which was perfectly clear. We could make out the increasing excitement on board the boat as the people, rushing to and fro, caused the deck lights to disappear and reappear as they passed in front of them.

▼ KEY WORD OR PHRASE	▼ WHAT IT CONVEYS
Fearful	This word conveys the pitiful state of the panicking passengers who were still on the ship.

▲ RMS *Titanic*

GENERAL VOCABULARY
stern rear of a boat
steerage the lower decks where the cheapest accommodation was provided

KEY POINT
The bigger your vocabulary, the more words you have to choose from and the easier it is to express yourself clearly. The best way to improve your vocabulary is by reading and taking an interest in the words that other people use.

WRITING SKILLS — VOCABULARY

LEARNING OBJECTIVES

This lesson will help you to:
- consider the effect of words and phrases
- demonstrate an ability to use words and phrases to good effect.

VOCABULARY FOR EFFECT

The words you use come from the vocabulary that you know and can use confidently and comfortably. Some words – *the*, *some*, *is*, *what*, for example – do not have the effect of other words such as *revolting*, *splendid*, *monster* and *eliminate*. Here you are going to look at the way writers choose words.

CONNOTATIONS

SUBJECT VOCABULARY

referend the thing or idea to which a word refers
connotations ideas linked to a word; ideas that have become associated with a word

GENERAL VOCABULARY

nauseous feeling sick

A word means more than just its **referend**. For example, the word 'grease' denotes or refers to an oily material often used to lubricate machinery or carry medication. Sometimes, however, the word is used to indicate distaste or revulsion, allowing the word's **connotations**, such as '**nauseous**', 'slimy' and 'sticky', to come into play.

Some words have positive or negative connotations, such as 'success' or 'regrets'.

> They talked all morning about her **success**.

In the first sentence, the use of the word 'success' means that you know that whatever she had done was approved of or appreciated as something positive.

> Now she was left only with her **regrets**.

However, in the second sentence, the use of the word 'regrets' lets you know that the subject now wishes that she had not done something which is seen in a negative light.

ACTIVITY 1

SKILLS ANALYSIS, INTERPRETATION, INNOVATION, COLLABORATION

▼ CHOOSING VOCABULARY IN PRACTICE

1. Work in small groups and discuss the effect of the following words and phrases:

    traitor   magic   cool   on the brink
    totally helpless   awesome   readily available
    desperate   cruel   adorable

2. Write complete sentences using each of the words and phrases listed in question 1.

3. Read the following extract and choose some of the words and phrases in it that have a particular effect on you as a reader. Then copy and complete the table that follows, adding your own ideas. Try to find at least another six examples.

    > Once upon a time it was said that three trolls lived in a forest. Local people lived in fear of them and avoided at night the twisting path that wound its way between the trees. From time to time late-night travellers would find themselves lost in the forest, alone and bewildered, and they would imagine the sound of a foot snapping a twig or catch in the corner of their eye something moving in the shadows.

    > These close encounters with the trolls were reported widely and fed the imaginations of the locals. None of them realised that nobody had ever been harmed in any way by these trolls, but that did not

WRITING SKILLS | VOCABULARY

restrain those people who really enjoyed terrifying their fellow citizens with outrageous tales of a death that could so easily catch up with them in the woods around the town.

The truth of the matter was that the three trolls were very shy. However, they craved the company of other beings and would approach them warily in the forest and then, before they could introduce themselves, their courage would fail and they would scuttle back into the undergrowth, safely out of sight.

▼ QUOTATION	▼ WHAT EFFECT IT HAS
Once upon a time…	This expression is frequently used to start fairy tales and so its use here alerts the reader to the possibility that this story follows key features of the genre.
Bewildered	This word creates a strong sense of uncertainty.

4 Complete the following sentence stem with six different words or phrases, indicating the effect you are aiming for in each case.

When it rains we…

5 Write a brief paragraph to finish the troll story. Before you start, state the effect that you would like to achieve; perhaps you would like to amuse your reader or shock them. Make it clear what your intention is before you start.

KEY POINT

In this section you have seen how words used thoughtfully enable the writer to achieve more. Powerful results are possible when words are effectively chosen.

SYNONYMS

A synonym is a word that means the same thing or nearly the same thing as another word. They can be used to echo or widen your understanding of a word or to reinforce an idea.

The young tree, **the sapling**, was the place chosen by the blackbird to build its nest.

Here the word 'sapling' provides a synonym for the tree. It helps to develop the referend (tree) by supplying more detail and further connotations.

▶ 'Sapling' provides a synonym for 'tree'. Can you think of any other synonyms?

WRITING SKILLS — VOCABULARY

LEARNING OBJECTIVES

This lesson will help you to:
- appreciate how language can be used to bring about a wide variety of effects.

LANGUAGE FOR DIFFERENT EFFECTS

As you read you become aware of the different ways in which language is used, and you might form preferences. When you read for a particular purpose, such as when looking for information on a holiday destination, you quickly learn to recognise the sort of material for which you are looking. This means that when you write something you should aim to make clear the purpose of the writing and the effect you want to achieve. It also helps to have examined and understood how other writers achieve different effects.

ACTIVITY 1 — SKILLS: PROBLEM SOLVING, ANALYSIS

▼ TYPE OF EFFECT IN WRITING

Visit a library and look for examples of written material that is informative, transactional, emotive, persuasive, discursive, entertaining, inspirational, descriptive, ironic and advisory.

Record the source for each type and be aware that one source may include more than one of these types. If necessary, a librarian should be able to help you.

SUBJECT VOCABULARY

transactional non-fiction writing for a purpose: to inform, explain, review, argue, persuade or advise

ironic using words to convey a meaning that is completely opposite to their apparent meaning

ACTIVITY 2 — SKILLS: CRITICAL THINKING, ANALYSIS, INTERPRETATION, CREATIVITY

▼ IDENTIFYING TYPES OF WRITING IN AN EXTRACT

1 Read the following extract and consider what effects the writer is trying to achieve. Look at some of the words used that indicate the writer's intentions. See if you can find and explain other ways in which the language is used to achieve important effects.

> I expect that you will have often heard warnings about the dangers to your health of smoking. One of my teachers once described handling the lungs of a victim of lung cancer; they resembled, he said, an old leather rugby ball[1] and they sat in his hands, hard and rough like a large lump of coal[2].
>
> Giving advice to young people is often difficult for parents and teachers[3]; it's part of growing up, to put aside advice and warnings from the older generation[4] and to trust your own judgement. One of the difficulties for young people, however, is "peer pressure," the need to fit in with their contemporaries, to meet their approval at least and, better still sometimes, to impress them. Daring to smoke, especially when it is forbidden, is part of this and it is probably as important for some young people as any pleasure to be gained from supposedly enjoying[5] a cigarette while watching nervously in case a teacher appears[6].

[1] Warning: this is what can happen to smokers.

[2] Description: shows the effects of smoking, to strengthen the warning.

[3] Information: plainly stated and aimed at readers who have yet to be parents or teachers.

[4] Explanation: rejecting adult advice is sometimes just a part of growing up.

[5] Ironic: suggests that the person is not really enjoying the cigarette when the purpose of smoking is supposedly to enjoy it.

[6] Description: shows the fear of a young person trying to show how grown-up he or she is.

WRITING SKILLS   VOCABULARY

Look at the following sentence.

>Now stop.

Which of the two words in this sentence is emphasised? What is the effect of this?

If the order of the words is altered, something changes.

>Stop now.

Instead of emphasising the action that is to be carried out, to stop, the emphasis is now on the timing of that action – it must be amended now, immediately.

The ordering of words in a sentence is important, particularly at the end of a sentence or before a pause. There is a brief moment before you hear the next word while the sound of the last word continues in your mind. Such a word is emphasised and brought to your attention.

Look at the following sentences. One is the first sentence of the extract in Activity 2, and the other is a re-ordered version. Consider the difference made by re-ordering the words. Which ending do you think is the more effective? Can you say why?

>I expect that you will have often heard warnings about the dangers to your health of smoking.

>I expect that you will have often heard warnings about the dangers of smoking to your health.

It may help you to analyse the phrases further by breaking them down into the following smaller phrases:

- about the dangers to your health / of smoking
- about the dangers of smoking / to your health.

There are three key words: 'dangers', 'health' and 'smoking'. Which of these should be most closely connected? Perhaps it would help to put the three words together like this: *Smoking endangers health.* Can you see now why smoking was left at the end of the original sentence?

KEY POINT

Your choice of words and phrases, and the way that you arrange and adapt them, are crucial if you want to communicate effectively.

SUBJECT VOCABULARY

rhetorical question a question that you ask as a way of making a statement, without expecting an answer
contrast where two objects, people or ideas are placed next to each other to highlight their differences
repetition saying the same thing more than once to highlight its importance
direct address using second person pronouns 'you' or 'your'
pattern of three where three things are linked or something is repeated three times in order to emphasise them and ensure they are memorable
hyperbole exaggerating for effect
alliteration the use of several words together that begin with the same sound or letter
similie a description that says that an object is like an image
personification when something which is not human is made to sound human by attributing human qualities to it

ACTIVITY 3   SKILLS INNOVATION, TEAMWORK

▼ OTHER LITERARY DEVICES

Look at the following literary devices. Can you think of an example of each? What effect do they have?

Rhetorical question
Contrast
Repetition
Direct address
Pattern of three
Hyperbole
Alliteration
Simile
Personification

WRITING SKILLS — VOCABULARY

LEARNING OBJECTIVES

This lesson will help you to:
- understand the importance of your choices when writing
- see how different choices can change meaning.

GENERAL VOCABULARY

clarity the quality of being expressed clearly

WHY YOUR CHOICES MATTER

You must take care when choosing words, when arranging them and when you incorporate them into the speech and writing.

- **Your choice of words** matters because it enables you to write with precision or exactness, clarity and an appropriate tone.
- **Your ordering of words** matters because it allows you to phrase points in a way that is effective and clear.
- **Your use of language and literary techniques** matters because it enables you to achieve particular effects with writing.

ACTIVITY 1
SKILLS PROBLEM SOLVING, ANALYSIS, INTERPRETATION, CREATIVITY, INNOVATION

▼ HOW ARRANGEMENT OF WORDS AFFECTS MEANING

1 William Carlos Williams was an American poet and doctor. Because his medical work took him into homes where families were facing emergencies, he was able to learn a lot about them. This is one of his most famous poems, 'This is just to say'.

> I have eaten 5
> the plums
> that were in
> the ice box
>
> and which 10
> you were probably
> saving
> for breakfast.
>
> Forgive me
> they were delicious 15
> so sweet
> and so cold.

It is not difficult to imagine 'This is just to say' as a hasty note of apology scrawled on a sticky note and stuck on a fridge door.

Now look at the words of the poem arranged as ordinary sentences.

> I have eaten the plums that were in the ice box and which you were probably saving for breakfast. Forgive me; they were delicious, so sweet and so cold.

▲ Even relatively simple poems such as 'This is just to say' can create strong images.

| WRITING SKILLS | VOCABULARY | 33 |

Work on your own and pick out key words in the poem which simply present clear facts. What words are left? What are the effects of these other words?

2 Work in a small group and consider the following questions.

▶ Which words describe the plums? What effect does this description have? Does it simply help you to imagine what the plums were like?

▶ What happens to the tone or mood of the poem after the first sentence?

▶ Which word is crucial here? What is the effect of the rest of the last sentence: 'they were delicious | so sweet | and so cold'? What would be the effect of describing the plums in the first sentence?

3 Write a cheeky note of mock apology along the lines of 'This is just to say'. For example, you could write an apology to a particular teacher for failing to do your homework.

4 Remember the different effects of, or purposes for writing: informative, transactional, emotive, persuasive, discursive, entertaining, inspirational, descriptive, ironic and advisory. How many of these can you find in Williams's poem? Explain how these effects are brought about.

ACTIVITY 2   SKILLS   CRITICAL THINKING, ANALYSIS

▼ CHECKING WRITTEN MATERIAL

To practise checking your own work, it helps to read other people's material critically. Read the following extract and the critical analysis of the text to see an example of critical reading. Can you suggest any other changes that should be made to the text?

> For some time, it suited the British authorities to sentence troublesome people[1] to transportation. Unfortunate poor people, who had found themselves starving and who had stolen food simply to stay alive, turned up[2] in the colonies in the country that would become Australia. Along with others who had chosen to settle in this new country[3], they made a go of things[4] and now take on[5] the English at games such as rugby and cricket and sometimes win.

[1] 'Convicts' would be a more precise way of referring to them and technically correct, whether or not they deserved conviction.

[2] '...turned up' is vague. They were sent.

[3] The reference to 'others who had chosen to settle in this new country' is verbose. They were settlers.

[4] 'made a go of things' is slang and may not be clear to all speakers of English. They succeeded.

[5] 'now take on' is inaccurate. It is their descendants who now take on the English.

▲ Transportation was often used as an alternative punishment to execution.

SUBJECT VOCABULARY
verbose excessively wordy or long-winded

KEY POINT
To write effectively, you must make sure your intention is clear to the reader.

WRITING SKILLS — SENTENCES

LEARNING OBJECTIVES

This lesson will help you to:
- understand the ways in which sentences can be assembled
- see the way that the meaning of a sentence is made effective.

SENTENCE TYPES

As you start to examine sentences it is important to remember what makes a sentence. A sentence is the most basic part of the written language and properly constructed sentences help you to communicate effectively, whatever your purpose.

A sentence is built around finite verbs, or action words, which indicate whether the action takes place in the past, present or future and which have some indication of the agent, the person or thing that carries out the action.

BUILDING SENTENCES

First look at sentences in a mechanical way. Here is a simple sentence. It has one main verb, *took*.

> They took their sunglasses.

To this you can add something more:

> They took their sunglasses and (they) enjoyed themselves.

The original sentence has become a compound sentence. Two simple sentences have become joined by a conjunction: *and*. They have become two coordinate **clauses** in a compound sentence. Each coordinate clause has a main verb; in this case, *took* and *enjoyed*.

You can develop the sentence further:

> They took their sunglasses and enjoyed themselves although it was raining.

To the compound sentence, with its two main verbs, a subordinate clause has been added: *although it was raining*. This clause also contains a verb, *was raining*; however, the clause, *although it was raining*, makes incomplete sense on its own. Without the main clause, you do not know what happened while it was raining.

This clause has to be joined to the main sentence with a subordinating conjunction, *although*. The sentence is now a complex sentence with two main verbs and a subordinate verb.

> They took their sunglasses and enjoyed themselves although it was raining.

You could link two of the components in other ways to form complex sentences:

> They took their sunglasses although it was raining.

> Although it was raining they took their sunglasses.

Each sentence here has a main clause and a subordinate clause.

Finally, look at another sentence:

> He looked at the menu which was badly written.

A simple sentence, *He looked at the menu*, has become a main clause to which a relative clause, *which was badly written* has been added. This relative clause has been linked with a relative conjunction, *which*, to form another complex sentence.

SUBJECT VOCABULARY

clause a group of words built around a finite verb

▲ 'They took their sunglasses and (they) enjoyed themselves' is a compound sentence.

WRITING SKILLS — SENTENCES

WHY EXAMINE SENTENCES LIKE THIS?

The purpose of examining sentences like this is to show you how you can build up ideas and communicate them effectively. By using subordinate, coordinate and relative clauses, you can add information without interrupting the flow of words and still indicate the most important aspects of what you are saying.

ACTIVITY 1
SKILLS: ANALYSIS

▼ IDENTIFYING FINITE VERBS

Identify the finite verbs in these sentences and decide what kind of sentence it is.
1. We should try to smile and try to laugh.
2. The program, which she had spent weeks developing, crashed.
3. Whenever they can all cows eat grass because grass is good for them.

ACTIVITY 2
SKILLS: ADAPTIVE LEARNING, INNOVATION

▼ VARYING SENTENCE TYPES

Try to write a short narrative, describing a short sequence of events, using simple, compound and complex sentences. You could start with these two sentences:

'His parents stood immediately in front of him. From beyond the closed door there came the sound of someone shouting and he decided to tell the truth.'

MINOR SENTENCES

You will sometimes find groups of words punctuated as if they were ordinary sentences when they are not.

Good. (A reaction to something.)
Over here! (A demonstration, some information.)
The boyfriend I ditched last week. (An answer to a question.)

In speech, such minor sentences are much more common and the listener can usually ask for clarification if required. When you write, it is better only to use minor sentences in direct or quoted speech to show what is actually said.

KEY POINT

Words and phrases can be built up into different types of sentences. By varying the sentences you use, you help the reader to stay engaged and strengthen the effect of what you write.

LEARNING OBJECTIVES

This lesson will help you to:
- find your opening words.

OPENING SENTENCES

Choosing the very first thing that you want to write or say can sometimes make it difficult to start. However, once you have taken that first step, you can continue more easily.

Opening sentences are very important as they set the tone for the reader. They are mainly used to introduce but can also be used to explain, attract attention or pose questions.

ACTIVITY 1 SKILLS CRITICAL THINKING, REASONING

▼ OPENING SENTENCE STYLE

Here are some opening sentences. Where would you expect to find them? In a novel, a newspaper, a text book or a television broadcast?

1. It was a man in front of them, a man with a gun.
2. Before being despatched to you, the contents of this package were carefully checked.
3. Hot pools can be found in Rotorua, on New Zealand's North Island, evidence of volcanic activity.
4. The views here are fantastic; we can see from the car park a long gentle slope down to a beach where Pacific rollers crash and spread themselves across the sand.
5. Once upon a time there was a wild goat who lived in the forest.
6. And European ministers gathered today in Brussels to update their latest agreement.
7. In order to update their latest agreement, European ministers gathered in Brussels.

Work in groups and match each of these opening sentences to the explanations that follow.

  i A newspaper article or an introduction to an item broadcast on radio or television. It's about an event that has already taken place, but is being reported very soon afterwards. The main point is conveyed early in the sentence to encourage the reader to continue to pay attention.
  ii An information slip. The sentence tells you what has been done and gives an explanation that is designed to reassure the reader.
  iii Travel writing. The reader is stopped by the drama of the opening which is followed by a description of a geographical feature.
  iv A history book. The sentence begins with an explanation of why the event took place with the main point made briefly at the end of the sentence, as if it is of less importance.

WRITING SKILLS — SENTENCES

v A narrative, the beginning of a novel or of a chapter in a novel. The reader is confronted with a simple but dramatic scene with only the bare essentials so that we are not distracted from the main image.

vi A geography book. The subject of the sentence is a geographical feature, introduced immediately and referred to as 'evidence', a matter of interest to geographers. This information is delivered in a straightforward manner.

vii A children's fairy story. The opening phrase is frequently used to introduce children's stories.

ACTIVITY 2

SKILLS: ANALYSIS, INNOVATION, COMMUNICATION

▼ KEY WORDS

Work in groups to copy and complete the table below. Look again at the sentences in Activity 1 and consider the essential words in each opening sentence and what effects they create.

▼ ESSENTIAL WORDS	▼ THE EFFECTS THEY CREATE
1 'in front', 'man', 'gun'	There is drama because the writer is confronted by an armed man.

After completing the table, work on your own or with a partner. Write another introductory sentence to match each of the explanations in Activity 1. Swap your opening sentences with a partner or with another pair. Write a sentence of your own to follow the introductory sentence that has been passed to you.

KEY POINT

To start a piece of writing you can:
- use particular words or phrases
- present something that is obviously new
- refer to something that has already been mentioned before saying something new about it.

▲ The Charlemagne building – part of the EU in Brussels

LEARNING OBJECTIVES

This lesson will help you to:
- understand the ways that sentences achieve their effects
- understand the way in which a sentence is constructed around its main points.

SENTENCES FOR EFFECT

You have already seen the mechanical ways in which sentences can be built up. Now look at the ways in which sentences achieve their effects.

ANALYSING SENTENCES

Here's a sentence from a book for young children:

> The cat sat on the mat.

To see how this sentence achieves its effect, consider the point of the sentence. What is it about? It's about the cat sitting on the mat. That is all you are told. This is a *periodic sentence*, a few simple words followed by a full stop (.) or, as it is called in American English, a period.

You can extend this sentence:

> The cat sat on the mat and smiled.

This time the question is more subtle: what main point or points is the writer making? You are told two main points.

A compound sentence is a sentence with more than one subject.

▲ What is the main point of this image?

SUBJECT VOCABULARY

periodic sentence a sentence that is not complete until the final word or clause

ACTIVITY 1

SKILLS ADAPTIVE LEARNING, INNOVATION, TEAMWORK

▼ PERIODIC SENTENCES

Write a few periodic sentences on individual slips of paper. Then work as a group and see how many balanced sentences you can form by joining the slips in pairs. You will probably need a few additional words.

Now look at a final development of the sentence.

> With a huge grin on her face the cat sat on the mat while from next door there came the sound of a dog digging its way under the fence.

The main point is still *The cat sat on the mat.* All the other information is of lesser importance and the main point is inserted among this additional information. This is a 'loose sentence'.

Each person in the group now writes one short periodic sentence. Pass your sentence to another member of the group who should add further information in order to make a balanced sentence. This should then be passed onto the next member of the group to be turned into a loose sentence.

WRITING SKILLS — SENTENCES

ACTIVITY 2

SKILLS: ADAPTIVE LEARNING, INNOVATION, TEAMWORK

▼ CONSTRUCTING VARIED SENTENCES

Work on your own and write three sentences as follows:
1. A periodic sentence including one of the following:
   - an important piece of information
   - a description of something that you find attractive
   - something in which you believe very strongly.
2. A balanced sentence developing the idea from your first sentence in two main points.
3. A loose sentence developing your idea further.

Then, in groups or as a class, listen to each other's sets of sentences read aloud and see how quickly you can identify the points they are trying to make.

MOVING ON

Look at two aspects of these examples: their length and their ordering.

> It was late. He had left home early, caught the early bus, but the accident on the main road meant he was alone now, after dark, in an area that he did not know.

A short opening sentence establishes the time in a dramatic fashion and the following sentence builds up to the next dramatic revelation, that the character is alone. It is then that more drama is revealed: the darkness and his lack of familiarity with the area.

> These instructions should be followed carefully. Operatives who fail to do this will be dealt with severely.

Here a simple sentence conveys information coupled with a warning at the end where it is more noticeable, more emphatic. The warning tone is maintained in the second sentence with its final warning that severe treatment is in prospect for operatives who fail to head the instructions.

> What would you do? You come home to find your house broken open, your goods stolen, and all the plumbing smashed. Then the sergeant down at the police station asks you to stay calm. Stay calm?

Confronted with a disaster, someone asks why they should be expected to stay calm. A short question holds the reader ready to respond. 'You' introduces the second sentence, an attempt to lead the reader into imagining the writer's feelings and aspects of the disaster are listed to build up the force of the description. In the next sentence, the tension is eased as you are told of the police sergeant's reaction, ready to hear the anger of the final, minor sentence, a simple question that is all the more direct and challenging in its brevity.

KEY POINT

In a periodic sentence the main point is found at the end, in a balanced sentence there is more than one main point and in a loose sentence the main point is not at the end. You can use this variety of sentence types to help convey effectively the things you wish to say in writing.

WRITING SKILLS — SENTENCES

LEARNING OBJECTIVES

This lesson will help you to:
- consider the purpose of sentences and the way you construct them to achieve your purposes.

SENTENCE PURPOSE

It is important to consider the purpose of sentences and the way in which they are constructed. By always being aware of this, it is possible to convey clear and strong ideas.

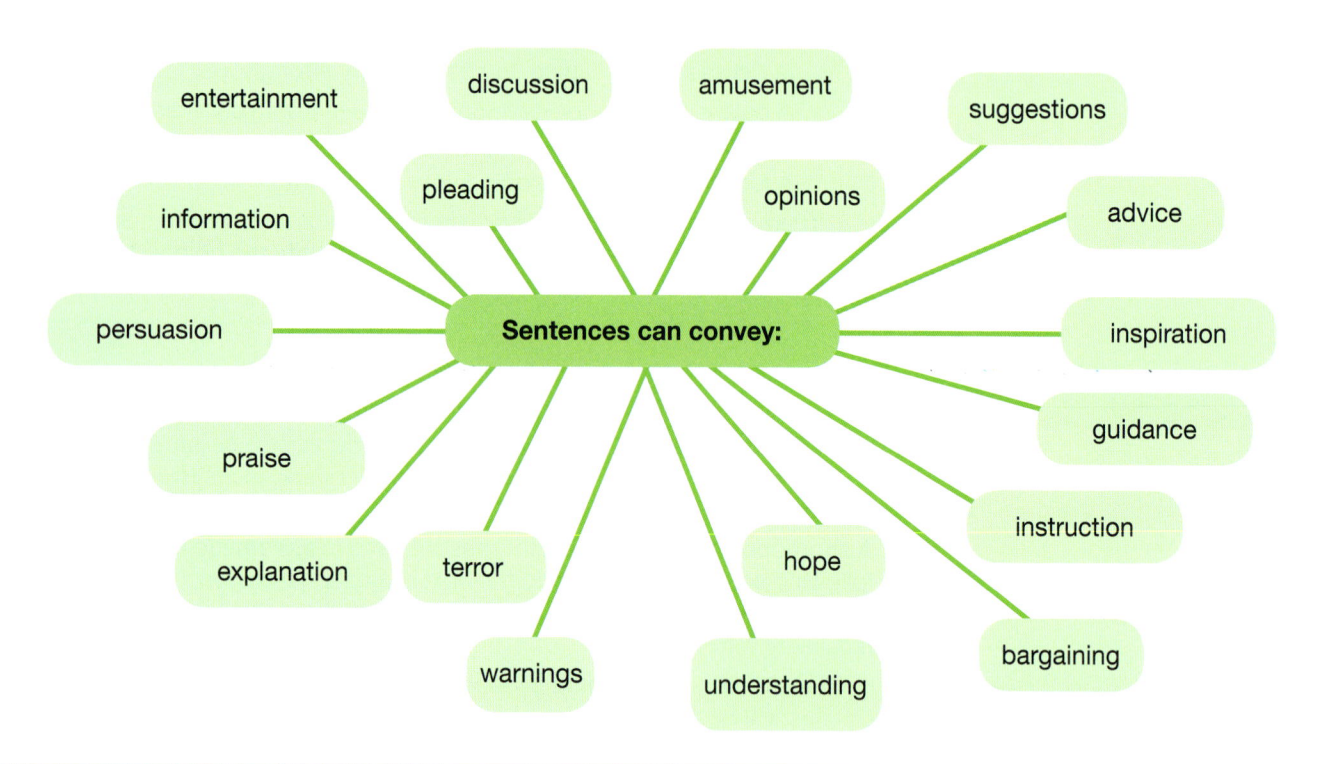

Sentences can convey:
- entertainment
- discussion
- amusement
- suggestions
- information
- pleading
- opinions
- advice
- persuasion
- inspiration
- guidance
- praise
- instruction
- explanation
- terror
- hope
- bargaining
- warnings
- understanding

BASIC SENTENCE TYPES

There are three basic types of sentence: sentences that are informative, descriptive or discursive.

EFFECTS OF DIFFERENT SENTENCES

Here you will look at the effects that can be achieved in an opening sentence.

Look at the development of a simple sentence that provides information.

> Our pets' favourite sleeping place was the dog's bed.

Now some description has been added.

> Our pets' favourite sleeping place was the dog's bed, nestled in a woollen blanket next to the radiator.

And now some discussion has been added.

> Our pets' favourite sleeping place was the dog's bed, nestled in a woollen blanket next to the radiator, which was not fair on the two cats, the guinea pigs and the mice which used to hide there when they managed to escape from their cage.

▶ Identify the key words that convey information, description and discussion.

▶ Divide this last sentence into three sentences, one informative, one descriptive and one discursive.

KEY POINT

Remember to always consider your audience, whether you are speaking directly to them or leaving something in writing for them to read later.

WRITING SKILLS SENTENCES

COMMENTARIES

Here are two passages for you to consider. The first one is measured, with quite long sentences.

> The news had arrived and it was not good. For many people in the crowd it was not bad news that they were expecting, but something better, the prospect of better rations at least. Better still would be release from this strange land and transport back to the border, if not all the way home. However, once they had listened to the commandant's words, there was nothing for it but to make their way back to the barracks and try to get some sleep.

The first, balanced sentence provides two items of information; the second item provides a response to the first, a natural flow of ideas. The second complex sentence contrasts this bad news with what they had perhaps been hoping for, 'something better'. This sentence is extended here with the phrase, 'the prospect of better rations at least', an important descriptive detail. The idea of hope is also extended in a complex sentence where a group of three items remind of this: release, transport to the border and transport home. The first, subordinate clause in the final sentence kills off any prospect of hope and leads to a main clause in which the inevitability of this is brought home to the reader and the prisoners' attempts to sleep bring closure to this episode.

The second passage is rather more dramatic.

> The hand of the clock moves to the vertical, like a sentinel arriving at his post. Now the moment has come. The referee looks around the pitch, catches the eye of each linesman and then raises his whistle to his lips. Mahama's boot makes contact. There is the beginning of a roar. The ball reaches a winger. He turns and sends the ball back towards the keeper who picks it up, as if concerned for its safety. The ball bounces once in front of him and he kicks it forwards. Razak it is now. He moves forward. Modi joins him. One kick and the ball is bouncing in the net.

A longer opening sentence holds the reader at the moment before the game begins. A short sentence hurries you towards the start, increasing the sense of drama, but then you are held still as the next sentence, a compound one, lists the referee's three actions as he prepares to unleash the players. Three short, simple sentences propel the action forward, then a longer, complex sentence allows the goalkeeper to slow things down. The reader watches as the ball is taken under his control and returned, a balanced sentence holding back the excitement until a series of short sentences, pared of any surplus information, conveys the essentials and the scoring of the goal provides a natural end to the passage.

▲ Different types of sentence can determine how something is read.

ACTIVITY 1

SKILLS ADAPTIVE LEARNING, INNOVATION, COMMUNICATION, TEAMWORK

▼ CONTROLLING YOUR WRITING

1 Work on your own and develop one of the following ideas into a paragraph of at least four sentences of varying length and complexity.
   - The approach of a stranger.
   - A surprise around a corner.
   - A glance from a window.
   - A clever idea.
2 Read this paragraph aloud, to your partner and ask them to comment.

WRITING SKILLS — STRUCTURE

LEARNING OBJECTIVES

This lesson will help you to:
- appreciate how you can structure or organise writing effectively, whether you are providing information, describing something, discussing something or providing entertainment.

PRINCIPLES OF STRUCTURE

When a piece of writing is judged by readers or marked by examiners, the purpose of the writing is considered, alongside the accuracy and clarity of the writing and with an overall sense of the writing's effectiveness.

Here you are going to consider the way that sentences and paragraphs are organised so that the structure of the writing is enhanced and made more effective.

UNDERSTANDING THE PRINCIPLES OF STRUCTURE

Read the following sentence.

> Zlatan, look out!

There is an urgent call to one person, the first name you read: Zlatan. The most important word is placed at the start of the sentence. Now look at the following sentence.

> After school I need to speak to you, Zlatan.

Here a teacher is making an announcement and wants all the class to listen until the name of the student concerned is revealed at the end of the sentence.

If you ask what a sentence is about, you can identify its subject. The subject of each of these sentences has been highlighted.

1 **The ice cream** was hidden in the freezer.
2 Hidden in the freezer was **the ice cream**.
3 **The ice cream**, which her brother had hidden in the freezer, was discovered.
4 Hidden in the freezer, which had been turned off, was **the ice cream**.

Those parts of the sentence that are not the subject are called the predicate. The predicate can be discovered by asking the question, 'What am I told about the subject of the sentence?'

Apply this question to the four sentences above.

▲ The structure of a sentence can alter the meaning and impact. Compare 'Zlatan, look out!' with 'After school I need to speak to you Zlatan.'

ACTIVITY 1   SKILLS INNOVATION, TEAMWORK

▼ PURPOSE AND PROGRESSION IN SENTENCES

Work in pairs and identify the key words and ideas in each of these sentences. Ask what seems to be the key ideas that link one sentence to another. Then look at the beginnings, middles and endings of these sentences.

> The ice cream was hidden in the freezer. Then the bananas were discovered in the bathroom and the marshmallows tucked away in Sophie's bedroom. Now there would have to be an inquiry.

Now identify the important stage in each sentence of this mini-narrative.

WRITING SKILLS — STRUCTURE

STAGES OF WRITING

The principle of stages in writing applies to any piece of writing that you create. Whether it is a brief email, a set of instructions for a piece of machinery, a text book or a novel, it will require an introduction, a middle section and an ending.

ACTIVITY 2
SKILLS CRITICAL THINKING, ANALYSIS

▼ STAGE TRANSITIONS

Work with a partner and identify the key words that show the transition from introduction, to mid-section, to the ending in the paragraph that follows.

> The Turkish teacher met them at the airport and introduced her husband, a company lawyer. Soon they were hurrying along the freeway and then there was a turning off, followed by miles bumping along worn back roads. For a while he wondered just what he had let himself in for and then the car slowed. Away from the road there was a large timber house, set in a large garden. Then he sighed with relief for this was to be his home for the next six weeks.

Now use those same words in a paragraph of your own construction, to show shifts from the introduction, to the middle section, to the conclusion.

KEY POINT

You have looked at how sentences can have an introduction, a middle section and an ending. The same is true of a more substantial piece of writing, including books.

ACTIVITY 3
SKILLS CRITICAL THINKING

▼ BREAKING DOWN STORIES

Work with a partner and identify any story that you know and that you think your classmates will know. It could be a television drama, a film you have watched, a story that you have read or a story that was read to you. Describe the three stages of the story (the introduction, the middle section and the ending) in three sentences.

Here is an example of three sentences that outline a well-known story (*The Cruel Sea* by Nicholas Montsarrat) in the same way.

> We meet Ericson, the captain of both the boats involved in the story, in a naval dockyard where the first of his two commands is still in the hands of the builders. Ericson's career, as captain of a warship that is sunk, and of another warship that survives the war, leads us through five years of naval warfare in what came to be known as *The Battle of the Atlantic*. At the end of this battle, Ericson finds himself in charge of captured submarines which are now incapable of threatening allied shipping any more.

LEARNING OBJECTIVES

This lesson will help you to:
- use paragraphs effectively.

PARAGRAPHING FOR EFFECT

There are no mechanical rules about the size or length of sentences or paragraphs, nor about the number of lines or words needed in each. The important thing is to ask yourself: how can I best organise sentences and paragraphs so that they are as clear as possible?

You have already looked at ideas that link sentences. Now, when you start a new paragraph you have to do two things: firstly, maintain contact with what you have already written and, secondly, develop ideas, sometimes by introducing new material, new ideas and new directions.

ACTIVITY 1

SKILLS: CRITICAL THINKING, ANALYSIS, INTERPRETATION

▼ **DEVELOPING NARRATIVES**

Work with a partner or in groups and read the passage below. There are three key items in the first paragraph: the tea, the woman and the newspaper. Follow these items from the first paragraph into the second paragraph. How is each developed?

> The woman offered him another cup of tea. She had been very friendly since he had stepped into the house. The room seemed all right and now there was another cup of tea. There was something slightly odd about the taste, not enough to worry him and, anyway, he wanted to find out what the rent would be. While she waited for his answer she glanced down at the newspaper and folded it away, hastily, out of sight, behind one of the cushions.
>
> There was a knock at the front door. The woman got up and went into the hall to see who it was and he could hear a conversation get under way. From behind the cushion he retrieved the newspaper and read the headline: *Missing students – poisoner suspected*. He took another sip of his tea. This time he screwed up his face and put down the cup. From one side he picked up his coat and stood up.

▶ What is new in the second paragraph?

▶ What changes about the young man in the second paragraph?

There is a balance in these two paragraphs. You learn why the young man has come to the house and that information needs no further development. The hints about the tea in the first paragraph prepare you for the dramatic newspaper headline revealed in the second paragraph.

WRITING SKILLS — STRUCTURE 45

ACTIVITY 2
SKILLS ▶ CRITICAL THINKING, ANALYSIS

▼ KEY CONTENT IN PARAGRAPHS

Work with a partner or on your own and identify the key words or ideas in each of the following two paragraphs. Copy and complete the table, commenting on the links between these words and ideas.

> At the foot of the hill there is a large spread of woodland, pine trees – dark green, that swarm upwards, almost to the top of the hill. Local people love this place, to which they bring their dogs and their children; on most days, providing the weather is reasonable, you will see them dotted about on the parkland, clearly in no hurry, clearly enjoying this special space.
>
> Now the county council has announced plans to extend the city ring-road to accommodate industrial traffic to the new factory sites as well as the growing rush-hour traffic associated with the expansion of the university. Councillors are divided about the threats to local people's leisure and the need to move traffic quickly around the city. Protests are planned for next week and locals hope that the council will be sufficiently embarrassed and will re-think the transport committee's recommendations.

▼ KEY WORDS AND IDEAS	▼ LINKS
Woodland/ring-road	Different types of location introducing each paragraph and contrasting what exists and what is proposed.

▶ A new paragraph can be used to shift tone or ideas.

ACTIVITY 3
SKILLS ▶ ADAPTIVE LEARNING, CREATIVITY

▼ DEVELOPMENT IDEAS

Work with a partner and develop the ideas listed below into sentences and paragraphs for a report in a newspaper. Remember to arrange the ideas in an order that suits the effect you want your report to have. Do you want to alert your readers, warn them or reassure them? Or something else completely?

> A burst water main, a busy road junction, freezing weather conditions, accidents and a busy hospital.

KEY POINT

As you move from one paragraph to another you should indicate clearly that you are either developing an idea or introducing a new one.

WRITING SKILLS — STRUCTURE

LEARNING OBJECTIVES

This lesson will help you to:
- organise the flow of ideas to maximise their effect.

LINKING IDEAS

Good writing flows and is easy to read. Here you will see how a writer can organise the flow of ideas to maximise their effect.

UNDERSTANDING HOW IDEAS LINK TOGETHER

Read this article about Nevil Shute, a 20th century British author. His best-known novel was *A Town Like Alice*.

Not many people[1] who enjoyed Shute's novels realised that he had started out as an engineer in the early days of aero-engineering after the First World War, not with aeroplanes, but with airships[2]. It was while he was working as an engineer that he began to write[3].

Although well-qualified[4], with an engineering degree from Oxford University, Shute, whose full name was Nevil Shute Norway was a practical man[5], interested in the ways that people from different backgrounds could get along well. In *A Town Like Alice*, a brief encounter during the Second World War between a brash Australian prisoner of war and an English girl who had also been taken prisoner by the Japanese, developed into a romance as the Australian travels to England after the war to find the woman he had known as Mrs Bong[6].

It is in his non-fiction[7], his auto-biography, *Slide Rule*, that we learn how to build an air-ship and he describes the ladder-way inside the craft[8] that enables engineers to climb out onto the top of the balloon while it is flying to sit and chat[9]. While the engineers hold on to a safety rope, passengers in the cabin slung below the balloon travel in comparative safety[10]. Shute also wrote authoritatively about the economics of air-ship construction and the politics that drove a government-controlled industry to compete with a private one[11].

In this book we also learn of[12] his terrible sadness in his early teens when his older brother was killed in the trenches of the First World War[13], as a result of the enemy's tunnelling under the British trenches and packing the space with high explosive. Shute watched as his brother, Fred, took two weeks to die in hospital in France; Shute's parents, unlike most people, were in a position to drive across France to visit their dying son. When Shute eventually wrote about this he was forty and still missing his brother terribly[14].

ACTIVITY 1

SKILLS: CRITICAL ANALYSIS, ANALYSIS, REASONING

▼ IDEA PROGRESSION

Read through the passage about Nevil Shute. Then look at each of the numbered sections along with the table which shows how each of these sections moves the reader along through the ideas conveyed.

Try to see how the flow is maintained. For example, the first point concerns the movement from the idea of Shute as a well-known novelist to the less well-known fact that he began his professional life as an

WRITING SKILLS | STRUCTURE

KEY POINT

Writing that flows helps the reader to enjoy and follow a piece of writing. Look at the second sentence of the piece about Shute that refers first to engineering, which has already been established, but also to his writing, a theme that is taken up in the next paragraph.

aeronautical engineer. The next direction of the flow of this passage is provided by the information that he worked, not with aeroplanes, which is what you might expect of aeronautical engineers, but with airships. It might help you to see your reading of the passage as a series of steps that lead you from one idea to the next, so that you follow the writer and understand what it is that they want to say.

1 Engaging the reader	Contrast novelist/engineer, surprising information
2 Contrast – unexpected	'not with' / 'airships' rather than 'aeroplanes'
3 Moving along	From engineering to writing
4 Anticipation	'Although well-qualified…'
5 Comparisons	Educated but practical, engineering and people
6 Adding detail	Summary of a novel
7 Adding ideas	Non-fiction as well as fiction
8 Explanation	Intriguing detail
9 Illustration	Engaging the imagination
10 Contrast	Passengers at ease, 'a safety rope'
11 Adding information	Expanding a point: economics and politics covered
12 Adding information	'We also learn': preparing for a new topic
13 Explanation	Details to help the reader understand this topic
14 Final comment	Distanced: 'eventually'

ACTIVITY 2 SKILLS CRITICAL THINKING, CREATIVITY

▼ LINKING KEY POINTS AND IDEAS

Find a piece of writing about a topic that you like that is between one and two pages long. It could be on sport, music, IT, engineering, fashion, cooking, travel or a piece of fiction. Mark or identify each of the main points as they are introduced and make a list of them. Re-order the list if you think the flow of writing could be improved then re-write the piece in your own words, taking care to link your points.

▲ You could try structuring your writing around these images.

LEARNING OBJECTIVES

This lesson will help you to:
- control sentences accurately so that what is written can be read easily and clearly understood.

ENDING A SENTENCE

The way in which a sentence finishes can have a dramatic impact on its purpose and content.

Read this passage aloud.

> there are three ways of ending a sentence this is very important if you do not punctuate sentences accurately they are very difficult to read then the meaning will not be clear do you understand this it is extremely important

Now read this passage aloud.

> There are three ways of ending a sentence. This is very important. If you do not punctuate sentences accurately they are very difficult to read. Then the meaning will not be clear. Do you understand this? It is extremely important!

Three ways of signalling the end of the sentences have been used in the second passage. Unless you use a question mark for a question or an exclamation mark to stress something important or dramatic, you should use a full stop. In American English, full stops are called 'periods'.

ACTIVITY 1 — SKILLS: INNOVATION

▼ CHOOSING CLOSING PUNCTUATION

Work on your own and punctuate the following passage. If you cannot read the passage aloud, try to imagine the sound of your voice as you read it. Remember, each sentence must have at least one main verb.

> it was night over the hill they could see the stars they had been told of the dangers of the area but they had decided to continue anyway soon they reached the first of the houses where the street took a sharp turn to the right soon they would be back home

KEY POINT

Punctuate the ends of sentences clearly so that they are easily read and easily understood.

Questions must be finished with a question mark. They are formed in two ways. They may be formed with auxiliary verbs such as *would*, *should*, *do*, *does*, and so on. For example: *Should we leave?* or *Does he take sugar?*

Another way of forming questions involves the reversal of the subject/verb order in a statement. For example, *Is it theirs?* This form of question may include question words such as *why*, *what*, *where*, *who*, *whom* and *how*. For example, *How do you like your coffee?*

Exclamation marks can be used to represent strong emotions, emphasise points or suggest volume. They should be used sparingly so as to not lessen their impact.

WRITING SKILLS — PUNCTUATION AND SPELLING

LEARNING OBJECTIVES

This lesson will help you to:
- understand that a comma is used to indicate a pause within a sentence.

COMMAS

Commas are essential for dictating the way in which sentences are read, spoken and understood. A single comma can change the entire meaning of a sentence.

Commas do the following:
- indicate a pause, to leave clear a main clause:

  While it was raining, they watched a film.
- separate items in a list:

  For breakfast he ate cereal, toast, baked beans and two apples.
- clarify meaning by separating ideas:

  His friend who had black hair was found with him. (*It was his friend with black hair who was found with him, not one of his other friends.*)

  His friend, who had black hair, was found with him. (*This friend just happened to have black hair.*)
  - Look at this sentence:

    The River Niger rises in the north of Nigeria, which takes its name from the river, to the north of Lake Oguta, and makes its way southwards towards the delta and out into the Gulf of Guinea.

    The first and second commas separate information about the origin of Nigeria's name and the second and third commas separate further information, about the place where the river rises. These three commas enclose additional information that does not impede the main flow of the sentence. Without this information the main sections of the sentence would still flow together.

    The River Niger rises to the north of Lake Oguta and makes its way southwards towards the delta and out into the Gulf of Guinea.
- open and close direct speech (notice how the actual words that are spoken are enclosed in speech marks, or inverted commas):

  'Come in,' said the doctor, 'do sit down.' The patient made himself comfortable and replied, 'Good to see you, doctor.'

  'You know,' said the doctor, 'it's a good job you made this appointment.'

ACTIVITY 1 — SKILLS: INNOVATION

▼ USING COMMAS

Insert commas where required in the following passage.

It was raining. Slowly very slowly the puddles filled dull and grey under the dull light. Look out! shouted Henry but it was too late. I told you to look where you were going. You never pay attention ever. Further down the road half a kilometre away an old truck started up misfired once or twice and began a struggle up the hill towards them.

KEY POINT

It is easy to read quickly from the start to the end of a sentence, as long as commas are used correctly to make clear the writer's intentions.

WRITING SKILLS — PUNCTUATION AND SPELLING

LEARNING OBJECTIVES

This lesson will help you to:
- understand how apostrophes are used.

APOSTROPHES

Apostrophes have two functions. They indicate the omission of one or more letters and, usually with the letter **s**, they indicate possession, meaning that something belongs to someone or something else. Like other punctuation marks, if they are used correctly, they help to make clear to the reader what the writer intended.

Read both these sentences aloud.

> It's going to be a long night and there's nowhere to go.
>
> It is going to be a long night and there is nowhere to go.

When you read the second sentence you have to make just a little more effort to read *It is* and *there is*. In speech people usually prefer to elide the *i* in *is*. That means the sound is suppressed or glided over for the sake of ease and speed. In writing, however, this is often seen as informal in style.

You can do this with other letters and, so long as you use the apostrophe, this will be clear to the reader. Here is another example.

> We haven't a penny between us but she's got plenty.

This time the *o* and *ha* sounds have been missed.

When an apostrophe is used to indicate possession, the apostrophe usually appears before the *s* if the subject is singular and afterwards if the subject is plural.

> Helen's mother hid all her brothers' bicycles.

With words that end in *s*, or words that do not take an *s* to show the plural there are two ways to punctuate possession, for example, *Chris' bike* and *the children's clothes*. Alternatively, an additional *'s* can be added to names ending with an *s*: *Chris's bike*. However, ensure that you remain consistent by only following one of these rules.

Finally, you have to remember *Its* and *It's*. When you omit the apostrophe in *its*, *it is* possessive. *It's* is a contraction of *it is*.

ACTIVITY 1 — SKILLS INNOVATION

USING APOSTROPHES

Insert the nine apostrophes required here.

> 'Glad youve come,' she said. 'Ive been lookin for you everywhere. I cant imagine whats the matter ere.'
>
> 'Troubles comin soon. Wed best go home.'

KEY POINT

Clear use of the apostrophe allows quick reading and clear meaning.

WRITING SKILLS — PUNCTUATION AND SPELLING

LEARNING OBJECTIVES

This lesson will help you to:
- understand how to use different punctuation marks.

COLONS, SEMI-COLONS, DASHES, BRACKETS, ELLIPSES

There is a range of different punctuation marks, each capable of achieving a particular effect or changing the meaning of a sentence. Being able to use them all will ensure your writing is varied and engaging.

COLONS

Colons are used to introduce evidence or examples.

> They could see what was stopping the car: a brick wedged under the tyre.

▶ Write three sentences using a colon like this.

SEMI-COLONS

Semi-colons are used to join closely related sentences or separate long items in a list.

> It was too late; slowly he raised his hands.

> They were all there; Billy who had broken his leg last year; Charlie who had rescued him, although he too had been wounded; and the dog.

▶ Write two sentences following the first example and two following the second example.

DASHES

Dashes are used to signal clearly the insertion of non-essential material into a sentence. Their purpose could be to add emphasis, to interrupt or to indicate an abrupt change of thought.

> They were all there – two men and a dog – and she realised that the police would have to be called.

▶ Write two sentences following the pattern of this example.

BRACKETS

Brackets are used to add additional material about a preceding item. Remember that, unlike dashes, brackets must be used in pairs.

> Kevin (lead singer) and Sharon were the band's best performers.

▶ Insert information in brackets about the asterisked words in the following sentence.

> 'Their guide* who had joined them at the airport helped two of them* to carry their bags.'

ELLIPSES

Ellipses are used where a word is omitted and are made up of three dots (like full stops). They are most useful in direct speech; when you speak, you are more likely to pause or break off in mid-sentence.

> He paused. 'I don't think I'm…' With that he turned away.

> 'If you don't stop that I'll, I'll…' Before she could finish they had drowned her in laughter.

▶ Work with a partner and construct two dialogues between two or more characters. Each of you should write the first line of a dialogue, then pass it to your partner who should write the second line. Continue like this until you have written at least ten lines.

KEY POINT

Remember that each of these punctuation marks has a distinctive function.

WRITING SKILLS — PUNCTUATION AND SPELLING

LEARNING OBJECTIVES

This lesson will help you to:
- avoid common spelling errors.

COMMON SPELLING ERRORS

It is easy to find lists of commonly misspelt words on the internet. These sites often provide reminders for some spellings and suggest that you make a list of the words that you find difficult to spell.

Correct spelling is something that depends on your visual memory so reading will help. You should also try to find ways of remembering something about the word, for example, station*a*ry and station*e*ry.

Where *a* is the final vowel the word *stationary* means *not moving* or *stopped*. Think of *stopped* as **a**rrested, a word which begins with an *a*.

Where *e* is the final vowel the word *stationery* refers to **e**nvelopes and writing paper.

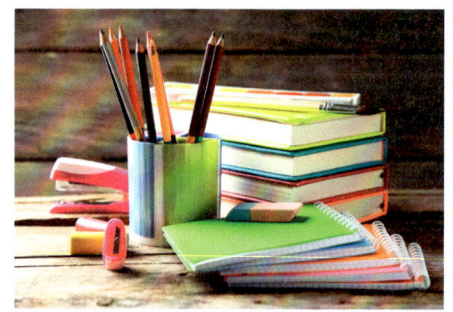

▲ Stationary/stationery; similar words, very different things

Another way to help yourself to remember difficult spellings is to look closely at the word, jotted down perhaps on a scrap of paper, and try to memorise it. Then cover up the word while you try to write it down accurately. Repeat this process if necessary. (Here's another difficult word, necessary. Remember, shirts are ne*c*e*ss*ary – one **c**ollar and two **s**leeves.)

Words that contain *e* and *i* together are sometimes easier to spell if you remember the following **mnemonic**:

i before e, except after c, unless the sound matches weigh.

So you have: *yield*, *receive*, *sleigh*. There are exceptions such as *seize*.

Particularly important words that you should make an effort to spell correctly include:

accompany	disguise	lightening	suspicious
agreeable	dumb	lightning	temperature
anxious	engineer	naughty	thorough
applaud	exhibition	neighbour	though
certificate	experiment	niece	thought
civilised	fulfil	occur	tremendous
compliment	government	occurred	vegetable
complement	fatigue	privilege	ventilation
conferred	height	prosperous	
deceitful	immediately	succession	
decision	language	suspicion	

SUBJECT VOCABULARY

mnemonic a device used to aid memory – usually in the form of a saying or rhyme

KEY POINT

Avoiding spelling mistakes will make your writing much more effective and engaging

WRITING SKILLS — PUNCTUATION AND SPELLING

LEARNING OBJECTIVES

This lesson will help you to:
- start checking your writing automatically.

IMPROVE YOUR WRITING

Like any practical activity, writing will improve with practice. Write regularly, at least ten minutes a day and always check your writing as you go. It's a good idea to check each paragraph as you proceed. That way you will also have a second look at your ideas and an opportunity to consider again how you will lead your ideas into the next paragraph.

Spelling, punctuation and grammar must all come together when you write. In practice you have been able to deal with them separately, but when you write you have to cope with all of them at once.

TIPS TO REMEMBER

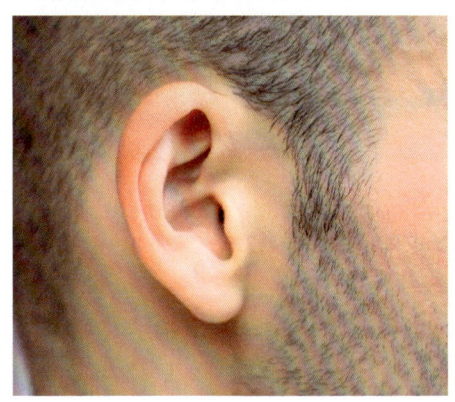

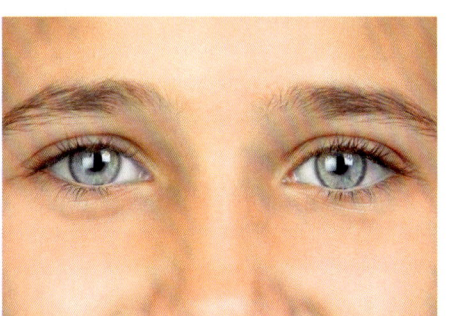

- Allow your hearing (or the imagined sound of reading) to check grammar and punctuation.
- Allow your sight to check spelling. If you are typing, don't rely on spell checkers.
- When you edit a piece of writing you have to consider the way words are used and put together so that you can correct errors. At the same time, you must consider the ideas that are conveyed and whether they could have been clearer and better organised.

Remember that you must do the following:

- Begin a sentence with a capital letter. A capital letter marks clearly the start of a new sentence. Capital letters must also be used to mark proper nouns and all components of a proper noun, such as Abdul, Singapore and Hong Kong Airport.
- Stop sentences clearly with a full stop, a question mark or an exclamation mark. Use these punctuation marks in direct speech to mark the end of a spoken sentence.
- Use commas for pauses and lists, as well as for clarifying information and in direct speech. Here the commas indicate the pauses as you read, to help indicate the words that are actually spoken.

   Marie uttered the words, 'You fool!' She swallowed hard before continuing. 'What do you think you're doing?' She raised her mobile. 'The police,' she said, 'the police will like this when I send it.'

When you want to include additional information without interrupting the flow of the sentence you must choose between dashes and brackets:

- Dashes lead the eye to the next word so that the additional information can be easily taken in as you read on. For example, 'It was light – the sort of morning that calls to early risers – so staying in bed seemed sinful.'
- Brackets allow the insertion of shorter, more practical items of information. For example, 'Take out the flour (wholemeal, remember) and weigh out 200 grams.'

▲ Listening to how your writing reads is almost as important as reading it thoroughly when checking your work.

KEY POINT

Remember that your aim should always be to write clearly, accurately and effectively. As you write ask yourself, is this clear, is this accurate, will this be effective when someone else reads it?

54 WRITING SKILLS — PUNCTUATION AND SPELLING

LEARNING OBJECTIVES

This lesson will help you to:
- detect items that require correction or that could be improved.

PROOF-READING, CHECKING AND EDITING

There are two important aspects of checking what has been written:

Proof-reading: marking errors in a draft

Editing: looking for opportunities to modify and improve the material

PROOF-READING: MECHANICAL ACCURACY

When proof-reading, ask yourself the following questions.
- Are words spelt and ordered correctly?
- Are words changed where necessary so that they work together?
- Do the words flow when read out loud? If you are unable to read aloud, try imagining reading aloud instead.
- Have you double checked?

ACTIVITY 1 — SKILLS: INNOVATION

▼ FINDING ERRORS

Work on your own or with a partner and correct the highlighted errors in the first sentence below. Then identify and correct the errors in the second sentence.

> There is a hard frost which have been anticipating for some days. Many of the smaler animals had burrow deeply but, fortunately for them, heavy rain then caused the river to bursted it's banks and many of them was drowned.

EDITING

When editing, ask yourself the following questions:
- Do the ideas flow?
- Are they easy to follow?
- Could more effective words be chosen?
- Could the presentation of ideas be more effective?

WRITING SKILLS — PUNCTUATION AND SPELLING

ACTIVITY 2
SKILLS: ADAPTIVE LEARNING, INNOVATION

▼ EDITING TEXT

Working on your own, read through these two sentences and edit them, choosing more effective words where you can and re-ordering them where this will improve the passage.

> Across the river he could see the old railway track which had been on the sea-wall. No trains had been seen there for half a century but now a bunch of men who gathered in the Railway Arms, a well-known public house, had decided to campaign for its restoration. One of his neighbours, now in his eighties, remembered the sound of the whistle from the midday train which was his signal to stop work in the fields and go home for lunch.

KEY POINT

Language is firstly a spoken matter, something understood through hearing before reading or writing. One of the best ways of checking written material is to read it aloud.

When checking your work, you should try to imagine the sound of a voice reading it aloud. Remember that the purpose of writing accurately is to make it easy for someone to read it and understand it with little effort. This is what you should check for when proof-reading and editing a piece of writing, whether it is your own or someone else's.

▶ An old-fashioned steam engine

Proof-reading and editing are essential to any form of writing. Even the best ideas or most carefully thought-out argument can benefit from these processes, ensuring they are as engaging and effective as possible. Spelling mistakes, grammatical errors or poorly constructed sentences can greatly lessen the impact of a piece of writing, so it is important to carefully check your work and ensure it is of the best possible quality.

بن قردان
BEN GUERDANE ↑

رأس الجدير
RAS AJDIR ↑

طرابلس
TRIPOLI ↑ 248

القاهرة
LE CAIRE ↑

PAPER 1: NON-FICTION AND TRANSACTIONAL WRITING

Assessment Objective 1

Read and understand a variety of texts, selecting and interpreting information, ideas and perspectives

Assessment Objective 2

Understand and analyse how writers use linguistic and structural devices to achieve their effects

Assessment Objective 3

Explore links and connections between writers' ideas and perspectives, as well as how these are conveyed

This chapter focuses on Paper 1: Non-fiction and Transactional Writing of the English Language A course. Working through these lessons and activities will help you to develop the reading and writing skills that you will need for the Paper 1 exam.

The chapter is split into the following sections:
- Non-fiction texts
- Text Anthology: Non-fiction
- Comparing texts
- Transactional writing.

Paper 1 is worth 60% of the total marks for the course and is split into two sections:
- Section A: Non-fiction
- Section B: Transactional writing.

In section A of your exam, you will need to be able to meet Assessment Objectives AO1, AO2 and AO3.

In section B of your exam, you will need to be able to meet Assessment Objectives AO4 and AO5.

Assessment Objective 4

Communicate effectively and imaginatively, adapting form, tone and register of writing for specific purposes and audiences

Assessment Objective 5

Write clearly, using a range of vocabulary and sentence structures, with appropriate paragraphing and accurate spelling, grammar and punctuation

In Paper 1, the assessment objectives are worth the following amounts.
AO1 – 7%
AO2 – 8%
AO3 – 15%
AO4 – 18%
AO5 – 12%

LEARNING OBJECTIVES

This lesson will help you to:
- understand some of the features of non-fiction texts and prepare you to answer exam questions on them.

TYPES OF TEXT

The types of non-fiction text that may appear in Paper 1 include examples of:

- biography or autobiography
- obituaries
- speeches
- newspaper or magazine articles
- travel writing
- diaries or letters
- reviews
- reference books.

KEY POINT

All non-fiction writing describes real events but, depending on the genre, the author gives their own account of events. This means that the 'truth' of their account can be questioned.

The texts that you will write about in Paper 1 will be non-fiction. Fiction describes scenes imagined (at least partly) by the writer. Non-fiction writing does the opposite: it is about things that really happened, although you cannot rely on all non-fiction to be accurate.

In an **autobiography**, the writer describes his or her own life. However, some events may not have been remembered accurately, or some events may be exaggerated for effect, perhaps to show the writer as positively as possible. Some autobiographies may be considered more like fiction than non-fiction by their readers because they are not very accurate.

A **biography** is the life story of a famous or interesting person, whether from history or from the present day. Today, there are also 'authorised biographies', in which the subject of the biography gives the writer specific legal permission to produce the biography. The subject can decide which events are included or omitted and how the writer describes them.

Another form of autobiographical writing is the **diary** or **journal**, or the modern equivalent, the **blog** (short for 'web log'). For example, *The Diary of a Young Girl* by Anne Frank contains important factual material about her daily life during the German occupation of the Netherlands. It is therefore more than just a personal account. However, not all diaries set out to be accurate or truthful. Many diaries have other purposes, such as to entertain, to give personal views and to communicate with friends.

News reports may appear in newspapers or magazines. News is expected to be objective or unbiased and based on clear evidence. As readers, you want to know whether a reporter is trying to present the material in a particular way because of their own opinions on the topic. However, some newspaper and magazine articles are undoubtedly biased. In all forms of non-fiction text, therefore, the question of truth and accuracy really matters. This means that part of the reader's analysis should include looking for any examples of bias or opinion that is not supported by evidence.

Feature articles are usually about a topic of interest to a large number of readers: they can be about almost anything, from family matters to global politics. They are usually based on research. Opinion or comment pieces will contain factual evidence and explanation, but aim to argue a case about a topic of general interest.

An **obituary** is a newspaper article, found most frequently in broadsheet newspapers, about a remarkable or well-known person who has just died. Its length depends on the fame or significance of the subject.

SUBJECT VOCABULARY

objective based on facts, or making a decision that is based on facts rather than on your feelings or beliefs
unbiased fair; not influenced by one's own or someone else's opinions
broadsheet a newspaper printed on large sheets of paper, especially a serious newspaper

| PAPER 1 | NON-FICTION TEXTS | 59 |

ACTIVITY 1 — AO1
SKILLS: CRITICAL THINKING, REASONING, DECISION MAKING

▼ IDENTIFYING TYPES OF NON-FICTION

Which of the types of non-fiction text described on page 58 do you think the following extracts come from? Give reasons for your decision. Which one do you think is more objective? Explain why you think this.

▼ FROM THE INDEPENDENT NEWSPAPER

Even the keenest gamers generally suffer nothing more than sore thumbs or tired eyes from their hobby. But scientists looking into the health effects of video game consoles have linked overplaying to dozens of injuries – some even life-threatening. The cases were uncovered after a team of Dutch researchers gathered all reported cases of Nintendo-related injuries, spanning 30 years.

▼ FROM IN THE EMPIRE OF GENGHIS KHAN BY STANLEY STEWART

On a low stool stood a mountainous plate of sheep parts, with the favoured cut, the great fatty tail, like a grey glacier on its summit. Younger sisters hustled in and out making last-minute preparations. While we were at breakfast the first lookouts were posted to watch for the return of the truck bearing the wedding party from the bride's camp.

BIOGRAPHY AND AUTOBIOGRAPHY

Read the following extract from an autobiography that tells Ellen MacArthur's account of her extraordinary life as a lone yachtswoman. While reading it, think about what MacArthur is writing about and how she has written her account.

▲ Yachtswoman Dame Ellen MacArthur

▼ FROM TAKING ON THE WORLD BY ELLEN MACARTHUR

The wind continued to rise during the first few days, and by the third I was changing down to the storm jib on the foredeck, and was thrown off my feet before cracking my head hard against the inner forestay rod, resulting in an instant lump and a strange nausea. Soon afterwards, the weather front passed, only to bring even stronger 55-knot gusts in a steady 45-knot wind. It was an unreal, crazy situation: just trying to hang on inside the boat took every ounce of strength. Food was hurled around the cabin along with water containers and spares, while I tried to scrape things up and put them back in the boxes. My hands stung, my eye was swollen, and my wrists were already covered in open sores...

Dawn brought some respite. My body temperature warmed after the freezing night, but if I sweated through the physical exertion of a sail change, when I stopped, I'd once again cool to a shiver. Sleep proved virtually impossible – just snatched ten-minute bursts ended by the cold.

jib A small sail.

foredeck The deck near the bows of the yacht.

forestay Another sail.

knot A nautical mile per hour.

> Just two days later conditions began to worsen again. Doing anything was not only difficult but painful. My hands were red-raw and swollen, and my head was aching – even more so when the freezing water washed breathtakingly over it each time I went forward to change sails. Shifting the sails was hard, brutal work. Whenever it was time to change one I would pull it forward, clipping myself on and hanging on for dear life. Waves would continuously power down the side-decks, often washing me and the sail back a couple of metres, and I had to hang on and tighten my grip on the sail tie even further. I would often cry out loud as I dragged the sail along; it was one way of letting out some of that frustration and of finding the strength to do it…
>
> After a week things finally began to calm, and with my legs red-hot and sore, and my wrists and fingers swollen, I finally enjoyed the first opportunity to remove my survival suit. Though the relief was wonderful, the smell was not!

KEY POINT

Read the exam questions carefully. Tailor your answer to the number of marks available and make sure you follow the key instructions.

HINT

You will need to analyse the techniques used by the writer in order to meet Assessment Objective 2. Think about:
- the story or narrative and what actually happened
- use of precise detail
- frequent use of personal pronouns
- first person perspective maintained throughout
- use of emotive language
- use of descriptive language.

ACTIVITY 2 — A02

SKILLS: CRITICAL THINKING, ANALYSIS, INTERPRETATION

▼ PREPARING FOR THE EXAM QUESTIONS

Questions 1, 2 and 3 in the exam require short answers, each of which is usually worth between 2 and 5 marks. The number of marks on offer will give you a good idea about how many points you should make and how much you should write.

Some questions will say that you should answer 'in your own words'. Copying phrases and sentences straight from the text is not a good idea, unless the question specifically says that it is acceptable to do so.

1. **In your own words, explain clearly the injury Ellen MacArthur suffered at the start of the passage.** **(2 marks)**

    In answering this question, you could begin: *Ellen was thrown by the storm against ….*

2. **Look again at the last paragraph (paragraph 4). In your own words, say what impressions you get of Ellen MacArthur's feelings at the end of the passage and why she felt like this.** **(3 marks)**

    Choose two or three of the techniques in the 'Hint' box, then find an example or two of each technique and describe what you think the effects are.

PAPER 1 — NON-FICTION TEXTS

OBITUARIES

GENERAL VOCABULARY

apartheid the former political and social system in South Africa, in which only white people had full political rights and people of other races, especially black people, were forced to go to separate schools, live in separate areas, and so on.

An obituary is a very abbreviated biographical sketch of a remarkable person in the form of a newspaper article. These are usually published in newspapers shortly after the person's death has been announced. The length of obituaries varies, but an important world leader is likely to get a full page. Here are extracts from two examples: one for Nelson Mandela, who after years of imprisonment eventually became president of post-apartheid South Africa, and the other for David Bowie, the famous musician. Both are taken from *The Guardian* newspaper.

▼ FROM 'NELSON MANDELA OBITUARY' FROM *THE GUARDIAN*

Mandela greatly enjoyed university, particularly boxing and athletics, and, on the strength of his first-year studies in English, anthropology, politics, native administration and Roman-Dutch law, nursed an ambition to become a civil servant and interpreter – about as high a position as a black man might aspire to in those days. But his ambition seemed to be crushed when, in 1940, in his second year, as a member of the student representative council he was expelled for his part in a rebellion over poor quality food. He returned to Mqhekezweni to find another potential disaster – an arranged marriage was being planned for him.

◀ Nelson Mandela

▼ FROM 'DAVID BOWIE OBITUARY' FROM *THE GUARDIAN*

In July 1969 Bowie released *Space Oddity*, the song that would give him his initial commercial breakthrough. Timed to coincide with the Apollo 11 moon landing, it was a top five UK hit. The accompanying album was originally called *Man of Words / Man of Music*, but was later reissued as *Space Oddity*.

The following year was a momentous one for Bowie. His brother Terry was committed to a psychiatric institution (and would kill himself in 1985), and his father died. In March, Bowie married Angela Barnett, an art student. He dumped Pitt [his manager] and recruited the driven and aggressive Tony DeFries, prompting Pitt to sue successfully for compensation. Artistically, Bowie was powering ahead. *The Man Who Sold the World* was released in the US in late 1970 and in the UK the following year under Bowie's new deal with RCA Victor, and with its daring songwriting and broody, hard-rock sound, it was the first album to do full justice to his writing and performing gifts.

◀ David Bowie

PAPER 1 — NON-FICTION TEXTS

ACTIVITY 3 — AO1 · AO2
SKILLS: CRITICAL THINKING, ANALYSIS, INTERPRETATION

▼ IDENTIFYING TECHNIQUES IN OBITUARIES

Obituaries are often sympathetic accounts of someone's achievements.

▶ How does the writer of the Mandela extract begin to influence the reader's sympathies?

▶ What makes these extracts more appropriate for obituaries than for biographies?

Copy and complete the following table, finding examples of the methods and techniques in the two extracts and commenting on their effect. Now identify some methods for yourself, remembering to back them up with evidence from the text and comment on their effect.

▼ METHOD OR TECHNIQUE	▼ EXAMPLE	▼ COMMENT ON EFFECT
Formal register		
Focus on factual information		
Conciseness of writing		

SUBJECT VOCABULARY

register the type or style of vocabulary used according to the situation

SPEECHES

Speeches can be given for many different reasons. Lawyers make speeches in court for the defence or the prosecution. People make speeches in debates or after formal dinners to entertain an audience. However, the most famous speeches are those made by politicians as part of campaigns. The purpose of such speeches is often to rally supporters and give listeners a sense of purpose and inspiration.

The following speech was made by the American civil rights campaigner, Martin Luther King Junior, who was later assassinated for his beliefs and his work on behalf of black Americans.

As you read the speech, think about how Martin Luther King shows his listeners that he is fighting for a better and fairer society in America, using techniques such as:

- repetition of key words
- repetition of the beginning of sentences
- reference to particular individuals
- use of geographical references (i.e. different parts of the United States)
- describing the difficulties black people have faced over the years
- the idea of bringing all people together
- the use of words from a patriotic song.

▲ Martin Luther King at the March on Washington rally in August 1963

PAPER 1 — NON-FICTION TEXTS

all men are created equal A quotation from the US Declaration of Independence, written just before the start of the war against Great Britain.

Georgia Southern American slave-owning state before the American Civil War.

colour of their skin but by the content of their character Note the alliteration of the sound /k/ five times.

let freedom ring Part of a patriotic American song.

New York New York State, which is very large.

Alleghenies A range of hills.

the old Negro spiritual A traditional hymn-like song of the Afro-Caribbeans, many of which originated during the era of slavery.

KEY POINT
Look at the way an author has used the technical devices of language to persuade the reader of a certain viewpoint.

HINT
Although you will be given credit for knowing and identifying techniques, many more marks go to good explanations of their **effects** and of **why they are used**, than to mere technique-spotting.

SUBJECT VOCABULARY
alliteration the use of several words together that begin with the same sound or letter
onomatopoeia where a word sounds like the noise it makes
simile a description that says that an object is *like* an image
metaphor describing something by comparing it to an image which it resembles, in a way that says the object *is* the image
personification when something which is not human is made to sound human by attributing human qualities to it
emotive language language that produces an emotional reaction

▼ 'I HAVE A DREAM', BY MARTIN LUTHER KING AT WASHINGTON DC, AUGUST 1963

I have a dream…

I have a dream that one day this nation will rise up and live out the true meaning of its creed: 'We hold these truths to be self-evident, that all men are created equal.'

I have a dream that one day on the red hills of Georgia, the sons of former slaves and the sons of former slave owners will be able to sit down together at the table of brotherhood.

I have a dream that my four little children will one day live in a nation where they will not be judged by the colour of their skin but by the content of their character.

I have a dream today!

And this will be the day – this will be the day when all of God's children will be able to sing with new meaning:

My country 'tis of thee, sweet land of liberty, of thee I sing.

Land where my fathers died, land of the Pilgrim's pride,

From every mountainside, let freedom ring!

And if America is to be a great nation, this must become true.

And so let freedom ring from the prodigious hilltops of New Hampshire.

Let freedom ring from the mighty mountains of New York.

Let freedom ring from the heightening Alleghenies of Pennsylvania.

Let freedom ring from every hill and molehill of Mississippi.

From every mountainside, let freedom ring.

And when this happens, when we allow freedom ring, when we let it ring from every village and every hamlet, from every state and every city, we will be able to speed up that day when all of God's children, black men and white men, Jews and Gentiles, Protestants and Catholics, will be able to join hands and sing in the words of the old Negro spiritual:

Free at last! Free at last!

Thank God Almighty, we are free at last!

The art of persuasive writing and speaking is called **rhetoric**. Rhetorical devices include many techniques used in poetry, since they can make all kinds of writing more memorable. These techniques include **alliteration**, **onomatopoeia**, figurative language (**similes**, **metaphors** and **personification**), **emotive language** and word choices.

PAPER 1 — NON-FICTION TEXTS

> **HINT**
>
> Some people find acronyms helpful in remembering lists of terms. We've suggested 'HER CRASH FACTOR'S L' for the following rhetorical techniques, but try to think of your own if you can.
>
> H Hyperbole or exaggeration
> E Emotive language
> R Register
> C Contrast
> R Repetition
> A Alliteration and assonance
> S Structure
> H Humour
> F Figurative language (similes, etc.)
> A Antithesis
> C Contrast
> T Tripling
> O Onomatopoeia
> R Rhetorical questions (and other rhetorical devices)
> S Short sentences or paragraphs
> L Lists

ACTIVITY 4 — A02
SKILLS: CRITICAL THINKING, ANALYSIS, INTERPRETATION

▼ IDENTIFYING TECHNIQUES USED IN SPEECHES

Look again at the bullet list of techniques on page 62. Copy and complete the following table, adding techniques and giving an example or two of each.

▼ METHOD OR TECHNIQUE	▼ EFFECT
Repetition of key words	
Geographical names	

▶ Pick out two quotations from the passage which give you the idea that Martin Luther King believes strongly in a fair society for people of all kinds. In each case, say why the language is so successful.

▶ Give three examples of rhetoric used in the extract and explain why they are effective.

ACTIVITY 5 — A02
SKILLS: CRITICAL THINKING, ANALYSIS, INTERPRETATION

▼ APPEALING TO LISTENERS' FEELINGS

Effective speeches will nearly always have a strong appeal to the listeners' feelings. Copy and complete the following table to help you to analyse how Martin Luther King achieves this.

▼ APPEALS TO	▼ QUOTATION	▼ COMMENT
Love of justice and fairness	'they will not be judged by the colour of their skin'	
Patriotism		
Idealism		

> **HINT**
>
> Structure is a key rhetorical method used to build up a feeling or an argument.

▶ How does Martin Luther King build up a strong impression of the rightness of his cause in this extract?

PAPER 1 — NON-FICTION TEXTS

DIARIES AND LETTERS

KEY POINT
The most famous published diaries show that the personal viewpoint can be an extremely powerful tool in non-fiction writing.

HINT
As you read the passage, think about:
- the age of the girl who is writing the diary
- signs of her ability to write in an unusually mature way about what she is experiencing
- her explanation as to why she writes the diary.

people Anne personifies the paper.

home Is it surprising to find that a diary is preoccupied with home life, family and friends?

time Notice the informal register here.

Many people express their most personal thoughts about their lives in writing that is less planned and more informal than an autobiography. This can be done either in a diary that they write regularly – often to an imaginary friend, such as Anne Frank's 'Kitty' – or in a letter to someone close: a friend, a lover or a relative. This means that the perspective of diaries and letters is personal, and many writers of diaries and letters did not originally intend them to be published. Remember that someone's thoughts and feelings can be an important part of a non-fiction text, just like in fiction.

Some of the most powerful diaries and letters that have been published give readers a remarkable understanding of the suffering of individuals in wartime. One example is Anne Frank's diary, published as *The Diary of a Young Girl*. Anne was a Dutch teenager who kept a diary over a period of two years during the Second World War. As she and her family were Jewish, they hid from the Nazis in a house in Amsterdam. The diary entries ended when the Frank family was eventually found and arrested. Anne was sent to a concentration camp, where she died. The following extract comes from the early months of Anne's period in hiding.

▼ THE DIARY OF A YOUNG GIRL BY ANNE FRANK

'Paper has more patience than people.' I thought of this saying on one of those days when I was feeling a little depressed and was sitting at home with my chin in my hands, bored and listless, wondering whether to stay in or go out. I finally stayed where I was, brooding. Yes, paper does have more patience, and since I'm not planning to let anyone else read this stiff-backed notebook grandly referred to as a 'diary', unless I should ever find a real friend, it probably won't make a bit of difference.

Now I'm back to the point that prompted me to keep a diary in the first place: I don't have a friend.

Let me put it more clearly, since no one will believe that a thirteen-year-old girl is completely alone in the world. And I'm not. I have loving parents and a sixteen-year-old sister, and there are about thirty people I can call friends. I have a throng of admirers who can't keep their adoring eyes off me and who sometimes have to resort to using a broken pocket mirror to try and catch a glimpse of me in the classroom. I have a family, loving aunts and a good home. No, on the surface I seem to have everything, except my one true friend. All I think about when I'm with friends is having a good time. I can't bring myself to talk about anything but ordinary everyday things. We don't seem to be able to get any closer, and that's the problem. Maybe it's my fault that we don't confide in each other. In any case, that's just how things are, and unfortunately they're not liable to change. This is why I've started the diary.

ACTIVITY 6 — A01 — SKILLS: CRITICAL THINKING, PROBLEM SOLVING, ANALYSIS, INTERPRETATION

▼ INTERPRETING WRITING

Write an answer for each of the following questions. A student answer for question 2 has been included to give you an idea of what you should be aiming to produce.

1. What reason does Anne give for keeping a diary? **(1 mark)**
2. In your own words, say how the final paragraph develops this thought. **(4 marks)**
3. Pick out two phrases which show that, at times, Anne is still quite young in her way of thinking and comment on each. **(4 marks)**

EXAMPLE STUDENT ANSWER TO QUESTION 2

> The statement that Anne does not have a friend is explored in an interesting way in the final paragraph. Anne distinguishes in quite a mature way between having a loving family and many people who admire her, although this may be ironic, and having someone in whom she can really confide. She recognises that her life is going to be extremely difficult, and that she risks feeling isolated from the community. She regrets the superficial relationships that she has with her friends, and is looking for some deeper and more trusting relationships.

▶ How many marks out of 4 might you give this answer and why? For example, do you think it is perceptive or superficial, well-developed or lacking in evidence?

D. H. Lawrence was an English novelist and poet. Born in 1885, his career was focused on writing poetry and fiction; most famously *Lady Chatterley's Lover*. His letters, sent to friends and family, are useful records into his life and history, particularly his traumatic wartime experiences despite not undertaking military service during the First World War on grounds of his personal beliefs and health.

The following extract from a letter that he wrote gives an insight into his feelings at the end of the war.

▼ FROM 'D. H. LAWRENCE TO LADY CYNTHIA ASQUITH, 30 JANUARY 1915'

It seems like another life – we *were* happy – four men. Then we came to Barrow in Furness, and saw that the war was declared. And we all went mad. I can remember soldiers kissing on Barrow station, and a woman shouting defiantly to her sweetheart 'When you get at 'em, Clem, let 'em have it', as the train drew off – and in all the tram-cars 'War'. – Messrs Vickers Maxim call in their workmen and the great notices on Vickers' gateways – and the thousands of men streaming over the bridges. Then I went down the coast a few miles. And I think of the amazing sunsets over flat sands and the smoky sea – then of sailing in a fisherman's boat, running in the wind against a

> heavy sea – and a French onion boat in with her sails set splendidly, in the morning sunshine – and the electric suspense everywhere – and the amazing, vivid, visionary beauty of everything, heightened by the immense pain everywhere.
>
> And since then, since I came back, things have not existed for me. I have spoken to no one, I have touched no one, I have seen no one. All the while, I swear, my soul lay in the tomb – not dead, but with the flat stone over it, a corpse, become corpse cold. And nobody existed because I did not exist myself.

KEY POINT

The strong impact of letters comes from their directness, often written soon after the author's experiences.

Read the passage again and think about:

- the locations that D. H. Lawrence describes
- how he describes his emotions
- his feelings about and attitudes towards death
- the reasons for these feelings.

ACTIVITY 7 — AO1 AO3 — SKILLS: CRITICAL THINKING, ANALYSIS, REASONING, DECISION MAKING

▼ **PREPARING FOR EXAM QUESTIONS**

Before answering the questions, pick out (by underlining, highlighting or writing out) the key sentences or phrases you will need for your answer. Think about how you can re-word them in your own words.

1. Explain in your own words why D. H. Lawrence finds nature so striking in the first paragraph.
2. Explain in your own words how the first paragraph gives a real sense of D. H. Lawrence's feelings towards the war.
3. Both the passages by Anne Frank and D. H. Lawrence are about experiences of difficulties and hardships in a time of war. What similarities and differences do you find in the attitudes of the two writers?
4. Fill in the gaps in the following answer with the suggested words in the box. In some cases, more than one of these words may be suitable.

Anne	writing	horrible	thoughts
dreadful	awful	Lawrence	experiences
feelings	events	friend	nature
ideas	war	differences	soldiers
trapped	similarities	person	

> There are more _____ than _____ in the way the two writers experience ____ and its horrors. This is partly because Anne is _____ indoors, so has not actually seen the suffering of the _____. D. H. Lawrence, however, experiences _____ conditions. Both write about themselves, and both are sharing their innermost _____ with someone special, even if in _____'s case this is not a real _____. The power of _____'s descriptions gives a really vivid impression of war, whereas in this extract, Anne seems more preoccupied with the act of _____ a diary than with recording important _____.

TRAVEL WRITING

A lot of both fiction and non-fiction writing deals with travel. When it is non-fiction, travel writing is generally autobiographical in form. Travel writers usually try to record their actual experiences. When analysing travel writing, ask yourself the following questions about the writing.

- Does the writer bring the events to life, so that you can really imagine the people, and picture the place and the way of life there? How do they do this?
- What attitudes does the writer show towards the places visited? Are there feelings of amazement, delight, humour or sadness?
- Why is the writer telling you about his or her travels? Is it to make you want to visit the place? To entertain you? To enable you to experience places and people that you may never be able to visit personally?
- Does the writer bring out the ways in which customs, clothing, food or traditions differ from those you are used to?

The following two extracts are about the writers' experiences in different places: one is describing Mongolia, while the other is describing Somalia.

In *In the Empire of Genghis Khan*, Stanley Stewart sees the beauty and fun of the wedding preparations he watches and wishes to share his enjoyment with the reader, by bringing events to life as vividly as he can. As you read the passage, think about:

- whether this wedding seems like weddings that you have witnessed
- how the writer felt as someone not used to these traditions
- signs that, at times, he found the celebrations very amusing
- the way it presents a detailed picture of events.

▼ A scene from a Mongolian wedding

FROM *IN THE EMPIRE OF GENGHIS KHAN* BY STANLEY STEWART

Throughout the evening people came to warn me about themselves. They sat on the grass outside my tent, unburdening themselves with pre-emptive confessions. The following day would be difficult, they said. Weddings were boisterous occasions. People became unpredictable. They counselled me about particular individuals, then admitted that they themselves could be as bad as the next fellow. I would be wise to get away early before things got out of hand.

In the morning the groom and his supporters, a party of about seven or eight relations, set off to fetch the bride from her ger, which lay some 15 miles away. An old Russian truck, the equivalent of the wedding Rolls, had been specially hired for the occasion.

When they arrived the groom would be obliged to search for his bride who by tradition must hide from him. It would not be too difficult. The tradition is that she hides under a bed in the neighbouring ger. While we waited for their return we were given breakfast in the newlyweds' ger. Over the past weeks it had been lovingly prepared by relations. It was like a show ger from Ideal Gers… Biscuits, slabs of white cheese and boiled sweets had been arrayed on every surface in dizzy tiers like wedding cakes. On a low stool stood a mountainous plate of sheep parts, with the favoured cut, the great fatty tail, like a grey glacier on its summit.

Younger sisters hustled in and out making last-minute preparations. While we were at breakfast the first lookouts were posted to watch for the return of the truck bearing the wedding party from the bride's camp. By mid-afternoon we were still waiting. Apparently a wedding breakfast would have been given to the groom and his accompanying party at the bride's camp, and complicated calculations were now performed concerning the number of miles to the bride's ger, divided by the speed of the truck combined with the probable duration of the breakfast, and finally multiplied by the estimated consumption of arkhi.

At four o'clock a spiral of dust finally appeared beyond a distant ridge. When the truck drew up in front of the wedding ger, it was clear that the lavish hospitality of the bride's camp had been the cause of the delay. The back of the truck was crammed with wedding guests in such a state of dishevelled merriment that we had some difficulty persuading them to disembark. The bride's mother, apparently convinced that they were at the wrong ger, required four men to convey her to terra firma. The bride's elder sister, shrugging off all assistance, fell headfirst from the tailgate, bounced twice and came to rest, smiling, against a door post.

---

ger Mongolian home.

Rolls Rolls Royce, a luxury make of car that is often used for weddings.

Ideal Gers A play on the name of a British magazine, Ideal Home.

arrayed Arranged.

arkhi A clear spirit distilled from milk.

lavish Very generous.

dishevelled Disordered, disarranged.

terra firma [Latin] Solid ground.

tailgate The back end of the truck.

ACTIVITY 8 — A01 A03
SKILLS: CRITICAL THINKING, ANALYSIS, REASONING, INTERPRETATION

▼ PREPARING FOR EXAM QUESTIONS

1 In paragraph 2, there is a custom involving a bride. What is it?
2 Describe the features of the preparations that take place in the newlyweds' ger.
3 Why is the description of the arrival of the truck humorous?

These three questions are similar to Questions 1–3 in Paper 1.

The following question is similar to Question 3 and is worth 12 marks in the exam.

▶ **In what ways does the writer make this passage entertaining?**

You should support your answer with close reference to the passage, including **brief** quotations.

In your answer you should write about:
- the writer's account of what happened
- his handling of pace and suspense or anticipation
- his descriptions of unusual things or customs
- his use of language.

The following passage is an example of a very different kind of travel writing. While you are reading it, consider what makes it different from the previous extract.

▼ FROM *A PASSAGE TO AFRICA* BY GEORGE ALAGIAH

I was in a little hamlet just outside Gufgaduud, a village in the back of beyond… In the ghoulish manner of journalists on the hunt for the most striking pictures, my cameraman and I tramped from one hut to another. What might have appalled us when we'd started our trip just a few days before no longer impressed us much.

There was Amina Abdirahman, who had gone out that morning in search of wild, edible roots, leaving her two young girls lying on the dirt floor of their hut. They had been sick for days, and were reaching the final, enervating stages of terminal hunger. Habiba was ten years old and her sister, Ayaan, was nine. By the time Amina returned, she had only one daughter. Habiba had died. No rage, no whimpering, just a passing away – that simple, frictionless, motionless deliverance from a state of half-life to death itself. It was, as I said at the time in my dispatch, a vision of 'famine away from the headlines, a famine of quiet suffering and lonely death'.

KEY POINT

Include details of the circumstances and events. You should not try to summarise the whole extract, but focus on key moments and explain why you think the writer included these details.

PAPER 1   NON-FICTION TEXTS

There was the old woman who lay in her hut, abandoned by relations who were too weak to carry her on their journey to find food. It was the smell that drew me to her doorway: the smell of decaying flesh. Where her shinbone should have been there was a festering wound the size of my hand. She'd been shot in the leg as the retreating army of the deposed dictator took revenge on whoever it found in its way. The shattered leg had fused into the gentle V-shape of a boomerang. It was rotting; she was rotting. You could see it in her sick, yellow eyes and smell it in the putrid air she recycled with every struggling breath she took.

ACTIVITY 9 — A03

SKILLS: CRITICAL THINKING, ANALYSIS, INTERPRETATION, DECISION MAKING

COMPARING TEXTS

This is the type of question you will have to answer when tackling Question 5 of Section A. It carries roughly half the marks for the section in the exam (22 marks out of 45).

1. Compare how the writers of these two travel pieces present their ideas and perspectives on their experiences. Support your answer with detailed examples from both texts including **brief** quotations.

(22 marks)

Read the information in the box in the margin, then copy and complete the table to help you plan your answer.

▼ METHOD/TECHNIQUE	▼ MONGOLIA	▼ SOMALIA	▼ COMPARISON
Type of detail or incident	Strange, odd or comical Example:	Distressing Example:	They are describing very different types of…
Communication of thoughts and attitudes	In describing the strange customs, his tone is… Example:	By focusing on the sad fates of individuals, he… Example:	
Language			

HINT

What particular effects do different writers use to interest the reader? For example, the use of emotive description in *A Passage to Africa* and the use of dramatic words and comic situations in *In the Empire of Genghis Khan*.

NEWSPAPER AND MAGAZINE ARTICLES

Reading newspapers or magazines regularly will not only improve your reading and writing skills; it will also steadily increase your general knowledge and understanding of current affairs. Many newspapers and magazines now exist in online versions, which makes them much easier to access.

Articles come in various types and lengths. They can be about anything of general current interest, from politics and economics to shopping and education. Articles may or may not express strong views or come to definite conclusions about the topic, but they usually inform you of developments, make you aware of things of interest and warn you of dangers. The following articles do express opinions meaning that they are known as 'opinion pieces'. In opinion pieces, it is particularly important that the views are well argued and backed up by evidence.

When you read the following extracts, or any newspaper or magazine articles, think about:

- what the writer is saying
- the aims of the writer
- how the writer achieves these aims
- how successful the writer has been.

Find some examples from the text as evidence for your points.

▼ 'SOCIAL MEDIA ADDICTION IS A BIGGER PROBLEM THAN YOU THINK' BY MIKE ELGAN FOR *COMPUTER WORLD*

Social networks are massively addictive. Most people I know check and interact on social sites constantly throughout the day. And they have no idea how much actual time they spend on social media.

If you're a social media addict, and your addiction is getting worse, there's a reason for that: Most of the major social network companies, as well as social content creators, are working hard every day to make their networks so addictive that you can't resist them.

Cornell Information Science published research earlier this month that looked at (among other things) the difficulty some people have in quitting Facebook and other social networks. They even have a label for the failure to quit: 'social media reversion.'

The study is interesting because they revealed the difficulty people have quitting Facebook because of addiction. Participants intended to quit, wanted to quit and believed they *could* quit (for 99 days), but many couldn't make more than a few days.

The addictive aspect of social networking is associated with FOMO – fear of missing out. Everyone is on Facebook. They're posting things, sharing news and content and talking to each other 24/7.

The network effect itself is addicting, according to Instagram software engineer Greg Hochmuth, 'A network effect is the idea that any network becomes more valuable as more people connect to that network. The phone system is the best example of this phenomenon – you have to have a phone because everybody else has a phone.

In the world of social networking, Facebook benefits most from network effect. Facebook happened to be the top social network when social networking busted out as a mainstream activity. Now, everybody's on Facebook because everybody's on Facebook. And even people who don't like the social network use it anyway, because that's where their family, friends and colleagues are – and because of addiction.

The contribution of network effect to the addictive quality of web sites is accidental. But social sites are also addictive by design.

▲ Changing social habits are a fertile subject for writers.

reversion Returning to something.

HINT

When you are thinking about structure, look at the paragraphs and try to say what the main idea is for each one. For example, in paragraph 1, it is that social media are addictive; in paragraph 2, it is that social media companies deliberately make their social networks addictive. Then ask yourself why some paragraphs are longer and where the writer brings in evidence. Finally, consider why the last paragraph is so short.

PAPER 1 — NON-FICTION TEXTS

ACTIVITY 10 — A01 A02
SKILLS: CRITICAL THINKING, INTERPRETATION

▼ UNDERSTANDING THE TEXT

Before answering the following questions, make sure that you have taken in the key points from the text. Think about:

- the use of detail (e.g. names and facts)
- the impact of the headline
- the problems that are mentioned
- the style and layout of the text.
- ▶ how, according to Elgan, are social networks addictive?
- ▶ how does he convey his own attitude to the problem?
- ▶ how does he structure his ideas in this extract?

KEY POINT

Analyse the structure of a passage and see how it helps the purpose of the writing. Ask how the different parts fit together and relate to each other.

▼ 'ARE HUMANS DEFINITELY CAUSING GLOBAL WARMING?' FROM *THE GUARDIAN*

Just as the world's most respected scientific bodies have confirmed that world is getting hotter, they have also stated that there is strong evidence that humans are driving the warming. The 2005 joint statement from the national academies of Brazil, Canada, China, France, Germany, India, Italy, Japan, Russia, the UK and the US said:

"It is likely that most of the warming in recent decades can be attributed to human activities."

Countless more recent statements and reports from the world's leading scientific bodies have said the same thing. For example, a 2010 summary of climate science by the Royal Society stated that:

"There is strong evidence that the warming of the Earth over the last half-century has been caused largely by human activity, such as the burning of fossil fuels and changes in land use, including agriculture and deforestation."

The idea that humans could change the planet's climate may be counter-intuitive, but the basic science is well understood. Each year, human activity causes billions of tonnes of greenhouse gases to be released into the atmosphere. As scientists have known for decades, these gases capture heat that would otherwise escape to space – the equivalent of wrapping the planet in an invisible blanket.

Of course, the planet's climate has always been in flux thanks to "natural" factors such as changes in solar or volcanic activity, or cycles relating the Earth's orbit around the sun. According to the scientific literature, however, the warming recorded to date matches the pattern of warming we would expect from a build up of greenhouse gas in the atmosphere – not the warming we would expect from other possible causes.

Now re-read the article on page 73, thinking about:
- the way that quotations are used
- how the writer tries to make their own views impossible to argue against
- the use of scientific and other technical language
- the kinds of evidence that the writer relies on to support the argument.

ACTIVITY 11 | **AO3** | **SKILLS** CRITICAL THINKING, ANALYSIS, INTERPRETATION, DECISION MAKING

▼ COMPARATIVE QUESTION

Studying the articles on pages 72–73 together, what do you learn about the writers' views on their chosen topic, the evidence that they are quoting and the seriousness of the way in which they are responding to it? Explain how each of the writers uses language to communicate their views.

Before answering the question, look back at a few of the tables that you have used in previous activities, then make one of your own to help you. It might look like this:

	▼ VIEW/OPINION	▼ EVIDENCE	▼ TONE/MOOD
Social media			
Climate change			

REVIEWS

Reviews play an important part in the relationship between an artistic product and the public. A series of good reviews can help a book, video game, television series or music album to succeed. A professional review performs several functions, such as:
- informing the reader about the product and its intended audience
- engaging the reader by the quality of the writing
- offering a series of critical judgements on aspects of the product
- making a recommendation as to whether the work is worth seeing, reading, hearing or buying.

PAPER 1 — NON-FICTION TEXTS

> **KEY POINT**
>
> In order to be trusted by readers, reviews need to strike a balance between being too positive and being overly critical.

immersive Involving.

epochal Helping to define a new era.

incandescent Filled with light from within.

▼ FROM A REVIEW OF *STAR WARS: EPISODE VII* BY MARK KERMODE IN *THE GUARDIAN*

The action takes place some years after the events of *Return of the Jedi*, and involves scavenger Rey (Daisy Ridley) teaming up with renegade 'First Order' Stormtrooper Finn (John Boyega) and globular droid BB-8. The opening scroll sets up an ongoing battle between the forces of good and evil and lays the groundwork for a quasi-mythical quest that will reunite friends old and new, and allow a grizzled Harrison Ford to deliver the line: 'Chewie, we're home…'

That sense of coming home runs throughout *The Force Awakens*, director JJ Abrams taking the series back to its roots while giving it a rocket-fuelled, 21st-century twist…The film feels very physical, scenes of dog-fighting TIE fighters and a relaunched Millennium Falcon crashing through trees possessing the kind of heft so sorely lacking from George Lucas's over-digitised prequels. The battle scenes are breathtakingly immersive…but also impressively joyous – the sight of a fleet of X-wings hurtling toward us over watery terrain brought a lump to my throat and a tear to my eye – just one of several occasions when I found myself welling up with unexpected emotion…

Having co-written the series's previous high-water mark, *The Empire Strikes Back*, Lawrence Kasdan here shares credits with Abrams and Michael Arndt on a screenplay… which subtly realigns its gender dynamics with Rey's proudly punchy, post-Hunger Games heroine. The spectre of Vader may live on in Adam Driver's Kylo Ren, but it's Rey in whom the film's true force resides, likeable newcomer Daisy Ridley carrying the heavily-mantled weight of the new series with aplomb. Plaudits, too, to John Boyega, who brings credibility and humour to the almost accidentally heroic role of Finn…

What's most striking about *Star Wars: The Force Awakens* is the fact that it has real heart and soul… Abrams breathes new life into Lucas's epochal creations in a manner that deftly looks back to the future. And it's a future that works. Watching the film in a packed auditorium with an audience almost incandescent with expectation, I found myself listening to a chorus of spontaneous gasps, cheers, laughs, whoops and even occasional cries of anguish.

What's really surprising is that many of them were coming from me.

ACTIVITY 12 — A01 — SKILLS: CRITICAL THINKING, ANALYSIS, INTERPRETATION

▼ LANGUAGE USED IN REVIEWS

Copy and complete the following table, finding examples of language used in the review that correspond with the categories in the first column. Then, using your examples, answer the questions.

▼ POSITIVE COMMENTS ABOUT…	▼ EXAMPLES FROM THE TEXT
the director/screenplay	
the audience reaction	
the acting	

▶ Explain two aspects of the film that the writer finds engaging.

▶ How does the writer build up or communicate his positive feelings about the film?

REFERENCE BOOKS AND WEBSITES

Reference books and websites are designed to be consulted, not read all the way through. They usually consist of a large number of articles, sometimes on a great variety of topics. Some reference books offer an overview of all knowledge, such as the famous *Encyclopaedia Britannica*. Other reference books have a much more specialised range – there are thousands of reference books covering every academic discipline and field of knowledge.

Read the following extracts from *Encyclopaedia Britannica*, considering how the writing style differs from the other types of non-fiction writing that you have encountered so far.

▼ 'ACQUISITION AND RECORDING OF INFORMATION IN DIGITAL FORM' FROM *ENCYCLOPAEDIA BRITANNICA*

The versatility of modern information systems stems from their ability to represent information electronically as digital signals and to manipulate it automatically at exceedingly high speeds. Information is stored in binary devices, which are the basic components of digital technology. Because these devices exist only in one of two states, information is represented in them either as the absence or the presence of energy (electric pulse). The two states of binary devices are conveniently designated by the binary digits, or bits, zero (0) and one (1).

▼ 'RAP' FROM *ENCYCLOPAEDIA BRITANNICA*

Rap, a musical style in which rhythmic and/or rhyming speech is chanted ('rapped') to musical accompaniment. This backing music, which can include digital sampling (music and sounds extracted from other recordings), is also called hip-hop, the name used to refer to a broader cultural movement that includes rap, deejaying (turntable manipulation), graffiti painting, and break dancing. Rap, which originated in African American communities in New York City, came to national prominence with the Sugar Hill Gang's 'Rapper's Delight' (1979). Rap's early stars included Grandmaster Flash and the Furious Five, Run-D.M.C., LL Cool J, Public Enemy (who espoused a radical political message), and the Beastie Boys. The late 1980s saw the advent of 'gangsta rap,' with lyrics that were often misogynistic or that glamorized violence and drug dealing. Later stars include Diddy, Snoop Dogg, Jay-Z, OutKast, Eminem, Kanye West, and Lil Wayne.

ACTIVITY 13 — A01
SKILLS: CRITICAL THINKING, ANALYSIS, INTERPRETATION

▼ CHARACTERISTICS OF REFERENCE WRITING

> **KEY POINT**
> Some reference works can be consulted by those with no subject knowledge at all. Others can be pitched at a higher level.

Characteristics of this kind of reference writing include those listed in the first column of the table below. Copy and complete the table and find another feature of your own.

▼ FEATURES	▼ EXAMPLES	▼ COMMENT ON EFFECT
A large amount of factual information		
Clusters of words from a specialised branch of knowledge		
A lack of emotive vocabulary		
Most sentences are complete statements		

LEARNING OBJECTIVES

This lesson will help you to:
- identify the writer's perspective
- understand how a writer communicates their perspective to a reader.

IDENTIFYING THE WRITER'S PERSPECTIVE

A writer's perspective is their point of view, or the angle from which they see the subject matter. Even the most purely informative articles, which show no personal angle at all, can be said to have a point of view, even if that point of view is objective or unbiased.

Many articles or pieces of writing that claim to be objective are not always unbiased, because everyone brings a personal, societal or national bias to bear on what they write. An article written for an encyclopaedia in the United States of America will be written from an American perspective, which means that the article may be different to one written in China, even though it is apparently unbiased. If the subject of the writing is politics, history or culture, national perspectives will often be very different. For example, in the travel writing extract on page 69, Stanley Stewart writes from the perspective of a curious British traveller, not from that of a native Mongolian. This fact means that his account of the wedding is entirely different from that of a native Mongolian.

There are many different types of perspective. The writer's origin in a particular community or ethnic group may give them a particular perspective. Having a certain job or occupation might also influence their perspective – you could say they write from the perspective of an economist, a student, a singer, and so on. Martin Luther King's famous speech, 'I have a dream...' is written from the point of view of a black American minister who has become the voice of a whole people.

DIFFERENCES IN PERSPECTIVE

In comparison, one of the commonest reasons for difference in perspective is the fact that people interact with others whom they do not necessarily understand. This may not be because of what they do or where they come from, but simply because people cannot know exactly what is going on in another person's thoughts. This is shown by the following accounts of the same event.

▼ DEV'S ACCOUNT

It was awful. He hit me hard in the face and all his friends laughed at me when I started to cry. I was just walking past and was trying to be helpful by pointing out that the bell had gone. They always laugh at me in the corridor and I thought if I tried to help they would like me more. I don't understand what is going on.

▼ DANIL'S ACCOUNT

This has nothing to do with my friends. They didn't even realise what had happened until after I hit him. I think they were laughing at a joke Adesh had made. I did punch him, but that was because he told me I was going to be late with this smirk on his face like he was going to tell the teacher. I have never really seen him before and I thought he was trying to show me up in front of my friends.

ACTIVITY 1 — A01
SKILLS: PROBLEM SOLVING, ANALYSIS, CREATIVITY

▼ THINKING ABOUT PERSPECTIVE

Neither Dev's nor Danil's account of the same incident is false, but the writer of each version of events has a different perspective.

1 Describe what happened in the corridor.
2 What might have influenced the two boys to view the events in such different ways? Write down your ideas.
3 Dev's perspective is that he has been bullied by this group for a long time. Write a sentence explaining Danil's perspective on Dev. Why is it important to have heard Danil's perspective?

DIFFERENT ATTITUDES

KEY POINT

Attitude affects language. When you read extracts, think about how the writer uses language to communicate certain things to you and what this reveals about the writer's purpose and personality.

Another way of thinking about perspectives is to think of the writer in relation to two or more groups of people with different attitudes – one group which shares their views and another group, or other groups, which do not share these views. Ask yourself which groups would agree with a particular idea or argument and which would disagree. For example, one group might be more conservative (resistant to change), while another group might be more progressive (looking for positive change). Another common opposition is that between the authoritarian or restrictive and the liberal or tolerant. Often, the older generation is seen as being authoritarian and young people are considered to be more liberal.

ACTIVITY 2 — A01
SKILLS: PROBLEM SOLVING, INNOVATION, EMPATHY

▼ DIFFERING ATTITUDES

Think of other ways in which people can be divided into groups whose attitudes are often different from each other.

Are these issues strictly defined so a person can only be in one group or the other? Or are some of them more complicated so that there is some overlap between them and some people can be placed more in between the groups?

▲ Kickz is a youth football programme in the UK.

the Premier League The highest league of English football.

Arsenal FC A Premier League football team based in London.

ACTIVITY 3 | A01 | SKILLS: CRITICAL THINKING, ANALYSIS, INTERPRETATION

▼ IDENTIFYING A WRITER'S PURPOSE

Read the following extracts. Identify the writer's purpose, making a note of the language choice and other writing techniques that allow you to identify the purpose. Then copy and complete the table, re-reading the extracts to find more examples to back up your ideas.

EXTRACT A

Kickz is a national programme, funded by the Premier League and Metropolitan Police, that uses football to work with young people at risk of offending in deprived areas. Arsenal FC delivers Kickz in Elthorne Park, getting kids off the street in the evening and playing football. The project has helped to transform the local area: there has been a reduction of 66% in youth crime within a one-mile radius of the project since it started.

… The projects are targeted at neighbourhoods with high levels of antisocial behaviour and crime… The sessions mostly involve football coaching, but they also provide coaching in other sports, such as basketball, and workshops on issues including drug awareness, healthy eating, volunteering, careers and weapons.

PAPER 1 — NON-FICTION TEXTS

the Grand National A famous British horse race over large jumps.

Eagle A British children's comic.

the Mekon A character in Eagle.

HINT
If an adult decides to write from the point of view of a child, then they will imitate the language of a child. Writers can write in their own voice, or they can write in the voice of someone else.

EXTRACT B
... If you saw your neighbour whipping a dog, you'd be on the phone to the police immediately, right? Of course, anyone with a shred of decency condemns hurting animals. Yet, inexplicably, some still turn a blind eye to the cruelty to horses during the Grand National, in which riders are required to carry a whip. Nearly every year, racehorses sustain injuries. Many have paid with their lives.

▲ Horse racing is a popular pastime across the world, but is it cruel?

EXTRACT C
Daddy says I have to eat to get well, even if it hurts. The nurse smiles at me when she brings the jam sandwiches. She smiles differently at the other nurses, and when she smiles at sister it is different again. I wish there were bubbles coming out of her head with words, like in Eagle… Thought bubbles would be a useful invention in real life. When you wake in the night there are strange slapping and scraping noises on the marble, and sometimes screams, but I close my eyes, and pretend I'm at home, and think of my presents, and imagine the Mekon in his bubble, and I do not cry, Daddy, I do not, I do not.

	▼ A	▼ B	▼ C
What attitude does the writer express?			
What is the likely age group of the writer?			
Why do you think the writer wrote the piece?			
What other types of people might share the attitude of each writer?			
What have you noticed about the language used in each extract?			

▶ How is the language of these extracts influenced by the writer's perspective? You could draw another table to help you answer this question, and remember to include examples.

LEARNING OBJECTIVES

This lesson will help you to:
- identify the text's audience and understand the purpose.

AUDIENCE AND PURPOSE

It is not always easy to appreciate a text unless you understand its purpose and who it was written for. Sometimes this is not difficult, such as when the reader is a member of the writer's intended audience. If you were a child born in Ghana or Jamaica, then the stories of Anansi the spider would be intended for you and there would be no additional context to learn about. However, in other cases, you may need some background knowledge: for example, Martin Luther King's speech, 'I have a dream...', does not mean all that it should if its reader is ignorant of the history and culture of the USA. Likewise, the poem, 'The Bright Lights of Sarajevo', means a great deal more if you know something about the Bosnian War of the 1990s.

HINT

Writers do not only write **from** a particular perspective. They also write with a particular '**view**' in front of them, which includes their purpose and audience, meaning that these three aspects are closely connected.

When you are reading, you should try to bear in mind the audience known as 'the general reader' or 'the general public'. These phrases are used to indicate that all kinds of people may want to read a book about an expedition to the Himalayas or up the River Amazon, and that you do not need to have any particular interests to find the book interesting. However, it would also be reasonable to suggest that such books will appeal to readers interested in adventurous travel. This group will cross boundaries of age, gender, race, and so on, as it is defined by interest only, although it may include more of one section of the population than another.

▶ **Do a survey of people you know and find out if, for example, outdoor adventure books such as *Between a Rock and a Hard Place* might appeal more to male readers than female, or more to younger readers than older ones. You could try this on other texts.**

ACTIVITY 1 — A01

SKILLS: CRITICAL THINKING, ANALYSIS, REASONING

▼ IDENTIFYING AUDIENCE AND PURPOSE

As you work through this book, you will read a wide range of texts written for different audiences and for very different reasons. The following table will help you to compare some of the passages that you have already encountered between pages 58 and 77. Copy and complete it as best you can.

▼ TEXT	▼ AUDIENCE	▼ PURPOSE
The Diary of a Young Girl	Herself; perhaps also for others.	To confide her thoughts with an imaginary friend.
Ellen MacArthur's autobiography	People interested in ocean yachting and racing or in tough sporting exploits.	
In the Empire of Genghis Khan		
Martin Luther King's 'I have a dream...' speech		

| PAPER 1 | NON-FICTION TEXTS | 83 |

Now do a similar exercise on some of the passages in the Anthology.

▼ TEXT	▼ AUDIENCE	▼ PURPOSE
'The Bright Lights of Sarajevo'	Those interested in the Bosnian war; those interested in the poetry of Tony Harrison and similar writers.	To communicate something of the way people went on living during the siege of Sarajevo.
'Explorers or boys messing about?'	Readers of *The Guardian*; those interested in human interest tales of endurance and hardship.	
Between a Rock and a Hard Place		

AUDIENCE, PURPOSE AND LANGUAGE

KEY POINT

Audience is always relevant to a text. The language is affected by the audience and vice versa.

Get into the habit of thinking about audience, purpose and language use whenever you read a text. Think about the relationship between these three aspects of the text. This skill will help you in the exam as well as in everyday life.

A writer's purpose has a good deal to do with their audience: a writer will never write for everyone. A writer's choice of language is also affected by both. Suppose that you were writing a story about a crime for a seven-year-old child. You would choose appropriate language for the reader, considering their age or level of understanding and the subject matter. Your choices would be very different if you had to write a script for a stand-up comedian.

ACTIVITY 2 — A01 — A02 — SKILLS: CRITICAL THINKING, ANALYSIS, REASONING

▼ CHOOSING LANGUAGE FOR AN AUDIENCE AND A PURPOSE

Copy and complete the following table with some of the ways in which language is affected by audience and purpose. Add more entries of your own to the table. The more you think about these aspects of a text, the better you will understand them.

▼ TEXT	▼ AUDIENCE	▼ PURPOSE	▼ LANGUAGE
Martin Luther King's 'I have a dream...' speech	The people at the rally for black civil rights.		
H is for Hawk (see pages 141–143)	Readers interested in hawks or birds; fans of non-fiction.		
A Passage to Africa (see pages 103–105)			
'Young and dyslexic?' (see pages 123–125)			
Chinese Cinderella (see pages 147–149)			

Re-read the extract from **The Diary of a Young Girl** (page 65) and answer the following question:

▶ **In what ways is the language of this passage affected by its audience and purpose?**

PAPER 1 — NON-FICTION TEXTS

LEARNING OBJECTIVES

This lesson will help you to:
- understand how writers use their expertise with language to create a range of varied effects.

LANGUAGE FOR DIFFERENT EFFECTS

Many writers think about their potential readers when they are writing. You have already looked at **purpose** and **perspective**, and now you are going to build on this by considering more of the effects that writers can achieve with their choice of words, phrases and sentences. Some of the examples in this section will be taken from the passages you have already looked at.

GETTING CLOSE TO THE READER

Some writers want to create a close relationship with their readers, while others do not. In autobiographies, writers may share very private thoughts and deal with difficult emotions. They can use chatty or colloquial speech if they feel that that is the best way to engage with their readers. Diaries can be good examples of this, whether their authors are writing only for themselves or for others.

EMOTIVE LANGUAGE

In *A Passage to Africa*, George Alagiah wants to shock the reader and to communicate the suffering that he sees in the villages that he visits. He wants you to see in your mind's eye the things he writes about.

Of the writers that you have read so far, which other writers have used emotive language?

ACTIVITY 1 — A02

SKILLS: CRITICAL THINKING, ANALYSIS, REASONING

▼ **THINKING ABOUT PURPOSE AND EFFECT**

Read the following quotations, taken from passages in this book, then copy and complete the table.

▼ QUOTATION	▼ LANGUAGE	▼ PURPOSE	▼ EFFECT
'I was 19. My American roommate was shocked by me. She asked where I had learned to speak English so well, and was confused when I said that Nigeria happened to have English as its official language.'	Narrative, with some emotive adjectives.	To show how people are prejudiced.	You learn from this anecdote how ordinary American people know little about distant foreign cultures (in this case, Nigeria).
'It was not a smile of greeting, it was not a smile of joy — how could it be? — but it was a smile nonetheless. It touched me in a way I could not explain. It moved me in a way that went beyond pity or revulsion.'	Emotive, focused on feelings.		
'The mattak or blubber of the whale is rich in necessary minerals and vitamins, and in a place where the climate prohibits the growth of vegetables or fruit, this rich source of vitamin C was the one reason that the Eskimos have never suffered from scurvy.'	Explanatory (or expository).		

PAPER 1 — NON-FICTION TEXTS

▼ QUOTATION	▼ LANGUAGE	▼ PURPOSE	▼ EFFECT
'The Royal Navy's ice patrol ship, HMS Endurance, which was 180 miles away surveying uncharted waters, began steaming towards the scene and dispatched its two Lynx helicopters.'	Narrative.		
'The big problem with the education system then was that there was no compassion, no understanding and no humanity.'	Thoughts and opinions.		
'Good God, my hand. The flaring agony throws me into a panic. I grimace and growl…'	Emotive, using sensational language and exclamations.		
'The hawk's wings, barred and beating, the sharp fingers of her dark-tipped primaries cutting the air, her feathers raised.'	Vividly descriptive.		

ACTIVITY 2 — A02

SKILLS: CRITICAL THINKING, ANALYSIS, INTERPRETATION

▼ THINKING ABOUT EFFECT AND LANGUAGE

Now think about this the other way around. What effect does the writer want to achieve with their choice of language? Copy and complete the following table, looking through passages in this book for examples of each purpose.

▼ PURPOSE	▼ LANGUAGE	▼ EXAMPLE	▼ EFFECT
To make the reader imagine something.	Vividly descriptive.	*A Passage to Africa*, lines…	You imagine the scene or person described.
To direct the reader's emotions.	Emotive, using the language of the emotions.		
To be friendly to the reader.	Chatty.		
To impress the reader with the writer's style.			
To amuse.	Humourous, jokey, playful.		
To inform.			
To argue.			
To create suspense.	Short sentences with mini-cliffhangers.	'And then the trouble began.'	

▲ A naval patrol ship

KEY POINT

The skilled writer can create a wide range of effects on the reader because they have an excellent command of the language.

LANGUAGE FOR PATTERN AND EFFECT

A lot of writing is concerned at least partly with creating patterns and certain effects within those patterns.

ACTIVITY 3 — AO2
SKILLS: CRITICAL THINKING, ANALYSIS, INTERPRETATION

▼ SIMPLE DESCRIPTIONS DESCRIBING THE AUTHOR'S CHOICE OF LANGUAGE

It is important that you can use the correct terminology when commenting on and describing language use.

1 Copy and complete this table.

▼ WRITER	▼ SUBJECT	▼ PHRASE	▼ TYPE OF LANGUAGE	▼ EFFECT
Helen Macdonald	A hawk	'A fallen angel. A griffon from the pages of an illuminated bestiary.'	Two metaphors with precise vocabulary.	The description is made more vivid and memorable.

2 Copy and complete the following table by finding examples of each technique and commenting on their effects.

	▼ TECHNIQUE	▼ EXAMPLE	▼ EFFECT
H	Hyperbole or exaggeration		
E	Emotive language		
R	Register		
C	Contrast		
R	Repetition		
A	Alliteration and assonance		
S	Structure		
H	Humour		
F	Figurative language (e.g. similes)		
A	Antithesis		
C	Contrast		
T	Tripling		
O	Onomatopoeia		
R	Rhetorical questions (and other rhetorical devices)		
S	Short sentences or paragraphs		
L	Lists		

PAPER 1 — NON-FICTION TEXTS

DESCRIPTORS FOR LANGUAGE

Many students find it difficult to think of ways to describe the effects of language and tend to overuse words like 'descriptive' when it is not strictly accurate, or rely on vague phrases such as 'draws the reader in'. Try using some of the following alternatives.

> **KEY POINT**
> Learning the technical terms for descriptive effects will allow you to express yourself more precisely in your analysis of writing.

Alliteration and assonance	Makes language more emphatic/more rhythmic/more memorable.
Onomatopoeia	Makes phrases more vivid and powerful.
Descriptive phrasing	Makes the reader imagine the scene.
Verbs of motion and action	Make the language more dynamic and energetic.
Wordplay, exaggeration	Makes writing light-hearted, amusing.
Abstract nouns	Make writing more intellectual or more to do with ideas.
Repetition	Emphasises a particular point or word.
A mixture of techniques	Makes language varied or lively.

Other techniques include:
- anaphora
- balanced phrases
- allusions
- juxtaposition.

Look these technical terms up in a dictionary and see if you can find examples in the texts in this book.

USING SENTENCE TYPES FOR EFFECT

There are two obvious ways of classifying sentence types: by their function and by their grammatical complexity.

SENTENCE FUNCTION

Statements	Dominate informative writing and narrative in stories.
Questions	Common in dialogue and in explorative articles. They can be used in speeches to engage the audience, particularly in the form of rhetorical questions.
Exclamations	Mainly found in dialogue, but also in first-person accounts of adventures, real-life experiences and so on.
Commands	Usually found in dialogue and instructions. They use the imperative form of the verb (for example, 'Come on, let's move.)'
Wishes	Expressions of thoughts and feelings often found in diaries, letters and dialogue (for example, 'If only I hadn't done that').

> **HINT**
> Help yourself to learn these different types of sentence by thinking of and writing an example of each one.

SENTENCE COMPLEXITY

Simple sentences	Consist of only one main clause.
Compound sentences	Two or more main clauses joined by 'and', 'but', 'so' or 'or'.
Complex sentences	Contain at least one subordinate clause.
Incomplete sentences	Do not have a complete main clause; used frequently in conversation and in writing for effect or emphasis or in one-word sentences such as, 'He stopped. Silence.'

LEARNING OBJECTIVES

This lesson will help you to:
- distinguish between these three types of writing
- distinguish facts from opinions.

FACT, OPINION AND EXPERT ADVICE

Often, the purpose of a text is to inform its audience about something. You have come across several texts with the purpose of informing readers about something, using a mixture of three main types of writing: description, reporting or narrative, and explanation. All of these are types of factual writing.

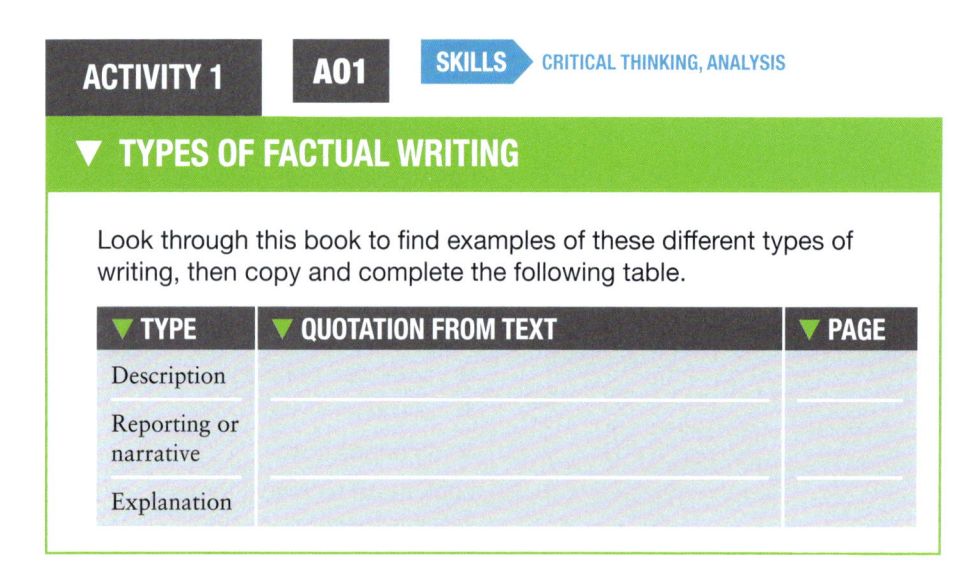

ACTIVITY 1 — A01 — SKILLS: CRITICAL THINKING, ANALYSIS

▼ **TYPES OF FACTUAL WRITING**

Look through this book to find examples of these different types of writing, then copy and complete the following table.

▼ TYPE	▼ QUOTATION FROM TEXT	▼ PAGE
Description		
Reporting or narrative		
Explanation		

FACTS AND OPINION

▲ 'The best sport in the world.' Is this a fact or an opinion?

As you have already seen, non-fiction texts often include people's opinions and beliefs, even if they may not be factually true. This includes:
- opinions as statements of belief, such as, 'I think football is the best sport in the world'
- opinions stated as fact such as 'Football is the best sport in the world'.

Be careful when someone states an opinion or belief as though it is a fact. For example, the second statement about football has the form of a factual statement, but it is still really just a statement of belief about football. People often make statements of belief as though they are facts, so you should always ask questions of what you read and analyse what people write as facts when they may in fact be statements of belief.

For example, advertisers may state opinion as fact. Washing products may be advertised as making clothes whiter than other brands of washing detergent, but it is unlikely that these statements can be said to be 'facts'.

In comparison, an argument is an opinion or set of opinions backed up by reasons and evidence. It would be easy to express an opinion that you are the President of the United States, but hard to construct an argument that proves that you are the President of the United States.

▶ Over a day or two, write down a collection of opinions stated as facts that you hear or see in the media, among your friends and family or in advertisements.

PAPER 1 — NON-FICTION TEXTS

ACTIVITY 2 — A01 — SKILLS: PROBLEM SOLVING

▼ FACT, OPINION OR ARGUMENT?

KEY POINT

You need to know how to recognise writing that states facts and then question whether the use of the factual form is justified.

Read the following extracts, then decide whether they are fact, opinion, argument, or opinion presented as fact.

'It's a fact that boys are stronger than girls.'
'Everyone knows that Britain will be better off outside the European Union. I don't know anyone who thinks otherwise.'
'We should encourage immigration into this country for three reasons: it supplies us with more skills, it helps us to understand other cultures and it is morally a good thing to do.'
'The USA is more powerful in military terms than Russia.'
'I think that all religions are equally valid: I don't know about all of them, but they all have their good points and their less good points.'

ADVICE

Non-fiction texts can contain examples of advice. For example, a book review may advise you to read or not to read a particular book. An online article may advise you how to save money, how to prepare for a hot summer, or recommend places to visit. An 'agony aunt' in a magazine could suggest ways of coping with problems in a personal relationship.

Generally speaking, people appreciate advice more if it comes from someone who knows what they are talking about: an expert. Advice is linked to persuasive writing, since it tries to influence the person being advised.

coolest The expert makes the advice seem more attractive by associating the recommended course of action with 'the coolest' people.

you can do it The tone is encouraging.

set... stick... try... keep These are imperatives: they are all commands. What effect does this have?

get some support Advice often suggests how to get more support and advice.

avoid the shops Advice is often both positive and negative ('dos and don'ts'); for example, 'avoid the shops' is a 'don't'.

Dear Billy,

Your letter shows you really want to give up smoking and that is the first step to making it happen. You won't be alone; all the coolest people are giving it up now.

Make no mistake, it is difficult to stop – but you can do it. Lots of people have managed to kick the habit.

Here's how you start.

Make a plan.

1. Set a date for your last cigarette and stick to it!
2. Try to get some support from a friend or relative. It always helps to talk to someone about problems – a problem shared is a problem halved!
3. Keep busy to help take your mind off ciggies. Perhaps take up a new hobby or sport, like cycling.
4. Try to change your routine, and avoid the shops where you usually buy cigarettes.
5. Save up the money that you normally spend on cigarettes and buy something special for yourself with it.

Good luck – I hope it all goes well. Quitting smoking will make you feel a lot better and, with the exercise from your cycling, you should be able to wave stress goodbye!

All the best,
Nadiya

LEARNING OBJECTIVES

This lesson will help you to:
- understand what structure in writing is and how you can write about it.

THE STRUCTURE OF A TEXT

What do you understand is meant by the word 'structure'? Try writing down a short definition of 'structure' in relation to a piece of writing. You could use one of the extracts in this book or another text that you know.

Most people respond to a skilfully structured piece of writing without understanding exactly why. When analysing structure, then, you have to understand the purpose of a passage, which can only be done by careful reading. The next task is to see the structure within it that helps put the purpose into effect. You can then write about:

- the writer's intention in the text
- the structure that the writer has used to achieve that intention
- the effects of each part of the structure.

Many students find it difficult to analyse structure in writing, but the following techniques should help you.

- Think in terms of the beginning, middle and end of the text or extract. How are they different from each other?
- Look at the paragraphs and identify the content of each one. Then consider what the writer is doing with that content and why he or she chose to put the content in that order.
- Look at the way in which the writer uses the basic types of writing that you find in non-fiction:
  - description (of the setting or the appearance of people and objects)
  - narrative (what happened or is happening)
  - dialogue or speech (including talking to one self)
  - thoughts and feelings (when not in direct speech)
  - background information, facts, or explanation.

HINT

Look also at the relative sizes of the paragraphs. If they vary quite noticeably then there is probably a good reason for it (a short paragraph might be an effective opening or conclusion, or used for emphasis elsewhere)

ACTIVITY 1 — A01 A02

SKILLS: CRITICAL THINKING, ANALYSIS, INTERPRETATION, CREATIVITY

▼ IDENTIFYING A PASSAGE'S STRUCTURE

Read the following passage, using the techniques you have just learned to help you think about the structure of the passage.

▼ FROM *CIDER WITH ROSIE* BY LAURIE LEE

I was set down from the carrier's cart at the age of three; and there with a sense of bewilderment and terror my life in the village began.

The June grass, amongst which I stood, was taller than I was, and I wept. I had never been so close to grass before. It towered above me and all around me, each blade tattooed with tiger-skins of sunlight. It was knife-edged, dark, and a wicked green, thick as a forest and alive with grasshoppers that chirped and chattered and leapt through the air like monkeys.

PAPER 1

NON-FICTION TEXTS

I was lost and didn't know where to move. A tropic heat oozed up from the ground, rank with sharp odours of roots and nettles. Snow-clouds of elder-blossom banked in the sky, showering upon me the fumes and flakes of their sweet and giddy suffocation. High overhead ran frenzied larks, screaming, as though the sky were tearing apart.

For the first time in my life I was out of the sight of humans. For the first time in my life I was alone in a world whose behaviour I could neither predict nor fathom: a world of birds that squealed, of plants that stank, of insects that sprang about without warning. I was lost and I did not expect to be found again. I put back my head and howled, and the sun hit me smartly on the face, like a bully.

▶ **Sum up, in three sentences, the beginning, middle and end of the extract. Use the third person ('he') in your summary. How is the first paragraph different from the others? Can you see a reason for this?**

▶ **Look again at the four paragraphs from *Cider with Rosie* and write a line about the purpose or effect of each paragraph. Then explain why you think Lee chose to put the content in that order.**

▶ **Can you identify more structural features? Use the correct terminology.**

▶ **What do you think is the effect of structuring the passage in these four paragraphs? Choose the comment from the following list that you think is most useful and accurate, and fill in the blanks.**

- The structure enables the writer to develop and _____ the narrator's feelings of _____ and _____ in slightly different ways _____.
- The structure arranges the description of the setting and the narrator's _____ in a way that _____ the feeling to _____.
- The structure gives the description a sense of _____ and _____.

HINT

Try to bring together your analytical and writing skills – think about how and why you would structure a piece of your own writing.

It can also be useful to consider the types of writing that the writer is using, such as description, narrative and so on. For example, a passage with some description of the setting, or a character, followed by some narrative in which something happens. As soon as you notice these different types of writing, you should be able to say something about why they are there in the passage. Many students do not consciously register when a writer is using dialogue or telling them a character's thoughts, so if you do notice these things, you will give yourself an immediate advantage.

KEY POINT

When people talk about the structure of a piece, they are not normally referring to sentence structure, which is usually regarded as a linguistic feature. However, there are two points worth bearing in mind.

1. You might notice that a piece ends or begins with a very short sentence, in which case the writer is using sentence structure as a deliberate part of the larger structure.
2. Sentence structure is still an important point to consider. If you can make a good point about sentence structure, then you should include it in your answer.

ACTIVITY 2 | **AO2** | **SKILLS** CRITICAL THINKING, INTERPRETATION

▼ IDENTIFYING DIFFERENT TYPES OF WRITING

Copy and complete the following table, using the analysis you have just made, to list four examples of different types of writing used by Lee in the passage that you have just read.

▼ TYPE OR FUNCTION	▼ QUOTATION	▼ EFFECT (OR PURPOSE)
Description		
Narrative		

LEARNING OBJECTIVES

This lesson will help you to:
- understand how to tackle Questions 1–3 on an unseen text.

UNSEEN TEXTS

The questions in Paper 1 Section A will be based on two non-fiction passages: one from the Anthology, with which you will be familiar, and another passage that you will not have seen before. Understanding and analysing this unseen text is critical to your success in this part of the exam.

READING UNSEEN TEXTS

The first thing to do when faced with an unseen text is to read it and start thinking about what it is saying. Try not to be scared by the fact that you have never seen it before. By using the skills that you have learned by studying other texts, you should have all the tools you need to understand it and analyse it effectively.

When you have read the text, use the following questions to help you think about what you have read.

- What sort of text is it?
- What is the text about?
- Who is the intended audience for the text?
- Is the writer trying to make a particular point?
- What literary and linguistic techniques does the writer use?
- What effects do these techniques have?
- How does the text make you feel personally?

Simply by answering these questions, you will find that you are able to say a lot about the unseen text. You should spend a short time reading the text and getting a good understanding of it. This will then allow you to focus on answering the specifics in the exam questions.

For this section, you will use the passage from *Cider with Rosie* on pages 90–91 as the unseen text.

ACTIVITY 1 — A01 A02 — SKILLS: CRITICAL THINKING, ANALYSIS, INTERPRETATION

▼ **UNDERSTANDING THE UNSEEN TEXT**

Read the passage from *Cider with Rosie*. Spend five minutes quickly answering the questions from the list above. Discuss your answers with a partner.

QUESTION 1

Question 1 is a comprehension question to check your understanding of the unseen text. It will ask you to find information from the text and to give two examples of this. You only need to provide two examples; there are no extra marks for providing more.

EXAM-STYLE QUESTION — A01 — SKILLS: ANALYSIS

1 From lines 3–9, select **two** words or phrases that describe the setting.

(2 marks)

PAPER 1 — NON-FICTION TEXTS

QUESTION 2

HINT

When answering, it is always better to explain a few techniques in detail rather than to list points without explaining them properly.

SUBJECT VOCABULARY

synonym a word that shares the same meaning as another word; for example, 'quick' might be a synonym for 'fast'

Question 2 concentrates on the writer's thoughts and feelings. You need to think about how you know what the writer is feeling – is this information given explicitly or is it implicit? You should also think about how you know this and the language that the writer uses in order to convey what they are thinking and how they feel.

ACTIVITY 2 | **A01** | **SKILLS** ADAPTIVE LEARNING, INNOVATION

▼ THOUGHTS AND FEELINGS

Thinking about the passage from *Cider with Rosie*, list all of the things that the author says about how he feels. In the exam you will be asked to use your own words to explain this, so write a list of synonyms for the words the author uses.

EXAM-STYLE QUESTION

A01 | **SKILLS** CRITICAL THINKING, INTERPRETATION

2 Look again at lines 7–13.

In your own words, explain what the writer's thoughts and feelings are of finding himself in a strange new place.

(4 marks)

QUESTION 3

HINT

For Question 3, rather than simply repeating the question, it might be better to find a way straight into the answer, such as 'At first the writer is not at all impressed with what he finds…'

Question 3 asks you to describe something that is happening in the text. You need to have an understanding of what the text is about and what the writer is saying. You should look to support your answer with short quotations from the text as evidence to back up your point. Point-Evidence-Explain (P-E-E) is a good model to use when answering this question.

ACTIVITY 3 | **A01** | **SKILLS** CRITICAL THINKING, ANALYSIS, INTERPRETATION

▼ USING QUOTATIONS

Looking at the passage from *Cider with Rosie*, complete the table below to list what the writer thinks about the village. Give examples from the text to support your point and explain how this is effective.

▼ FEELING	▼ QUOTATION	▼ EXPLANATION
He feels overwhelmed by the experience.	"I put my head back and howled"	This is an instinctive primal reaction to the unknown situation and he resorts to a basic impulse to cry.

EXAM-STYLE QUESTION

A01 | **SKILLS** CRITICAL THINKING, ANALYSIS, INTERPRETATION

3 From lines 1–15, describe the writer's first impressions of the village. You may support your points with **brief** quotations.

(5 marks)

94 PAPER 1 — NON-FICTION TEXTS

LEARNING OBJECTIVES

This lesson will help you to:
- prepare for answering non-fiction exam questions.

PUTTING IT INTO PRACTICE

The passages you will be given for Paper 1 are likely to be between 800 and 1400 words long, or at least 60 lines in length. The following example is shorter than this, but you can use it to practise your reading, planning and writing skills in preparation for the exam. Read the unseen passage and answer the questions that follow. One of the questions also requires you to consider *Beyond the Sky and the Earth* from the Anthology. Aim to complete all five questions from Section A in 90 minutes.

KEY POINT

To ensure the most efficient use of time, a direct approach to answering the question is usually best, rather than spending a long time getting to your main points.

humitas A sweet, steamed fresh corn cake, traditional in the Ande, similar to the Mexican tamale. What is the effect of using these South American words?

red Why are they 'disturbingly red'? What is the effect?

usual suspects What is the tone here? Where does this phrase come from?

gizzards Stomach parts.

maize Crop from which sweetcorn grows.

like freshly run over roadkill An unusual simile – what is the effect?

▲ A street scene in Quito, Ecuador

▼ FROM *THE HUNGRY CYCLIST* BY TOM KEVILL-DAVIES

Sheltering from torrential rain in a dirty roadside hamlet just north of Quito, I surveyed my options for dinner. A few limp limbed chickens did another turn in their mechanical rotisserie; a plate of worn-out humitas, a sweet tamale, waited for that unlucky customer to save them from another night under the heat lamp; a bored teenager with too much hair-gel prodded and probed a row of disturbingly red hotdog sausages. Not at all tempted by the usual suspects that made up the options in these small Ecuadorian towns, I began to wonder if my hunger could hold out until breakfast.

But hello! What's this?

At the end of the street, sheltering from the rain under a tatty umbrella, an old lady was fanning frantically at the coals of her small grill. I took a seat on the cold steps of the grocery store from which she served, and watched her work while a steady stream of customers pulled in from the rain.

I ordered a bowl of grilled chicken gizzards, served on a heap of sweet corn and fried kernels of salted maize and it was immediately clear that she knew what she was doing. As the evening passed by the buses, trucks and pick-ups splashed through the rain filled potholes of the main street. We didn't talk much, but that seemed normal here in Ecuador, but from what little was said, and my persistent interest in the secret of her giblets, it was obvious we enjoyed a common love of food, and it wasn't long before our conversation turned to Cuy. I expressed my dismay at having only found this traditional dish strung up like freshly run over roadkill in front of the tourist restaurants en route from Otavalo to Quito, and my keenness to see how these rodents were prepared at home. I was invited for lunch the next day.

Cuy, conejillo de Indias – Indian rabbits, or guinea pigs as we know them in the pet shop – have been an important food source in Peru and Ecuador since pre-Inca times. Fifteen centuries later, they still remain an Andean delicacy, and on average Peruvians and Ecuadorians gobble down twenty-two million of these tasty rodents every year. Most Andean households keep cuy at home in the same way that we might keep chickens. Considered a speciality, they are mostly saved for special occasions. Rather like a bottle of champagne or perhaps

PAPER 1 — NON-FICTION TEXTS

conejillo de Indias What is the effect of using this Spanish phrase?

delicacy A much-prized dish.

Ferrero Rocher Italian chocolates wrapped in gold foil.

a box of Ferrero Rocher, a mating pair of guinea pigs are a typical house warming gift for a newlywed couple. Playing an integral role in Andean religious and ceremonial practices, as well as providing dinner, cuy are also used in the traditional medicine of the region. A live cuy is rubbed over the body of someone sick. The cuy's squeaking indicates the diseased area of the human patient.

EXAM-STYLE QUESTIONS

The following questions are based on Text One: *The Hungry Cyclist* and Text Two: *Beyond the Sky and the Earth: A Journey into Bhutan*.

Text One: *The Hungry Cyclist*

A01 | SKILLS | ANALYSIS

1. From the last two paragraphs, select **two** words or phrases that describe the uses of Cuy. **(2 marks)**

A01 | SKILLS | CRITICAL THINKING, INTERPRETATION

2. Look again at the first paragraph.
   In your own words, explain what the writer's thoughts and feelings are before he finds the lady who was grilling chicken. **(4 marks)**

A01 | SKILLS | CRITICAL THINKING, ANALYSIS, INTERPRETATION

3. From the fourth paragraph, describe the writer's impressions of Ecuadorian cuisine.
   You may support your points with **brief** quotations. **(5 marks)**

---

he seems to understand that her food is good quality when the 'steady stream of customers pulled in from the rain'... The student has used inference here to sum up what the writer thinks of Ecuadorian cuisine. Remember to link all ideas to the question.

She serves quite humble food such as 'chicken gizzards', but it's clear that it tastes good...The final point again uses inference, and links back to the question. Remember, you need to make five points to achieve five marks.

> The writer is intrigued by the old lady cooking further down the street; he seems to understand that her food is good quality when the 'steady stream of customers pulled in from the rain'. The writer is interested in what the locals eat, rather than what is offered to tourists. The old lady is described as fanning the coals 'frantically' on a simple outside grill; the writer seems fascinated by the authenticity of this. He watches her work and is clearly impressed as he remarks that 'it was immediately clear that she knew what she was doing'. She serves quite humble food such as 'chicken gizzards', but it's clear that it tastes good as the writer asks her about the recipe afterwards, which shows his interest in genuine Ecuadorian cooking.

Remind yourself of the passage from *Beyond the Sky and the Earth* (pages 134–136).

A02 | SKILLS | CRITICAL THINKING, ANALYSIS, REASONING, INTERPRETATION

4. How does the writer create an interesting and engaging atmosphere and sense of place?
   You should support your answer with close reference to the passage, including **brief** quotations. **(12 marks)**

Question 5 is based on both *The Hungry Cyclist* and *Beyond the Sky and the Earth*.

A03 | SKILLS | CRITICAL THINKING, ANALYSIS, INTERPRETATION, DECISION MAKING

5. Compare how the writers present their ideas and perspectives about their experiences.
   Support your answer with detailed examples from both texts, including **brief** quotations. **(22 marks)**

HINT
Use connectives that help you make comparisons. For example, 'Both travellers are exploring new places, but whereas Zeppa ... , Kevill-Davies ...'

'THE DANGER OF A SINGLE STORY' CHIMAMANDA NGOZI ADICHIE

BACKGROUND AND CONTEXT
Chimamanda Ngozi Adichie was born the fifth of six children in the town of Nsukka in south-eastern Nigeria, where the University of Nigeria is situated. Her father was a professor of statistics at the university and her mother was the university's first female registrar.

Adichie studied medicine and pharmacy at the University of Nigeria for a year and a half. Then she left Nigeria to study communications and political science in the USA. Now she divides her time between Nigeria, where she teaches writing workshops, and the United States.

She has published poetry and fiction and her novels have won several awards. For example, her first novel, *Purple Hibiscus* (2003), was awarded the Commonwealth Writers' Prize for Best First Book (2005). Adichie says of feminism and writing, 'I think of myself as a storyteller, but I would not mind at all if someone were to think of me as a feminist writer... I'm very feminist in the way I look at the world, and that world view must somehow be part of my work.'

GENERAL VOCABULARY
registrar keeping official records of the students

BEFORE YOU START READING
1. Think of an ethnic group about which you have a few ideas but about which you know very few actual facts. Write down your honest views of the stereotype of that ethnic group.
2. Find out as much about this group as you can. Write down some new things that surprise you.
3. Do you think others see you in a stereotyped way? Write down some of the stereotypes they might have.

▼ FROM 'THE DANGER OF A SINGLE STORY' BY CHIMAMANDA NGOZI ADICHIE

Adichie, a successful novelist, delivered this speech at a TED conference. She speaks about the power of storytelling and the danger of a single view.

I'm a storyteller. And I would like to tell you a few personal stories about what I like to call "the danger of the single story." I grew up on a university campus in eastern Nigeria. My mother says that I started reading at the age of two, although I think four is probably close to the truth. So I was an early reader, and what I read were British and American children's books.

TED A nonprofit organisation devoted to spreading ideas, usually in the form of short, powerful talks (18 minutes or less); TED stands for Technology, Entertainment and Design.

campus The complex of buildings that make up a university.

I was also an early writer, and when I began to write, at about the age of seven, stories in pencil with crayon illustrations that my poor mother was obligated to read, I wrote exactly the kinds of stories I was reading: all my characters were white and blue-eyed, they played in the snow, they ate apples, and they talked a lot about the weather, how lovely it was that the sun had come out.

Now, this despite the fact that I lived in Nigeria. I had never been outside Nigeria. We didn't have snow, we ate mangoes, and we never talked about the weather, because there was no need to. …

What this demonstrates, I think, is how impressionable and vulnerable we are in the face of a story, particularly as children. Because all I had read were books in which characters were foreign, I had become convinced that books by their very nature had to have foreigners in them and had to be about things with which I could not personally identify. Now, things changed when I discovered African books. There weren't many of them available, and they weren't quite as easy to find as the foreign books.

But because of writers like Chinua Achebe and Camara Laye, I went through a mental shift in my perception of literature. I realized that people like me, girls with skin the colour of chocolate, whose kinky hair could not form ponytails, could also exist in literature. I started to write about things I recognized.

Now, I loved those American and British books I read. They stirred my imagination. They opened up new worlds for me. But the unintended consequence was that I did not know that people like me could exist in literature. So what the discovery of African writers did for me was this: it saved me from having a single story of what books are.

I come from a conventional, middle-class Nigerian family. My father was a professor. My mother was an administrator. And so we had, as was the norm, live-in domestic help, who would often come from nearby rural villages. So, the year I turned eight, we got a new house boy. His name was Fide. The only thing my mother told us about him was that his family was very poor. My mother sent yams and rice, and our old clothes, to his family. And when I didn't finish my dinner, my mother would say, "Finish your food! Don't you know? People like Fide's family have nothing." So I felt enormous pity for Fide's family.

Then one Saturday, we went to his village to visit, and his mother showed us a beautifully patterned basket made of dyed raffia that his brother had made. I was startled. It had not occurred to me that anybody in his family could actually make something. All I had heard about them was how poor they were, so that it had become impossible for me to see them as anything else but poor. Their poverty was my single story of them.

Years later, I thought about this when I left Nigeria to go to university in the United States. I was 19. My American roommate was shocked by me. She asked where I had learned to speak English so well, and was confused when I said that Nigeria happened to have English as its official language. She asked if she could listen to what she called my "tribal music", and was consequently very disappointed when I produced my tape of Mariah Carey.

---

impressionable Easily influenced.

Chinua Achebe and Camara Laye Prominent and pioneering Nigerian authors in the second half of the 20th century.

▲ Nigerian poet and novelist Chimamanda Ngozi Adichie

raffia Dry palm leaves.

Mariah Carey Popular American singer.

stove What do you notice about this paragraph?

AIDS Auto-immune Deficiency Syndrome, a threat to life in some African countries.

fleecing Exploiting someone financially; robbing someone of their money

Guadalajara City in Mexico popular with tourists.

Alice Walker 20th-century African-American writer.

She assumed that I did not know how to use a stove.

What struck me was this: she had felt sorry for me even before she saw me. Her default position toward me, as an African, was a kind of patronising, well-meaning pity. My roommate had a single story of Africa: a single story of catastrophe. In this single story, there was no possibility of Africans being similar to her in any way, no possibility of feelings more complex than pity, no possibility of a connection as human equals. …

So, after I had spent some years in the U.S. as an African, I began to understand my roommate's response to me. If I had not grown up in Nigeria, and if all I knew about Africa were from popular images, I too would think that Africa was a place of beautiful landscapes, beautiful animals, and incomprehensible people, fighting senseless wars, dying of poverty and AIDS, unable to speak for themselves and waiting to be saved by a kind, white foreigner. I would see Africans in the same way that I, as a child, had seen Fide's family. …

But I must quickly add that I too am just as guilty in the question of the single story. A few years ago, I visited Mexico from the U.S. The political climate in the U.S. at the time was tense, and there were debates going on about immigration. And, as often happens in America, immigration became synonymous with Mexicans. There were endless stories of Mexicans as people who were fleecing the healthcare system, sneaking across the border, being arrested at the border, that sort of thing.

I remember walking around on my first day in Guadalajara, watching the people going to work, rolling up tortillas in the marketplace, smoking, laughing. I remember first feeling slight surprise. And then, I was overwhelmed with shame. I realised that I had been so immersed in the media coverage of Mexicans that they had become one thing in my mind, the abject immigrant. I had bought into the single story of Mexicans and I could not have been more ashamed of myself.

So that is how to create a single story, show a people as one thing, as only one thing, over and over again, and that is what they become. …

Stories matter. Many stories matter. Stories have been used to dispossess and to malign, but stories can also be used to empower and to humanise. Stories can break the dignity of a people, but stories can also repair that broken dignity.

The American writer Alice Walker wrote this about her Southern relatives who had moved to the North. She introduced them to a book about the Southern life that they had left behind. "They sat around, reading the book themselves, listening to me read the book, and a kind of paradise was regained."

I would like to end with this thought: That when we reject the single story, when we realise that there is never a single story about any place, we regain a kind of paradise.

PAPER 1 — TEXT ANTHOLOGY: NON-FICTION

UNDERSTANDING THE TEXT

This is a speech delivered to a conference with an educational theme. In it, Adichie discusses the power and influence that simple storytelling can have, particularly on the young. She shows from her own experience how stories can cause prejudices and that new stories are then needed to redress the balance. Her argument is even more compelling because she shows how she herself was vulnerable to just such influences.

She explains how all the stories she knew when she was growing up were European in outlook, perspective and characterisation, which led her to think that all stories had to be about white people. Then she shows that some Americans tend to have a very limited and simplified impression of Africa, not realising, for example, that there is such a thing as an educated Nigerian middle class. In the last part she explains how she herself had an equally limited view of Mexican culture, influenced by American worries about illegal immigration and drugs.

In this speech, Adichie uses personal stories, or anecdotes, to persuade people that they need to hear or read a wide variety of stories to understand the peoples of the world. To rely on what she calls the 'single story' will never be enough.

▲ Simple storytelling can have a powerful influence on young children.

ACTIVITY 1 — AO1 — SKILLS: ANALYSIS, INTERPRETATION

▼ IDENTIFYING KEY POINTS

Find key parts of the speech and consider what Adichie is trying to tell the reader (or in this case, the listener). Copy and complete the table, adding examples of your own.

▼ DETAIL	▼ WHAT IT TELLS THE READER
'my characters were white and blue-eyed, they played in the snow' ….	That she took the material for her stories from her reading, not from her surroundings.
'whose kinky hair could not form ponytails'	
'a beautifully patterned basket made of dyed raffia'	

ACTIVITY 2 — AO1 — SKILLS: CRITICAL THINKING, ANALYSIS, INTERPRETATION

▼ IDENTIFYING KEY THEMES

Copy and complete the following table, identifying the themes of Adichie's speech and adding any examples of your own.

▼ THEME	▼ QUOTATION	▼ COMMENT
Ignorance	'She… was confused when I said that Nigeria happened to have English as its official language.'	Like other examples in the speech, Adichie's room-mate knows nothing about another culture.
Prejudice		
Self-knowledge		
Importance of stories		

PAPER 1 — TEXT ANTHOLOGY: NON-FICTION

EXAM-STYLE QUESTION

AO2 — SKILLS: CRITICAL THINKING, ANALYSIS, ADAPTIVE LEARNING, CREATIVITY

How does the writer use language and structure to explore identity?

You should support your answer with close reference to the passage, including **brief** quotations.

(12 marks)

EXPLORING LANGUAGE

SUBJECT VOCABULARY

anecdotal consisting of short stories based on someone's personal experience
persuasive able to make other people believe something or do what you ask

The language of this passage is **anecdotal** and **persuasive**: it is evident that the writer is trying hard to communicate some linked experiences that were important to her in making her examine the way that people form prejudiced views of others. She tries to do this as concisely as possible. She uses narrative, detail, emotive language and makes comments about her thoughts and feelings.

The sentence structure is varied in the speech: compare the sentence beginning, 'If I had not grown up in Nigeria…', with the short simple sentence with which the passage begins. What do you think such variety contributes to a piece such as this? Speech-writing also offers the opportunity for less formal sentence structures than you would find in most written English. Can you find evidence of this in the passage?

ACTIVITY 3 — **AO2** — SKILLS: CRITICAL THINKING, ANALYSIS, INTERPRETATION

▼ IDENTIFYING LINGUISTIC TECHNIQUES AND DEVICES

Copy and complete the following table, explaining as precisely as you can what you think the effect that each technique has on the audience. A simple way to start this is to put your finger at random on the passage, and try to find a linguistic technique or device in the sentence you've landed on.

▼ LINGUISTIC TECHNIQUES OR DEVICES	▼ QUOTATION	▼ EFFECT CREATED
Personal anecdote	'I visited Mexico from the U.S…'	By explaining how she discovered that she has the kind of prejudice that she has experienced from others, she shows how universal prejudice is, and also that she doesn't see herself as superior to others.
Anaphora (repetition of opening words of phrases which are next to each other)	'no possibility…'	
Emotive language		
Use of short sentences		

PAPER 1 — TEXT ANTHOLOGY: NON-FICTION

STRUCTURE

KEY POINT

Persuasion is not only about language in terms of words used, but also about using structure to build credibility point by point.

All good persuasive speeches have a clear structure, enabling the audience to follow the points linked together in an argument. The structure of this speech is simple and effective. You can soon see that it is written in 18 paragraphs. One way of analysing the structure would be to summarise the content of each paragraph in a sentence. Another way would be to divide the speech into sections and chart it that way.

ACTIVITY 4 — AO2 — SKILLS: CRITICAL THINKING, ANALYSIS, INTERPRETATION

▼ IDENTIFYING EFFECTS OF STRUCTURE

Copy and complete the table, noting how the content is divided up.

▼ PARAGRAPHS	▼ CONTENT	▼ COMMENT ON RELEVANCE TO ARGUMENT
1–3	Her childhood reading and writing.	This introduces the key theme and shows its impact on herself when very young.

Analyse the structure of the paragraphs as well and you will see that they are not all identical. Short paragraphs have an effect on the way you read them.

ACTIVITY 5 — AO1 — SKILLS: CRITICAL THINKING, ANALYSIS, ADAPTIVE LEARNING, CREATIVITY

▼ UNDERSTANDING ANOTHER'S CULTURE

Imagine (if it is not true!) that you and your partner come from different cultures or countries and that you are meeting for the first time. Talk as honestly as you can about your expectations of each other, your prejudices and stereotypes.

ACTIVITY 6 — AO2 — SKILLS: PROBLEM SOLVING, ADAPTIVE LEARNING, CREATIVITY, INNOVATION

▼ WRITING TASKS

1 'A student cannot be regarded as educated unless they are equipped with the ability both to examine cultural prejudice critically when they come across it and also to challenge it in discussion.'

You have been asked to give a speech to your class in which you express your views on this statement. The speech may consider:

- whether there is adequate provision in the curriculum and, if not, how it should be improved
- how the quality of discussion and debate on these issues might be improved
- any other points you wish to make.

Your response will be marked for the accurate and appropriate use of vocabulary, spelling, punctuation and grammar.

2 Write about a time when you have been surprised by someone's views or realised that your own views were wrong.

Your response could be real or imagined.

EXAMPLE STUDENT ANSWER A TO QUESTION 2

> In a school assembly the headteacher talked about an appalling civil war that had happened in part of Africa, and in which hundreds of thousands of people had been massacred, just because they were an ethnic minority. I had got used to people saying that we ought to respect the beliefs of others and I thought that pretty much all countries accepted this by now. I mean, I knew something about the holocaust in Europe during the Second World War – it was so terrible that it was a warning to the rest of the world never to do anything like that ever again. But this was another attempt at genocide, in my own lifetime. I realised that I had been wrong. It was going to take much longer for the whole world to learn. If they ever did.

Assess the answer above. Some of the aspects you might want to consider are: how does it manage information and ideas, does it address the intended reader, is it well structured, how accurate is the spelling and grammar, and generally how well has the text fulfilled the task set by the question?

EXAMPLE STUDENT ANSWER B TO QUESTION 2

> I supposed I'd always envied him in a way, I mean he was good at sports, I mean I'm alright but he was obviusly excellent, and he was quite clever as well. I sort of resented the way he could do things quite easily. So I never really gave him much of a chance. I slagged him off to my friends saying he was arrogant and such (using some nice slangy phrases of course).
> Later though he did me a good turn, though I didn't deserve it. He spoke up for me when I was trying hard to get into the first XI, and said I deserved a chance. I honestly dont know why he did, but it made a diffrence.
> It happened like this……

Now look at the answer above. How well does the writer communicate? Do you think the writer understands the needs of their reader? What do you think of the tone and the vocabulary used?

EXAM-STYLE QUESTION

A02 SKILLS CRITICAL THINKING, ANALYSIS, ADAPTIVE LEARNING, CREATIVITY

How does Adiche develop a persuasive argument?

You should support your answer with close reference to the passage, including **brief** quotations.

(12 marks)

A PASSAGE TO AFRICA
GEORGE ALAGIAH

BACKGROUND AND CONTEXT

George Alagiah was born in Sri Lanka, but when he was five years old his family moved to live in West Africa. He now lives in the United Kingdom and works as a newscaster for the BBC.

This passage comes from his book *A Passage to Africa*. In this autobiography, he writes about his life and experiences as a TV reporter working mainly across Africa. In this extract, he writes about a report he made when he was covering the civil war in Somalia for the BBC.

▲ BBC newscaster George Alagiah

BEFORE YOU START READING

1. Find some information about George Alagiah. You can look at the BBC website.
2. Find out something about the civil war in Somalia, which began in the 1990s.
3. In a small group or with a partner, share your ideas on the following questions.
   ▶ Why do you think people watch news on television? Do you watch it? If you don't, why not?
   ▶ Have you ever watched a news programme reporting a war or a humanitarian crisis, such as a famine or an earthquake? What do you remember about it and the effect it had on you?
   ▶ Does television reporting of terrible events, such as floods or famines, help the people who are suffering?

FROM *A PASSAGE TO AFRICA* BY GEORGE ALAGIAH

Alagiah writes about his experiences as a television reporter during the war in Somalia, Africa in the 1990s. He won a special award for his report on the incidents described in this passage.

I saw a thousand hungry, lean, scared and betrayed faces as I criss-crossed Somalia between the end of 1991 and December 1992, but there is one I will never forget.

I was in a little hamlet just outside Gufgaduud, a village in the back of beyond, a place the aid agencies had yet to reach. In my notebook I had jotted down instructions on how to get there. 'Take the Badale Road for a few kilometres til the end of the tarmac, turn right on to a dirt track, stay on it for about forty-five minutes – Gufgaduud. Go another fifteen minutes approx. – like a ghost village.'…

In the ghoulish manner of journalists on the hunt for the most striking pictures, my cameraman … and I tramped from one hut to another. What might have appalled us when we'd started our trip just a few days before no longer impressed us much. The search for the shocking is like the craving for a drug: you require heavier and more frequent doses the longer you're at it. Pictures that stun the editors one day are written off as the same old stuff the next. This sounds callous, but it is just a fact of life. It's how we collect and compile the images that so move people in the comfort of their sitting rooms back home.

There was Amina Abdirahman, who had gone out that morning in search of wild, edible roots, leaving her two young girls lying on the dirt floor of their hut. They had been sick for days, and were reaching the final, enervating stages of terminal hunger. Habiba was ten years old and her sister, Ayaan, was nine. By the time Amina returned, she had only one daughter. Habiba had died. No rage, no whimpering, just a passing away – that simple, frictionless, motionless deliverance from a state of half-life to death itself. It was, as I said at the time in my dispatch, a vision of 'famine away from the headlines, a famine of quiet suffering and lonely death'.

There was the old woman who lay in her hut, abandoned by relations who were too weak to carry her on their journey to find food. It was the smell that drew me to her doorway: the smell of decaying flesh. Where her shinbone should have been there was a festering wound the size of my hand. She'd been shot in the leg as the retreating army of the deposed dictator took revenge on whoever it found in its way. The shattered leg had fused into the gentle V-shape of a boomerang. It was rotting; she was rotting. You could see it in her sick, yellow eyes and smell it in the putrid air she recycled with every struggling breath she took.

And then there was the face I will never forget.

My reaction to everyone else I met that day was a mixture of pity and revulsion. Yes, revulsion. The degeneration of the human body, sucked of its natural vitality by the twin evils of hunger and disease, is a disgusting thing. We never say so in our TV reports. It's a taboo that has yet to be breached. To be in a feeding centre is to hear and smell the excretion of fluids by people who are beyond controlling their bodily functions. To be in a feeding centre is surreptitiously to wipe your hands on the back of your trousers after you've held the clammy palm of a mother who has just cleaned vomit from her child's mouth.

---

revulsion Disgust.

surreptitiously Secretly.

There's pity, too, because even in this state of utter despair they aspire to a dignity that is almost impossible to achieve. An old woman will cover her shrivelled body with a soiled cloth as your gaze turns towards her. Or the old and dying man who keeps his hoe next to the mat with which, one day soon, they will shroud his corpse, as if he means to go out and till the soil once all this is over.

I saw that face for only a few seconds, a fleeting meeting of eyes before the face turned away, as its owner retreated into the darkness of another hut. In those brief moments there had been a smile, not from me, but from the face. It was not a smile of greeting, it was not a smile of joy – how could it be? – but it was a smile nonetheless. It touched me in a way I could not explain. It moved me in a way that went beyond pity or revulsion.

What was it about that smile? I had to find out. I urged my translator to ask the man why he had smiled. He came back with an answer. 'It's just that he was embarrassed to be found in this condition,' the translator explained. And then it clicked. That's what the smile had been about. It was the feeble smile that goes with apology, the kind of smile you might give if you felt you had done something wrong.

Normally **inured** to stories of suffering, accustomed to the evidence of deprivation, I was unsettled by this one smile in a way I had never been before. There is an unwritten code between the journalist and his subjects in these situations. The journalist observes, the subject is observed. The journalist is active, the subject is passive. But this smile had turned the tables on that tacit agreement. Without uttering a single word, the man had posed a question that cut to the heart of the relationship between me and him, between us and them, between the rich world and the poor world. If he was embarrassed to be found weakened by hunger and ground down by conflict, how should I feel to be standing there so strong and confident?

I resolved there and then that I would write the story of Gufgaduud with all the power and purpose I could muster. It seemed at the time, and still does, the only adequate answer a reporter can give to the man's question.

I have one regret about that brief encounter in Gufgaduud. Having searched through my notes and studied the dispatch that the BBC broadcast, I see that I never found out what the man's name was. Yet meeting him was a seminal moment in the gradual collection of experiences we call context. Facts and figures are the easy part of journalism. Knowing where they sit in the great scheme of things is much harder. So, my nameless friend, if you are still alive, I owe you one.

inured Hardened.

▶ The civil war in Somalia began in 1991.

UNDERSTANDING THE TEXT

George Alagiah's purpose is to explain his role as a reporter, giving his thoughts and feelings about a particularly challenging incident. He is also trying to challenge his readers, to make you think about your role.

The questions in the following table will help you approach this aspect of the text. Read the text again and find answers to the questions in the table. Remember, more than one point can be made in answer to each question.

▼ QUESTION	▼ ANSWER AND EVIDENCE
What kinds of pictures and stories do the television news companies want?	1 Powerful images – 'the most striking pictures' 2 3
What do the television news companies **not** want to show or report?	1 Yesterday's news – old pictures are 'written off as the same old stuff' 2 3
What do we learn about TV audiences from this passage?	1 2 3

KEY POINT

The author of this passage used the smile as the central focus of the passage, to encourage the reader to discover its significance.

ACTIVITY 1 — A01 — SKILLS: CRITICAL THINKING

▼ **THE MAN'S SMILE**

This smile is the key to a full understanding of the passage because it makes such an impact on the writer.

▶ Look at the following list of statements about the smile and then find a quotation to illustrate each one:
- it reverses roles
- it asks questions
- it stimulates actions
- it affects the writer very powerfully.

▶ Now try to put into your own words what you think the importance of the smile is.

▶ In the extract from *A Passage to Africa*, can you find any other examples of things that seem to be the opposite of what they should be?

EXAM-STYLE QUESTION

A02

SKILLS: CRITICAL THINKING, ANALYSIS, ADAPTIVE LEARNING, CREATIVITY

How does the writer use language and structure to create a sense of atmosphere?

You should support your answer with close reference to the passage, including **brief** quotations.

(12 marks)

PAPER 1 — TEXT ANTHOLOGY: NON-FICTION

EXPLORING LANGUAGE

In this passage, George Alagiah is writing both as a journalist and about being a journalist. He describes what he saw in a vivid way, but at the same time he gives the reader an insight into the world of reporting, where journalists compete with each other to get the largest audience.

Complete the following table to think about the differing uses and kinds of language in the passage.

▼ LANGUAGE USE	▼ EXAMPLE
Emotive words are used to convey the world of the victims.	1 Adjectives emphasise their poverty – for example, 'hungry', 'lean', 'scared'. 2 3
Words give you a vivid image of the world of the television journalist.	1 They are like predators 'on the hunt'. 2 3
Sentence structure is varied to engage the reader.	1 Incomplete sentences are used for effect. 2 3

ACTIVITY 2 — AO4 AO5

SKILLS: ADAPTIVE LEARNING, INTERPRETATION, CREATIVITY, INNOVATION

▼ **WRITING TASKS**

1 Imagine that you are a television or radio news reporter.
   ▶ **Describe a vivid and dramatic scene for a news item. You can either give this account live to the class or write the script for it.**
   ▶ **Write an entry for a personal diary giving your real thoughts and feelings about what you saw.**

2 In his book, George Alagiah writes, 'In global terms, if you have a roof over your head, food on the table, a doctor who will not charge you when you are ill and a school place that does not depend on your ability to pay, then, my friend, you are rich.' Comment on this, giving your ideas on what makes you rich.

3 Write a short story entitled 'The Smile'.

PAPER 1

TEXT ANTHOLOGY: NON-FICTION

THE EXPLORER'S DAUGHTER
KARI HERBERT

BACKGROUND AND CONTEXT

Kari Herbert's father was a polar explorer. She lived as a child with her family in northwest Greenland in the Arctic. She was so fascinated by the place that she returned there later as an adult to write about it.

The book from which this extract is taken is partly a **memoir** and partly a travel book, giving the reader information about this strange and beautiful place, its people and its animals. She found that the way of life of the Inughuit people of Greenland was changing due to the impact of the modern world. However they still retained aspects of their traditional way of life, such as hunting for food and driving teams of dogs.

A major part of the extract is an account of a hunt for **narwhal**. Hunting is a very emotive issue and many conservationists argue that whales should be protected. Kari Herbert's feelings on this topic are divided. She sympathises with both the narwhal and the hunters, who face incredible danger. They hunt in **kayaks** in water so cold that they would die quickly if their kayak overturned.

SUBJECT VOCABULARY

memoir a form of autobiography

GENERAL VOCABULARY

narwhal a species of whale, famous for the long single tusk on its head
kayak a type of canoe

▲ The Inughuit of the Arctic understand the intelligence of the narwhal.

BEFORE YOU START READING

1 Do some research.

▶ Find some information about Kari Herbert. You can visit her website.

▶ Find out as much as you can about the Inughuit people (sometimes spelt Inuit and formerly known as Eskimo) and their way of life.

▶ Find pictures of narwhal and information about them.

2 Some people think that hunting animals should be banned. In a small group or with a partner, share your ideas on the following questions.

▶ **What arguments can you think of in favour of hunting animals?**

▶ **What arguments can you think of against hunting animals?**

▶ **Do you think hunting wild animals should be banned?**

▶ **How important is it to protect endangered species?**

▼ FROM *THE EXPLORER'S DAUGHTER* BY KARI HERBERT

As a small child, Herbert lived, with her family, among the Inughuit people (sometimes called Inuits, or Eskimos) in the harsh environment of the Arctic. In 2002 she revisited the area, staying near Thule, a remote settlement in North Greenland. In this passage she writes about her experience of watching a hunt for the narwhal, a toothed whale, and what she thought and felt about it.

Two hours after the last of the hunters had returned and eaten, narwhal were spotted again, this time very close. Within an hour even those of us on shore could with the naked eye see the plumes of spray from the narwhal catching the light in a spectral play of colour. Two large pods of narwhal circled in the fjord, often looking as if they were going to merge, but always slowly, methodically passing each other by. Scrambling back up to the lookout I looked across the glittering kingdom in front of me and took a sharp intake of breath. The hunters were dotted all around the fjord. The evening light was turning butter-gold, glinting off man and whale and catching the soft billows of smoke from a lone hunter's pipe. From where we sat at the lookout it looked as though the hunters were close enough to touch the narwhal with their bare hands and yet they never moved. Distances are always deceptive in the Arctic, and I fell to wondering if the narwhal existed at all or were instead mischievous tricks of the shifting light…

The narwhal rarely stray from High Arctic waters, escaping only to the slightly more temperate waters towards the Arctic Circle in the dead of winter, but never entering the warmer southern seas. In summer the hunters of Thule are fortunate to witness the annual return of the narwhal to the Inglefield Fjord, on the side of which we now sat.

The narwhal… is an essential contributor to the survival of the hunters in the High Arctic. The mattak or blubber of the whale is rich in necessary minerals and vitamins, and in a place where the climate prohibits the growth of vegetables or fruit, this rich source of vitamin C was the one reason that the Eskimos have never suffered from scurvy… For centuries the blubber of the whales was also the only source of light and heat, and the dark rich meat is still a valuable part of the diet for both man and dogs (a single narwhal can feed a team of dogs for an entire month). Its single ivory tusk, which can grow up to six feet in length, was used for harpoon tips and handles for other hunting implements (although the ivory was found to be brittle and not hugely satisfactory as a weapon), for carving protective tupilaks, and even as a central beam for their small ancient dwellings. Strangely, the tusk seems to have little use for the narwhal itself; they do not use the tusk to break through ice as a breathing hole, nor will they use it to catch or attack prey, but rather the primary use seems to be to disturb the top of the sea bed in order to catch Arctic halibut for which they have a particular predilection. Often the ends of their tusks are worn down or even broken from such usage.

---

pods Small groups of whales.

fjord A long, narrow strip of the sea, between steep mountains.

mattak or blubber The fat of the whale.

scurvy A painful, weakening disease caused by lack of vitamin C.

tupilaks Charms or figures with magical powers.

predilection Liking.

The women clustered on the knoll of the lookout, binoculars pointing in every direction, each woman focusing on her husband or family member, occasionally spinning round at a small gasp or jump as one of the women saw a hunter near a narwhal… Each wife knew her husband instinctively and watched their progress intently; it was crucial to her that her husband catch a narwhal – it was part of their staple diet, and some of the mattak and meat could be sold to other hunters who hadn't been so lucky, bringing in some much-needed extra income. Every hunter was on the water. It was like watching a vast, waterborne game with the hunters spread like a net around the sound.

The narwhal… are intelligent creatures, their senses are keen and they talk to one another under the water. Their hearing is particularly developed and they can hear the sound of a paddling kayak from a great distance. That was why the hunters had to sit so very still in the water.

One hunter was almost on top of a pair of narwhal, and they were huge. He gently picked up his harpoon and aimed – in that split second my heart leapt for both hunter and narwhal. I urged the man on in my head; he was so close, and so brave to attempt what he was about to do – he was miles from land in a flimsy kayak, and could easily be capsized and drowned. The hunter had no rifle, only one harpoon with two heads and one bladder. It was a foolhardy exercise and one that could only inspire respect. And yet at the same time my heart also urged the narwhal to dive, to leave, to survive.

This dilemma stayed with me the whole time that I was in Greenland. I understand the harshness of life in the Arctic and the needs of the hunters and their families to hunt and live on animals and sea mammals that we demand to be protected because of their beauty. And I know that one cannot afford to be sentimental in the Arctic. 'How can you possibly eat seal?' I have been asked over and over again. True, the images that bombarded us several years ago of men battering seals for their fur hasn't helped the issue of polar hunting, but the Inughuit do not kill seals using this method, nor do they kill for sport. They use every part of the animals they kill, and most of the food in Thule is still brought in by the hunter-gatherers and fishermen. Imported goods can only ever account for part of the food supply; there is still only one annual supply ship that makes it through the ice to Qaanaaq, and the small twice-weekly plane from West Greenland can only carry a certain amount of goods. Hunting is still an absolute necessity in Thule.

▼ Traditional ways of life in the Arctic are under threat.

PAPER 1 — TEXT ANTHOLOGY: NON-FICTION

111

UNDERSTANDING THE TEXT

Kari Herbert sympathises with both hunter and hunted. The writer's central purposes are to convey the tension of the subject but also its beauty. You need to examine the different ways in which the writer does these things within the same passage. Copy and complete the following table with answers and evidence from the extract.

▼ QUESTION	▼ ANSWER AND EVIDENCE
Why do the Inughuit hunt the narwhal? Find as many reasons as you can.	1 Narwhal meat provides food – 'a valuable part of the diet for both man and dogs'. 2 3
What details show the difficulties and dangers faced by the Inughuit in the hunt?	1 2 3
What details show the writer's respect and sympathy for the narwhal?	1 2 3

EXPLORING LANGUAGE

The extract has many purposes and the writer uses language in different ways to fulfil these. She uses description to convey the beauty of the setting, gives the reader information about the Inughuit and the narwhal, dramatises the hunt and gives the reader an insight into her own thoughts and feelings. Copy and complete the following table to help you sort out these various strands.

▼ LANGUAGE USE	▼ EVIDENCE
Language to convey the effects of light.	1 A 'glittering kingdom'. 2 3
Language to give information: factual, scientific, other specialised language.	1 Precise scientific language makes the information more authoritative – for example, '[Its] mattak or blubber… is rich in necessary minerals and vitamins'. 2 3
Language to create tension.	1 The way the women react suggests their nervousness – for example, 'spinning round at a small gasp'. 2 3
Language to show the conflict in the writer's personal feelings and thoughts.	1 2 3

ACTIVITY 1 — A04 A05 — SKILLS: REASONING, CREATIVITY, INNOVATION

▼ WRITING TASKS

1 Write about a place you know well, or have recently re-visited, that has changed significantly in the time that you have known it. Analyse the ways in which it has changed, giving your thoughts about these changes.

2 Some people think that not enough is being done to preserve traditions and customs. What aspects of your way of life would you most want to keep and why?

EXAM-STYLE QUESTION

A02

SKILLS: CRITICAL THINKING, ANALYSIS, ADAPTIVE LEARNING, CREATIVITY

How does the writer use language and structure to explore the hunters' way of life?

You should support your answer with close reference to the passage, including **brief** quotations.

(12 marks)

▲ The Fjords of Greenland are a challenging place to explore, let alone live.

PAPER 1 — TEXT ANTHOLOGY: NON-FICTION

EXPLORERS OR BOYS MESSING ABOUT?
STEVEN MORRIS

BACKGROUND AND CONTEXT
This is a newspaper article that tells the story of two men rescued by the Chilean Navy when their helicopter crashed in the sea in the Antarctic.

BEFORE YOU START READING

1 Do some research. You might want to look at the original article.
   Compare this with how it was reported at the time by doing an internet search for 'antarctic helicopter crash 2003'.

2 In a small group or with a partner, share your ideas on the following questions.

   ▶ **Do you think that it is fair that the taxpayers have to pay for these explorers and others like them to be rescued?**

   ▶ **What do you see as the advantages and disadvantages of:**

   ■ requiring all explorers to buy additional insurance

   ■ requiring all explorers to buy licences from the government, without which they would not be allowed to explore

   ■ requiring explorers to do community work to repay any taxpayers' money spent on rescuing them?

▲ Sunset over the Antarctic Ocean

'EXPLORERS OR BOYS MESSING ABOUT? EITHER WAY, TAXPAYER GETS RESCUE BILL' BY STEVEN MORRIS

Adapted from an article published in The Guardian newspaper, January 28, 2003: Helicopter duo plucked from liferaft after Antarctic crash.

Their last expedition ended in farce when the Russians threatened to send in military planes to intercept them as they tried to cross into Siberia via the icebound Bering Strait.

Yesterday a new adventure undertaken by British explorers Steve Brooks and Quentin Smith almost led to tragedy when their helicopter plunged into the sea off Antarctica.

The men were plucked from the icy water by a Chilean naval ship after a nine-hour rescue which began when Mr Brooks contacted his wife, Jo Vestey, on his satellite phone asking for assistance. The rescue involved the Royal Navy, the RAF and British coastguards.

Last night there was resentment in some quarters that the men's adventure had cost the taxpayers of Britain and Chile tens of thousands of pounds.

Experts questioned the wisdom of taking a small helicopter – the four-seater Robinson R44 has a single engine – into such a hostile environment.

There was also confusion about what exactly the men were trying to achieve. A website set up to promote the Bering Strait expedition claims the team were planning to fly from the north to south pole in their "trusty helicopter".

But Ms Vestey claimed she did not know what the pair were up to, describing them as 'boys messing about with a helicopter'.

The drama began at around 1am British time when Mr Brooks, 42, and 40-year-old Mr Smith, also known as Q, ditched into the sea 100 miles off Antarctica, about 36 miles north of Smith Island, and scrambled into their liferaft.

Mr Brooks called his wife in London on his satellite phone. She said: 'He said they were both in the liferaft but were okay and could I call the emergency people?'

Meanwhile, distress signals were being beamed from the ditched helicopter and from Mr Brooks' Breitling emergency watch, a wedding present.

The signals from the aircraft were deciphered by Falmouth coastguard and passed on to the rescue coordination centre at RAF Kinloss in Scotland.

The Royal Navy's ice patrol ship, HMS Endurance, which was 180 miles away surveying uncharted waters, began steaming towards the scene and dispatched its two Lynx helicopters.

One was driven back because of poor visibility but the second was on its way when the men were picked up by a Chilean naval vessel at about 10.20 am British time.

Though the pair wore survival suits and the weather at the spot where they ditched was clear, one Antarctic explorer told Mr Brooks' wife it was 'nothing short of a miracle' that they had survived.

Falmouth Coastal town in Cornwall, England.

Both men are experienced adventurers. Mr Brooks, a property developer from London, has taken part in expeditions to 70 countries in 15 years. He has trekked solo to Everest base camp and walked barefoot for three days in the Himalayas. He has negotiated the white water rapids of the Zambezi river by kayak and survived a charge by a silver back gorilla in the Congo. He is also a qualified mechanical engineer and pilot.

He and his wife spent their honeymoon flying the helicopter from Alaska to Chile. The 16,000-mile trip took three months.

Mr Smith, also from London, claims to have been flying since the age of five. He has twice flown a helicopter around the globe and won the world freestyle helicopter flying championship.

Despite their experience, it is not the first time they have hit the headlines for the wrong reasons.

In April, Mr Brooks and another explorer, Graham Stratford, were poised to become the first to complete a crossing of the 56-mile wide frozen Bering Strait between the US and Russia in an amphibious vehicle, Snowbird VI, which could carve its way through ice floes and float in the water in between.

But they were forced to call a halt after the Russian authorities told them they would scramble military helicopters to lift them off the ice if they crossed the border.

Ironically, one of the aims of the expedition, for which Mr Smith provided air back-up, was to demonstrate how good relations between east and west had become.

The wisdom of the team's latest adventure was questioned by, among others, Günter Endres, editor of *Jane's Helicopter Markets and Systems*, who said: 'I'm surprised they used the R44. I wouldn't use a helicopter like that to go so far over the sea. It sounds as if they were pushing it to the maximum.'

A spokesman for the pair said it was not known what had gone wrong. The flying conditions had been 'excellent'.

The Ministry of Defence said the taxpayer would pick up the bill, as was normal in rescues in the UK and abroad. The spokesperson said it was 'highly unlikely' it would recover any of the money.

Last night the men were on their way to the Chilean naval base Eduardo Frei, where HMS Endurance was to pick them up. Ms Vestey said: 'They have been checked and appear to be well. I don't know what will happen to them once they have been picked up by HMS Endurance – they'll probably have their bottoms kicked and be sent home the long way.'

> **UNDERSTANDING THE TEXT**
>
> On the surface, this may appear to be an information text, as the article explains what happened to the two men and how they were rescued. However, the writer also takes a strongly critical stance on what he sees as irresponsible behaviour on the part of the two explorers. The key to understanding the article is in recognising how the writer makes his opinions clear.

PAPER 1 — TEXT ANTHOLOGY: NON-FICTION

ACTIVITY 1 — A01 — SKILLS: CRITICAL THINKING

▼ EXPLORING OPINIONS

Copy and complete the following table, finding explanations and evidence of the writer's opinions.

▼ THE WRITER'S OPINIONS	▼ EXPLANATION AND EVIDENCE
The two explorers are presented as childish.	1 Mr Smith has a nickname, which suggests a juvenile nature. 2 When they get in trouble they phone home, like running home to their mother. 3 Ms Vestey dismisses them as 'boys' and describes their behaviour as 'messing about'.
The writer uses irony to express his opinions.	1 Mr Smith's nickname is ironic as Q is the character from the James Bond films who is good with technical devices. 2 3
The two explorers are not really as expert as they claim to be.	1 2 3
The Royal Navy is used to criticise the two men.	1 2 3
The writer uses experts to voice his criticisms for him.	1 2 3
The writer uses emotive language.	1 2 3

▶ Write a single paragraph that directly expresses how the writer feels, rather than using the range of indirect criticisms that the writer uses in the text.

GENERAL VOCABULARY

irony using words to convey a meaning that is completely opposite to their apparent meaning

ACTIVITY 2 — A04 — A05 — SKILLS: CRITICAL THINKING, ANALYSIS, ADAPTIVE LEARNING, CREATIVITY

▼ OPINION AND FACT

Think of a recent event or situation of which you have personal experience, and about which you have a critical opinion. Write a short account, including factual details, but use what you have learnt from the extract to find ways to express your opinions as well.

EXAM-STYLE QUESTION — A02 — SKILLS: CRITICAL THINKING, ANALYSIS, ADAPTIVE LEARNING, CREATIVITY

How does the writer use language and structure to detail their opinion on the event?

You should support your answer with close reference to the passage, including **brief** quotations. **(12 marks)**

BETWEEN A ROCK AND A HARD PLACE
ARON RALSTON

BACKGROUND AND CONTEXT

Between a Rock and a Hard Place is an autobiography written by Aron Ralston, an engineer turned outdoorsman and motivational speaker. It relates his experience in 2003 of being trapped for five days and seven hours in Blue John Canyon, in the Utah desert in the southern United States.

His right arm was trapped by a boulder and, unable to free himself, he amputated his arm using a blunt pocketknife. He then had to return through the canyon and climb down a 20-metre slope before he could reach safety and receive medical care.

BEFORE YOU START READING

1 Read about Aron Ralston and his experience. If you are able to, watch *127 Hours*, the 2010 film on the same subject.
2 Think about what attracts people to potentially dangerous outdoor activities and sports. Is it a love of adventure? A sense of boredom? Or something else entirely?
3 Share any accounts of survival or lucky escapes that you have heard or read about.

▲ Blue John Canyon, Utah, USA

FROM *BETWEEN A ROCK AND A HARD PLACE* BY ARON RALSTON

In this first-hand account, Ralston describes how a boulder crushed his right hand while he was climbing and hiking in a canyon. He had not informed anyone of his hiking plans.

I come to another drop-off. This one is maybe eleven or twelve feet high, a foot higher and of a different geometry than the overhang I descended ten minutes ago. Another refrigerator chockstone is wedged between the walls, ten feet downstream from and at the same height as the ledge. It gives the space below the drop-off the claustrophobic feel of a short tunnel. Instead of the walls widening after the drop-off, or opening into a bowl at the bottom of the canyon, here the slot narrows to a consistent three feet across at the lip of the drop-off and continues at that width for fifty feet down the canyon.

Sometimes in narrow passages like this one, it's possible for me to stem my body across the slot, with my feet and back pushing out in opposite directions against the walls. Controlling this counterpressure by switching my hands and feet on the opposing walls, I can move up or down the shoulder width crevice fairly easily as long as the friction contact stays solid between the walls and my hands, feet, and back. This technique is known as stemming or chimneying; you can imagine using it to climb up the inside of a chimney.

Just below the ledge where I'm standing is a chockstone the size of a large bus tire, stuck fast in the channel between the walls, a few feet out from the lip. If I can step onto it, then I'll have a nine-foot height to descend, less than that of the first overhang. I'll dangle off the chockstone, then take a short fall onto the rounded rocks piled on the canyon floor.

Stemming across the canyon at the lip of the drop-off, with one foot and one hand on each of the walls, I traverse out to the chockstone. I press my back against the south wall and lock my left knee, which pushes my foot tight against the north wall. With my right foot, I kick at the boulder to test how stuck it is. It's jammed tightly enough to hold my weight. I lower myself from the chimneying position and step onto the chockstone. It supports me but teeters slightly. After confirming that I don't want to chimney down from the chockstone's height, I squat and grip the rear of the lodged boulder, turning to face back upcanyon. Sliding my belly over the front edge, I can lower myself and hang from my fully extended arms, akin to climbing down from the roof of a house.

As I dangle, I feel the stone respond to my adjusting grip with a scraping quake as my body's weight applies enough torque to disturb it from its position. Instantly, I know this is trouble, and instinctively, I let go of the rotating boulder to land on the round rocks below. When I look up, the backlit chockstone falling toward my head consumes the sky. Fear shoots my hands over my head. I can't move backward or I'll fall over a small ledge. My only hope is to push off the falling rock and get my head out of its way.

The next three seconds play out at a tenth of their normal speed. Time dilates, as if I'm dreaming, and my reactions decelerate. In slow motion: the rock smashes my left hand against the south wall; my eyes register the collision, and I yank my left arm back as the rock ricochets; the boulder then crushes my right hand and ensnares my right arm at the wrist, palm

---

drop-off A sheer downward slope.

chockstone A stone that has become stuck between rocks.

overhang A part of something (in this case, the rock) that extends over something else.

traverse Cross.

teeters Balance unsteadily.

torque Rotating force.

ricochets Bounces off.

in, thumb up, fingers extended; the rock slides another foot down the wall with my arm in tow, tearing the skin off the lateral side of my forearm. Then silence.

My disbelief paralyzes me temporarily as I stare at the sight of my arm vanishing into an implausibly small gap between the fallen boulder and the canyon wall. Within moments, my nervous system's pain response overcomes the initial shock. Good God, my hand. The flaring agony throws me into a panic. I grimace and growl… My mind commands my body, 'Get your hand out of there!' I yank my arm three times in a naive attempt to pull it out. But I'm stuck.

Anxiety has my brain tweaking; searing-hot pain shoots from my wrist up my arm. I'm frantic, and I cry out… My desperate brain conjures up a probably apocryphal story in which an adrenaline-stoked mom lifts an overturned car to free her baby. I'd give it even odds that it's made up, but I do know for certain that *right now*, while my body's chemicals are raging at full flood, is the best chance I'll have to free myself with brute force. I shove against the large boulder, heaving against it, pushing with my left hand, lifting with my knees pressed under the rock. I get good leverage with the aid of a twelve-inch shelf in front of my feet. Standing on that, I brace my thighs under the boulder and thrust upward repeatedly, grunting, 'Come on… move!' Nothing.

| apocryphal | Doubtful, untrue. |

UNDERSTANDING THE TEXT

This extract from *Between a Rock and a Hard Place* describes the place where the accident occurred and the event itself. Aron Ralston describes the events in great detail. He recreates the scene of the accident effectively. As he is writing for a general audience, he explains the terminology related to climbing as well as the reasons behind the different things he does. His clearheaded and analytical thinking pattern is effectively brought out as well as his ability to react quickly and to take action in the face of an unexpected problem.

As this is an autobiography, it is written in the first person and has many factual details that makes it feel authentic. Because it narrates a stressful situation, the present tense is used. This gives it a sense of immediacy and makes the reader feel as though they are there with the writer as the events unfold.

▲ 'Another chockstone is wedged between the walls…'

ACTIVITY 1 — AO1
SKILLS: ANALYSIS, INTERPRETATION

▼ DESCRIPTIVE LANGUAGE

1. Copy and complete the following table, identifying different pieces of information or descriptive detail given in the passage. Explain how each detail helps us to understand the writer's character or feelings.

▼ INFORMATION/DESCRIPTION	▼ ANSWER AND COMMENT
'Instead of the walls widening after the drop-off, or opening into a bowl at the bottom of the canyon, here the slot narrows to a consistent three feet across at the lip of the drop-off and continues at that width for fifty feet down the canyon.'	This information shows us that he is able to assess his surroundings in an accurate and analytical manner. He uses terms such as 'consistent three feet' which shows that he is skilled at gauging distance – a necessary skill for a climber.
'With my right foot, I kick at the boulder to test how stuck it is.'	

2. From the second paragraph, find two phrases that show the writer is careful.

EXPLORING LANGUAGE

Ralston's style is largely factual and analytical. He is very clear and precise in what he says about the events and his reactions. His use of minute details and his step-by-step narrative style are strong techniques that he uses to make his writing effective and interesting.

ACTIVITY 2 — AO2
SKILLS: ANALYSIS, INTERPRETATION

▼ LANGUAGE FOR EFFECT

Copy and complete the following table, thinking about other techniques that the writer has used and their effect.

▼ TECHNIQUE	▼ EXAMPLE	▼ EFFECT
Emotive language	'flaring agony'	This phrase shows the extent of the pain the writer feels as the first shock wears off. The word 'flaring' shows how the pain rapidly grows and spreads, while the word 'agony' shows how extremely painful it is.
Direct speech		
Variety in punctuation		
	'akin to climbing down from the roof of a house'	
Personification		

PAPER 1 — TEXT ANTHOLOGY: NON-FICTION

ACTIVITY 3 — AO2
SKILLS: CRITICAL THINKING, ANALYSIS, INTERPRETATION

▼ SENTENCE TYPE

Ralston uses a variety of sentence types to make his writing interesting. Copy and complete the following table with examples of each type and explain the effect.

▼ TYPE OF SENTENCE	▼ EXAMPLE	▼ EFFECT
Long complex sentences		
Short sentences		
Incomplete sentences		

EXAM-STYLE QUESTION

AO2

SKILLS: CRITICAL THINKING, ANALYSIS, ADAPTIVE LEARNING, CREATIVITY

How does the writer use language and structure to engage of the reader?

You should support your answer with close reference to the passage, including **brief** quotations. **(12 marks)**

ACTIVITY 4 — AO4 AO5
SKILLS: PROBLEM SOLVING, CREATIVITY, INNOVATION

▼ WRITING TASKS

1. Write a magazine article giving your views on the statement: 'Extreme situations bring out the best in all of us'. In the article, you may include:
   - anecdotal incidents that support this statement
   - the positives and negatives of facing extreme situations
   - any other points you wish to make.
2. In 1910, Robert Scott, an English naval officer and explorer, led an expedition to the South Pole. Three explorers from this group set out in July 1911 to collect emperor penguin eggs to be studied by scientists back home. After 35 days they managed to return to base camp with three eggs. During this trip, the three explorers faced extreme hardship due to cold and weather. Imagine that you are one of the explorers and write a diary entry detailing one day of the journey.

KEY POINT

First-person narration is often noted for its level of detail. This can enable the writer to write with immediacy and power.

HOW TO WRITE A SUCCESSFUL ANSWER

The following is a candidate's answer to the question, 'In your own words explain what the writer's thoughts and feelings are in paragraph 5'. The annotations show some of the strengths of the answer.

> **In this paragraph** the writer feels worried as he is **unsure** whether the stone that he is balancing on will hold. The movement of the stone alerts him to danger and reacts quickly. He is very frightened as he watches the stone falling towards him, but **he is also able to make a quick decision and react**. He doesn't give up and wait but thinks of what action he can take and picks the only option available to him which is to push the stone away.

in this paragraph Addresses the question directly.

unsure Focuses on a specific feeling.

he is also able to make a quick decision and react His thoughts are given in the candidate's own words.

Using this answer as a guide, write your own answer to the following question.

▶ In your own words, explain the writer's feelings and reactions in paragraph 7.

'YOUNG AND DYSLEXIC? YOU'VE GOT IT GOING ON'
BENJAMIN ZEPHANIAH

BACKGROUND AND CONTEXT
Benjamin Zephaniah has earned widespread respect for his ability to overcome spite, prejudice and ridicule. Because of his difficulties with reading, his teachers dismissed him as unintelligent and not worthy of their attention. Rejected by a number of schools, he was unable to read when he left education at the age of 13. Unusually and bravely, he refused to give in to despair, acknowledged his difficulties and joined an adult reading class. Since then, he has taken an imaginative and constructive approach to life's challenges.

In this article from *The Guardian* newspaper, Zephaniah explains how this happened, from his early difficulties in school to his determination to write. He performed some of his early work in church at the age of 11, but found himself with a criminal record two years later. Despite this troubled period, he has gone on to become a successful poet and writer. His publication within a well-regarded national newspaper can be seen as an ironic contrast to his earlier life.

▲ Poet Benjamin Zephaniah

BEFORE YOU START READING

1. Find out more about the author and his very unusual background before he became a highly regarded poet and author. Find out what you can about borstals, reform schools and life in poor inner-city areas of Britain. Write down your thoughts and highlight what you think makes a typical writer. Is Zephaniah what you would consider to be a 'traditional' writer?

2. Read the following example of Zephaniah's poetry, entitled *White Comedy*. Look at the way that Zephaniah uses the words 'white' and 'black' and the way that they affect other words. Look at some other examples of his poetry. What common themes can you identify within his poems?

I waz whitemailed
By a white witch,
Wid white magic
An white lies,
Branded by a white sheep
I slaved as a whitesmith
Near a white spot
Where I suffered whitewater fever.
Whitelisted as a whiteleg
I waz in de white book
As a master of white art,
It waz like white death.

People called me white jack
Some hailed me as a white wog,
So I joined de white watch
Trained as a white guard
Lived off the white economy.
Caught and beaten by de
    whiteshirts
I waz condemned to a white mass,
Don't worry,
I shall be writing to de Black
    House.

▼ 'YOUNG AND DYSLEXIC? YOU'VE GOT IT GOING ON' BY BENJAMIN ZEPHANIAH

This article was published in *The Guardian*, 2 October 2015, and is adapted from Zephaniah's contribution to *Creative, Successful, Dyslexic* (Jessica Kingsley, 2015).

As a child I suffered, but learned to turn dyslexia to my advantage, to see the world more creatively. We are the architects, we are the designers.

I'm of the generation where teachers didn't know what dyslexia was. The big problem with the education system then was that there was no compassion, no understanding and no humanity. I don't look back and feel angry with the teachers. The ones who wanted to have an individual approach weren't allowed to. The idea of being kind and thoughtful and listening to problems just wasn't done: the past is a different kind of country.

At school my ideas always contradicted the teachers'. I remember one teacher saying that human beings sleep for one-third of their life and I put my hand up and said, "If there's a God isn't that a design fault? If you've built something, you want efficiency. If I was God I would have designed sleep so we could stay awake. Then good people could do one-third more good in the world."

The teacher said, "Shut up, stupid boy. Bad people would do one-third more bad." I thought I'd put in a good idea. I was just being creative. She also had a point, but the thing was she called me stupid for even thinking about it.

I remember a teacher talking about Africa and the 'local savages' and I would say, "Who are you to talk about savages?" She would say, "How dare you challenge me?" – and that would get me into trouble.

Once, when I was finding it difficult to engage with writing and had asked for some help, a teacher said, "It's all right. We can't all be intelligent, but you'll end up being a good sportsperson, so why don't you go outside and play some football?" I thought, "Oh great", but now I realise he was stereotyping me.

I had poems in my head even then, and when I was 10 or 11 my sister wrote some of them down for me. When I was 13 I could read very basically but it would be such hard work that I would give up. I thought that so long as you could read how much the banknote was worth, you knew enough or you could ask a mate.

I got thrown out of a lot of schools, the last one at 13. I was expelled partly because of arguing with teachers on an intellectual level and partly for being a rude boy and fighting. I didn't stab anybody, but I did take revenge on a teacher once. I stole his car and drove it into his front garden. I remember him telling us the Nazis weren't that bad. He could say that in the classroom. When I was in borstal I used to do this thing of looking at people I didn't want to be like. I saw a guy who spent all his time sitting stooped over and I thought, "I don't want to be like that", so I learned to sit with a straight back. Being observant helped me make the right choices.

A high percentage of the prison population are dyslexic, and a high percentage of the architect population. If you look at the statistics, I should

---

dyslexia Difficulties with reading despite normal intelligence.

the past is a different kind of country A phrase meaning that life was different in the past.

contradict Challenge what someone has said.

stereotyping Making unwarranted assumptions about someone or something.

borstal A residential training centre for young people who are in trouble.

be in prison: a black man brought up on the wrong side of town whose family fell apart, in trouble with the police when I was a kid, unable to read and write, with no qualifications and, on top of that, dyslexic. But I think staying out of prison is about conquering your fears and finding your path in life.

When I go into prisons to talk to people I see men and women who, in intelligence and other qualities, are the same as me. But opportunities opened for me and they missed theirs, didn't notice them or didn't take them.

I never thought I was stupid. I didn't have that struggle. If I have someone in front of me who doesn't have a problem reading and writing telling me that black people are savages I just think, "I'm not stupid – you're the one who's stupid." I just had self-belief.

For my first book I told my poems to my girlfriend, who wrote them down for me. It really took off, especially within the black community. I wrote "wid luv" for "with love". People didn't think they were dyslexic poems, they just thought I wrote phonetically.

At 21 I went to an adult education class in London to learn to read and write. The teacher told me, "You are dyslexic," and I was like, "Do I need an operation?" She explained to me what it meant and I suddenly thought, "Ah, I get it. I thought I was going crazy."

I wrote more poetry, novels for teenagers, plays, other books and recorded music. I take poetry to people who do not read poetry. Still now, when I'm writing the word "knot", I have to stop and think, "How do I write that?" I have to draw something to let me know what the word is to come back to it later. If I can't spell "question" I just put a question mark and come back to it later.

When I look at a book, the first thing I see is the size of it, and I know that's what it's like for a lot of young people who find reading tough. When Brunel University offered me the job of professor of poetry and creative writing, I knew my students would be officially more educated than me. I tell them, "You can do this course and get the right grade because you have a good memory – but if you don't have passion, creativity, individuality, there's no point." In my life now, I find that people **accommodate** my dyslexia. I can perform my poetry because it doesn't have to be word perfect, but I never read one of my novels in public. When I go to literary festivals I always get an actor to read it out for me. Otherwise all my energy goes into reading the book and the mood is lost.

If someone can't understand dyslexia it's their problem. In the same way, if someone **oppresses** me because of my race I don't sit down and think, "How can I become white?" It's not my problem, it's theirs and they are the ones who have to come to terms with it.

If you're dyslexic and you feel there's something holding you back, just remember: it's not you. In many ways being dyslexic is a natural way to be.

What's unnatural is the way we read and write. If you look at a pictorial language like Chinese, you can see the word for a woman because the character looks like a woman. The word for a house looks like a house. It is a strange step to go from that to a squiggle that represents a sound.

So don't be heavy on yourself. And if you are a parent of someone with

---

accommodate Make adjustments for someone or something.

oppresses Makes someone feel inadequate or worthless and limits their freedom.

defect Something that prevents proper functioning or a problem.

dyslexia don't think of it as a **defect**. Dyslexia is not a measure of intelligence: you may have a genius on your hands. Having dyslexia can make you creative. If you want to construct a sentence and can't find the word you are searching for, you have to think of a way to write round it. This requires being creative and so your 'creativity muscle' gets bigger.

Kids come up to me and say, "I'm dyslexic too," and I say to them, "Use it to your advantage, see the world differently. Us dyslexic people, we've got it going on – we are the architects. We are the designers." It's like these kids are proud to be like me and if that helps them, that is great. I didn't have that as a child. I say to them, "Bloody nondyslexics … who do they think they are?"

UNDERSTANDING THE TEXT

This newspaper article is drawn from Zephaniah's contribution to a book about how dyslexic people can be successful. He presents himself as someone who has found ways of coping with dyslexia, persuading other dyslexics that they should not regard dyslexia as an obstacle, but as an opportunity to be creative, rather than restricted.

In a relatively short space, Zephaniah introduces a number of important points. Mainly, he does this by using short, tightly-written paragraphs so that in a matter of a few minutes you learn what the author understands as the essential elements of his coping with dyslexia.

ACTIVITY 1 | A01 | SKILLS: CRITICAL THINKING

▼ ANALYSING THE ARTICLE

Copy and complete the following table, analysing what the writer is saying in each of the examples from the article.

▼ EXAMPLE	▼ WHAT THE WRITER IS SAYING
'no compassion, no understanding and no humanity'	These words show Zephaniah's view of his time in school.
'She also had a point'	
'such hard work that I would give up'	
'But opportunities opened for me and they missed theirs'	
'Do I need an operation?'	
'I don't sit down and think, "How can I become white?"'	

ACTIVITY 2 — A01
SKILLS: ANALYSIS, INTERPRETATION

▼ THEMES AND IDEAS

Copy and complete the following table. Find evidence of each theme in the article and discuss your findings.

▼ THEME	▼ COMMENT	▼ EVIDENCE
Failed schooling	Zephaniah describes his poor start in life, which contrasts with what he achieves later despite the difficulties faced at school.	
Challenging teachers		
Things not being what they seemed / what people would expect them to be		
Escaping, avoiding things and coping		
Turning things round		
Creativity		

EXPLORING LANGUAGE

An even tone is maintained in the opening paragraphs, despite the fact that Zephaniah is describing events that troubled him at the time. He reports events without reacting to them. In this way, readers are encouraged to draw their own conclusions, and this makes Zephaniah's points more convincing. On two occasions, he simply tells readers what he thought when faced with a teacher whose comments troubled him. This shows the reader an example of his reacting without making things worse. Zephaniah shows his self-restraint when provoked. In his final two paragraphs, he provides encouragement and a challenge with the striking phrases, 'creativity muscle' and 'Bloody nondyslexics … who do they think they are?'.

A short, introductory paragraph conveys Zephaniah's conclusion from the outset and engages with the reader: 'We are the architects, we are the designers'. The writing is matter-of-fact and lacks self-pity. From being thrown out of schools to his appointment as a professor of poetry at a university, he presents important events in his life in chronological order, to show how he came to see beyond his troubles as a teenager and turned them into something positive, from which both he and the reader can learn.

KEY POINT

Sometimes, non-fiction writers hold back from giving their full reaction to create a space in which the reader can fill with their own reaction.

ACTIVITY 3 — A02 — SKILLS: ANALYSIS

▼ LANGUAGE FOR EFFECT

Copy and complete the following table, explaining the techniques that Zephaniah uses in these extracts to achieve his purposes. A clue has been provided in each case.

▼ EXAMPLE	▼ CLUE	▼ TECHNIQUE
'I had poems in my head even then.'	Think about metaphor.	
'I saw a guy who spent all his time sitting stooped over and I thought, "I don't want to be like that," so I learned to sit with a straight back.'	Look at the main verbs.	
'If you look at the statistics, I should be in prison: a black man brought up on the wrong side of town whose family fell apart, in trouble with the police when I was a kid, unable to read and write, with no qualifications and, on top of that, dyslexic.'	Look at the list.	

ACTIVITY 4 — A01 — SKILLS: COLLABORATION, EMPATHY, NEGOTIATION

▼ AUDIENCE AND LANGUAGE

Make notes on your answers to the following questions. Discuss them with others if possible.

1. Why does Zephaniah think architects are important? What does he think about 'beating the odds'?
2. How inspiring do you think other dyslexics would find this piece? Why?
3. Zephaniah thinks a pictorial written language, such as the Chinese system, is easier to understand – do you agree? Can you think of any other examples? Think about how a letter represents a thing, and about representing sound.

| ACTIVITY 5 | A04 | A05 | SKILLS: CREATIVITY, INNOVATION |

▼ WRITING TASKS

1 A friend has been told that they are dyslexic. Write about what you would do to help and encourage them.
2 Someone in your class is being treated badly by a teacher. Write a story in which this classmate deals with the problem, not by becoming angry, but by thinking creatively.

EXAM-STYLE QUESTIONS

A02

SKILLS: CRITICAL THINKING, ANALYSIS, ADAPTIVE LEARNING, CREATIVITY

How does the writer explore his early life and relationship with reading?

You should support your answer with close reference to the passage, including **brief** quotations.

(12 marks)

How does the writer use language and structure to encourage the reader to challenge unfair treatment?

You should support your answer with close reference to the passage, including **brief** quotations.

(12 marks)

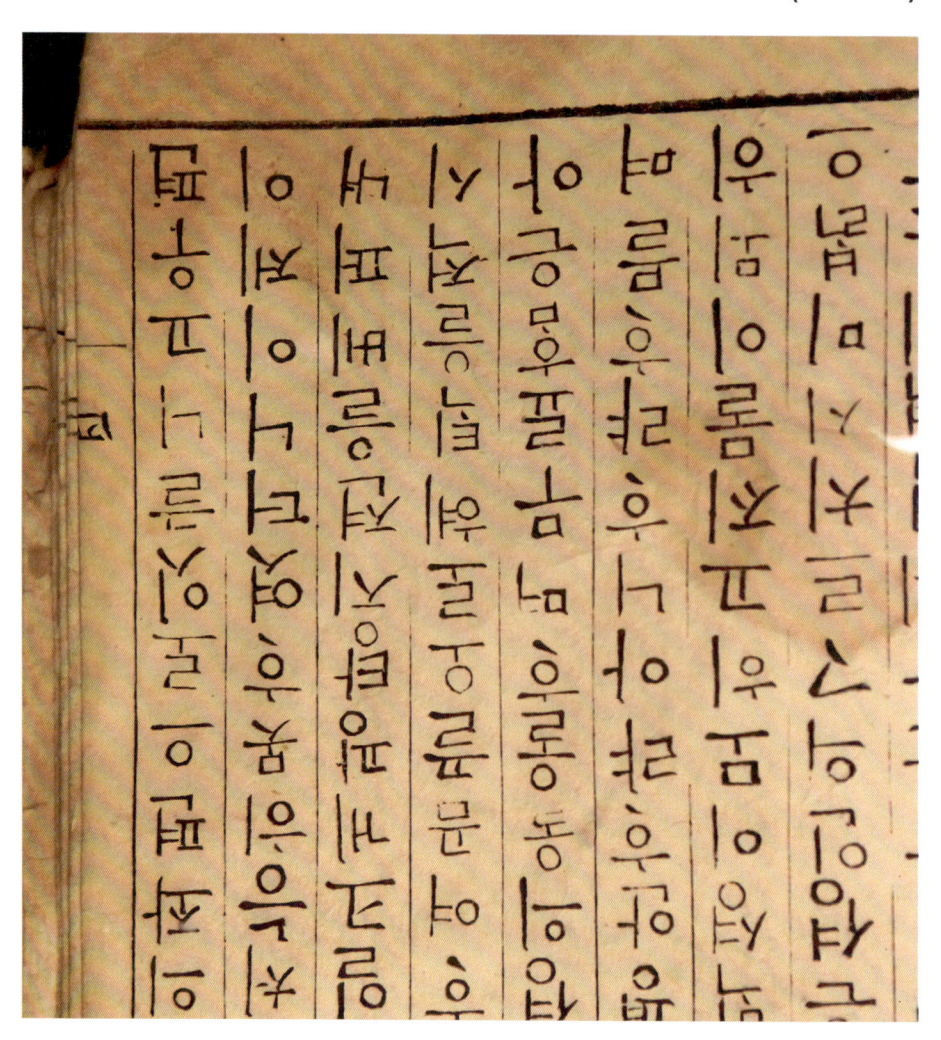

▶ Some languages make more sense to people than others.

PAPER 1 — TEXT ANTHOLOGY: NON-FICTION

SUBJECT VOCABULARY

travelogue a book that describes a travel experience

A GAME OF POLO WITH A HEADLESS GOAT
EMMA LEVINE

BACKGROUND AND CONTEXT

This extract comes from a book which was written as a spin-off from Emma Levine's television series about strange and unusual sports. It is a **travelogue** in which she describes these sports, the people involved and her experiences of filming them. In doing so, she gives an insight not just into the sports themselves, but into the lives and culture of the people who take part in and watch them.

BEFORE YOU START READING

1 Do some research.
- Find some information about Emma Levine. You can visit her website by searching for her name.
- Find a newspaper report on a motor race, perhaps a Formula 1 Grand Prix, and make some notes about the way in which it has been written.
- What is the strangest sport or game you know or can find information about?

2 In a small group or with a partner, share your ideas on the following questions.
- Do you prefer to take part in sport or watch it?
- How important is sport in your life?
- Do you think the involvement of money in sport (for example, gambling or excessive pay for sportspeople) ruins sport?

▼ FROM *A GAME OF POLO WITH A HEADLESS GOAT* BY EMMA LEVINE

Levine travelled throughout Asia researching and filming unusual sports. In this passage she writes about a donkey race in Karachi, Pakistan.

We drove off to find the best viewing spot, which turned out to be the crest of the hill so we could see the approaching race. I asked the lads if we could join in the 'Wacky Races' and follow the donkeys, and they loved the idea. 'We'll open the car boot, you climb inside and point your camera towards the race. As the donkeys overtake us, we'll join the cars.' 'But will you try and get to the front?' 'Oh yes, that's no problem.'

The two lads who had never been interested in this Karachi sport were suddenly fired up with enthusiasm. We waited for eternity on the brow of the hill, me perched in the boot with a zoom lens pointing out. Nearly one hour later I was beginning to feel rather silly when the only action was a villager on a wobbly bicycle, who nearly fell off as he cycled past and gazed around at us.

Several vehicles went past, and some donkey-carts carrying spectators. 'Are they coming?' we called out to them. 'Coming, coming,' came the reply. I was beginning to lose faith in its happening, but the lads remained confident.

Just as I was assuming that the race had been cancelled, we spotted two approaching donkey-carts in front of a cloud of fumes and dust created by some fifty vehicles roaring up in their wake. As they drew nearer, Yaqoob revved up the engine and began to inch the car out of the lay-by. The two donkeys were almost dwarfed by their entourage; but there was no denying their speed – the Kibla donkey is said to achieve speeds of up to 40 kph, and this looked close. The two were neck-and-neck, their jockeys perched on top of the tiny carts using their whips energetically, although not cruelly.

The noise of the approaching vehicles grew; horns tooting, bells ringing, and the special rattles used just for this purpose (like maracas, a metal container filled with dried beans). Men standing on top of their cars and vans, hanging out of taxis and perched on lorries, all cheered and shouted, while the vehicles jostled to get to the front of the convoy.

Yaqoob chose exactly the right moment to edge out of the road and swerve in front of the nearest car, finding the perfect place to see the two donkeys and at the front of the vehicles. This was Formula One without rules, or a city-centre rush hour gone anarchic; a complete flouting of every type of traffic rule and common sense.

Our young driver relished this unusual test of driving skills. It was survival of the fittest, and depended upon the ability to cut in front of a vehicle with a sharp flick of the steering wheel (no lane discipline here); quick reflexes to spot a gap in the traffic for a couple of seconds; nerves of steel, and an effective horn. There were two races – the motorized spectators at the back; in front, the two donkeys, still running close and amazingly not put off by the uproar just behind them. Ahead of the donkeys, oncoming traffic – for it was a main road – had to dive into the ditch and wait there until we had passed. Yaqoob loved it. We stayed near to the front, his hand permanently on the horn and his language growing more colourful with every vehicle that tried to cut in front.

The road straightened and levelled, and everyone picked up speed as we neared the end of the race. But just as they were reaching the finishing line,

anarchic Lawless.

flouting Breaking.

▲ Emma Levine writes about the ancient sports of Asia.

the hospital gate, there was a near pile-up as the leading donkey swerved, lost his footing and he and the cart tumbled over. The race was over.

And then the trouble began. I assumed the winner was the one who completed the race but it was not seen that way by everyone. Apart from the two jockeys and 'officials' (who, it turned out, were actually monitoring the race) there were over a hundred punters who had all staked money on the race, and therefore had strong opinions. Some were claiming that the donkey had fallen because the other one had been ridden too close to him. Voices were raised, fists were out and tempers rising. Everyone gathered around one jockey and official, while the bookmakers were trying to insist that the race should be re-run.

Yaqoob and Iqbal were nervous of hanging around a volatile situation. They agreed to find out for me what was happening, ordering me to stay inside the car as they were swallowed up by the crowd. They emerged sometime later. 'It's still not resolved,' said Iqbal, 'but it's starting to get nasty. I think we should leave.' As we drove away, Yaqoob reflected on his driving skills. 'I really enjoyed that,' he said as we drove off at a more sedate pace. 'But I don't even have my licence yet because I'm underage!'

They both found this hilarious, but I was glad he hadn't told me before; an inexperienced, underage driver causing a massive pile-up in the middle of the high-stakes donkey race could have caused problems.

UNDERSTANDING THE TEXT

Emma Levine's purpose in writing her book was to describe and inform. She obviously has to engage the reader and hold their interest. As you study this text, you need to think about how she does this.

ACTIVITY 1 — A01 — SKILLS: CRITICAL THINKING, ANALYSIS

▼ THREE RACES

The passage seems a straightforward description and narrative of the race, but it isn't. First of all, there is not just one race happening, but three:

- the donkey race
- the spectators' race
- the writer's race to get the best pictures.

1. Find one quotation for each of these in order to show that there are three races taking place.
2. Is the main focus of the reader's interest the race, or the people involved in it? What do you think? Find some evidence to support your point of view.

STRUCTURE

The passage can be defined as a series of linked paragraphs, describing events in chronological order and concluding with the end of the race and the writer's overview of what happened. The internal structure is much more complex than this simple outline suggests.

ACTIVITY 2 — A01 — SKILLS: ANALYSIS, INTERPRETATION

▼ TYPES OF WRITING

Copy and complete the following table, finding examples of each of the different kinds of writing used in the passage. How does each of the examples that you have found add to the reader's interest in the passage?

▼ TYPE OF WRITING	▼ EXAMPLE(S)
Description	
Dialogue	
Informational writing	
Narrative	
Evaluation	
Commentary	

EXPLORING LANGUAGE

Most newspaper reports of sports races are serious in tone, and try to give the facts of the race and what it was like. Emma Levine's purpose is much more complicated than that. This passage is a mixture of comic writing and serious reportage, with a lot of information given as well. Consider each of these elements carefully.

KEY POINT

The subject matter of this passage lends itself to both comedy and drama and the writer exploits both to great effect.

▲ The Kibla donkey is said to achieve speeds of up to 40 kph.

PAPER 1   TEXT ANTHOLOGY: NON-FICTION   133

ACTIVITY 3 — A02 — SKILLS: ANALYSIS

▼ LANGUAGE FOR EFFECT

KEY POINT

Sport, which essentially shows adults playing games, is a fertile subject for writers.

Copy and complete the following table to help you understand how language is used in the passage.

▼ QUESTION		▼ ANSWER AND EVIDENCE
What words and phrases does Levine use to bring out the humour of the race?		1 'the "Wacky Races"' – this reference to a famous television cartoon series puts the race in a comic context. 2 3
What words and phrases help to convey the excitement of the races?	Words that convey movement	1 'some fifty vehicles roaring up in their wake' – this conveys the speed of the cars and the speed of the donkeys. 2 3
	Words that suggest sound	1 2 3
	Words that create visual images	1 2 3
What words and phrases help show that the passage contains some serious moments?		1 'Yaqoob and Iqbal were nervous of hanging around a volatile situation' – this shows the danger of the situation and how quickly the mood of the spectators might change. 2 3

ACTIVITY 4 — A04 — A05 — SKILLS: REASONING, CREATIVITY, INNOVATION

▼ WRITING TASKS

1 Write a short story about a race or a hunt.
2 Write a newspaper report on a game involving a team sport, such as football, cricket or basketball.
3 'Taking part in sport is more important than winning'. Argue either in favour of this statement or against it.

EXAM-STYLE QUESTION

A02 SKILLS: CRITICAL THINKING, ANALYSIS, ADAPTIVE LEARNING, CREATIVITY

How does the writer use language and structure to create excitement and interest?

You should support your answer with close reference to the passage, including **brief** quotations.

(12 marks)

SUBJECT VOCABULARY

memoir a form of autobiography

GENERAL VOCABULARY

landlocked without a coastline

BEYOND THE SKY AND THE EARTH: A JOURNEY INTO BHUTAN
JAMIE ZEPPA

BACKGROUND AND CONTEXT

Jamie Zeppa is a Canadian writer and college professor. *Beyond the Sky and Earth: A Journey into Bhutan* is an autobiography that recounts her experiences on a two-year assignment as an English lecturer in the 1980s in the mountainous kingdom of Bhutan. It is a **memoir**, but it should also be classed as travel writing. It is a record of the culture and life of a Himalayan village and her initial reactions and growing attachment to this remote and unexplored part of the world.

Bhutan is a **landlocked** country in South Asia and was not exposed to western influences until the second half of the 20th century, which enabled it to retain much of its unique identity and charm. It is a country that has been named the happiest in Asia and the eighth happiest in the world.

BEFORE YOU START READING

1 Do some research about the history and geography of Bhutan.
2 In groups, talk about what makes your own culture different from that of other countries. Are there many differences, or only a few? Talk about the different things that people discuss when describing a culture, such as language, clothing and practices.
3 Quite often the names of countries and cities have very interesting stories behind their origin. Share any that you know with the rest of your class.

▼ FROM *BEYOND THE SKY AND THE EARTH: A JOURNEY INTO BHUTAN* BY JAMIE ZEPPA

When Zeppa was 24 years old she left Canada to teach in Bhutan. This memoir grew out of an essay she wrote about her early days in the country.

Mountains all around, climbing up to peaks, rolling into valleys, again and again. Bhutan is all and only mountains. I know the technical explanation for the landscape, landmass meeting landmass, the Indian subcontinent colliding into Asia thirty or forty million years ago, but I cannot imagine it. It is easier to picture a giant child gathering earth in great armfuls, piling up rock, pinching mud into ridges and sharp peaks, knuckling out little valleys and gorges, poking holes for water to fall through.

It is my first night in Thimphu, the capital, a ninety-minute drive from the airport in Paro. It took five different flights over four days to get there, from Toronto to Montreal to Amsterdam to New Delhi to Calcutta to Paro. I am exhausted but I cannot sleep. From my simple, pine-panelled room at the

Paro A valley in Bhutan that contains the country's only international airport.

| PAPER 1 | TEXT ANTHOLOGY: NON-FICTION | 135 |

flavorless Zeppa uses American English spellings.

Saskatchewan A province in Canada known for its harsh winters.

British Columbia A Canadian province on the west coast, containing the city of Vancouver.

impish Mischievous; the term comes from the name of a mythological creature, 'imp', believed to cause trouble.

WUSC World University Service of Canada, a non-profit organisation that works with local bodies to strengthen educational systems and economic opportunities.

Willie Nelson A well-known American musician of country music whose career was at its height in the 1970s.

Rambo The American main character from the Rambo films.

dzong A type of fortress found in the present and former Tibetan Buddhist kingdoms of the Himalayas, particularly Bhutan and south Tibet.

emissary A diplomat or representative for a country.

George Bogle A Scottish traveller and diplomat who was the first to establish diplomatic relations with Tibet.

Druk Sherig hotel, I watch mountains rise to meet the moon. I used to wonder what was on the other side of mountains, how the landscape resolved itself beyond the immediate wall in front of you. Flying in from the baked-brown plains of India this morning, I found out: on the other side of mountains are mountains, more mountains and mountains again. The entire earth below us was a convulsion of crests and gorges and wind sharpened pinnacles. Just past Everest, I caught a glimpse of the Tibetan plateau, the edge of a frozen desert 4,500 meters above sea level. Thimphu's altitude is about half of that but even here, the winter air is thin and dry and very cold.

The next morning, I share breakfast of instant coffee, powdered milk, plasticky white bread and flavorless red jam in the hotel with two other Canadians who have signed on to teach in Bhutan for two years. Lorna has golden brown hair, freckles and a no nonsense, home-on-the-farm demeanour that is frequently shattered by her ringing laughter and stories of wild characters that populate her life in Saskatchewan. Sasha from British Columbia is slight and dark, with an impish smile. After breakfast, we have a brief meeting with Gordon, the field director of the WUSC program in Bhutan, and then walk along the main road of Thimpu. Both Lorna and Sasha have traveled extensively; Lorna trekked all over Europe and northern Africa and Sasha worked for a year in an orphanage in Bombay. They are both ecstatic about Bhutan so far, and I stay close to them, hoping to pick up some of their enthusiasm.

Although Thimphu's official population is 20,000, it seems even smaller. It doesn't even have traffic lights. Blue-suited policemen stationed at two intersections along the main street direct the occasional truck or land cruiser using incomprehensible but graceful hand gestures. The buildings all have the same pitched roof, trefoil windows and heavy beams painted with lotus flowers, jewels and clouds. One-storied shops with wooden-shuttered windows open onto the street. They seem to be selling the same things: onions, rice, milk powder, dried fish, plastic buckets and metal plates, quilts and packages of stale, soft cookies from India – Bourbon Biscuits, Coconut Crunchies and the hideously colored Orange Cream Biscuits. There are more signs of the outside world than I had expected: teenagers in acid washed jeans, Willie Nelson's greatest hits after the news in English on the Bhutan Broadcasting Service, a Rambo poster in a bar. Overall, these signs of cultural infiltration are few, but they are startling against the Bhutanese-ness of everything else.

The town itself looks very old, with cracked sidewalks and faded paintwork but Gordon told us that it didn't exist thirty-odd years ago. Before the sixties, when the third king decided to make it the capital, it was nothing but rice paddies, a few farm houses, and a dzong – one of the fortresses that are scattered throughout the country. Thimphu is actually new. "Thimphu will look like New York to you when you come back after a year in the east," he said.

At the end of the main road is Tashichho Dzong, the seat of the Royal Government of Bhutan, a grand, whitewashed, red-roofed, golden-tipped fortress, built in the traditional way, without blueprints or nails. Beyond, hamlets are connected by footpaths, and terraced fields, barren now, climb steadily from the river and merge into forest. Thimphu will never look like New York to me, I think.

The Bhutanese are a very handsome people, 'the best built race of men I ever saw,' wrote emissary George Bogle on his way to Tibet in 1774, and I find I

▶

agree. Of medium height and sturdily built, they have beautiful aristocratic faces with dark, almond-shaped eyes, high cheekbones and gentle smiles. Both men and women wear their black hair short. The women wear a *kira*, a brightly striped, ankle-length dress and the men a *gho*, a knee-length robe that resembles a kimono, except the top part is exceptionally voluminous. The Bhutanese of Nepali origin tend to be taller, with sharper features and darker complexions. They too wear the gho and kira. People look at us curiously, but they do not seem surprised at our presence. Although we see few other foreigners in town, we know they are here. Gordon said something this morning about Thimphu's small but friendly 'ex-pat' community.

When we stop and ask for directions at a hotel, the young man behind the counter walks with us to the street, pointing out the way, explaining politely in impeccable English. I search for the right word to describe the people, for the quality that impresses me most – dignity, unselfconsciousness, good humor, grace – but can find no single word to hold all of my impressions.

In Thimpu, we attended a week-long orientation session with twelve other Irish, British, Australian and New Zealand teachers new to Bhutan. Our first lessons, in Bhutanese history, are the most interesting. Historical records show that waves of Tibetan immigrants settled in Bhutan sometime before the tenth century, but the area is thought to have been inhabited long before that. In the eighth century, the Indian saint Padmasambhava brought Buddhism to the area, where it absorbed many elements of Bon, the indigenous shamanistic religion. The new religion took hold but was not a unifying force. The area remained a collection of isolated valleys, each ruled by its own king. When the Tibetan lama Ngawang Namgyel arrived in 1616, he set about unifying the valleys under one central authority and gave the country the name Druk Yul, meaning Land of the Thunder Dragon. Earlier names for Bhutan are just as beautiful – the Tibetans knew the country as the Southern Land of Medicinal Herbs and the South Sandalwood Country. Districts within Bhutan were even more felicitously-named: Rainbow District of Desires, Lotus Grove of the Gods, Blooming Valley of Luxuriant Fruits, the Land of Longing and Silver Pines. Bhutan, the name by which the country became known to the outside world, is thought to be derived from *Bhotanta*, meaning the 'end of Tibet' or from the Sanskrit *Bhu-uttan*, meaning 'highlands'.

While the rest of Asia was being overrun by Europeans of varying hue but similar cry, only a handful of Westerners found their way into Bhutan. Two Portuguese Jesuits came to call in 1627, and six British missions paid brief but cordial visits from the late 1700s until the middle of the next century. Relations with the British took a nasty turn during the disastrous visit of Ashley Eden in 1864. Eden, who had gone to sort out a small problem of the Bhutanese raids on British territory, had his back slapped, his hair pulled, and his face rubbed with wet dough, and was then forced to sign an outrageous treaty that led to a brief war between the British and the Bhutanese. Considering the consolidated British empire in the south, and the Great Game being played out in the north between the colonial powers, Bhutan's preservation of its independence was remarkable. I am full of admiration for this small country that has managed to look after itself so well.

Padmasambhava An Indian Buddhist master.

shamanistic religion A religion that has a belief in natural phenomenon and in powerful spirits that can be influenced by shamans (a person who acts as an intermediary between natural and supernatural worlds).

lama A Buddhist monk from Tibet or Mongolia.

Sandalwood A tree grown for its fragrant wood and oil in the Indian subcontinent.

felicitously Pleasingly or well-chosen.

Sanskrit An ancient Indian language.

Jesuits Members of a Roman Catholic order devoted to missionary work.

cordial Friendly and polite.

Ashley Eden An official and diplomat in India under British rule.

Great Game The economic and political conflict between the British Empire and the Russian Empire for supremacy in Central Asia in the 19th century.

| PAPER 1 | TEXT ANTHOLOGY: NON-FICTION | 137 |

UNDERSTANDING THE TEXT

This extract gives the reader a vivid description of the writer's first impressions of a foreign land. It conveys the way in which the writer's reaction changes from an initial lukewarm attitude to a gradual fascination as she begins to learn about the country's history and observe its culture.

Travel writing gives personal accounts of explorations and travel experiences. Examples of the genre contain many factual details. Terms that are specific to that culture are explained and opinions are conveyed. Like most travel writing, this extract describes a key event and includes background details and research that was most likely conducted after the travel experience has ended.

ACTIVITY 1 — A01 — SKILLS: ANALYSIS

▼ FEATURES OF TRAVEL WRITING

Copy and complete the following table, finding examples of these features of travel writing in the passage.

▼ FEATURE	▼ EXAMPLE
Central event	
Factual details	
Background details	
Terminology and explanation	
Opinions	
Evidence of research	

ACTIVITY 2 — A02 — SKILLS: CRITICAL THINKING, ANALYSIS, INTERPRETATION

▼ LANGUAGE FOR EFFECT

Because this is a memoir, the reader learns about Bhutan through the eyes of the narrator, and it conveys her mixed feelings effectively. While the text is full of information intended to give the reader a sense of place, it is also her personal view of Bhutan and everything that she sees and experiences.

Copy and complete the following table, making a list of the writer's feelings, giving an example and explaining their effect.

▼ FEELING/ATTITUDE	▼ EXAMPLE	▼ COMMENT
A sense of being unable to understand the experience.	'… but I cannot imagine it'	The writer seems unable to even understand the geography of the area, as if it is so different from what she is used to that she needs to visualise it in different ways.
A lack of enthusiasm for the country.		
	'teenagers in acid washed jeans, Willie Nelson's greatest hits after the news in English on the Bhutan Broadcasting Service…'	

EXPLORING LANGUAGE

In this extract, Jamie Zeppa is both an observer and a participant. She is looking at and reflecting on the elements of culture that she sees around her, but she is also beginning to participate by attending the training session as part of her work as a lecturer. These aspects are reflected in the language choices she makes.

This is mainly an informative piece full of factual information. If it was too full of facts, the reader might find it boring or dry. However, Zeppa is able to make it lively and capture the reader's attention. One reason for this is her love for the place. Another reason is her skilled use of techniques and the language choices she makes.

- **In the second paragraph, find two phrases that show that the writer is observing her surroundings.**
- **Look at paragraph three and explain in your own words what the writer thinks about Thimphu.**

▲ The mountains of the Paro Valley, Bhutan

PAPER 1 — TEXT ANTHOLOGY: NON-FICTION

KEY POINT

Look at the ways in which the writer uses language to perform the dual roles of observer and participant.

ACTIVITY 3 — AO2
SKILLS: ANALYSIS, INTERPRETATION

▼ TECHNIQUES FOR EFFECT

Copy and complete the following table, thinking about the techniques used in the extract and their effect on the reader.

▼ TECHNIQUE	▼ EXAMPLE	▼ EFFECT
Repetition		
Hyphenated words		
Imagery		
Original phrases		

Now copy and complete the next table, picking out some words or phrases that Zeppa uses to make her text feel lively and to add vivid detail.

▼ WORDS OR PHRASES	▼ COMMENT
'hideously coloured Orange Cream Biscuits'	A small amount of humour is added by this phrase. It also creates a picture in the reader's mind of the brightness of the food dye used and creates an impression that the writer finds some aspects of what she sees very different from home.

The writer uses lists extensively as a technique. This is particularly useful because she is describing the varied and fascinating world that she is being exposed to. Lists can be of two types:

1. syndetic lists – a list connected by the use of conjunctions between each term, for example, 'apples and oranges and grapes'
2. asyndetic lists – a list connected by commas, for example, 'umbrellas, shoes, prams and all sorts of things'. At times, even the final conjunction 'and' can be omitted, for example, 'articles, adjectives, nouns, phrases, clauses, verbs... the list was endless'.

Copy and complete the following table, finding an example of each type of list in the passage and explaining why it might have been used.

▼ TYPE	▼ EXAMPLE	▼ EFFECT
Syndetic		
Asyndetic		

ACTIVITY 4 — A04 A05 — SKILLS: TEAMWORK, SELF-PRESENTATION

▼ TEN THINGS I NEED …

1 Give a speech on the topic, 'The ten things I need in order to be happy'. When planning, think of all the little things as well as the important things that you should have in your list. Try to add one item or idea that is really different from other people's, as this can be used to comic effect.

2 In pairs, create the text for a radio commercial advertising an exotic or interesting place to visit, then perform it for the class.

ACTIVITY 5 — A04 A05 — SKILLS: PROBLEM SOLVING, CREATIVITY, INNOVATION

▼ WRITING TASKS

1 Write an article for your school newspaper persuading senior students to take a gap year after their final exams. During this year, they should provide some service to the community before beginning their university education. How will you convince them to do so?

2 Look at the following images. Write a narrative beginning with the words, 'I wanted to get away to a place that was different from any that I had known until now'.

▲ 'A place that was different from any that I had known'

EXAM-STYLE QUESTION

A02

SKILLS: CRITICAL THINKING, ANALYSIS, ADAPTIVE LEARNING, CREATIVITY

How does the writer use language and structure to convey her growing fascination with Bhutan?

You should support your answer with close reference to the passage, including **brief** quotations.

(12 marks)

H IS FOR HAWK
HELEN MACDONALD

BACKGROUND AND CONTEXT

Helen Macdonald is a very experienced and enthusiastic falconer. When her father died suddenly on a London street, she was devastated. In an attempt to cope with her grief, she decided to buy and train one of the most difficult and aggressive of birds of prey, the goshawk. The experience changed her life. She said: 'The book is a memoir about that year when I lost my father and trained a hawk'.

Macdonald's book, published in 2013, won the Samuel Johnson Prize and Costa Book of the Year Award (both highly prestigious awards in the UK and Ireland). One reviewer, Mark Cocker, said: 'More than any other writer I know, Macdonald is able to summon the mental world of a bird of prey... As a naturalist she has somehow acquired her bird's laser-like visual acuity'. In addition, he praised her writing for its verbal inventiveness and precision.

GENERAL VOCABULARY

summon in this case, bring an image into the reader's mind
acuity the keenness or sharpness of something such as sight

BEFORE YOU START READING

1. Find out what you can about goshawks and what makes them different from other birds of prey.
2. Find some pictures of hawks on the internet. Try to think of some words or phrases to describe them and their apparent 'personalities'.
3. What is hawking? What do you think might be the rewards of training a goshawk with which to go hawking?

▼ FROM *H IS FOR HAWK* BY HELEN MACDONALD

When Macdonald's father died suddenly of a heart attack, Macdonald was devastated. An experienced falconer, she adopted a goshawk to distract her from her grief. In this extract Macdonald meets her hawk for the first time.

'We'll check the ring numbers against the Article 10s,' he explained, pulling a sheaf of yellow paper from his rucksack and unfolding two of the official forms that accompany captive-bred rare birds throughout their lives. 'Don't want you going home with the wrong bird.'

We noted the numbers. We stared down at the boxes, at their parcel-tape handles, their doors of thin plywood and hinges of carefully tied string. Then he knelt on the concrete, untied a hinge on the smaller box and squinted into its dark interior. A sudden *thump* of feathered shoulders and the box shook as if someone had punched it, hard, from within. 'She's got her hood off,' he said, and frowned. That light, leather hood was to keep the hawk from fearful sights. Like us.

Another hinge untied. Concentration. Infinite caution. Daylight irrigating the box. Scratching talons, another thump. And another.

Article 10s Certificates required for rare or endangered species sold in the UK.

▲ The goshawk, an aggressive bird of prey

primaries Large feathers at the ends of the wings.

fretful porpentine A defensive porcupine (the phrase is borrowed from Shakespeare's *Hamlet*).

illuminated bestiary A beautifully illustrated medieval book about mythical and real animals.

marionette A puppet worked by strings.

jesses Short leather straps fastened to the legs.

point-source glitter Glitter made up of many points of light.

tautly Tensely, tightly.

hackles Small feathers at the back of the neck.

Thump. The air turned syrupy, slow, flecked with dust. The last few seconds before a battle. And with the last bow pulled free, he reached inside, and amidst a whirring, chaotic clatter of wings and feet and talons and a high-pitched twittering and it's all happening at once, the man pulls an enormous, enormous hawk out of the box and in a strange coincidence of world and deed a great flood of sunlight drenches us and everything is brilliance and fury. The hawk's wings, barred and beating, the sharp fingers of her dark-tipped primaries cutting the air, her feathers raised like the scattered quills of a fretful porpentine. Two enormous eyes. My heart jumps sideways. She is a conjuring trick. A reptile. A fallen angel. A griffon from the pages of an illuminated bestiary. Something bright and distant, like gold falling through water. A broken marionette of wings, legs and light-splashed feathers. She is wearing jesses, and the man holds them. For one awful, long moment she is hanging head-downward, wings open, like a turkey in a butcher's shop, only her head is turned right-way-up and she is seeing more than she has ever seen before in her whole short life. Her world was an aviary no larger than a living room. Then it was a box. But now it is this; and she can see *everything*: the point-source glitter on the waves, a diving cormorant a hundred yards out; pigment flakes under wax on the lines of parked cars; far hills and the heather on them and miles and miles of sky where the sun spreads on dust and water and illegible things moving in it that are white scraps of gulls. Everything startling and new-stamped on her entirely astonished brain.

Through all this the man was perfectly calm. He gathered up the hawk in one practised movement, folding her wings, anchoring her broad feathered back against his chest, gripping her scaled yellow legs in one hand. 'Let's get that hood back on,' he said tautly. There was concern in his face. It was born of care. This hawk had been hatched in an incubator, had broken from a frail bluish eggshell into a humid perspex box, and for the first few days of her life this man had fed her with scraps of meat held in a pair of tweezers, waiting patiently for the lumpen, fluffy chick to notice the food and eat, her new neck wobbling with the effort of keeping her head in the air. All at once I loved this man, and fiercely. I grabbed the hood from the box and turned to the hawk. Her beak was open, her hackles raised; her wild eyes were the colour of sun on white paper, and they stared because the whole world had fallen into them at once. One, two, three. I tucked the hood over her head. There was a brief intimation of a thin, angular skull under her feathers, of an alien brain fizzing and fusing with terror, then I drew the braces closed. We checked the ring numbers against the form.

It was the wrong bird. This was the younger one. The smaller one. This was not my hawk.

Oh.

So we put her back and opened the other box, which was meant to hold the larger, older bird. And dear God, it did. Everything about this second hawk was different. She came out like a Victorian melodrama: a sort of madwoman in the attack. She was smokier and darker and much, much bigger, and instead of twittering, she wailed; great, awful gouts of sound like a thing in pain, and the sound was unbearable. *This is my hawk*, I was telling myself and it was all I could do to breathe. She too was bareheaded, and I grabbed the hood from the box as before. But as I brought it up to her face I looked into her eyes and saw

| PAPER 1 | TEXT ANTHOLOGY: NON-FICTION | 143 |

something blank and crazy in her stare. Some madness from a distant country. I didn't recognise her. *This isn't my hawk.* The hood was on, the ring numbers checked, the bird back in the box, the yellow form folded, the money exchanged, and all I could think was, *But this isn't my hawk*. Slow panic. I knew what I had to say, and it was a monstrous breach of etiquette. 'This is really awkward,' I began. 'But I really liked the first one. Do you think there's any chance I could take that one instead… ?' I tailed off. His eyebrows were raised. I started again, saying stupider things: 'I'm sure the other falconer would like the larger bird? She's more beautiful than the first one, isn't she? I know this is out of order, but I… Could I? Would it be all right, do you think?' And on and on, a desperate, crazy barrage of incoherent appeals.

I'm sure nothing I said persuaded him more than the look on my face as I said it. A tall, white-faced woman with wind-wrecked hair and exhausted eyes was pleading with him on a quayside, hands held out as if she were in a seaside production of Medea. Looking at me he must have sensed that my stuttered request wasn't a simple one. That there was something behind it that was very important. There was a moment of total silence.

Medea Greek revenge tragedy about a woman with magical powers.

UNDERSTANDING THE TEXT

This extract from the book describes the moment when Macdonald first meets the hawk she has decided to train. It is a moment of great significance – the relationship that she builds with this bird is the main topic of the book and is the method that she adopts for dealing with her grief for her father.

KEY POINT

Non-fiction can incorporate elements more associated with fiction, such as creative use of narrative.

Although the second hawk that is pulled out is the one that she has reserved for herself, Macdonald makes a very quick decision on instinct. There is something she does not like about the larger bird and she decides to ask for the one that the man brought out first. She describes both birds in detail.

This kind of writing is sometimes called 'creative non-fiction'. This is because, although it is factual, it is also imaginative and highly-crafted writing. When you re-read the extract, look out for the same kinds of writing that you get in fiction – description, narrative, dialogue, thoughts and feelings, as well as more fact-based explanation.

ACTIVITY 1 | AO1 | SKILLS: ANALYSIS

▼ EXAMINING THE DETAIL

Much of the success of creative non-fiction is in the detail. Copy and complete the following table, examining details from the extract and considering what they tell the reader.

▼ LINES	▼ DETAILS	▼ WHAT DOES THIS TELL THE READER?
9–11	'a sudden thump… as if someone had punched it, hard, from within'	The bird is powerful and aggressive.
	'…in one practised movement, folding her wings, anchoring her broad feathered back against his chest…'	
	'Her beak was open, her hackles raised; her wild eyes were the colour of sun on white paper…'	

ACTIVITY 2 — A01 — SKILLS: ANALYSIS

▼ THEMES

Copy and complete the following table, thinking carefully about the themes of the extract. Add some more themes that you noticed in the extract.

▼ THEME	▼ EXAMPLE	▼ COMMENT
Beauty of the bird	Lines 24–26: 'She is a conjuring trick… a fallen angel… like gold…'.	Macdonald is completely fascinated, almost overwhelmed, by the bird.
Fierce personality of the bird		
Emotional reaction		

EXPLORING LANGUAGE

GENERAL VOCABULARY

lexicographer writer of dictionaries
curated objects objects in a museum

The language of this passage is inventive and intense. It is clear that the writer was concentrating hard on communicating as vividly as possible an experience that was important in her life and in the story that she is telling. You can see this in a number of ways such as in the precision of the vocabulary, the originality of the imagery (the figurative language); and the variety of sentence structures.

Mark Cocker wrote that Macdonald 'combines a **lexicographer**'s pleasure in words as carefully **curated objects** with an inventive passion for words or for ways of releasing fresh effects from the old stock'. Can you see why he said this?

ACTIVITY 3 — A02 — SKILLS: CRITICAL THINKING, ANALYSIS, INTERPRETATION

▼ LANGUAGE FOR EFFECT

Copy and complete the following table, finding examples of the different linguistic techniques and devices and considering the effect that they create. Then identify some more linguistic techniques, quotations and effects for yourself.

▼ TECHNIQUES OR DEVICES	▼ QUOTATION	▼ EFFECT CREATED
Lists	'glitter on the waves, a diving cormorant…'	This makes you understand in detail the range and precision of the bird's vision.
Similes		
Metaphors		
Short incomplete sentences		

| PAPER 1 | TEXT ANTHOLOGY: NON-FICTION | 145 |

STRUCTURE

To understand the structure of the extract, you can either look at the content of each of the eight paragraphs or think of it as being composed of a smaller number of sections.

ACTIVITY 4 | **AO2** | **SKILLS** CRITICAL THINKING

KEY POINT
One of the most individual aspects of creative non-fiction is the extent to which the author uses figurative language.

▼ **UNDERSTANDING THE STRUCTURE**

1 Copy and complete the following table, dividing the extract into four or five sections as you think appropriate.

▼ SECTIONS	▼ WHAT THE SECTION IS ABOUT (CONTENT)
First section: Line _____ to line _____. [Hint: Think about which paragraph shifts into a different stage in the account. Where does the hawk actually appear?]	
Second section: Line _____ to line _____. [Hint: Is the focus always on the bird itself?]	
Third section: Line _____ to line _____.	

2 You know that the content is structured. What does this structure help to achieve?

EXAMPLE STUDENT ANSWER A TO THE EXAM-STYLE QUESTION

> Macdonald is clearly excited about seeing the hawk: you can tell this by the way she exaggerates, saying that the hawk is 'enormous, enormous'.

If this is typical of the whole response, it would justify a Level 2 mark with the following comments.
- Some understanding of and comment on language and structure and how these are used by writers to achieve effects, including use of vocabulary.
- The selection of references is valid, but not developed.

PAPER 1 — **TEXT ANTHOLOGY: NON-FICTION**

EXAMPLE STUDENT ANSWER B TO THE EXAM-STYLE QUESTION

> Macdonald creates excitement through a range of linguistic techniques. Her language is emotive and figurative, creating a forceful effect. For example, in the lines beginning, 'the man pulls an enormous, enormous hawk… 'the words 'brilliance and fury' express her strong feelings while the repetition of 'enormous' shows she is surprised.

If this is typical of the whole response, it would justify a Level 3 mark with the following comment.

- Clear understanding and explanation of language and how it is used to achieve effects, including use of vocabulary and sentence structure.

ACTIVITY 5 | **A04** | **A05** | **SKILLS** CRITICAL THINKING, ANALYSIS, REASONING, INTERPRETATION

▼ WRITING TASKS

1. 'Making personal relationships with animals is the only way we can understand their nature'. Write a magazine article giving your views on this statement. The article may include:
   - the advantages and disadvantages of such relationships
   - any other points you wish to make.

   Your response will be marked for the accurate and appropriate use of vocabulary, as well as accuracy of spelling and grammar.

2. How does the writer present the character of the hawks in the passage from *H is for Hawk*?

   You should write about:
   - the description of their appearance
   - the way they behave
   - the writer's use of language and techniques to convey these.

   You should refer closely to the text to support your answer and use **brief** quotations.

EXAM-STYLE QUESTIONS

A02

SKILLS CRITICAL THINKING, ANALYSIS, ADAPTIVE LEARNING, CREATIVITY

How does the writer use language and structure to portray the birds and setting?

You should support your answer with close reference to the passage, including **brief** quotations. **(12 marks)**

How does the writer create a sense of excitement?

You should support your answer with close reference to the passage, including **brief** quotations.

(12 marks)

CHINESE CINDERELLA
ADELINE YEN MAH

BACKGROUND AND CONTEXT
Chinese Cinderella is an autobiography by Adeline Yen Mah in which she describes growing up in a wealthy family in Hong Kong in the 1950s. She is rejected by her stepmother and her father is a distant, though powerful, character. She spends much of her time at boarding school.

BEFORE YOU START READING
Do some research.
- Look up Adeline Yen Mah on the internet.
- Can you find other examples of childhood autobiographies?

▼ FROM *CHINESE CINDERELLA* BY ADELINE YEN MAH

Growing up in a wealthy family in 1950s Hong Kong, Mah should have had an enviable childhood, but she was rejected by her dominating stepmother and despised by her brothers and sisters. She was sent to a boarding school and left there. In this extract from her autobiography she relates one of the few occasions when she went home.

Time went by relentlessly and it was Saturday again. Eight weeks more and it would be the end of term … in my case perhaps the end of school forever.

Four of us were playing Monopoly. My heart was not in it and I was losing steadily. Outside it was hot and there was a warm wind blowing. The radio warned of a possible typhoon the next day. It was my turn and I threw the dice. As I played, the thought of leaving school throbbed at the back of my mind like a persistent toothache.

'Adeline!' Ma-mien Valentino was calling.

'You can't go now,' Mary protested. 'For once I'm winning. One, two, three, four. Good! You've landed on my property. Thirty-five dollars, please. Oh, good afternoon, Mother Valentino!'

We all stood up and greeted her.

'Adeline, didn't you hear me call you? Hurry up downstairs! Your chauffeur is waiting to take you home!'

Full of foreboding, I ran downstairs as in a nightmare, wondering who had died this time. Father's chauffeur assured me everyone was healthy.

'Then why are you taking me home?' I asked.

'How should *I* know?' he answered defensively, shrugging his shoulders. 'Your guess is as good as mine. They give the orders and I carry them out.'

During the short drive home, my heart was full of dread and I wondered what I had done wrong. Our car stopped at an elegant villa at mid-level, halfway up the hill between the peak and the harbour.

'Where are we?' I asked foolishly.

▲ Chinese-American author and physician Adeline Yen Mah

typhoon A storm in the Indian or Western Pacific Oceans.

'Don't you know anything?' the chauffeur replied rudely. 'This is your new home. Your parents moved here a few months ago.'

'I had forgotten,' I said as I got out.

Ah Gum opened the door. Inside, it was quiet and cool.

'Where is everyone?'

'Your mother is out playing bridge. Your two brothers and Little Sister are sunbathing by the swimming pool. Your father is in his room and wants to see you as soon as you get home.'

> bridge A card game played with four people.

'See me in his room?' I was overwhelmed by the thought that I had been summoned by Father to enter the Holy of Holies – a place to which I had never been invited. Why? …

Timidly, I knocked on the door. Father was alone, looking relaxed in his slippers and bathrobe, reading a newspaper. He smiled as I entered and I saw he was in a happy mood. I breathed a small sigh of relief at first but became uneasy when I wondered why he was being so nice, thinking, Is this a giant ruse on his part to trick me? Dare I let my guard down?

'Sit down! Sit down!' He pointed to a chair. 'Don't look so scared. Here, take a look at this! They're writing about someone we both know, I think.'

He handed me the day's newspaper and there, in one corner, I saw my name ADELINE YEN in capital letters prominently displayed.

'It was announced today that 14-year-old Hong Kong schoolgirl ADELINE JUN-LING YEN of Sacred Heart Canossian School, Caine Road, Hong Kong, has won first prize in the International Play-writing Competition held in London, England, for the 1951–1952 school year. It is the first time that any local Chinese student from Hong Kong has won such a prestigious event. Besides a medal, the prize comes with a cash reward of FIFTY ENGLISH POUNDS. Our sincere congratulations, ADELINE YEN, for bringing honour to Hong Kong. We are proud of you.'

Is it possible? Am I dreaming? Me, the winner?

'I was going up the lift this morning with my friend C.Y. Tung when he showed me this article and asked me, "Is the winner Adeline Jun-ling Yen related to you? The two of you have the same uncommon last name." Now C.Y. himself has a few children about your age but so far none of them has won an international literary prize, as far as I know. So I was quite pleased to tell him you are my daughter. Well done!'

He looked radiant. For once, he was proud of me. In front of his revered colleague, C.Y. Tung, a prominent fellow businessman also from Shanghai, I had given him face. I thought, Is this the big moment I have been waiting for? My whole being vibrated with all the joy in the world. I only had to stretch out my hand to reach the stars.

> face In this context, a positive successful appearance in the eyes of other people.

'Tell me, how did you do it?' he continued. 'How come *you* won?'

'Well, the rules and regulations were so very complicated. One really has to be dedicated just to understand what they want. Perhaps I was the only one determined enough to enter and there were no other competitors!'

He laughed approvingly. 'I doubt it very much but that's a good answer.'

'Please, Father,' I asked boldly, thinking it was now or never. 'May I go to university in England too, just like my brothers?'

'I do believe you have potential. Tell me, what would you study?'

My heart gave a giant lurch as it dawned on me that he was agreeing to let me go. How marvellous it was simply to be alive! Study? I thought. Going to England is like entering heaven. Does it matter what you do after you get to heaven?

But Father was expecting an answer. What about creative writing? After all, I had just won first prize in an international writing competition!

'I plan to study literature. I'll be a writer.'

'Writer!' he scoffed. 'You are going to starve! What language are you going to write in and who is going to read your writing? Though you may think you're an expert in both Chinese and English, your Chinese is actually rather elementary. As for your English, don't you think the native English speakers can write better than you?'

I waited in silence. I did not wish to contradict him.

'You will go to England with Third Brother this summer and you will go to medical school. After you graduate, you will specialise in obstetrics. Women will always be having babies. Women patients prefer women doctors. You will learn to deliver their babies. That's a foolproof profession for you. Don't you agree?'

Agree? Of course I agreed. Apparently, he had it all planned out. As long as he let me go to university in England, I would study anything he wished. How did that line go in Wordsworth's poem? *Bliss was it in that dawn to be alive.*

'Father, I shall go to medical school in England and become a doctor. Thank you very, very much.'

obstetrics Caring for women who are having babies.

Wordsworth A Romantic poet who wrote during the 18th and 19th centuries.

ACTIVITY 1 — AO1 — SKILLS: REASONING, CREATIVITY, INTERPERSONAL SKILLS

▼ CHILDHOOD AUTOBIOGRAPHIES

In a small group or with a partner, discuss the following questions.

1 Do you think that adults always remember the incidents of their childhood accurately? Do you think that this matters when reading a book like *Chinese Cinderella*?

2 Some critics think that characters in *Chinese Cinderella* are either all good or all bad, and that very few of the characters are realistic. What do you think of this point of view?

UNDERSTANDING THE TEXT

Adeline Yen Mah writes to inform, explain and describe. She is writing for a general audience which may be interested in childhood memoirs, or perhaps in understanding the culture that Yen Mah comes from. Yen Mah writes in such a way that you can understand not only what is happening, but also the emotional impact of each incident in the passage.

The key to understanding the piece is to understand Adeline and her thoughts and feelings about boarding school and her ambition to travel to England. Most important of all is her relationship with her father.

PAPER 1 — TEXT ANTHOLOGY: NON-FICTION

ACTIVITY 2 — A01
SKILLS: CRITICAL THINKING

▼ ANALYSING EMOTIONS

Copy and complete the following tables, finding evidence in the extract for Adeline's feelings.

▼ ADELINE'S FEELINGS BEFORE SHE MEETS HER FATHER	▼ EVIDENCE
Her first reaction on hearing that he wants to see her.	She is 'overwhelmed'.
She suggests her father's room is somewhere uniquely special, a place to be revered, an inner sanctum to which few, if any, are admitted.	1 'the Holy of Holies' 2 'a place to which I had never been invited' 3
Her feelings on entering her father's room.	1 She knocks 'timidly'. 2 3

▼ ADELINE'S FEELINGS AS SHE MEETS HER FATHER	▼ EVIDENCE
He is commanding, as indicated by the repetition and use of exclamation.	1 Use of exclamation marks 2 He orders her to 'Sit down!' and repeats it. 3
He is reassuring.	1 2 3
Their relationship lacks warmth and closeness.	1 2 3
He appears to be relaxed and at ease, in contrast to her tension.	1 2 3
She is desperate to please her father and her reaction to his pleasure is overwhelming.	1 2 3
She emphasises her shyness.	1 2 3
She emphasises that she is wary of him.	1 2 3

PAPER 1 — TEXT ANTHOLOGY: NON-FICTION

EXPLORING LANGUAGE

Like all writers, Adeline Yen Mah uses certain effects in order to create a response in the reader. Copy and complete the following table, explaining the effect(s) that you think she was trying to achieve with each technique.

TECHNIQUE	INTENDED EFFECT
Moves into the present tense.	Emphasises her lack of confidence and how worried she was.
Use of repetition by her father.	Indicates either impatience or vigour.
Use of punctuation and short sentences.	Develops the reader's understanding of character.
Use of triple rhetorical questions all written in the present tense.	
Use of cliché.	
Use of numbers rather than names for children.	
The passage starts in the past tense, moves through the present tense and ends with the past tense.	

GENERAL VOCABULARY
cliché An overused, unoriginal phrase or saying.

KEY POINT
Writers are highly skilled at using language to achieve particular psychological responses in the reader. Try to become aware of your own responses when reading to understand what the writer is doing.

ACTIVITY 3 — AO4 AO5
SKILLS: REASONING, CREATIVITY, INNOVATION

▼ WRITING TASKS

1 Consider the following two statements. Write an argument in favour of one of these statements.
   - 'Boarding schools teach young people to become confident and well-rounded adults.'
   - 'Sending young children away to boarding school is cruel and unnatural.'
2 Describe your hopes and dreams for your future and how you would feel if someone made your dreams come true.

EXAM-STYLE QUESTION
AO2

SKILLS: CRITICAL THINKING, ANALYSIS, ADAPTIVE LEARNING, CREATIVITY

How does the writer use language and structure to convey her emotions?

You should support your answer with close reference to the passage, including **brief** quotations.

(12 marks)

LEARNING OBJECTIVES

This lesson will help you to:
- read and interpret non-fiction texts.

IDENTIFYING KEY INFORMATION

In Paper 1, the passages will be non-fiction and one of the passages will be an 'unseen text' which will be unfamiliar to you. When dealing with the unseen text, you must give yourself plenty of time to read it carefully. However, you won't have time to read and re-read the passage lots of times so try to apply some of the following active reading strategies.
- Before you read the passage, read the title carefully and think about what it suggests. Based on the title, what do you think the passage may be about?
- If there are a few lines of introduction, read and consider these carefully.
- Read the passage to get a sense of the tone and content.
- Read the passage again. While you read, use your pen or highlighter to circle different things of interest. This is to highlight key words and phrases to help you answer the questions.

TAP IT!

When you read an unseen text for the first time you should **TAP** it!
- **T**ype: What type of text is it?
- **A**udience: Who is the intended audience? How do you know this?
- **P**urpose: What is the purpose of this passage? Is it informing you, explaining to you or persuading you?

TYPE OF TEXT

You should be able to establish the type of text that you are reading very quickly. There are three things that will help you here: the subject, the narrative perspective and the tense.
- **Subject**: What is the subject of the text? Is the subject matter aimed at a particular age group? Where does the text come from?
- **Narrative perspective**: If it is a first-person autobiographical narrative, for example, it is likely to be a personal account. Does it seem to be an autobiography?
- **Tense**: Is it written in the present tense or is it retrospective?

GENERAL VOCABULARY
retrospective looking back at a past event
conventions features normally associated with something

ACTIVITY 1 — AO1 — SKILLS: CRITICAL THINKING

▼ **TYPES OF NON-FICTION TEXT**

Cover the list below with your hand or a piece of paper, then see how many different types of non-fiction text can you name

newspaper article	autobiography	interview	advertorial feature
magazine article	biography	report	newspaper column
travel writing	text book	journal	

▶ Select one of the types of non-fiction above. What does it look like? Add any conventions of this text type that you think are important.

PAPER 1 — **COMPARING TEXTS** — 153

AUDIENCE

KEY POINT

Clues as to the writer's intended audience include the level of difficulty of the language and the assumed knowledge contained in the text.

A writer will usually have a particular audience in mind when they write. Look for any clues that might tell you about the intended reader for example.

- **Age**: Is the subject matter aimed at a particular age group? Does the difficulty of the language suggest a certain readership?
- **Knowledge**: What do you need to know to make sense of the passage?
- **Tone**: What kind of tone is the piece written in? Is the language used formal or informal?

PURPOSE

The main difference between fiction and non-fiction is that non-fiction is usually written for a precise practical purpose, whereas fiction is usually written to entertain. You will need to identify the writer's intention in order to establish the purpose of a non-fiction text. It may help you to think of these 'writing triplets' in order to give you a system for thinking about purpose.

- **Inform, explain, describe**: Is the writer writing to make something clear or to give information?
- **Argue, persuade, advise**: Is the writer writing to discuss an issue or persuade someone to share their views?
- **Explore, imagine, entertain**: Is the writer writing with no other purpose than to entertain the reader?

ACTIVITY 2 | **A01** | **SKILLS** CRITICAL THINKING, PROBLEM SOLVING, INTERPRETATION

▼ TEXT TYPE, AUDIENCE AND PURPOSE

1 Read the extract from *Touching The Void* on pages 163–164 and TAP it. What is the type, audience and purpose of the text? Remember that texts usually have a combination of several purposes. Use highlighters to colour code any evidence of different purposes.

EXAMPLE STUDENT ANSWER

> **Type**: First person account.
> **Audience**: Anyone who is interested in the story. Joe does not use any technical language associated with mountaineering and in this way he does not seek to exclude the general reader.
> **Purpose**: To engage and inform.

2 Summarise briefly in your own words:
- what happened to Joe
- what choices face Simon.

EXAMPLE STUDENT ANSWER

> *Touching the Void* is a book by Joe Simpson. It is a true story of how he and his climbing partner, Simon Yates, set out to become the first people to climb Siula Grande in Peru. They were nearing the end of their climb in the Peruvian Andes when a disastrous accident occurred in which Joe broke his leg. Simon, who was tied to Joe with a rope, felt that if he did not break free, they would both die. As a result, he cut the rope supporting Joe and returned down the mountain, believing Joe to be dead. Although his leg was broken, Joe crawled his way back down the mountain and was eventually rescued.

▲ Siula Grande, Peru

LEARNING OBJECTIVES

This lesson will help you to:
- look at unseen texts in detail, considering language and structure.

ANALYSING THE TEXTS

Once you have read the unseen extract and used the TAP technique to begin analysing it, you need to consider the writer's technique. How has the writer used language and sentence structure to influence the reader?

COPING WITH UNSEEN TEXTS

- Before you read the unseen passage, read the title carefully. What does it suggest the passage may be about? What might you infer, predict or expect from the passage after reading the title?
- Consider the beginning and ending of the passage carefully.
- Read the text in full to get a sense of the passage's tone and content. Underline:
  - words you don't understand
  - words or phrases that you feel are important – you may choose to come back and comment on these.
- What type of text is it? A first-person autobiographical narrative, for example? What about the tense – is it written in the present tense or is it retrospective?
- Who is the intended audience? How do you know this?
- What is the purpose of the passage? Is it informing you, explaining to you or persuading you?
- How has the writer used language and sentence structure to create effect?
- Also consider what effect is created by the narrative perspective and the tone.

WRITER'S TECHNIQUE

Once you are clear about what the piece is about and what the writer is trying to achieve, you will be able to consider technique. A good writer will have a range of techniques that they use in order to create effect. You should look for a variety of techniques but always relate them back to **audience** and **purpose**. A useful way to identify and understand writers' techniques is to consider the different levels at which devices are used:

- word level
- sentence level
- text level.

PAPER 1 — COMPARING TEXTS

ACTIVITY 1 — AO2 — SKILLS: ANALYSIS

▼ FEATURES AT WORD LEVEL

Read the following short lines of text. What do you notice about the language used? Can you identify which of the techniques in the Hint box are being used in each?

> Nine out of ten dogs would recommend Doggibix.

> Best Ever Mega Monday Amazing 200% Discount Sale!

> Work, work, work? Get the laughs back in your life this Thursday at the Comedy Club.

> Sunshine Spas: simply the best!

> This film was fast, funny and full of surprises! ★★★★★

> Is your girlfriend afraid of your mother?

HINT

It may help you if you think about these specific devices:
- rhetorical questions
- hyperbole
- facts and statistics
- rule of three
- superlative
- repetition.

ACTIVITY 2 — AO1 — SKILLS: CRITICAL THINKING, ANALYSIS, INTERPRETATION

▼ TOUCHING THE VOID

Imagine that the extract from *Touching the Void* on pages 163–164 is the unseen passage. What words or phrases in Joe's account most vividly shows:
- the pain he suffers as a result of his injuries
- his thoughts and feelings?

STRUCTURING YOUR RESPONSE

Copy and complete the following table, adding your own examples of word level features to comment on. Review the section, 'Use of Language' (pages 16–23), if you need help thinking about language features in more detail.

▼ WORD LEVEL FEATURE	▼ EXAMPLE	▼ EFFECT
Simple language	'He would leave me. He had no choice.'	Joe's simple language portrays the starkness of the choices available to Simon and how life-threatening Joe's injury really is.
Use of direct speech	'"You're dead" "I'm dead." Everyone said it… if there's just two of you a broken ankle could turn into a death sentence.'	Direct speech helps to convey the immediacy of thought and to bring other perspectives into the first-person narrative.

155

COMPARING TEXTS

ACTIVITY 3 — A02
SKILLS: CRITICAL THINKING, ANALYSIS, INTERPRETATION

▼ FEATURES AT SENTENCE LEVEL

The way in which a writer combines words and phrases into sentences is important. Look again at the extract from *Touching the Void*, considering it as a typical unseen passage. Look at the example in the table below, then find two more examples of sentence level features that you could comment on. Go back to the section, 'Use of Language' (pages 16–23), if you need a reminder of sentence structure features.

▼ SENTENCE LEVEL FEATURE	▼ EXAMPLE	▼ EFFECT
Simple sentences	'My leg!… My leg!'	Joe's account uses a number of short, simple exclamatory sentences that show the sudden horror of the situation. Here, the two exclamation marks and ellipsis convey the panic he is feeling while the repeated simple sentence is sharp, mirroring the sudden pain he feels.

> **HINT**
>
> The grammatical construction of a sentence is called its syntax. This includes both punctuation and sentence type. For example: 'Robbed!' The syntax of this exclamatory, one-word simple sentence evokes a sense of emotion and drama. The message is conveyed quickly to the reader and in an emotive manner.

ACTIVITY 4 — A02
SKILLS: CRITICAL THINKING, ANALYSIS, INTERPRETATION

▼ FEATURES AT TEXT LEVEL

The appearance of the text on the page can also be used to create meaning, such as the use of subheadings and paragraphing. There will be less to say about this when analysing some texts; however, always be aware of text level features how the writer creates an effect at the level of the whole text. Copy and complete the following table, adding examples and explaining their effects.

▼ TEXT LEVEL FEATURE	▼ EXAMPLE	▼ EFFECT
First person narrative		
Two different perspectives	'I hit the slope…' 'Joe had disappeared…'	By using two different perspectives, *Touching the Void* allows the reader to appreciate the horror from the perspective of the victim and the friend. As such, the suspense and discomfort is even more acute as the reader is forced to engage with Joe's physical pain but also Simon's grief as he believes his friend is dead.

> **HINT**
>
> Your aim is not simply to identify techniques, but to explain the *effects* of the author's craft. A weak answer simply re-tells the events of the passage; a strong answer comments on the way in which language is used to create meaning and prompt reader response.

| PAPER 1 | COMPARING TEXTS | 157 |

ACTIVITY 5 — AO2 — SKILLS: CRITICAL THINKING, ANALYSIS, INTERPRETATION

▼ CONSIDERING LANGUAGE

Refer back to the extract from Ellen MacArthur's autobiography on pages 59–60. It deals with an emergency she faced on the 44th day of the Vendée Globe yacht race when she had to replace an essential sail. How does this passage bring out the thoughts and feelings of Ellen MacArthur as she sails alone in a race around the world?

INDICATIVE CONTENT

> **KEY POINT**
>
> In analysing texts, try to cultivate the skill of registering effects at different levels, including the syntax and the text. This is like zooming in and panning out.

MacArthur's style is unaffected and frank, and seems very powerful because it is a very personal narrative. The passage highlights the enormous physical and psychological challenges in sailing alone in heavy seas. Because the narrative focuses on the physical effects of the bad weather, it makes the fact that MacArthur finds the strength to continue seem even more extraordinary. The challenge seems almost superhuman, but MacArthur's narrative shows that she is very human and subject to the same feelings as other people. This leads the reader to marvel at her strength and motivation. There is much use of the first-person pronoun. Other features include:

- use of technical details ('the storm jib', 'the inner forestay rod') gives the reader a sense of the reality of the situation, although this is not overdone
- plenty of active verbs ('continued', 'snatched', 'dragged', 'enjoyed') give the reader a sense of immediacy and action
- straightforward, direct language; the limited use of adjectives and adverbs means that they have an impact when used ('unreal, crazy situation')
- use of words, phrases and clauses that suggest struggle, effort or challenge ('not only difficult but painful', 'hang on')
- conversational features, such as contractions ('I'd') and repetition of the same words for emphasis ('freezing night', 'freezing water'), all of which add immediacy to the writing

▲ Ellen MacArthur's yacht *Kingfisher* competing in the Vendeé Globe race

KEY POINT

Even though Ellen MacArthur is a yachtswoman, not a writer, and her style is not 'literary', it is still complex

- varying lengths of sentence keeps the reader's attention; they often alternate between short, punchy sentences and more complex descriptive sentences ('Dawn brought some respite. My body temperature warmed after the freezing night, but if I sweated through the physical exertion of a sail change, when I stopped, I'd once again cool to a shiver.')
- little figurative language gives the impression of unrelenting action
- simple, clear descriptions of her sensations ('My hands were red-raw', 'my head was aching', 'the freezing water washed breathtakingly over [me]') make the reader imagine how she must have felt
- the use of familiar phrases or clichés ('ounce of strength', 'hanging on for dear life') ensure that the reader can understand what MacArthur is explaining immediately, without having to devote time to considering a new or innovative use of language
- personification of the weather as someone throwing MacArthur's possessions around the yacht ('Food was hurled') gives the impression that the weather is fighting with MacArthur
- the lack of speech emphasises the fact that MacArthur is all alone; the only sound described ('I would often cry out loud') is just a wordless noise that is relayed to the reader indirectly, rather than as direct speech
- humorous lightening of tone at the end, juxtaposing the 'wonderful' relief of being out of her survival suit with the smell from her body and survival suit. The comedy of the moment is emphasised by MacArthur's use of litotes, or ironic understatement, to describe the smell as 'not... wonderful', which is funnier than if the smell had been described directly.

▼ FROM *HOW THE POOR DIE* BY GEORGE ORWELL

After some days I grew well enough to sit up and study the surrounding patients. The stuffy room, with its narrow beds so close together that you could easily touch your neighbour's hand, had every sort of disease in it except, I suppose, acutely infectious cases. My right-hand neighbour was a little red-haired cobbler with one leg shorter than the other, who used to announce the death of any other patient (this happened a number of times, and my neighbour was always the first to hear of it) by whistling to me, exclaiming 'Numéro 43!' (or whatever it was) and flinging his arms above his head. This man had not much wrong with him, but in most of the other beds within my angle of vision some squalid tragedy or some plain horror was being enacted. In the bed that was foot to foot with mine there lay, until he died (I didn't see him die — they moved him to another bed), a little weazened man who was suffering from I do not know what disease, but something that made his whole body so intensely sensitive that any movement from side to side, sometimes even the weight of the bedclothes, would make him shout out with pain. His worst suffering was when he urinated, which he did with the greatest difficulty. A nurse would bring him the bedbottle and then for a long time stand beside his bed, whistling, as grooms are said to do with horses, until at last with an agonized shriek of 'Je fissel' he would get started. In the bed next to him the sandy-haired man whom I had seen being cupped used to cough up blood-streaked mucus at all hours. My left-hand neighbour was a tall, flaccid-looking young man who used periodically to have a tube inserted into his back and astonishing quantities of frothy liquid drawn off from some part of his

Orwell wrote *How the Poor Die* in 1929 after being in hospital in Paris.

body. In the bed beyond that a veteran of the war of 1870 was dying, a handsome old man with a white imperial, round whose bed, at all hours when visiting was allowed, four elderly female relatives dressed all in black sat exactly like crows, obviously scheming for some pitiful legacy. In the bed opposite me in the farther row was an old bald-headed man with drooping moustaches and greatly swollen face and body, who was suffering from some disease that made him urinate almost incessantly. A huge glass receptacle stood always beside his bed. One day his wife and daughter came to visit him. At sight of them the old man's bloated face lit up with a smile of surprising sweetness, and as his daughter, a pretty girl of about twenty, approached the bed I saw that his hand was slowly working its way from under the bedclothes. I seemed to see in advance the gesture that was coming — the girl kneeling beside the bed, the old man's hand laid on her head in his dying blessing. But no, he merely handed her the bedbottle, which she promptly took from him and emptied into the receptacle.

About a dozen beds away from me was Numéro 57 — I think that was his number — a cirrhosis-of-the-liver case. Everyone in the ward knew him by sight because he was sometimes the subject of a medical lecture. On two afternoons a week the tall, grave doctor would lecture in the ward to a party of students, and on more than one occasion old Numéro 57 was wheeled in on a sort of trolley into the middle of the ward, where the doctor would roll back his nightshirt, dilate with his fingers a huge flabby protruberance on the man's belly — the diseased liver, I suppose — and explain solemnly that this was a disease attributable to alcoholism, commoner in the wine-drinking countries. As usual he neither spoke to his patient nor gave him a smile, a nod or any kind of recognition. While he talked, very grave and upright, he would hold the wasted body beneath his two hands, sometimes giving it a gentle roll to and fro, in just the attitude of a woman handling a rolling-pin. Not that Numéro 57 minded this kind of thing. Obviously he was an old hospital inmate, a regular exhibit at lectures, his liver long since marked down for a bottle in some pathological museum. Utterly uninterested in what was said about him, he would lie with his colourless eyes gazing at nothing, while the doctor showed him off like a piece of antique china. He was a man of about sixty, astonishingly shrunken. His face, pale as vellum, had shrunken away till it seemed no bigger than a doll's.

One morning my cobbler neighbour woke me up plucking at my pillow before the nurses arrived. 'Numéro 57!' — he flung his arms above his head. There was a light in the ward, enough to see by. I could see old Numéro 57 lying crumpled up on his side, his face sticking out over the side of the bed, and towards me. He had died some time during the night, nobody knew when. When the nurses came they received the news of his death indifferently and went about their work. After a long time, an hour or more, two other nurses marched in abreast like soldiers, with a great clumping of sabots, and knotted the corpse up in the sheets, but it was not removed till some time later. Meanwhile, in the better light, I had had time for a good look at Numéro 57. Indeed I lay on my side to look at him. Curiously enough he was the first dead European I had seen. I had seen dead men before, but always Asiatics and usually people who had died violent deaths. Numéro 57's eyes were still open, his mouth also open, his small face contorted into an expression of agony. What most impressed me, however, was the whiteness of his face. It had been pale before, but now it was little darker than die sheets. As I gazed at the tiny, screwed-up face it struck me that this disgusting piece of refuse, waiting to be carted away and dumped on a slab in the dissecting room, was an example of 'natural' death, one of the things you pray for in the Litany. There you are, then, I thought, that's what is waiting for you, twenty, thirty, forty years hence: that is how the lucky ones die, the ones who live to be old. One wants to live, of course, indeed one only stays alive by virtue of the fear of death, but I think now, as I thought then, that it's better to die violently and not too old. People talk about the horrors of war, but what weapon has man invented that even approaches in cruelty some of the commoner diseases? 'Natural' death, almost by definition, means something slow, smelly and painful. Even at that, it makes a difference if you can achieve it in your own home and not in a public institution. This poor old wretch who had just flickered out like a candle-end was not even important enough to have anyone watching by his deathbed. He was merely a number, then a 'subject' for the students' scalpels.

EXAM-STYLE QUESTIONS

Re-read the passage from *How the Poor Die*, then answer these questions.

A01 — SKILLS: ANALYSIS

A01 — SKILLS: CRITICAL THINKING, INTERPRETATION

A01 — SKILLS: CRITICAL THINKING, ANALYSIS, INTERPRETATION

A02 — SKILLS: CRITICAL THINKING, ANALYSIS, REASONING, INTERPRETATION

1 Select **two** phrases that the narrator uses to describe his neighbouring patients in the first paragraph. **(2 marks)**

2 In the final paragraph and **in your own words**, explain the conclusions Orwell draws from his experiences of how the poor die? **(4 marks)**

3 Describe the attitudes towards the sick in this hospital. You may support your points with **brief** quotations. **(5 marks)**

4 How does the writer use language and structure to create sympathy for the patients in this extract?

You should support your answer with close reference to the passage, including **brief** quotations. **(12 marks)**

INTERPRETING TEXT

The text below is an extract from a review of a car, the Capybara, when it first went on sale. Read the extract and answer the questions below.

▼ FROM REVIEW OF THE 'CAPYBARA'

First impressions count for a lot, and unfortunately, the first impression of the Capybara isn't great. The styling can at best be described as 'challenging' and at worst 'capable of frightening small children'. Things do get better on climbing through the oddly proportioned door, but the shocked look of passers-by acts as a constant reminder of the styling.

So it's safe to say the exterior is an acquired taste and relocating to the driver's seat is recommended. The interior quality is incredibly strong and suggests the manufacturer's money has been directed here whilst the designers were left to play outside. Beautifully finished equipment and finishes suggest that this is a much more expensive car than it actually is. Anyone sat in the sculpted seats is likely to feel reassured that they are experiencing a quality product and have invested their funds wisely.

PAPER 1 — COMPARING TEXTS — 161

> Inserting the futuristic key into the central console, you are greeted with a gentle murmur, rather than the expected rasping shout of other cars in this class. This lack of soundtrack continues as you smoothly drive away. Road noise is often an issue for small cars, but there is none here.
>
> The longer you spend in the Capybara, the more you can appreciate its character. This is a happy car, unhampered by its looks and far more focused on transporting you in comfort and luxury. State of the art safety features including laser-guided cruise control, ABS+ and a GPS controlled gearbox cocoon the driver in a relaxed environment that you would expect in luxury cars.
>
> But this isn't a luxury car, this is a relatively cheap, well-engineered small car that does its best to defy the first impressions the exterior styling inspires. If you can look beyond these, you have one of the best small cars on the road.
>
> Remember, first impressions can also be misleading – it's what's on the inside that counts.

SUBJECT VOCABULARY

premodified a noun with a description before it, e.g. 'the big blue car'

dynamic verb: a verb that describes actions or events that are happening, e.g. 'I go'

modal auxiliary verb a verb that helps another verb to express a meaning, e.g. 'can', 'would', 'should'

personification when something which is not human is made to sound human by attributing human qualities to it

phonological relating to the sound structure of words

▶ How does the writer use language to convey information and ideas to the reader? How does this language try to influence the reader's response? Use these questions to help you to identify relevant points.

▶ How does this text address the reader? Why does it do this?

▶ This is a car review, but does it remind you of any other kind of speech or writing? Why might it be trying not to seem too obviously like an advert?

▶ Does the review use many technical terms? Why? Why not?

▶ Identify some of the adjectives and adverbs which are used. What is their purpose here?

▶ Can you identify any nouns which are extensively **premodified**? Why might adverts tend to use a lot of premodification of nouns?

▶ Can you identify any rhetorical devices which are used to persuade the reader?

▶ Can you identify and comment on any **dynamic verbs** that are used? Look also at the use of **modal auxiliary verbs**.

▶ Where does the advert use **personification**? Why does it use this metaphorical device?

▶ What **phonological** feature is employed and why?

LEARNING OBJECTIVES

This lesson will help you to:
- explore links and connections between writers' ideas and perspectives and how these are conveyed.

COMPARISONS

Before you start, read or re-read the 10 pieces of contemporary non-fiction from the Pearson Edexcel International GCSE Anthology.
- From 'The Danger of a Single Story' by Chimamanda Ngozi Adichie.
- From *A Passage to Africa* by George Alagiah.
- From *The Explorer's Daughter* by Kari Herbert.
- 'Explorers or boys messing about?' by Steven Morris.
- From *Between a Rock and a Hard Place* by Aron Ralston.
- 'Young and dyslexic?' by Benjamin Zephaniah.
- From *A Game of Polo with a Headless Goat* by Emma Levine.
- From *Beyond the Sky and the Earth* by Jamie Zeppa.
- From *H is for Hawk* by Helen Macdonald.
- From *Chinese Cinderella* by Adeline Yen Mah.

QUESTION 5

HINT

The final question is worth approximately half of the marks for the whole section. You should divide your time accordingly.

SUBJECT VOCABULARY

implicit suggested or understood without being stated directly
explicit expressed in a way that is very clear and direct

HINT

Make sure you select information that is relevant to the question.

Question 5 is the final question of Section A, and it will ask you to compare the unseen text that you have been given with one of the texts from the Anthology. This question is the longest and most complex and represents about half of the marks available in Section A.

5 STEPS TO SUCCESS

STEP 1: Remember that the essay that you write in response to the question will be comparative, based on both Text One and Text Two from the Extracts Booklet. One will be a text from the Anthology, the other will be a text that you have not seen before. The question is likely to focus on:
- what the texts are about, key themes and the authors' conclusions
- the authors' use of language, character and other effects.

STEP 2: Make sure that you focus on the question. Begin by stating what the texts are about, both obviously and at a deeper level, considering **implicit** and **explicit** meaning.

STEP 3: Make sure you refer to interesting or relevant points of detail, as a very general answer will not be as successful. It is not enough to point things out and 'translate' the text; avoid retelling the story and make sure you explain how the devices and features work, what their effect is on the reader, and so on. Ask yourself why the author might have used that kind of language, imagery and so on. Remember: Point-Evidence-Explain.

STEP 4: Draw clear links and contrasts between the texts. Depending on which texts you are given, you may also be able to draw contrasts and links within the texts as well. Make sure that you compare and contrast the texts by using words and phrases such as 'similarly', 'in comparison' or 'on the other hand'.

STEP 5: Quote briefly, using a single word or phrase, to support your comments. You may refer to a whole paragraph or long section, but do not copy it out in full. Show that you are quoting by using inverted commas. Because you should only use short quotations, you should integrate them into your sentences and introduce them with a comma or colon. Whenever you quote, always explain in your own words what the quotation means and comment on its effect, with particular focus on language and structure.

STARTING TO COMPARE

Touching the Void is an autobiography by Joe Simpson. Unusually for an autobiography, it is presented from both the perspective of Joe, and of his climbing partner, Simon Yates, in the first person.

Published in 2003, it is a true story of how he and Simon set out to become the first people to climb Siula Grande in Peru. However, the pair are involved in a terrible accident which results in Joe breaking his leg and becoming separated from his partner. Simon is forced to cut the rope connecting the pair as he believes Joe to be dead and his only chance of survival.

Read the following extract that details the accident from both perspectives.

▼ FROM *TOUCHING THE VOID* BY JOE SIMPSON

Joe's account

I hit the slope at the base of the cliff before I saw it coming. I was facing into the slope and both knees locked as I struck it. I felt a shattering blow in my knee, felt bones splitting, and screamed. The impact catapulted me over backwards and down the slope of the East Face. I slid, head-first, on my back. The rushing speed of it confused me. I thought of the drop below but felt nothing. Simon would be ripped off the mountain. He couldn't hold this. I screamed again as I jerked to a sudden violent stop.

Everything was still, silent. My thoughts raced madly. Then pain flooded down my thigh – a fierce burning fire coming down the inside of my thigh, seeming to ball in my groin, building and building until I cried out at it, and my breathing came in ragged gasps. My leg!… My leg!

I hung, head down, on my back, left leg tangled in the rope above me and my right leg hanging slackly to one side. I lifted my head from the snow and stared, up across my chest, at a grotesque distortion in the right knee, twisting the leg into a strange zigzag. I didn't connect it with the pain which burnt my groin. That had nothing to do with my knee. I kicked my left leg free of the rope and swung round until I was hanging against the snow on my chest, feet down. The pain eased. I kicked my left foot into the slope and stood up.

A wave of nausea surged over me. I pressed my face into the snow, and the sharp cold seemed to calm me. Something terrible, something dark with dread occurred to me, and as I thought about it I felt the dark thought break into panic: 'I've broken my leg, that's it. I'm dead. Everyone said it… if there's just two of you a broken ankle could turn into a death sentence… if it's broken… if… It doesn't hurt so much, maybe I've just ripped something.'

I kicked my right leg against the slope, feeling sure it wasn't broken. My knee exploded. Bone grated, and the fireball rushed from groin to knee. I screamed. I looked down at the knee and could see it was broken, yet I tried not to believe what I was seeing. It wasn't just broken, it was ruptured, twisted, crushed, and I could see the kink in the joint and knew what had happened. The impact had driven my lower leg up through the knee joint. …

I dug my axes into the snow, and pounded my good leg deeply into the soft slope until I felt sure it wouldn't slip. The effort brought back the nausea and I felt my head spin giddily to the point of fainting. I moved and a searing spasm of pain cleared away the faintness. I could see the summit of Seria Norte away to the west. I was not far below it. The sight drove home how desperately things had changed. We were above 19,000 feet, still on the ridge, and very much alone. I looked south at the small rise I had hoped to scale quickly and it seemed to grow with every second that I stared. I would never get over it. Simon would not be able to get me up it. He would leave me. He had no choice. I held my breath, thinking about it. Left here? Alone?… For an age I felt overwhelmed at the notion of being left; I felt like screaming, and I felt like swearing, but stayed silent. If I said a word, I would panic. I could feel myself teetering on the edge of it.

Simon's account

Joe had disappeared behind a rise in the ridge and began moving faster than I could go. I was glad we had put the steep section behind us at last. … I felt tired and was grateful to be able to follow Joe's tracks instead of breaking trail.

I rested a while when I saw that Joe had stopped moving. Obviously he had found an obstacle and I thought I would wait until he started moving again. When the rope moved again I trudged forward after it, slowly.

Suddenly there was a sharp tug as the rope lashed out taut across the slope. I was pulled forward several feet as I pushed my axes into the snow and braced myself for another jerk. Nothing happened. I knew that Joe had fallen, but I couldn't see him, so I stayed put. I waited for about ten minutes until the tautened rope went slack on the snow and I felt sure that Joe had got his weight off me. I began to move along his footsteps cautiously, half expecting something else to happen. I kept tensed up and ready to dig my axes in at the first sign of trouble.

As I crested the rise, I could see down a slope to where the rope disappeared over the edge of a drop. I approached slowly, wondering what had happened. When I reached the top of the drop I saw Joe below me. He had one foot dug in and was leaning against the slope with his face buried in the snow. I asked him what had happened and he looked at me in surprise. I knew he was injured, but the significance didn't hit me at first.

He told me very calmly that he had broken his leg. He looked pathetic, and my immediate thought came without any emotion. … You're dead… no two ways about it! I think he knew it too. I could see it in his face. It was all totally rational. I knew where we were, I took in everything around me instantly, and knew he was dead. It never occurred to me that I might also die. I accepted without question that I could get off the mountain alone. I had no doubt about that.

… Below him I could see thousands of feet of open face falling into the eastern glacier bay. I watched him quite dispassionately. I couldn't help him, and it occurred to me that in all likelihood he would fall to his death. I wasn't disturbed by the thought. In a way I hoped he would fall. I knew I couldn't leave him while he was still fighting for it, but I had no idea how I might help him. I could get down. If I tried to get him down I might die with him. It didn't frighten me. It just seemed a waste. It would be pointless. I kept staring at him, expecting him to fall…

---

breaking trail The process of making a trail through deep snow.

PAPER 1 — COMPARING TEXTS

ACTIVITY 1 — AO3
SKILLS: ANALYSIS, INTERPRETATION

▼ COMPARING JOE AND SIMON'S ACCOUNTS

To help you to develop comparative skills, look back at the *Touching the Void* extract again in order to make comparisons within the text. Work with a partner to copy and complete the following table, considering Simon's account.

▼ WHAT WORDS OR PHRASES IN JOE'S ACCOUNT MOST VIVIDLY SHOW HIS PAIN AND HIS THOUGHTS AND FEELINGS?	▼ WHAT WORDS OR PHRASES IN SIMON'S ACCOUNT SHOW MOST CLEARLY THE DIFFICULT DECISION HE FACES? EXPLAIN THE REASONS FOR YOUR CHOICES.
Joe's account focuses on pain and shock: agony, panic and fear. He is obsessed with pain and the extremity of the damage, using powerful and emotive verbs: 'it was ruptured, twisted, crushed'. This uses the rule of three and emotive language to make the reader feel his pain.	
Sharp, onomatopoeic sounds, such as 'bones splitting' and 'shattering blow', using emotive verbs.	
Sometimes uncompromisingly direct to intensify sense of reality: 'the impact had driven my lower leg up through the knee joint'; 'we were above 19,000 feet… and very much alone'. Sometimes detailed descriptions involve the reader and put them in his shoes.	
Words and images that convey thoughts and feelings vividly and frankly, sometimes in a sequence that conveys dramatic changes of mood and thought (paragraph 4: 'A wave of nausea… I'm dead.'); phrasing becomes abstract and almost vague at times, suggesting trauma: 'something terrible, something dark with dread'; 'teetering on the edge of (panic)'.	
Uses rhetorical questions, such as 'Left here? Alone?'. This creates an atmosphere of uncertainty, putting the reader in his shoes and creating a sense of drama and suspense.	

KEY POINT
The individuality of your answer will lie in your choices of which details to highlight and the effect you think they have on the reader. Focus your energy on these aspects rather than making very general comments.

ACTIVITY 2 — AO1 AO2 AO3
SKILLS: CRITICAL THINKING, REASONING, DECISION MAKING

▼ MEETING ASSESSMENT OBJECTIVES

Read the two following student responses to the exam-style question on page 167. How well do you think they meet the following assessment objectives?

- AO1: Read and understand a variety of texts, selecting and interpreting information, ideas and perspectives
- AO2: Understand and analyse how writers use linguistic and structural devices to achieve their effects
- AO3: Explore links and connections between writers' ideas and perspectives, as well as how these are conveyed

▲ Joe Simpson's is a great story of mountaineering survival.

EXAMPLE STUDENT ANSWER A

Joe's account of the climb is very matter of fact and doesn't spare us the grim details of the injury that he sustained earlier in the climb: 'I felt a shattering blow in my knee, felt bones splitting, and screamed'. This indicates that he isn't really too badly affected currently by the psychological trauma of his ordeal. In Simon's account he is also very matter of fact about the experiences of Siula Grande, but the way in which he presents it isn't so horrific, more clinical. As if he isn't really there and is just doing a commentary on someone else climbing the mountain.

Joe's account of the climb uses a lot more exciting language and a richer vocabulary to keep the reader interested: 'Everything was still, silent. My thoughts raced madly'. Whereas Simon's account only uses very simple language and is more factual rather than exciting: 'I rested a while when I saw that Joe had stopped moving'. I think this suggests that Joe is perhaps more experienced at writing or was more affected by the incident on the Siula Grande. This helps us to understand that Joe and Simon aren't professional writers; I feel that this does take some of the possible atmosphere away from the story.

In conclusion I think that there really aren't that many differences between the two accounts, other than the ones that I have stated. I think this is because they are both about the same incident and are both written from the same aspect of climbers.

EXAMPLE STUDENT ANSWER B

Both Simon and Joe use ellipses in their accounts: 'I kept staring at him expecting him to fall…'. The ellipses help to add tension and makes the reader wonder what will happen next. It keeps you on the edge of your seat and introduces the idea of an unfortunate event, which can help to build up to a climax point. Simon's account ends with an ellipsis, leaving it up to your imagination and making you want to find out more.

This extract consists of two pieces of autobiographical prose narrative (or monologues) giving different perspectives on the same event. Relatively short paragraphs follow a sequence of time, but the real demarcations are provided by crucial developments in thought. The key to understanding the piece is to appreciate the different ways Joe and Simon respond to the accident. Though both accounts are very similar in style, there are significant differences to be explored.

Simon and Joe both use exclamatory sentences in their accounts. 'My leg!… my leg!' Joe uses this in particular to emphasise a thought and to bring a greater level of attention to the phrase. In this example it

PAPER 1 — COMPARING TEXTS

highlights how painful this experience is for him and forces an emotional response from the reader.

In keeping with this idea, emotive language is used more frequently by Joe: 'something dark with dread occurred to me, as I thought about it I felt the dark thought break into a panic'. The use of words like 'dread', 'dark' and 'break' create a semantic field of horror and sadness.

In comparison with Joe's account, Simon is less emotional and more objective in considering the situation in hand: 'I could see it in his face. It was all totally rational'. The use of short simple sentences helps keep his point of view very black and white and provokes a less emotional response from the reader. It seems fitting that Simon, as the observer, is more pragmatic in his analysis of the situation – the reader is aware that he feels a responsibility to act and is weighing up his decisions in as calm and factual a way as he is able to.

In conclusion, the juxtaposition between Simon and Joe's narratives illuminates the pathos in the two accounts. The starkly different tones force the reader to take sides. The reader is more likely to side with Joe's emotive and deeply personal account.

> **HINT**
> You must COMPARE and CONTRAST. To do this, use phrases that show you are comparing, such as, 'in comparison', 'in contrast', 'similarly', 'however'.

ACTIVITY 3 — A03
SKILLS: CRITICAL THINKING, ANALYSIS, INTERPRETATION, DECISION MAKING

▼ **HOW WRITERS PRESENT THEIR IDEAS**

Reread the two Anthology texts, *The Explorer's Daughter* and *Chinese Cinderella*. Compare and contrast how the writers present their ideas and perspectives about their experiences.

You should support your answer with detailed examples from both texts. **(22 marks)**

You might like to consider some of the following points: biographical and autobiographical writing, style, structure, viewpoint, selection of detail, presentation of fact/opinion.

> **KEY POINT**
> Both of these extracts involve father/daughter relations but there are differences in perspective and choice of detail that reflect the different priorities of each writer.

EXAM-STYLE QUESTION — A03
SKILLS: CRITICAL THINKING, ANALYSIS, INTERPRETATION, DECISION MAKING

Compare and contrast Joe and Simon's attitudes towards the accident described in the passage from *Touching the Void*. Support your answer with detailed examples, including brief quotations. **(22 marks)**

PAPER 1 — COMPARING TEXTS

LEARNING OBJECTIVES

This lesson will help you to:
- practise and perfect skills to respond effectively to unseen non-fiction in the exam.

SELECTING EVIDENCE

You will need to locate quotations in order to support your points quickly, under exam conditions. It is important that the quotations that you use are short and directly relevant to your point.

ACTIVITY 1 — **A01** — **SKILLS** ANALYSIS

▼ SELECTING EVIDENCE FROM *TOUCHING THE VOID*

Read the passage from *Touching the Void* on pages 163–164. Copy and complete the following tables, finding evidence of each technique or stylistic choice in the passage.

HINT

Remember to always use quotation marks to indicate direct quotation. Wherever possible, quotations should be integrated into the main body of your own sentences. Longer quotations should be used sparingly and set off from the main paragraph.

▼ JOE'S ACCOUNT	▼ EVIDENCE
Short sentences	
Description of how physically painful the accident is	
Descriptions of feeling lonely	
Use of modal verbs (*must*, *could*, *should*, *would*, *shall*, *will*) to speculate about the future	
Punctuation for effect	

▼ SIMON'S ACCOUNT	▼ EVIDENCE
Careful and considered tone	
Realistic understanding of the situation	
Unsympathetic descriptions	
Use of modal verbs (*must*, *could*, *should*, *would*, *shall*, *will*) to speculate about the future	
Punctuation for effect	

PAPER 1 | **COMPARING TEXTS** | 169

ACTIVITY 2 — A02 — SKILLS: ANALYSIS

▼ **BEAT THE CLOCK!**

You have three minutes to find an example of each of the following techniques in the *Touching the Void* extract on pages 163–164:

- ellipsis
- exclamation mark
- direct speech
- emotive language
- rhetorical question
- use of first person narrative
- colloquial language.

HINT

The exam involves a mixture of short and longer answer questions. You will need to locate the relevant part of the passage for each question, but you do not need to offer direct quotation for the shorter questions. Read the question carefully and look at the number of marks available to help you to determine how much information to include and whether you need to quote.

ACTIVITY 3 — A02 — SKILLS: CRITICAL THINKING, ANALYSIS, INTERPRETATION

▼ **POINT-EVIDENCE-EXPLAIN**

For each of the techniques listed in Activity 2, construct a P-E-E paragraph exploring the effect that the technique has on the context of the story and its effect on the reader. Start by completing the following example.

Point: Both Simon and Joe use ellipses in their accounts. Joe's passage even ends with it.

Evidence: 'I kept staring at him, expecting him to fall…'

Explanation: Ellipsis is used as a structural device to create suspense and anticipation.

EXAM-STYLE QUESTIONS

A01

SKILLS: ANALYSIS, CRITICAL THINKING, INTERPRETATION

1. Select **two** words or phrases that describe why Simon almost hopes that Joe falls. **(2 marks)**
2. **In your own words**, explain why Simon is feeling good at the beginning of his account. **(4 marks)**

▲ 'I kept staring at him, expecting him to fall…'

COMPARING TEXTS

LEARNING OBJECTIVES

This lesson will help you to:
- prepare for Section A of the Paper 1 exam.

PUTTING IT INTO PRACTICE

You should prepare for Section A of the Paper 1 exam by answering questions on an unprepared non-fiction reading passage (Text 1) and questions on a passage from the Anthology (Text 2). Text 1 could be drawn from a range of contemporary non-fiction, including autobiography, travel writing, reportage, media articles, letters, diary entries and opinion pieces.

PREPARING FOR THE EXAM: NEED TO KNOW

- All questions are compulsory.
- Questions will test reading skills: factual comprehension; inference and an understanding of how writers use language; evaluation of how writers use linguistic and structural devices to achieve effect and comparative skills.
- The pattern of questioning consists of short, specific questions on Texts 1 and 2 (separately targeted) followed by a more sustained comparative question drawing on the two passages as a whole.
- Questions will be phrased so that they are understandable and clear. The shorter questions will be more factually-based and phrased more directly, for example, 'What similarities and differences… does the writer note?' or 'Find four examples of…'. Questions 4 and 5 are longer and will require more overall interpretation, for example, 'Show how the writer is successful in using language to make the situation real to the reader'.
- Section A is worth 50% of the total marks for Paper 1.
- Anthologies may not be taken into the exam, but the relevant passage will be reprinted in the extracts booklet that you will get with your exam paper.
- Further examples can be found in the Pearson Edexcel exemplar assessment materials.

HINT

Timing is crucial for exam success. As one of the texts will be unfamiliar, you should give Section A more time than Section B, being very careful to leave yourself enough time to complete the paper. It is recommended that you spend 15 minutes reading the extracts, leaving one hour and 15 minutes for Section A and 45 minutes for Section B.

EXAM-STYLE QUESTIONS

AO1	SKILLS	ANALYSIS
AO1	SKILLS	CRITICAL THINKING, INTERPRETATION
AO1	SKILLS	CRITICAL THINKING, ANALYSIS, INTERPRETATION
AO2	SKILLS	CRITICAL THINKING, ANALYSIS, REASONING, INTERPRETATION
AO3	SKILLS	CRITICAL THINKING, ANALYSIS, INTERPRETATION, DECISION MAKING

Read the passage from *How the Poor Die* by George Orwell (pages 158–160).

1. Select two words or phrases that describe the patient known as 'Numéro 57'. **(2 marks)**

2. **In your own words**, explain what the writer's thoughts and feelings are towards the other patients. **(4 marks)**

3. Describe what we learn about the writer's character from his thoughts about the other patients and how he describes them. You may support your points with brief quotations. **(5 marks)**

4. Remind yourself of the passage from *A Passage to Africa* (pages 104–105). How does the writer present his views about his experiences as a television reporter in Somalia? You should support your answer with close reference to the passage, including brief quotations. **(12 marks)**

5. [Question 5 is based on both *How the Poor Die* and *A Passage to Africa*.] Compare how the writers present their ideas and perspectives about their experiences. Support your answer with detailed examples from both texts. **(22 marks)**

PAPER 1 — COMPARING TEXTS

ANSWERS

1. One mark each for any of the following: 'wasted', 'Utterly uninterested', 'colourless eyes', 'like a piece of antique china', 'about sixty', 'astonishingly shrunken', 'pale as vellum', 'shrunken away', 'his face… seemed no bigger than a doll's'.

2. Marks will be awarded for any reasonable interpretation of the writer's thoughts and feelings. One mark each for examples including (up to a maximum of two):
   - sadness at the tragedy of the suffering that he sees
   - horror at the squalor of the environment and the dehumanising treatment of the patients
   - astonishment at his left-hand neighbour's illness
   - sympathy towards the old veteran with the apparently scheming relatives

3. As the question is worth five marks, aim to make five points about the writer's character. You do not have to include quotations, but they may help to support your points. Remember to keep quotations short. Answers may include:
   - the writer is a curious person who is interested in everything he sees around him, even things that are morbid or disgusting, which you can see from the detailed descriptions of the other patients' illnesses
   - the writer is a sympathetic person who pities Numéro 57 and the way in which he dies ('poor old wretch'/'merely a number')
   - the writer is truthful; he would like to be idealistic or romantic about the actions of the patients ('his dying blessing') but reports what actually happens ('But no…')
   - the writer is not squeamish or easily upset by horrible sights ('I had time for a good look').

4. Marks awarded for discussion of the writer's presentation of a war-torn country in the autobiographical account, considering how information is conveyed; structure; viewpoint and tone.

   Read the following sample student answer and then consider the examiner's comments.

George Alagiah has clearly been struck in a powerful way by what he encountered in Somalia. He wants to make his readers see what terrible conditions existed there and how fortunate we are to live in such a different world. He also shows that journalists often just start out by looking for the best stories they can find. But in this case, the stories affected him on a deeply emotional level.

The most powerful effect of Alagiah's writing is **the way he focuses on particular individuals and their tragedies**. He describes the death of the ten year-old Habiba in a graphic way: 'No rage, no whimpering, just a passing away'. He is also skilled at creating not only images of the terrible sights he saw but also uses the other senses to convey the horror, as when he writes: 'the smell of decaying flesh'.

One of the striking ways he presents his experiences is by **drawing attention to a particular moment or sight**. He does this especially when writing about the smile of the unknown man. His translator's explanation that he was 'embarrassed to be found in this condition' disturbed him and he could not get it out of his mind. He also realises that he never even found the man's name, and feels guilty about

---

the way he focuses on particular individuals and their tragedies. This shows an understanding of structure, and the different possibilities of writing about this subject.

He describes the death of the ten year-old Habiba… Here, the student begins to analyse language. Is there anything else you could say about this quotation to show a deeper analysis?

He is also skilled at creating not only images of the terrible sights he saw… This is an excellent point; sensory description is a key feature of this text.

drawing attention to a particular moment or sight. The student shows insight into structure again here.

This response precisely analyses key aspects of language and structure from the text, demonstrating an excellent understanding of the writer's intentions. Points are supported by well-chosen quotations.

that, too. He almost seems ashamed of his life as a journalist and the way in which he was normally able to report on such events in a detached way. Overall, Alagiah communicates to the reader the way in which people in that situation lack basic necessities and human respect. However, he also reflects on how he felt to be witnessing and reporting on these events.

> **EXAMINER'S COMMENTS**
> This is a well-focused response that makes very thoughtful points about the writer's views and experiences. There are excellent examples focusing on the detail of Alagiah's language. The writing is accurate, and engaging.

5   Reward responses that compare how the writers present their ideas about their experiences.

Responses may include the following elements or points.

- Both texts describe a memorable experience from a retrospective first-person perspective.
- Both texts describe events seen from an adult's perspective.
- *How the Poor Die* begins with a short narrative sentence about how the writer comes to see the things that he goes on to report to the reader ('After some days…'). The second sentence then focuses on immediate descriptive details ('stuffy room'; 'narrow beds') rather than looking ahead to the deeper reflections that Orwell will discuss later. In comparison, *A Passage to Africa* begins with a list ('hungry, lean, scared and betrayed'), a rhetorical device that emphasises the overwhelmingly difficult conditions of Somalia.
- *How the Poor Die* has a shocking, abrupt title that leads the reader to expect a description of a death and makes the text sound like a matter-of-fact report into the lives of the poor. On the other hand, the title of *A Passage to Africa* makes the reader expect to read a travelogue about a journey to or within Africa, but does not alert the reader to the horror of the writer's journey.
- Orwell uses metaphorical and figurative language in his descriptions to emphasise the points he is making ('as grooms are said to do with horses'; 'in just the attitude of a woman handling a rolling-pin'; 'flickered out like a candle-end'). In comparison, *A Passage to Africa* is written like a piece of journalism and uses careful, predominantly objective descriptions.
- The structure of both texts is quite similar, working slowly through descriptions of a number of characters but creating suspense: in *A Passage to Africa*, as the reader waits for the unforgettable face; in *How the Poor Die*, as the reader waits for a description of the deaths suggested by the title. Similarly, both texts end with searching reflections on humanity and life.
- Neither of the texts uses much direct speech. The only direct speech in *How the Poor Die* is that of the patient who announces the deaths of others ('Numéro 43!' and 'Numéro 57!'), which focuses the reader's attention on seeing and hearing everything through Orwell's eyes and ears, rather than hearing for themselves. Similarly, *A Passage to Africa* only uses direct speech to give directions to the hamlet, which makes it feel immediate, as though the reader could also navigate there using these directions.

> **HINT**
> Aim for economical and relevant use of quotation in Questions 4 and 5.
> Avoid drifting away from the topic or question – for example, by projecting modern ideas about health care onto your reading of the hospital passage.

| PAPER 1 | COMPARING TEXTS | 173 |

ACTIVITY 1 — **A01** — **SKILLS**: REASONING, COLLABORATION, COOPERATION, EMPATHY, NEGOTIATION

▼ CONSOLIDATING YOUR KNOWLEDGE

Imagine that the Pearson Edexcel exam board have asked a group of students to give them some feedback on their selection of Anthology texts. In groups of five, complete the following tasks.

1. Each of you should choose two or three of the pieces in the Anthology. Using your skimming and scanning skills, summarise what each piece is about.
2. Stage a group discussion to decide which three pieces are the most educational and should definitely stay in the Anthology.
3. Decide as a group which three pieces you would like removed from the Anthology. Make sure you give specific reasons for your choices.
4. Working individually, research and choose one other non-fiction text you would like to be included in the Anthology. Why would you like this to be included? You may wish to include newspaper and magazine articles, extracts from websites, autobiographies or biographies and encyclopaedia entries.
5. Share your ideas with the rest of your group. Your group of five can only include three new pieces to replace those that you have chosen to remove, which means that you will need to persuade others in your group to choose your suggested piece. Now hold a vote on which three pieces should be included.
6. Debate the following statements, with two of the group arguing for each statement, and three arguing against.
   - 'The Anthology extracts are negative tales of hardship or danger.'
   - 'It is not necessary to give young people a say in what they study; teachers will always make better decisions for them.'

HINT

All non-fiction texts involve language and structure and the writers will present their idea. Think about how best to compare these things in the given texts when working under exam conditions.

ACTIVITY 2 — **A01** **A02** **A03** — **SKILLS**: CRITICAL THINKING, CREATIVITY

▼ TOP TEN EXAM TIPS

Imagine that you are the teacher in charge of your class. Can you write your own top ten exam tips for Section A?

▲ What are your top ten exam tips?

LEARNING OBJECTIVES

This lesson will help you to:
- understand what is meant by 'transactional writing'.

HINT

The examiners want to see how well you can write, not how much you know about something.

AN INTRODUCTION TO TRANSACTIONAL WRITING

Transactional writing is non-fiction writing for a purpose: to inform, explain, review, argue, persuade or advise. Each task will be aimed at dealing with one or two of these purposes (for example, 'to explain' will involve some informing).

Section B of Paper 1 will give you a choice of one of two tasks of this kind. Typically, it will present you with a debatable statement in inverted commas and ask you to write an article, a speech or a letter in which you express your views. You will have about an hour to plan and write it and it is worth half of the total marks for the whole paper. The topic will not require any specialised knowledge. Topics might include aspects of school life, transport and travel, common leisure activities such as sports and the internet, and aspects of the media.

TYPES OF TRANSACTIONAL WRITING

▲ Gamers need informative texts.

The six types of transactional writing covered in Section B of the paper can be defined as follows.

- To **inform**: to pass on information (this includes descriptive writing).
- To **explain**: to make clear how or why something is as it is.
- To **review**: to outline a piece of work, or an event, and comment on it.
- To **argue**: to produce an organised sequence of reasons to support a point of view.
- To **persuade**: to convince an audience or reader to think or act in a certain way.
- To **advise**: to give useful suggestions and ideas to help someone or some people.

ACTIVITY 1 | A01 | A02
SKILLS CRITICAL THINKING, PROBLEM SOLVING, ANALYSIS, ADAPTIVE WRITING

▼ **TEXTS WITH DIFFERENT PURPOSES**

1. Read the following extracts from texts with different purposes. Identify the language techniques that are used in each text to help it achieve its purpose.
   - **Inform**: A videogame console is an interactive entertainment computer or electronic device that produces a video display signal which can be used with a display device (a television, computer monitor, etc.) to display a videogame.
   - **Persuade**: Nintendo changes the way you play by maximising the fun and minimising the fuss. The Wii console makes you feel less like a player and more like you're in the game.
   - **Explain**: Why do we play videogames? The need for play is a primary component of human development and has been with us since the dawn of intelligence. Even in the brains of animals can be seen the impetus that leads to play. So, before we tackle videogaming, we should assess why we, as a species, need playtime so strongly.
2. Choose a computer game, television programme or book that you particularly like. Write three short paragraphs like the paragraphs above. One should inform your reader, one should persuade your reader, and one should explain to your reader.

PAPER 1 — TRANSACTIONAL WRITING

ACTIVITY 2 — A01 — SKILLS: CRITICAL THINKING

TYPES OF TRANSACTIONAL WRITING

Look back over the following texts from the Anthology, then copy and complete the table. Which types of transactional writing can you find in each text?

	INFORM	EXPLAIN	REVIEW	ARGUE	PERSUADE	ADVISE
From *The Explorer's Daughter* by Kari Herbert	✓	✓		✓	✓	
From 'The Danger of a Single Story' by Chimamanda Ngozi Adichie						
From *A Passage to Africa* by George Alagiah						
'Explorers, or boys messing about?' by Steven Morris						
'Young and dyslexic?' by Benjamin Zephaniah						
From *Chinese Cinderella* by Adeline Yen Mah						
'I have a dream' speech by Martin Luther King						

HINT

When reading more widely, try to identify different types of transactional writing. This will help prepare you for the exam.

ACTIVITY 3 — A01 — SKILLS: CRITICAL THINKING

IDENTIFY TRANSACTIONAL WRITING

Identify types of transactional writing in other passages that you have read in this book to add more examples to the table in Activity 2.

LEARNING OBJECTIVES

This lesson will help you to:
- understand in more detail the features of writing to inform, explain and review, and how you should tackle these writing tasks.

WRITING FOR A PURPOSE: INFORM, EXPLAIN, REVIEW

In many ways, writing to inform is the most straightforward writing task. Its main requirements are that it should be accurate, clear and well organised. Explanation also involves giving information, of course, but there is a greater need to select the information required and organise it so that you explain the topic clearly. A review informs you about a product or event and gives you a reasoned opinion on it.

WRITING TO INFORM

In informative text, it is important to think about your readers and make sure that they will be able to understand what you write.

▲ Informative writing is in some ways the most straightforward writing task, but does have its own challenges.

ACTIVITY 1 | **A02** | **SKILLS** ADAPTIVE LEARNING, CREATIVITY

▼ **FOCUSING ON THE READER**

Read the following question and sample student response.

▶ A young person from another country is coming to spend a term at your school or college. Write to inform them about your school or college and what happens in an ordinary day there.

> Dear Emilja,
> Our school is called New City High School. The school has been built on the outskirts of our town and it is quite a new building. The school has 1200 young people from the age of 11 up to 18. The school site has been landscaped and there are lawns and trees on it. There are playgrounds and sports facilities which are very popular.
> The day starts at 8.30 am. Most students get there by bus and walk up from the bus turning point outside the school gates. Registration is from 8.30 until 8.45 with your form teacher. All sorts of things go on in registration time. You can hand in notes if you have been off sick, or money if you are paying to go on a school trip. Some days you can go out to the library and return your books. On Tuesday and Friday there is assembly in the hall. This is where we have a speech from the Headteacher and sometimes she gives out prizes and cups to the sports teams that have won. We might have some music if the choir or the school bands have practised something to play to the school. Following that lesson 1 starts at 8.45 and what you have will depend upon your timetable and what day it is.

| PAPER 1 | TRANSACTIONAL WRITING | 177 |

> Students are supposed to line up outside classrooms if the teacher is not there. When the teacher arrives you are supposed to: go in quietly; stand behind your chair; wait until the teacher has said 'good morning'; and then you can sit down. Outdoor coats should not be worn in class. Students are supposed to take them off and put them on the back of the chair. There is a cloakroom where they can be left but most students don't because it is not very convenient.
>
> Yours sincerely,
> Takuma

Annotate the sample answer, labelling all the positive things you can find in it (such as good sentences, clear writing, good vocabulary and punctuation). Now read the mark scheme (page 206) carefully and decide what mark you think this answer deserves.

ACTIVITY 2 — A02 — SKILLS: CRITICAL THINKING, ANALYSIS, INTERPRETATION

▼ TECHNIQUES FOR INFORMATIVE WRITING

Look again at the letter in Activity 1. Identify an example of each of the techniques listed in the following table and explain the effect of each technique.

▼ ELEMENTS/TECHNIQUES	▼ EXAMPLE	▼ EFFECT
Headings		
Facts		
Statistics		
Language choices		
Structure		
Tone		
Description*		

* Remember that **description** is a type of informative writing (since it tells you what something looks like), which means that your understanding of this skill acquired from creative writing and from analysis of the Anthology and other texts will be useful.

WRITING TO EXPLAIN

Any question that contains the word 'how' or 'why' expects you to do some sort of explanation. Use clear paragraphs to organise your response. In the 45 minutes that you will have in the exam, you will probably have time to include four to six paragraphs. Try to link your paragraphs using signposting words such as 'firstly', 'therefore' and 'in addition'.

ACTIVITY 3 — A02
SKILLS: CRITICAL THINKING, ANALYSIS, INTERPRETATION

▼ FEATURES OF EXPLANATORY WRITING

A number of features will be found in explanatory writing. Copy and complete the following table using examples of your own or examples that you have found in the texts in this book.

▼ 'EXPLAIN' FEATURES	▼ EXAMPLES	▼ INTENDED EFFECT
Texts have a title that asks 'how' or 'why'.		
Texts use features such as clear paragraphs, bullet points, bold font and subheadings.		
Texts use connectives to show a series of points or events (for example, 'firstly').		
Texts use connectives to explain cause and effect (for example, 'because').		
Texts may contain diagrams.		
Texts may use technical or specialist vocabulary.		
Texts use formal or impersonal style in which neither the writer nor reader is directly involved.		
Texts are clearly structured and reach a conclusion that reminds the reader of the question.		

ACTIVITY 4 — A04 A05
SKILLS: PROBLEM SOLVING, ADAPTIVE LEARNING, CREATIVITY, INNOVATION

▼ WRITING A PRACTICE ANSWER

The topic you may be asked to explain will be something general like this.

▶ **Write an article for your school magazine explaining how you make your decisions with regard to either your GCSE or your A level subjects.**

Plan and write an answer to this question in no more than 45 minutes. Complete a table based on the one in Activity 2 to help you use some of the techniques listed in the table.

HINT
The strategies in Activity 5 can be applied to any writing task.

ACTIVITY 5 — A04 A05
SKILLS: ADAPTIVE LEARNING, CREATIVITY

▼ ADAPTING YOUR LANGUAGE FOR CHILDREN

Try writing the same piece that you wrote in response to Activity 4 for a group of 11-year-olds. How would you adapt your language for them?

PAPER 1 — **TRANSACTIONAL WRITING**

WRITING TO REVIEW

Since reviews are written for commercial publications such as newspapers, reviews need to be well written in order to engage the reader. This also means that the register can change depending on the readership: if the readers are teenagers, the language will probably be more colloquial and 'teenager-friendly'.

If you are asked to write a review in Section B, it is likely that it will be about a book, a film, an event or a computer game of your own choice. As part of the review, you should describe the overall qualities and effects of the subject that you have chosen.

▶ **Look back at the review of *Star Wars* on page 75 and write down a list of the points that the reviewer makes about the film.**

The key to writing successfully is to make a plan in manageable sections so that you have less thinking to do while you are writing. In the 45 minutes that you have to complete Section B, you are expected to write 400–600 words (2–3 sides).

> **KEY POINT**
>
> Although a review is inevitably personal, readers need to trust your opinion, so assertions need to be evidenced in some way, without bias.

ACTIVITY 6 | **AO4** | **SKILLS** CRITICAL THINKING, PROBLEM SOLVING

▼ **STRUCTURING A REVIEW**

Think of a film that you have enjoyed recently and use the table below to plan a review of it in no more than six paragraphs. Look at your list of points made in the review of *Star Wars* for guidance. Things to write about will include the story, the characters, the dialogue or screenplay, the acting, the visual elements (settings, cinematography, effects), the pace, the music and so on.

Paragraph 1	
Paragraph 2	
Paragraph 3	
Paragraph 4	
Paragraph 5	
Paragraph 6	

Once you have created an outline, it should be quite easy to fill it in. See if you can do this now. Copy and complete the table below to structure your ideas and key points.

▼ STORY-LINE	▼ SCRIPT/ DIALOGUE	▼ CINEMATO- GRAPHY	▼ ACTING	▼ VISUAL ELEMENTS
Take care! No spoilers!		Including CGI		

180 PAPER 1 — TRANSACTIONAL WRITING

LEARNING OBJECTIVES

This lesson will help you to:
- understand how to distinguish between writing to argue, writing to persuade and writing to advise, and how to approach these writing tasks.

WRITING FOR A PURPOSE: ARGUE, PERSUADE, ADVISE

In each of these types of writing, the aim is to persuade the reader using various techniques. There are many kinds of 'argue' question, but they will generally ask you to do one or both of the following:
- present reasons, with evidence, in support of (or against) a viewpoint
- develop a point of view.

WRITING TO ARGUE

A typical 'argue' exam question might be:

> 'Some experts believe that a school uniform creates more problems than it solves and should be abolished in all schools.'
>
> Give your views on this topic, arguing either in favour of school uniform or against it. Your argument may include:
> - the advantages and disadvantages of uniforms
> - the potential problems caused by uniforms
> - any other points you wish to make. **(45 marks)**

Look at the following students' attempts to begin an answer to this question.

EXAMPLE STUDENT ANSWER A

> Some experts say school uniform creates more problems than it solves, i am going to tell u my views. My first opinion about school uniform is very clear and I am against the school uniform, School uniforms are horrible,
> i hate ours. Teachers say that it is smart but i couldn't disagree more. It makes me look fat. And the colour is soo bad it makes u feel ill. There are lots of other reasons why it is rubbish e.g. it is not cheap and it is not good kwality, they say that school uniform makes us look the same so nobody can tell the difference between rich kidz and poor kidz, but u can becos the rich ones still make there uniform look like designer wear always.
> School uniform makes us look like zombies.

EXAMPLE STUDENT ANSWER B

> In my opinion, school uniform should not be abolished. This is because it makes our school look neat and tidy. The ties keep our collars in check, while the shoes make us look like young businessmen and women. This is important as it helps to build a healthy relationship for our college which is what we should be striving to do.
> In my view, the uniform defines us as a school; it distinguishes from others. I appreciate that we are not seen as individuals, but it is important that we are seen as easily recognised out of school and in school. This gives us a sense of pride and belonging. I think it also makes us behave better; nobody gains if our school has a reputation for bad behaviour. Moreover, uniform also has

▲ Does school uniform create more problems than it solves?

PAPER 1 — TRANSACTIONAL WRITING

> very practical advantages. For instance, we have different ties in our school for prefects and for other students. This is useful when prefects do their duties because they are easily identifiable.

Even if you don't agree with the point of view expressed, it is easy to see that one of these answers is much better than the other.

- What makes Answer B better than Answer A?

ACTIVITY 1 — A03
SKILLS: CRITICAL THINKING, DECISION MAKING

▼ WHAT MAKES A GOOD ANSWER?

Read the 10 statements given in the following table. Five apply to Answer A and five to Answer B. After reading each statement, put a tick in the correct column depending on whether you think the statement applies to Answer A or Answer B.

▼ STATEMENT	▼ ANSWER A	▼ ANSWER B
Sentences are badly punctuated and there are several spelling mistakes.		
A wide range of words and sentence structures is used to engage the reader.		
Text speak, abbreviations and slang are inappropriately used.		
The first sentence repeats the question and there is a limited range of words and sentence structures.		
It is firmly structured in paragraphs and ideas are carefully linked by words and phrases.		
The tone is serious and the argument is very logical.		
The tone is too informal and ideas are not linked clearly.		
The structure is weak and there are no paragraphs.		
The spelling, punctuation and grammar are correct.		
Points are made clearly, and reasons and evidence are given for them.		

WRITING TO PERSUADE

To persuade means trying to influence someone to:
- accept a point of view
- behave in a certain way.

The first type of question might ask you to argue persuasively in favour of a statement in a class debate (for example, 'Smoking should be banned in all public places'). The second type of question might ask you to write a letter to persuade one or more people to do something (for example, take part in a charity event).

If you want to persuade someone successfully, you will need to use a strong argument, but you will be even more successful if you use language to make them agree with you.

KEY POINT

You can persuade with the ideas in your argument, but you can also persuade with intelligent use of language itself.

Persuasive writing techniques include:
- linking your ideas with words that connect and develop them, such as, 'moreover', 'furthermore', 'in addition', 'on the other hand'
- using words like 'this' or 'these' to link new paragraphs with previous paragraphs
- using evidence or supporting points from personal knowledge or experience
- making your language choices expressive and lively.

ACTIVITY 2 — A02 — SKILLS: CRITICAL THINKING, INTERPRETATION

▼ ANSWERING A 'PERSUADE' QUESTION

Here is an example of a persuasive speech in answer to the following question.

▶ How would you persuade the Governors to redecorate the school?

> I am here today to tell you that I believe there should be many changes to help students. I know that these ideas will cost a lot of money but I reckon they will greatly improve the facilities and the atmosphere.
> First I believe we should redecorate the school. If we made the place look more pleasant then students will be happier and they will work better too. In particular the toilets are in urgent need of refurbishment. It would be a good idea to introduce some new subjects in the curriculum that are more relevant to the students. Teaching methods need to be looked at, so that students can have more modern ways of learning things.
> You could also look into methods of making people want to come to school. Perhaps you could give special privileges to students who regularly attend. The school rules need to be looked at as many are out of date. Why not have a special area set aside for smokers, as long as they bring a letter from their parents?

What do you think of this speech? Copy and complete the table, adding points of your own.

▼ MERITS	▼ WEAKNESSES	▼ HOW YOU COULD IMPROVE IT
It is accurately written.	It does not go into much detail.	Give more reasons for the ideas.
The advice is generally clear and structured.	Some of the ideas are controversial and the writer should justify them.	Quote more evident to support the ideas.
The tone is appropriate and the words are formal (suitable for this audience).	It ends very suddenly.	Show more awareness of the audience for whom it is intended.

WRITING TO ADVISE

Most people give and receive advice almost every day. This advice is often social or moral (for example, how to deal with a personal problem). In general, in an exam, you will have to:

- give helpful opinions, suggestions or information to a specified person or group of people
- recommend a course of action to someone, perhaps guiding or warning them.

A question may be worded to combine both these possibilities, but the advice will almost always be targeted at a specific audience or reader.

| PAPER 1 | TRANSACTIONAL WRITING | 183 |

HINT

Do:
- choose words and sentence structures that will influence your reader
- use good examples and details to support your main points.

Don't:
- use too many emotive words – this can have the opposite effect to that intended
- use statistics that are obviously nonsense – this will weaken your argument!

▲ Advising someone involves trying to influence them.

KEY POINT

You don't just need to choose influencing words, but also influencing sentence structure.

'Writing to advise' is linked to 'writing to argue and persuade'. If you give advice to someone, you will also be trying to influence them to follow your advice, so persuasion and reasoning play a part.

ACTIVITY 3 | A04 | A05 | SKILLS PROBLEM SOLVING, ADAPTIVE LEARNING, CREATIVITY, INNOVATION

▼ **ANSWERING AN 'ADVISE' QUESTION**

Imagine you are an expert who gives advice on a website. Write your replies to these questions from a teenager and a parent.

> Hello,
> I am being bullied by some people in my form at school. They aren't hitting me, they're just calling me names and I'm fed up with it. What can I do?
> Mohammed

> Hello,
> My fourteen-year-old daughter seems to spend all her time on social media. I am really worried about her. I don't understand it. How can I help her?
> Mrs P

ACTIVITY 4 | A02 | SKILLS CRITICAL THINKING

▼ **ANALYSING AN ANSWER**

Look at this exam-style question and the first part of an example student answer. How good do you think this answer is?

▶ You have been asked to speak to younger students at your school or college, giving advice on how to cope with exams. Write the talk you would give.

> To some people, examinations are the most difficult situation to go through. Others find them easy, an opportunity to show off what they have learned. Whichever category you believe that you fall into, it really does not matter. The idea is to realise which category you fall into then understand how to conquer your weaknesses and maximise your strengths. However, what I tell you today will be useful for all of you. The first stage for any examination is to prepare for it. If you fail to prepare, you prepare to fail. It really is a simple as that…

ACTIVITY 5 | A04 | A05 | SKILLS PROBLEM SOLVING, ADAPTIVE LEARNING, CREATIVITY

▼ **WRITING A SPEECH**

Write your own speech in answer to the question in Activity 4. Your speech should be about 350–400 words long.

LEARNING OBJECTIVES

This lesson will help you to:
- understand how to write for different audiences.

WRITING FOR AN AUDIENCE

The Section B tasks will specify your target audience or readership. Possible tasks include writing to a school class or assembly, writing a letter to a headteacher or school governors or to a teenager abroad, and writing an article for a school or local magazine. As a writer, you need to make decisions about such things as register, style and tone, all of which will depend on your audience.

ACTIVITY 1 — A01 A02 — SKILLS: CRITICAL THINKING, ANALYSIS, INTERPRETATION

▼ **THINKING ABOUT YOUR AUDIENCE**

'Certain gases that trap heat are building up in Earth's atmosphere...'

Consider the following extracts about climate change. What audience do you think each one is written for?

1 Highlight any words or phrases that are particularly suitable for the audience.
2 Circle words and phrases that show the register of the piece of writing.
3 List the decisions that the writer has made to make the writing suitable for the intended audience.

EXTRACT A

Certain gases that trap heat are building up in Earth's atmosphere. The primary culprit is carbon dioxide, released from burning coal, oil and natural gas in power plants, cars, factories etc. (and to a lesser extent when forests are cleared). The second is methane, released from rice paddies, both ends of cows, rotting garbage in landfills, mining operations, and gas pipelines. Third are chlorofluorocarbons (CFCs) and similar chemicals, which are also implicated in the separate problem of ozone depletion … Nitrous oxide (from fertilizers and other chemicals) is fourth…

EXTRACT B

People are seeing change all over the world. Arctic sea ice is melting earlier and forming later. Glaciers are disappearing. Heat waves, storms and floods are becoming more extreme. Insects are emerging sooner and flowers are blooming earlier. In some places, birds are laying eggs before they're expected and bears have stopped hibernating.

EXTRACT C

So what's going on?

For real, all it takes is a couple degrees
Before floods, droughts, and hurricanes are not anomalies
And all these catastrophes become our new realities
Comin' down on the world just like the Sword of Damocles.

PAPER 1　　TRANSACTIONAL WRITING　　185

> We need smarter ideas for sustainable policies
> New technologies for a new green economy.
> New discoveries, and new questions to ask
> 'Cuz we can figure out the future by examining the past.
>
> So we sail to the Poles, and sample the extremes,
> And drill into the ice, and discover what it means.
> So use that brain, and make science a priority
> And you can work on stopping global warming with authority.

ACTIVITY 2 — A01 — SKILLS: ANALYSIS

▼ USING SOPHISTICATED TECHNIQUES TO PERSUADE

Read the following extract from the Royal Society for the Prevention of Cruelty to Animals (RSPCA), which aims to persuade people to give money to the charity. Charities depend on people giving money to them so their appeals need to be very persuasive. When you have read it, copy and complete the table that follows.

> Have you ever thought about how the RSPCA is truly amazing?
>
> We've been saving animals from cruelty for nearly 200 years. We lead the world in showing how to live with animals in harmony and respect. And all because enough people in our country care about protecting animals from cruelty. Animals cannot speak out for themselves. So we do.
>
> RSPCA inspectors have always been the most visible part of our work to prevent animals suffering. Today our 370 inspectors and animal welfare officers collect and rescue around 119,000 animals every year. It seems like people are conscious of animals' needs, and they are prepared to bring suffering animals to our attention.
>
> Looking after pitilessly abused and abandoned animals, and finding them new homes is just part of the daily task we face. For instance, our 24-hour cruelty and advice line receives over 3,000 calls on average, every day, that's one call every 29 seconds. And each week our inspectors have to investigate around 2,750 complaints about suspected cruelty to animals. Multiply that by weeks in a month, and then by every month in a year.
>
> The RSPCA could not survive without public support. Thank you for helping to make the RSPCA truly amazing!

HINT

Always think about the purpose of your writing. The words in this charity appeal have been carefully chosen:

- to make you feel the horror of animal cruelty
- to stress the positive effect that the RSPCA has on animal welfare
- to emphasise the importance of RSPCA inspectors.

▼ QUESTIONS TO CONSIDER	▼ EXAMPLES FROM THE TEXT
What words in this piece emphasise the cruel way in which some animals are treated?	1 'pitilessly abused' 2 3
What words emphasise the positive aspects of the RSPCA's work?	1 'harmony and respect' 2 3
What words and details emphasise the strengths of the RSPCA inspectors?	1 'the most visible part of our work' 2 3

▶ Find an example of each of the following techniques:

- rhetorical questions
- short sentences for dramatic effect
- the use of statistics to prove what is being said
- repetition of words, or use of similar words, for effect.

ACTIVITY 3 — AO2 — SKILLS: CRITICAL THINKING, ANALYSIS, INTERPRETATION

▼ WRITING TO A FRIEND

Sometimes the context for advice or persuasion is much more personal. The following extract is by a teenager who has been told by a friend that she is going alone to meet someone she only knows from a social networking site. She is writing to persuade her friend not to go. Would you expect her style (or register) to be informal? Why might it use some conversational features?

> Dear Ella,
>
> Please don't shout at me for writing this letter, but I doubt if you would let me talk directly to you. I know I am being uptight and intruding on your private life but I am sick with worry, since you told me that you were going to meet this 'boy'. We have always been close friends and you have always trusted me in the past. So listen to me now. What you are doing is plain stupid. Insane, even.

This letter uses different techniques from the RSPCA charity appeal. Link the statements about techniques on the left with the correct explanation for each one on the right.

TECHNIQUE	EXPLANATION
1 The style is very informal and uses conversational language such as 'uptight' and 'plain stupid'.	A This is to make the friend feel guilty and also to reassure her.
2 It uses a variety of personal pronouns.	B This is to emphasise what the writer is saying.
3 It uses a variety of sentence structures, including commands and sentences with no verbs.	C This makes the letter more personal and establishes a direct link with the friend.
4 It appeals to the friend on various emotional levels.	D This is appropriate because it is written to a close friend.

▲ Writing to a friend will use a personal style and structure.

ACTIVITY 4 — AO4 AO5 — SKILLS: PROBLEM SOLVING, ADAPTIVE LEARNING, CREATIVITY

▼ WRITING IN A SERIOUS STYLE

The extract about the RSPCA in Activity 2 could be easily adapted to be a speech, a leaflet or a part of an article. Write a brief piece in a similarly serious and adult style on a charity of your choice.

LEARNING OBJECTIVES

This lesson will help you to:
- understand how an appreciation of form can help you to write what is needed.

HINT

It is unlikely that you will be asked to write a very chatty letter to a close friend in the exam, because the examiners want to see that you can write with a good command of standard English.

HINT

These examples are all in similar fonts because you are not expected to try to imitate any of the visual features of the form in your exam. For example, if you are writing an article you would not need to imitate the visual appearance of a large headline.

FORM

The form of a text is the set of conventions that distinguish one type of text from another. Think about what makes a review different from a news article. Form is partly a matter of layout or appearance, partly the approach to the content, and partly the style or the way that the piece is written.

For example, in terms of the content or subject matter, the form of a feature article requires that all the content is clearly relevant to the topic, organised in a logical and clear way. In comparison, the form of a personal letter allows complete freedom to write about anything of interest to both the writer and reader (though there are still certain conventions) and not necessarily in any particular order. In terms of style, a feature article usually needs to be reasonably formal, whereas a personal letter can, of course, be very casual and colloquial.

ACTIVITY 1 | A01 | SKILLS: CRITICAL THINKING

▼ **IDENTIFYING FORM**

Look at the following openings of various pieces of writing.

EXTRACT A

What's in a name?

Names, common as many of them are, are like little codes: they tell people certain things about us, about where we come from.

EXTRACT B

Hi Pierre,

I expect the weather over there in Lyon is loads better than here in Canada. You don't want to be out in the sticks here I can tell you.

EXTRACT C

Dear Sirs,

I write concerning the recent plans for improvements in the local environment.

EXTRACT D

Thrills, spills and a gender twist

If you are a fan of Liam Hearn's books you won't be disappointed by the latest adventure.

PAPER 1 — TRANSACTIONAL WRITING

189

Now copy and complete the following table, writing down the things that you notice about the layout and content in extracts A–D.

	▼ TYPE OF FORM	▼ FEATURES OF THE FORM
A		
B		
C		
D		

IDENTIFYING FORM BY ITS PHYSICAL LAYOUT

In many cases, the layout is the most obvious indication of form. However, it is unlikely to be the most important aspect of form.

KEY POINT

Distinguishing one form of writing from another goes beyond the sort of layout differences that one can see at a glance.

NEWSPAPER AND MAGAZINE ARTICLES	■ Short paragraphs ■ Conform to a series of conventional lengths, for example, short articles of 600–800 words; full-length features of around 1,500 or so words ■ Use headlines and subheadings ■ Short introductory summaries
FILM AND BOOK REVIEWS	■ Most commonly around 300–700 words, though can be longer ■ Tend to have a punchy or clever headline and sometimes subheadings
LETTERS	■ If official or business, writer's address top right and date below; addressee's address top left ■ Begin with 'Dear…' ■ Short paragraphs ■ End with 'Yours sincerely', 'All best wishes' or similar, depending on level of familiarity with the reader
SPEECHES	■ Begin with a form of greeting, for example, 'Ladies and gentlemen…' ■ End with a form of farewell, a conclusion suitable to a spoken address rather than a written one: this could take the form of thanks to the audience for listening

IDENTIFYING FORM BY ITS CONTENT

It is the combination of the layout and content that makes forms identifiable. Even without the layout of a letter, the words, 'Dear John', at the start of a piece of writing would identify it as a letter. Similarly, when you read a summarising opening sentence such as, 'Yesterday evening, the Prime Minister announced that there would be a referendum…', you recognise it as the start of a news article.

FORM: NEWSPAPER ARTICLES

> **HINT**
> You are not expected to lay out an article as it would appear in print, such as in columns and with large fonts for headlines. You are being tested on the way that you use language, not the visual layout. You should still include paragraphs or headings if appropriate, though.

- Headlines tell you what the article is about in a concise, attention-grabbing way. For example, it might use wordplay or alliteration and leave out any words that are not vital to the meaning.
- A standfirst or summary sub-heading gives more detail, engaging the reader further.
- Opening paragraphs summarise the gist of the piece, which is very different from the opening of short stories or letters.
- Experts or people involved are often quoted as evidence and to add weight to an argument.

THE TRUTH ABOUT LYING: IT'S THE HANDS THAT BETRAY YOU, NOT THE EYES

By analysing videos of liars, the team found there was no link between lying and eye movements.

ADAM SHERWIN

It is often claimed that even the most stone-faced liar will be betrayed by an unwitting eye movement.

But new research suggests that 'lying eyes', which no fibber can avoid revealing, are actually a myth.

Verbal hesitations and excessive hand gestures may prove a better guide to whether a person is telling untruths, according to research conducted by Professor Richard Wiseman.

ACTIVITY 2 | **AO4** | **AO5** | **SKILLS**: PROBLEM SOLVING, ADAPTIVE LEARNING, CREATIVITY

▼ **WRITING AN ARTICLE**

> **HINT**
> If you cannot remember the facts, then try inventing some. The aim here is to practise the form of your writing, rather than to focus on accuracy.

Write a short article that contains the features listed, you could write about aspects of climate change, changes in nutritional advice or an interesting discovery arising from research.

FORM: FILM AND BOOK REVIEWS

- Titles of reviews are usually catchy to engage the reader and indicate the reviewer's opinion.
- A sub-heading gives more details of the reviewer's opinion.
- Ratings give an opinion on how good the book, film or event is.
- An engaging opening paragraph sometimes uses figurative language to give the reader a taste of what the film or event is like.

THE HORSE AS HERO

War Horse, by Michael Morpurgo, is a powerful and emotive story about the trenches of the First World War from an entirely original perspective. It is one of the best books of this year for younger readers.

Most readers will know that millions died in the horrors of the `war to end wars'; few will know that six million horses were also killed in the atrocious carnage. The tale tracks the experiences of Joey, the much-loved horse of a young recruit named Albert, who is separated from him…

PAPER 1 — TRANSACTIONAL WRITING

▲ What was the last film you enjoyed watching?

ACTIVITY 3 — A04 — A05
SKILLS: PROBLEM SOLVING, ADAPTIVE LEARNING, CREATIVITY

▼ WRITING A REVIEW

Write a brief review of a book or film you have enjoyed, using the features listed on page 190 and appropriate language.

FORM: LETTERS

▼ LAYOUT OR PHYSICAL FORM
- Writer's address and the date go in the top right corner.
- Addressee's name and address go on the left, lower down.
- Start with 'Dear…'.
- Can use a subject line to draw the reader's attention to the topic.
- End with 'Yours faithfully' if started with 'Dear Sir or Madam'. If started with the addressee's name, end with 'Yours sincerely'. If informal, could end with 'All the best' or 'With love'.

▼ CONTENT
- Formal letters normally begin with the reason for writing ('I write concerning the…').
- Informal letters often begin with a thought for the addressee, such as, 'I hope all is well with you'.
- Formal letters contain information and make points. They may also express thanks or make a complaint.
- Informal letters usually contain personal news and plans.
- The last paragraph before signing off usually expresses hopes or good wishes, for example, formally, 'I hope you will give this matter your serious consideration' or, informally, 'all the best until then'.

ACTIVITY 4 — A04 — A05
SKILLS: PROBLEM SOLVING, ADAPTIVE LEARNING, CREATIVITY

▼ WRITING A LETTER

Write a letter, to the governors of your school, requesting that they improve the school in two ways that you think are important. In this case, you should use the opening greeting, 'Dear Governors'.

KEY POINT
Formal letters require adherence to certain rules but there is still scope for your own choices.

FORM: REPORTS

A report is a response to a request for detailed information about a place, institution, event or other project. It differs from a newspaper article because it requires extensive research into the background and often then gives a recommendation as to what should happen next. Governments commission numerous reports on all aspects of modern life as the basis for forming policy and making decisions. For example, a town council might need a report on the roads in a part of the town or the way that schools are fulfilling the needs of the community.

PAPER 1 — TRANSACTIONAL WRITING

ACTIVITY 5 — AO4, AO5 — SKILLS: PROBLEM SOLVING, ADAPTIVE LEARNING, CREATIVITY

WRITING A REPORT

Write a response to the following question.

▶ **Your school or borough has been allotted a significant amount of extra funding to improve its facilities, which would be enough to pay for some new buildings. You have been asked to write a report on the state of facilities, in either your local community or your school, in one of the following areas:**

- **sports**
- **leisure**
- **arts**
- **provision for pedestrians and cyclists.**

HINT

As with other writing questions, you can invent details to make it sound more convincing and knowledgeable. However, you should try to make them realistic.

FORM: BLOGS

A blog, short for 'web log', is a cross between a diary and a personal magazine. They vary from those written and designed by professional journalists and other writers, which resemble online newspapers, to very informal ones written by students or young people. They are found on many sites on the internet.

This is an example of a blog post from a blogger who reviews computer games.

> Still only available as an early alpha build on Steam, but already immensely popular, Dean Hall's bleak, utterly unsentimental zombie survival game is unbearably tense and atmospheric. Players are pitched together into a stark landscape, and must survive for as long as possible, ransacking buildings for guns and food and avoiding the undead. But just as in all the best zombie fiction, it's not the rotting monsters you often have to worry about, it's the other survivors. Each server houses up to 40 players, all desperately scavenging for the same meagre supplies. And if you kill another participant, you can take their stuff. There is a clear benefit to adopting a 'shoot first' policy.

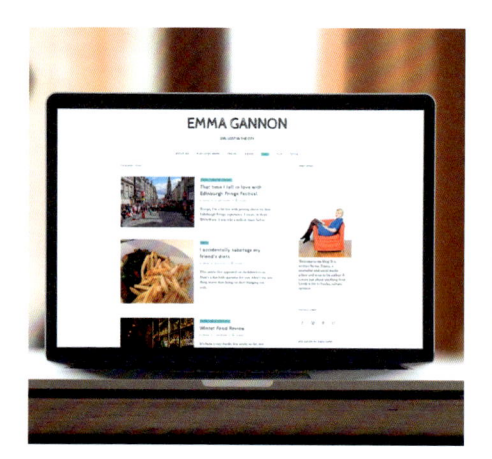

▲ A popular lifestyle and fashion blog

ACTIVITY 6 — AO4, AO5 — SKILLS: PROBLEM SOLVING, ADAPTIVE LEARNING, CREATIVITY

WRITING A BLOG POST

Write a blog post on a hobby or interest that you would like to share with others. Try to use standard English, but you may need to tailor your language to the needs of your audience and use more informal language.

FORM: INFORMATION GUIDES

These are leaflets designed to offer the reader a brief guide to a place, a process, a system and so on. Read the following question and think about the information that you might need to include in the guide that you write.

▶ **Write a brief guide to your home town, village or district for new residents or a visitor.**

PAPER 1   TRANSACTIONAL WRITING   193

> **HINT**
>
> Remember that you can introduce a statistic with phrases such as, 'It is believed that...' or 'One expert has said that...'.

As well as providing information, you should organise this information logically using subheadings and bullet points. Include some facts, statistics and opinions, any of which could be quotations. They do not need to be completely accurate you can invent things. However, remember that this is supposed to be non-fiction, so keep it realistic.

ACTIVITY 7 — A04 A05 — SKILLS: PROBLEM SOLVING, ADAPTIVE LEARNING, CREATIVITY

▼ WRITING AN INFORMATION LEAFLET

Write an answer to the question on page 192, planning it first using something like the following table.

Introduction	
Paragraph 2	The neighbourhood.
Paragraph 3	The wider town or environment.
Paragraph 4	Things worth seeing and doing.
Conclusion	

Alternatively, you could choose to use a spider diagram to help you plan.

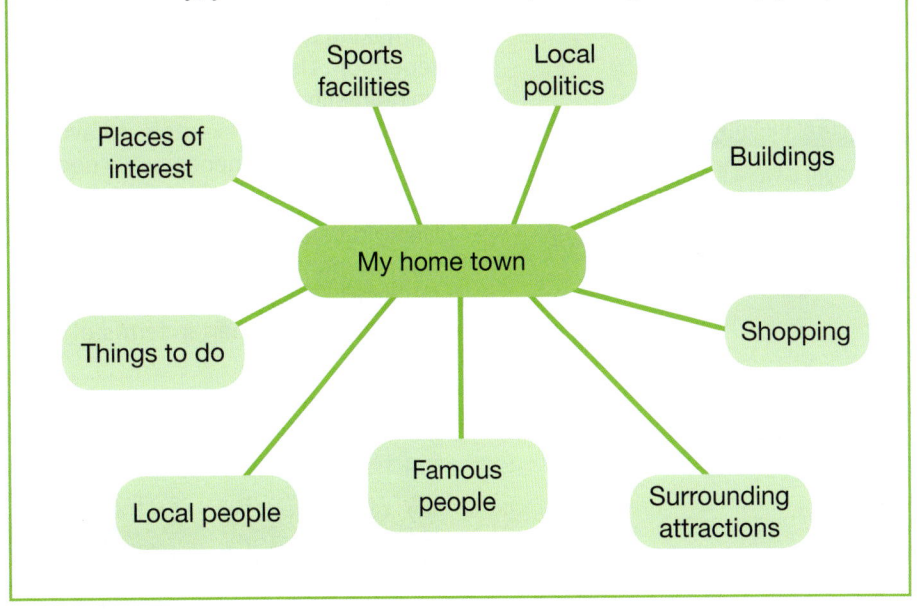

Spider diagram centred on "My home town" with branches to: Sports facilities, Local politics, Buildings, Shopping, Surrounding attractions, Famous people, Local people, Things to do, Places of interest.

ACTIVITY 8 — A02 A04 — SKILLS: ANALYSIS, ADAPTIVE LEARNING, CREATIVITY

▼ EXTENDED DESCRIPTION

An information guide can include some descriptive writing. The main aim is to bring the topic to life with some vivid phrasing and interesting word choices.

Re-read the information guide that you wrote for Activity 7. Have you included any extended descriptive sections? Could you add some now? Look back at some of the extracts in the Anthology to remind yourself of some examples of good descriptive writing.

LEARNING OBJECTIVES

This lesson will help you to:
- select the right vocabulary to make your writing more precise, clear and effective.

VOCABULARY FOR EFFECT

Vocabulary choice improves with reading and practice. When an author's use of vocabulary is excellent, it makes the text engaging and interesting and it makes the writer appear skilful and authoritative. It is a matter of choosing individual words and the phrases into which they are combined. When thinking about vocabulary choice, it can be helpful to subdivide it into different aspects: register, variety, impact, the context of word, decoration or colour and signposting.

REGISTER

The register of a text is the way in which vocabulary is chosen for a particular audience. For example, if you are writing a letter to a friend or giving a talk to your class, you will use a more informal register than if you are writing a formal letter to the school governors or headteacher.

VARIETY

Variety can be achieved by finding alternative ways of saying similar things or making similar points. For example, you could use **synonyms** instead of repetition. Using the same word more than once can make your writing feel uninteresting and repetitive. Most words offer you plenty of synonyms to choose from. For example, to avoid repeating the word 'important', you could use 'significant', 'necessary', 'needed', 'vital', 'crucial', 'non-negotiable' or 'top priority'.

Using different synonyms is not just for the sake of variety – words of similar but not identical meaning may suit the content better than others. For example, the word 'imaginative' has different associations to 'ingenious', even though they are not far apart in terms of their meaning.

SUBJECT VOCABULARY

synonym a word that shares the same meaning as another word; for example, 'quick' might be a synonym for 'fast'.

ACTIVITY 1 — AO1 — SKILLS: ANALYSIS

▼ FINDING AND CHOOSING SYNONYMS

Use your own knowledge, a thesaurus or dictionary to find several synonyms each for the following common words: 'bad', 'terrible', 'good', 'brilliant', 'idea', 'interesting'.

ACTIVITY 2 — AO1 — SKILLS: ANALYSIS

▼ LOOKING FOR SYNONYMS

Find more synonyms for the following words: 'happy', 'unhappy', 'success', 'failure', 'do', 'go', 'achieve'. Make sure the words are grammatically equivalent (that is, if you are looking for a synonym for an adjective, you find other adjectives).

PAPER 1 — TRANSACTIONAL WRITING 195

GENERAL VOCABULARY

repetition saying the same thing more than once to highlight its importance

ACTIVITY 3 — AO4 AO5 — SKILLS: ANALYSIS, INNOVATION

▼ REPETITION AS A RHETORICAL TECHNIQUE

Repetition can be a good rhetorical technique if it is used skilfully, but if it is used badly it can weaken the impact of your writing. Re-write the following text, replacing the words 'point' and 'people' with different synonyms and trying to make the sentences more interesting.

> Social networking does have many good points. One is that it helps friends stay in touch; another point is that you can talk to people whenever you like, and this helps people in many ways; a third point is that people can introduce friends to other people very easily.

WORDS IN CONTEXT

Words do not create much impact on their own. They react with those around them in the mind of the reader. A chain of words may be linked by their subject matter if, for example, they are taken from the specialist vocabulary of the topic. A chain of words could also be linked by tone or feeling: for example, a group of positive words and phrases, or a group of words and phrases that create a dramatic effect. If you look through any of the texts featured in this book, you will find examples of different word chains.

IMPACT

Your vocabulary choice can be crucial in creating impact, especially in text that is intended to be heard, such as a speech. For example, whether you are aiming to describe or persuade, techniques such as onomatopoeia and alliteration can add force to a sentence. For example, 'lead us towards a *dark* and *desperate* situation' uses alliteration to draw attention to the adjectives describing the nature of the situation.

EMOTIVE LANGUAGE

Using emotive language can certainly add impact to your argument. For example, you may be writing about climate change and want to shock your reader into action. To do this, you need to emphasise the scale of the problem by choosing a more powerful word than 'problem'. For example, you could use 'catastrophe', 'disaster' or 'calamity'.

KEY POINT

Using words for impact has to be judged carefully. If a word is too weak then there is not enough power in the sentence, but if a word is too strong you risk sounding melodramatic.

Compare the following sentences. Which one do you think has a greater impact?

> If we ignore alternative energy sources now, we will soon be facing a problem.

> If we ignore alternative energy sources now, we will soon be facing a catastrophe.

CONNOTATIONS

You can guide your reader's reactions by thinking about the connotations of your vocabulary choice. Look at the table on page 196. Each of the suggested adjectives could be used to finish the sentences, as they have similar meanings, but they have different connotations that may affect your reader's response.

PAPER 1 — TRANSACTIONAL WRITING

▲ Which adjective would you use to complete the sentence 'Having a job outside school makes me...'?

▼ SENTENCE	▼ ADJECTIVE	▼ CONNOTATIONS
'Having a job outside school makes me…'	exhausted	extreme physical fatigue
	drained	emptiness, suggesting that there is nothing left in the speaker
	sleepy	childishness that should not be taken too seriously
'Computer games are often…'	ruthless	lack of feeling or regard for others
	barbaric	uncivilised
	brutal	uncaring violence

The words in the table are also emotive words, meaning that they trigger an emotional response and therefore engage the audience. Such words are essential in storytelling, as well as in writing to argue and persuade.

Using words with particular connotations can be very effective in arguing for or against a statement. For example, if you are arguing in favour of euthanasia, you could describe it as 'a humane method'. However, if you are arguing against it, you could describe it as 'a licence to murder'. The connotations of the words 'humane' and 'murder' will influence the way in which your audience thinks about the subject.

Look at pages 304–305 to remind yourself of other ways in which vocabulary can be used for effect.

ACTIVITY 4 — AO4 AO5

SKILLS: PROBLEM SOLVING, ADAPTIVE LEARNING, CREATIVITY

▼ PERSUASIVE VOCABULARY

Write an opening paragraph for the following exam-style question, focusing on vocabulary to persuade the reader.

▶ The editor of your school newspaper has asked for contributions in response to this topic:

'Computer games are good for you as well as fun.'

You can write in favour of the statement or against it. Remember to choose vocabulary for its impact and for its connotations.

DECORATION OR COLOUR

In writing to describe, you often appeal to the reader's senses by including details such as sounds, smells, feelings and tastes. In other forms of writing, where you may not use description (for example, when you are writing to argue), you can introduce similar sensory effects by using figurative language.

This is why a writer might say that an unpopular idea went down 'like a lead balloon', or that a good leader is a 'knight in shining armour'. Although both of these phrases are clichés, they still enliven the writing, and more original phrases will have a greater effect.

SUBJECT VOCABULARY

clichés phrases that are used so often that they start to lose their impact

PAPER 1 — TRANSACTIONAL WRITING

Decorative language can also be used in informative writing. An information guide such as the one that you wrote in response to Activity 7 on page 193 can be livened up and made more interesting for the reader by using some of the following techniques.

SUBJECT VOCABULARY

pun an amusing use of a word or phrase that has two meanings, or of words that have the same sound but different meanings

irony using words to convey a meaning that is completely opposite to their apparent meaning

litotes ironic understatement used to mean something by saying its opposite

▼ TECHNIQUE	▼ EXAMPLE
Make the description vivid	Varied adjectives and adverbs.
Exaggerate	'…has some of the finest views in the south-west…'
Use humour	This might include puns, or exaggerated or unusual vocabulary.
Invent quotations, within reason	'The manager of the local football club says that it is "the ideal place for a new sports pitch"…'
Use irony or litotes	'…perhaps not the most inviting of buildings…'

SIGNPOSTING

Try to use 'signposting' vocabulary so that your points are more clearly structured. This is especially useful in speeches, where the paragraphing has to be heard, not seen. Some examples are given in the following table.

▼ PURPOSE	▼ EXAMPLES
To order ideas	'Firstly', 'secondly', 'moreover', 'furthermore', 'in addition', 'finally'…
To introduce reasons or consequences	'Therefore', 'as a result', 'consequently'…
To give alternatives	'On the other hand', 'nevertheless', 'however', 'in contrast'…
To develop ideas	'To develop this further', 'what this means is', 'in support of this'…

ACTIVITY 5 — A04 — A05 — SKILLS: ANALYSIS, ADAPTIVE LEARNING, CREATIVITY

▼ USING VOCABULARY FOR EFFECT

Re-write the information guide that you wrote in response to Activity 7 on page 193. Try to improve its readability by including more vocabulary for effect.

LEARNING OBJECTIVES

This lesson will help you to:
- understand how you can control sentences for greater impact.

SENTENCES FOR EFFECT

Consciously structuring your sentences will help your writing to make an impression on readers.

SENTENCE OPENINGS

The simplest way to ensure variety in your sentence structure is to think about the first words of each sentence and try to make them different from the others. Less experienced writers often start their sentences in similar ways, but the following table lists some different methods of opening sentences.

▼ TYPE OF WORD	▼ EXAMPLES
A pronoun I, you, he, she, it, we, they, my, your	'I write to you as a concerned…'
A preposition above, behind, between, near, for, with	'In all of our towns, there are…'
A present participle (or -ing word) thinking, watching, caring, making	'Looking at the state of the parks in our area…'
An adjective huge, beautiful, terrible, strange	'Noisy, threatening lorries rumble past…'
An adverb (usually end in -ly) happily, unfortunately, unhelpfully	'Alarmingly, the facts are…'
A conjunction (subordinate clause + main clause) if, although, because, when, while	'Although there are limits to the amount of money available…'

ACTIVITY 1 — A04 A05 — SKILLS: PROBLEM SOLVING, ADAPTIVE LEARNING, CREATIVITY

▼ VARYING YOUR SENTENCE OPENINGS

Using at least five of the styles of sentence opener in the table, write different openings for an answer to this exam-style question.

▶ **Explain how you think we could improve our efficiency in recycling.**

STRUCTURING SENTENCES

LONG COMPLEX SENTENCES

Complex sentences, containing one or more subordinate clauses, are good for conveying information or ideas, so try using them in explanations and arguments. They give an impression of fluent thinking, although you should be careful not to let a sentence ramble as you may lose your reader's attention. The following text is an example of a complex sentence. What impression does it give?

> While some people think that global warming is a natural phenomenon that has happened many times before in the Earth's history, others, looking hard at the scientific evidence, are convinced that we are mainly responsible.

| PAPER 1 | TRANSACTIONAL WRITING | 199 |

> **KEY POINT**
>
> Concentrate on the ends of your sentences to make maximum effect. Short sentences ending with the main point or a memorable phrase make more impact.

Many subordinate clauses begin with adverbial conjunctions, such as 'because', 'if', 'while', 'when', 'so that', 'after', 'before' and so on. These conjunctions play an important part in putting your ideas in order and linking thoughts together in a complex sentence.

ENDING FOR IMPACT

You can structure your sentences to ensure that the main point is emphasised. The last words of a sentence tend to stand out because they are read or heard most recently, so it is a good technique to place important words at the end of a sentence. Compare the following sentences and their endings.

> The government can just ignore it, despite all the work and research.
>
> The final insult is that, after all the work and research, the government can just ignore it.

The second sentence places the main point of the sentence at the end, where it is emphasised, and is therefore a bit more powerful than the first.

THE LONG AND THE SHORT

Short, punchy, single-clause sentences can add impact to an argument, or add variety or surprise to a description or piece of information. Short sentences are particularly effective when they follow a longer multi-clause sentence.

For example, if you used a long and complex sentence to explain a particular point, you could follow it with a simple statement such as 'They are right' or 'We need it now' to emphasise the point.

ACTIVITY 2 — A04 — A05 — **SKILLS** ▶ CRITICAL THINKING, ANALYSIS

▼ WRITING TO MAKE AN IMPRESSION

Look at the exam-style question.

▶ 'Television is mostly a waste of time and distracts us from better things we could be doing.' Write an argument giving your views on this statement.

Write an introduction, using the skills that you have just learned, to make an impression on the reader.

▲ A waste of time?

THE IMPORTANCE OF PUNCTUATION

Punctuating sentences correctly is not just for the sake of showing that you can do it. It also directly affects the impact you have on the reader.

One of the errors that many students make is using the comma splice, which is the name given to a comma used where there should be a full stop, a semi-colon or colon, or a comma with a conjunction. For many readers, the comma splice interrupts fluent reading.

▼ THE COMMA SPLICE	▼ CORRECT ALTERNATIVES
The school sets too much homework, this is why a lot of students are demotivated.	…too much homework. This is why…
	…too much homework: this is why…
	…too much homework, which is why…

LEARNING OBJECTIVES

This lesson will help you to:
- understand how to write effective openings and conclusions to your writing.

OPENINGS AND CONCLUSIONS

One of the benefits of planning is that you are less likely to write a weak or uncertain opening because you have thought about what you are going to write. A mistake that students can make if they have not planned their response is to simply repeat words from the question with a phrase such as, 'In this article I am going to write about…'. Since your reader already knows this, it is a waste of time and is uninteresting.

OPENINGS

When you read a text, you probably expect the opening to be interesting, and to grab your attention in some way. The following table lists some effective techniques that you can use to improve your openings. Which technique you use will depend on the task.

TECHNIQUE	EXAMPLE
A rhetorical question	'How often do you take action when you feel something ought to be done?'
An arresting or controversial statement	'It's not children who need educating about recycling – it's the grown-ups who ought to know better.'
A surprising or shocking fact or statistic	'The unreleased energy contained in the average dustbin each year could power a television for 5,000 hours.'
A relevant quotation	'We live in a disposable society. It's easier to throw things out than to fix them.'
A short and relevant anecdote	'I have found it saves money to reuse the plastic containers…'

HINT

Remember that your statistics do not have to be accurate in the exam; they just have to sound plausible. However, if you are writing for homework, you should check that your statistics are correct.

KEY POINT

The pressure of getting started can often lead to a bland opening, written just to get something on the page. It pays to resist this pressure and think through your first words.

ACTIVITY 1 — AO4 AO5

SKILLS: PROBLEM SOLVING, ADAPTIVE LEARNING, CREATIVITY

USING DIFFERENT KINDS OF OPENING

Write two possible openings to a response to the following question.

▶ Write an article arguing for or against the proposal that the smacking of children should be made illegal.

PAPER 1 — TRANSACTIONAL WRITING

ACTIVITY 2 — A01 A02 — SKILLS: CRITICAL THINKING, ANALYSIS

▼ EFFECTIVE OPENINGS

The following extracts are the openings of some of the texts in this book. Read each one and then write down the features that make them effective openings.

EXTRACT A
'I'm a storyteller. And I would like to tell you a few personal stories about what I like to call "the danger of the single story."'

EXTRACT B
'I saw a thousand hungry, lean, scared and betrayed faces as I criss-crossed Somalia between the end of 1991 and December 1992, but there is one I will never forget.'

EXTRACT C
'I have a dream…I have a dream that one day this nation will rise up and live out the true meaning of its creed.'

EXTRACT D
'Paper has more patience than people.'

CONCLUSIONS

An effective conclusion will leave the reader with a strong impression and should make them remember the point that you have made. A weak conclusion will leave them with less to remember. Different techniques can be used to achieve a strong conclusion, as shown in the following table.

▼ TECHNIQUE	▼ EXAMPLE
A positive, upbeat note	'This is surely a recipe for success.'
A warning	'If we do not act soon, then it may be too late to save…'
An appeal for action	'We must act now – and act quickly – to save our heritage.'
A question for people to think about	'Couldn't that be the best outcome of them all?'
A vivid image	'Just a single light, shining in the dark.'
A link with the opening, though not repeating the wording	'Perhaps the question that we asked at the outset was the wrong question. Perhaps we should ask instead…'

ACTIVITY 3 — A04 A05 — SKILLS: PROBLEM SOLVING, ADAPTIVE LEARNING, CREATIVITY

▼ USING DIFFERENT KINDS OF CONCLUSION

Look back at the two openings that you wrote in Activity 1. Write two possible conclusions to the pieces, using different techniques.

ACTIVITY 4 — A02 — SKILLS: ANALYSIS, REASONING

▼ EFFECTIVE CONCLUSIONS

Find three examples of conclusions from extracts in this book and explain why they are effective.

LEARNING OBJECTIVES

This lesson will help you to:
- understand the importance of planning
- improve your planning techniques.

IDEAS AND PLANNING

It is very helpful to plan before writing. Once you have a plan, you will feel more confident that you can write a successful piece and this confidence will show in your writing. Since you have about 45 minutes for Section B, you can spend 5–10 minutes planning.

PLANNING TECHNIQUES

You can plan using spider diagrams, thought clouds, lists and so on: it doesn't matter what you use as long as it works for you.

A good idea to start with is to jot down the three primary things about any piece you write: the **purpose**, the **audience** and the **form**. You can base some ideas on this triplet. For example, refer to the audience, especially when writing a speech; state your purpose clearly; and use appropriate language for the form. Jotting down your ideas will also help ensure that you do not forget them.

Once you have planned, the next thing to do is to generate some ideas. One idea per paragraph is a good start.

▲ Spider diagrams can be useful for planning.

ACTIVITY 1 — AO4

SKILLS: PROBLEM SOLVING, REASONING, ADAPTIVE LEARNING, CREATIVITY

▼ STRATEGIES FOR PLANNING

If you can think of two contrasting approaches to the topic, it will help you to make relevant points. Consider the following question.

▶ **Write an article for a local or school magazine on the topic: 'Not enough attention is paid to the problem of stress in the lives of modern teenagers'.**

A student has used the following table to plan their response to this question. If you choose to use this method, you do not need to fill out all the rows: five or six should be enough for the essay that you write in the exam. You will know when your plan is detailed enough, because at that stage you should feel that the essay will be straightforward to write.

▼ POINT	▼ APPROACH 1	▼ APPROACH 2
Time perspective	The past – was life less stressful and how? Working hours? Less competition? More stability in work and communities?	The present and the future – we are healthier, but are we under more pressure in hearts and minds? If so why? Less family stability?
Views of different groups		Group B: Working class young people – more worried about the future of the planet and their own future etc.?
Anecdotes to tell	Things that involved you or a friend.	Something that involved someone you have heard of.
Different aspects of the subject	Types and causes of stress: work, health.	
How to tackle problem	Step 1: understand causes.	
Gender angle	Boys.	Girls.

Possible benefits or problems		
Timeframe	Stage 1.	
What to do now – warning for future?	Can't avoid stress but must organise life so that each individual is not overloaded.	

ACTIVITY 2 — AO4
SKILLS: PROBLEM SOLVING, REASONING, ADAPTIVE LEARNING, CREATIVITY

▼ PLANNING A REPORT WITH RECOMMENDATIONS

> Your local council wants to improve provisions for teenagers in the neighbourhood. Write a report for the council explaining how, in your view, the local facilities might be improved.

Plan the report first. You could include:
- what facilities exist at present
- your ideas about how they can be improved
- ideas about providing new facilities.

Consider the following plan. What would you do differently?

Introduction
- facilities which are widely believed to be inadequate
- many ideas are being discussed
- motivate and engage teenagers: anecdotes or statistics of recent problems

Main point 1: Present facilities
- present state: what we have now (e.g. not enough land)
- poor conditions: e.g. football pitch / tennis court (quote expert views)

Main point 2: Improvements suggested
- youth centre: redecorate with help of teenagers
- repair sports pitch: apply for sponsorship from sports company
- provide more computers and video games in local library

Main point 3: New facilities
- bowling alley: give an estimate of how much money this could generate
- café to be managed by volunteers

Conclusion
- summarise the benefits of suggestions

HINT
Some exam questions will contain prompts of this kind. They give a useful place to start structuring your answer. In terms of the previous planning table, the three main points opposite would fit the 'time perspective' approach. Notice that, although this is mainly a piece of writing to explain, it clearly gives opportunities to inform, to describe and to persuade.

ACTIVITY 3 — AO4
SKILLS: PROBLEM SOLVING, REASONING, ADAPTIVE LEARNING, CREATIVITY

▼ PRACTISE YOUR PLANNING

> Write a speech for your class or year group, in which you try to persuade them to participate in the school's extra-curricular activities.

Plan your response to this question. You could try using the planning table or another strategy, such as spider diagrams or lists. Consider your own experiences and how you could use them to persuade others that the extra-curricular activities at your school are valuable.

204 PAPER 1 — TRANSACTIONAL WRITING

LEARNING OBJECTIVES

This lesson will help you to:
- understand how the methods and techniques discussed in this chapter can combine to make a good answer.

PUTTING IT INTO PRACTICE

In the exam in Section B you will have to answer one question from a choice of two. You should aim to spend 45 minutes writing your response to the transactional writing question.

EXAM-STYLE QUESTION

AO4 AO5

SKILLS CRITICAL THINKING, ANALYSIS, ADAPTIVE LEARNING, CREATIVITY

'Schools have a duty to continually improve conditions for students.'

You have been asked to give a speech in which you express your views on this statement.

Your speech may include:
- who should have responsibility for improvements
- whether improvements would help students
- any other points you wish to make.

Your response will be marked for the accurate and appropriate use of vocabulary, spelling, punctuation and grammar. **(45 marks)**

ACTIVITY 1 — AO4
SKILLS PROBLEM SOLVING, REASONING, ADAPTIVE LEARNING, CREATIVITY

▼ IDEAS AND PLANNING

Using the following table to help you, make your own plan for the exam-style question.

▼ PARAGRAPH PLAN	▼ TECHNIQUES TO USE
■ Intro: mention poor conditions – suggest there is an answer.	■ Rhetorical questions.
■ Para 1: argue link between environment and work (Ofsted, etc.).	■ Direct address to reader.
■ Para 2: what some people think (to counter).	■ Alliteration – 'dreary dining rooms'.
■ Para 3: persuasive questions.	■ Imperatives – short final sentence.
■ Para 4: argue what is minimum needed now – joint action needed.	■ Connectives – 'moreover', 'firstly', so on.
■ Para 5: What are current plans to improve?	■ Use 'us' and 'we'.
■ Conclusion: politicians, etc.	■ Variety of sentences.
	■ Facts and statistics.
	■ Some informal vocab.

HINT

Think of planning first. Notice that the question asks you to argue and persuade: 'argue' means that you should present your own views and explain why others are wrong; 'persuade' means that you need to think about your audience and how to encourage them to think the way that you do.

SAMPLE ANSWER

Read through the following answer to the exam-style question and the comments.

For how much longer must students in school put up with dilapidated classrooms, sub-standard social areas and dreary dining rooms? Starting with a rhetorical question is a good way to engage the audience from the start.

a poor quality environment leads to poor quality work Repetition of 'poor quality' makes this point more powerful.

INTRODUCTION
For how much longer must students in school put up with dilapidated classrooms, sub-standard social areas and dreary dining rooms? Ambitious and hardworking students like your children and students deserve better.

DEVELOP IDEAS
The first reason why conditions must improve is that **a poor quality environment leads to poor quality work.** Substandard work restricts students' chances of

PAPER 1 — TRANSACTIONAL WRITING

With an under-qualified workforce, the whole nation will suffer. The student is using a formal register and referring to large scale ideas, which adds weight to the argument. linked statements to develop a strong point.

Cluttered classrooms, foul toilet facilities and inadequate outdoor space Here, the student has chosen adjectives carefully as emotive language.

ver 60% of schools operate out of shoddy buildings. Statistics make the argument sound more assured and well-researched.

you The focus has shifted away from facts, to the audience. Using second person is highly persuasive and makes the issue more personal.

The minimum that our children deserve is this: attractive, airy buildings with no hiding-room for bullies; adequate indoor and outdoor recreational space; appealing eating areas, offering a variety of good value, high quality meals and snacks; sufficient hygienic and well-maintained toilet facilities so that no-one wastes time in queues. A list of detailed, well thought out ideas adds momentum to the argument here.

Our children's future depends upon it. Ending with a short sentence and emotive language is a powerful way to conclude.

This argument is well-written and highly persuasive due to judicious use of techniques such as rhetorical questions, statistics and repetition. The formal register and statistics adds weight to the points made. Sentence structures have been chosen for effect, and often help to build momentum.

---

achieving good qualifications. With an under-qualified workforce, the whole nation will suffer.

Ofsted reports repeatedly expose the grim quality of Britain's school premises. Cluttered classrooms, foul toilet facilities and inadequate outdoor space are all too commonly reported: over 60% of schools operate out of shoddy buildings. It is time that the school authorities took action.

Some people think that it is not worth providing decent facilities for children. They think that youngsters won't take care of expensive resources. But how are children ever to learn to value such resources, if they never encounter them?

MOVE ONTO PERSUASION

Have you ever asked yourself why school are so shoddily equipped? Do you want your children to be educated in buildings as dreary as the ones you attended? Or are you prepared to stand up and demand that something is done?

The citizens of a rich and modern state deserve up-to-date conditions in which to study and work. Your children are the future citizens of such a state and if we want their best efforts and loyalty to the nation, we must show them that we value them. How better to do this than to provide them with schools fit for the 21st century? The last Labour government started the Building Schools for the Future project. What a pity that the money ran out in the recession.

We're coming out of that now. If we all pull together we can make change happen. The minimum that our children deserve is this: attractive, airy buildings with no hiding-room for bullies; adequate indoor and outdoor recreational space; appealing eating areas, offering a variety of good value, high quality meals and snacks; sufficient hygienic and well-maintained toilet facilities so that no-one wastes time in queues. Surely you would not settle for less for your children? Let us demand from our politicians that they tell us what plans they have to improve schools. If they cannot answer satisfactorily, then we will not elect them.

CONCLUSION

Undoubtedly we are agreed that something must be done. Indeed, we are agreed on what must be done. Politicians will try to block us by pleading poverty and putting off the time for action. Do not be deflected. If we act now to insist on upgraded school conditions, our children will thrive; if we do not, they will suffer and may never forgive us. Ladies and gentlemen, use your influence now. Our children's future depends upon it.

ACTIVITY 2 | **AO4** **AO5** | **SKILLS** CRITICAL THINKING, ANALYSIS, REASONING

▼ MARKING AN ANSWER

Using the following mark scheme, assess sample answer and give it two marks: one for AO4, out of 27, and one for AO5, out of 18.

MARK SCHEME FOR AO4 (UP TO 27 MARKS)

Level 3: 12–17 marks
- Communicates clearly.
- Expectations/requirements of the intended reader.
- Appropriate use of form, tone and register.

Level 4: 18–22 marks
- Communicates successfully.
- A secure realisation of the writing task according to the writer's purpose and the expectations/requirements of the intended reader is shown.
- Effective use of form, tone and register.

Level 5: 23–27 marks
- Communication is perceptive and subtle.
- Task is sharply focused on purpose and the expectations/requirements of the intended reader.
- Sophisticated control of text structure, skilfully sustained paragraphing as appropriate and/or assured application of a range of cohesive devices.

MARK SCHEME FOR AO5 (UP TO 18 MARKS)

Level 3: 8–11 marks
- Develops and connects appropriate information and ideas; structural and grammatical features and paragraphing make the meaning clear.
- Uses accurate and varied punctuation, adapting sentence structure as appropriate.

Level 4: 12–15 marks
- Manages information and ideas, with structural and grammatical features used cohesively and deliberately across the text.
- Positions a range of punctuation for clarity, managing sentence structures for deliberate effect.

Level 5: 16–18 marks
- Manipulates complex ideas, utilising a range of structural and grammatical features to support coherence and cohesion.
- Uses extensive vocabulary strategically; rare spelling errors do not detract from overall meaning.
- Punctuates writing with accuracy to aid emphasis and precision, using a range of sentence structures accurately and selectively to achieve particular effects.

| PAPER 1 | TRANSACTIONAL WRITING | 207 |

ACTIVITY 3 — AO4 AO5
SKILLS: CRITICAL THINKING, ANALYSIS, REASONING

▼ MARKING AN ANSWER

Now read the following sample answer and mark it the same way that you marked the previous sample answer. Remember to give it one mark for AO4, out of 27, and a second mark for AO5, out of 18.

> **Why is school so badly equipped? Do you want your children to be educated in buildings as boring as the ones you attended? Perhaps you should be willing to try to take some action to improve the situation.**
>
> **The people of a rich and modern state need up-to-date conditions in their schools. Your children are the future of this country and we need to show them that we value them.**
>
> **So we need schools fit for the 21st century? We've got a few, but where are the rest?**
>
> **What we want is: spacious buildings we're not always bumping into people; plenty of space outdoors too; good food and snacks; better toilet facilities – these are what you'd like for your children.**
>
> **If we do something about it we can make things happen. We need to get our politicians to improve schools, but if they don't come up with the goods, then we don't have to elect them.**

ACTIVITY 4 — AO4 AO5
SKILLS: PROBLEM SOLVING, ADAPTIVE LEARNING, CREATIVITY

▼ PRACTISE YOUR WRITING

The government is encouraging debate on how to tackle the problem of poor diet and lack of exercise. Write an article explaining some of the actions that they could take and arguing that they should act quickly and effectively.

KEY POINT

Include a clear and urgent call to action. The writing can be figurative, but make sure it is imperative.

▲ Poor diet and lack of exercise is a problem in the UK

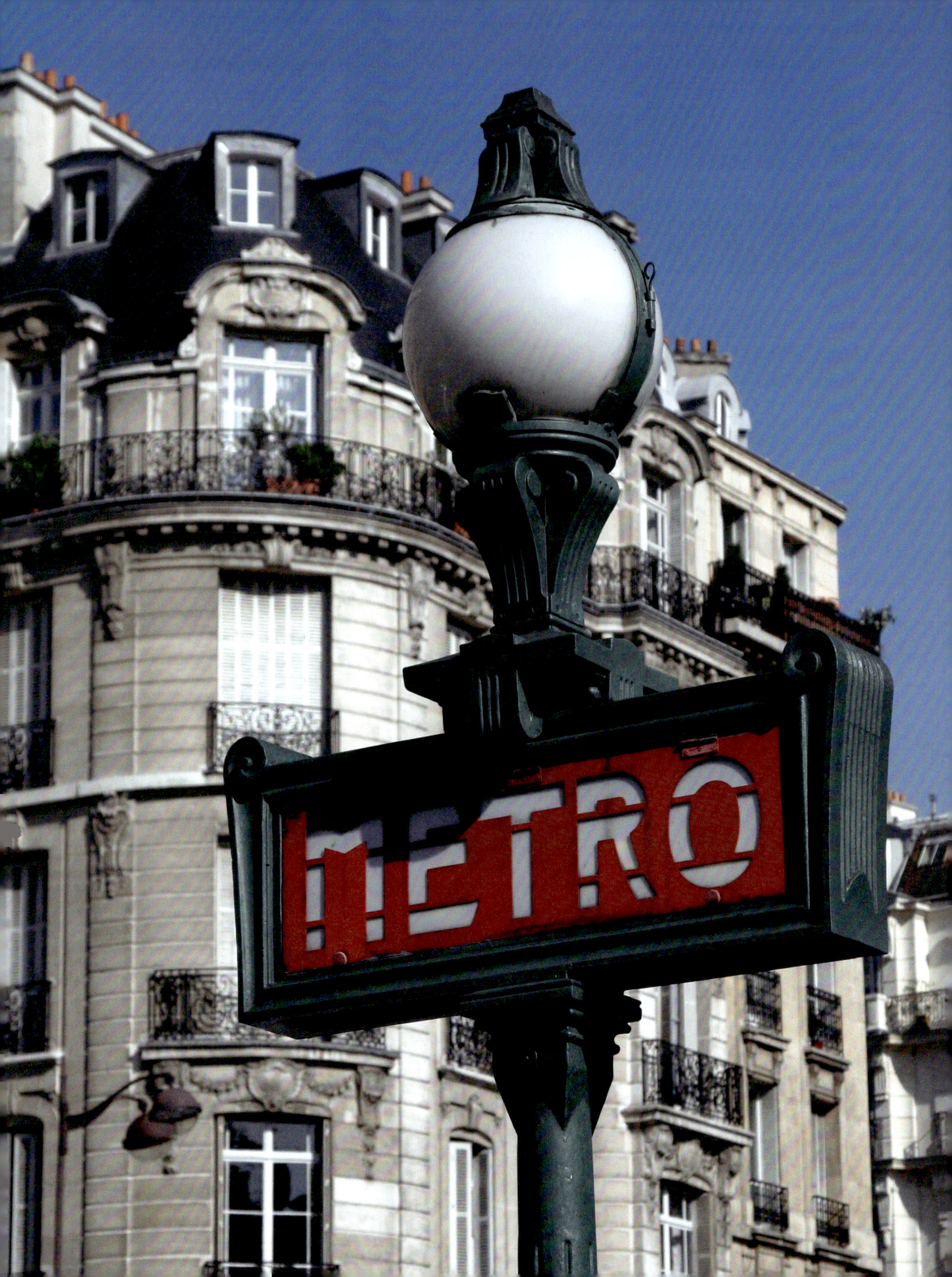
METRO

PAPER 2: POETRY AND PROSE TEXTS AND IMAGINATIVE WRITING

Assessment Objective 1

Read and understand a variety of texts, selecting and interpreting information, ideas and perspectives

Assessment Objective 2

Understand and analyse how writers use linguistic and structural devices to achieve their effects

This chapter focuses on Paper 2: Poetry and Prose Texts and Imaginative Writing of the English Language A course. Working through these lessons and activities will help you to develop the reading and writing skills that you will need for the Paper 2 exam.

The chapter is split into the following sections:
- Fiction texts
- Text Anthology: Poetry and prose texts
- Imaginative writing.

Paper 2 is worth 40% of the total marks for the course and is split into two sections:
- Section A: Poetry and prose texts
- Section B: Imaginative writing.

In section A of your exam, you will need to be able to meet the Assessment Objectives AO1 and AO2.

In section B of your exam, you will need to be able to meet the Assessment Objectives AO4 and AO5.

Assessment Objective 4

Communicate effectively and imaginatively, adapting form, tone and register of writing for specific purposes and audiences

Assessment Objective 5

Write clearly, using a range of vocabulary and sentence structures, with appropriate paragraphing and accurate spelling, grammar and punctuation

In Paper 2, the assessment objectives are worth the following amounts.
AO1 – 8%
AO2 – 12%
AO4 – 12%
AO5 – 8%

210 PAPER 2 — READING SKILLS: FICTION TEXTS

LEARNING OBJECTIVES

This lesson will help you to:
- begin reading and interpreting poetry and prose texts.

TYPES OF TEXT

In the Pearson Edexcel Anthology, you will read a variety of poetry and prose extracts. You will need to analyse and interpret them in order to answer questions in the exam.

APPROACHING PROSE

When you read a prose text, start thinking about it by asking yourself the following questions.
- How is the story told?
- Who is telling it?
- Where is it located?

Next, considering the features of the text will help you to analyse what the writer is doing. These features could include:
- setting
- narrative perspective
- characterisation
- descriptive techniques
- effect, or how it makes the reader feel
- possible interpretation or interpretations of the text's implicit meanings.

KEY POINT

It is useful to have a series of questions in your mind when approaching any prose text. These are some examples, but you can think of more.

APPROACHING POETRY

When you read a poem, you should also start by considering the following questions.
- What is it about?
- How does it make you feel?
- What does it mean to you personally?

Then consider how the poet communicates meaning and feeling. This could be achieved by:
- imagery
- linguistic techniques
- rhythm and rhyme
- structure and form
- possible interpretation or interpretations of the text's implicit meaning.

Read the following poem and then complete Activity 1.

▼ 'LINES WRITTEN IN EARLY SPRING' BY WILLIAM WORDSWORTH

I heard a thousand blended notes,
While in a grove I sate reclined,
In that sweet mood when pleasant thoughts
Bring sad thoughts to the mind.

To her fair works did nature link
The human soul that through me ran;

5

And much it grieved my heart to think
What man has made of man.

Through primrose-tufts, in that sweet bower,
The periwinkle trailed its wreathes; 10
And 'tis my faith that every flower
Enjoys the air it breathes.

The birds around me hopped and played:
Their thoughts I cannot measure,
But the least motion which they made, 15
It seemed a thrill of pleasure.

The budding twigs spread out their fan,
To catch the breezy air;
And I think, do all I can,
That there was pleasure there. 20

If I these thoughts may not prevent,
If such be of my creed the plan,
Have I not reason to lament
What man has made of man?

creed Belief, particularly religious belief.

ACTIVITY 1 — AO1 — SKILLS: CRITICAL THINKING, ANALYSIS, INTERPRETATION

▼ APPROACHING POETRY

'Lines Written in Early Spring' is a famous poem by the British poet, William Wordsworth. It was first published in 1798 and explores the speaker's thoughts on nature and their surroundings before focusing on darker thoughts about humanity.

Re-read the poem carefully, then answer the following questions.

1 What do you think of the poem?
2 Which words or phrases do you particularly like?
3 Why are these words or phrases effective?
4 Where is the poem set?
5 Who is the narrator and what are they like?
6 What themes does the poem explore?
7 Write three Point-Evidence-Explain paragraphs exploring the ways in which the poet presents nature.

LEARNING OBJECTIVES

This lesson will help you to:

- understand how to identify figurative language
- consider how figurative language is used for effect in creating character, atmosphere and emotion.

FIGURATIVE LANGUAGE

Figurative language is used to create powerful imagery in texts. It can be used by writers or poets to create atmosphere, mood, tone and emotion, or to add to readers' understanding or to descriptions of character or setting.

Figurative language works by making comparisons between two things. It therefore provides the reader with a strong visual image to identify with. The most common figurative techniques are metaphor, simile and personification.

SUBJECT VOCABULARY

metaphor describing something by comparing it to an image which it resembles, in a way that says the object *is* the image
simile a description that says that an object is *like* an image rather than that *it is* the image
personification when something which is not human is made to sound human by attributing human qualities to it

ACTIVITY 1 — A04 — SKILLS: ANALYSIS, INNOVATION

▼ USING FIGURATIVE LANGUAGE

Look at the photos and write your own figurative descriptions of each. For example: *The amber flames leapt and danced*. 'Leapt' and 'danced' are personification, emphasising the active nature of the fire and likening it to a person dancing. *The beach was like a white ribbon of paper*. This simile conveys the colour and shape of the beach.

FIGURATIVE LANGUAGE IN POETRY

The following poems are excellent examples of how metaphor can be used in poetry.

READING SKILLS: FICTION TEXTS

> **KEY POINT**
>
> Similes and metaphors are sometimes confused. Remember that similes compare using 'like' or 'as', while metaphors make a more direct comparison of one thing to another. For example, 'She's as fierce as a tiger' is a simile, but 'She's a tiger when she's angry.' is a metaphor.

▼ 'LOVE IS...' BY ADRIAN HENRI

Love is feeling cold in the back of vans
Love is a fanclub with only two fans
Love is walking holding paintstained hands
Love is.

Love is fish and chips on winter nights 5
Love is blankets full of strange delights
Love is when you don't put out the light
Love is

Love is the presents in Christmas shops
Love is when you're feeling Top of the Pops 10
Love is what happens when the music stops
Love is

Love is white panties lying all forlorn
Love is pink nightdresses still slightly warm
Love is when you have to leave at dawn 15
Love is

Love is you and love is me
Love is prison and love is free
Love's what's there when you are away from me
Love is... 20

▼ 'VALENTINE' BY CAROL ANN DUFFY

Not a red rose or a satin heart.

I give you an onion.
It is a moon wrapped in brown paper.
It promises light
like the careful undressing of love. 5

Here.
It will blind you with tears
like a lover.
It will make your reflection
a wobbling photo of grief. 10

I am trying to be truthful.

Not a cute card or a kissogram.

I give you an onion.
Its fierce kiss will stay on your lips,
possessive and faithful 15
as we are,
for as long as we are.

Take it.
Its platinum loops shrink to a wedding-ring,
if you like. 20

Lethal.
Its scent will cling to your fingers,
cling to your knife.

ACTIVITY 2 — A03 A04 A05 — SKILLS: ANALYSIS, REASONING, INTERPRETATION, DECISION MAKING, CREATIVITY

▼ USING FIGURATIVE LANGUAGE IN POETRY

1. Re-read 'Love is...' and 'Valentine'. What similarities and differences can you find between the two poems' uses of metaphor?
2. Write your own metaphorical poem. Start with the words, 'All the world's a…'. Write it in pairs of lines, each pair introducing a metaphor and then explaining its relevance. For example:

    All the world's a rollercoaster,
    It spins around, its ups and downs…

FIGURATIVE LANGUAGE IN PROSE

In a text, settings can also be used to suggest a mood, ideas or feelings that are important to your wider reading of that text. Read the following extract carefully, considering the way in which the setting is described.

DID YOU KNOW?
Pathetic fallacy is very similar to personification. It is usually used to make inanimate objects or things reflect what is going on in the scene. For example, if the weather is hot and sunny, it usually represents a 'happy' story. If the weather is dark, cold and stormy, you can usually guess that something bad is going to happen.

▼ FROM *LORD OF THE FLIES*, BY WILLIAM GOLDING

Ralph disentangled himself cautiously and stole away through the branches. In a few seconds the fat boy's grunts were behind him and he was hurrying towards the screen that laid between him and the lagoon. He climbed over a broken trunk and was out of the jungle.

The shore was fledged with palm trees. These stood or leaned or reclined against the light and their green feathers were a hundred feet up in the air. The ground beneath them was a bank covered with coarse grass, torn everywhere by the upheavals of fallen trees, scattered with decaying coconuts and palm saplings. Behind this was the darkness of the forest proper and the open space of the scar. Ralph stood, one hand against a grey trunk, and screwed up his eyes against the shimmering water. Out there, perhaps a mile away, the white surf flinked on a coral reef, and beyond that the open sea was a dark blue. Within the irregular arc of the coral lagoon was still as a mountain lake – blue of all the shades a shadowy green and purple. The beach between the palm terrace and the water was a thin bow stave, endless apparently, for to Ralph's left the perspectives of palm and beach and water drew to a point at infinity; and always, almost visible was the heat.

| PAPER 2 | READING SKILLS: FICTION TEXTS | 215 |

DID YOU KNOW?

A Socratic circle has the following rules.

- Divide your class into two groups.
- The inner circle sits around desks and discusses the question amongst themselves. Only one person may speak at a time. Use an object to indicate who has the power to speak at any given moment.
- The outer circle must remain silent, but should take notes. Whose argument is the most persuasive? Who do you disagree with? Why?
- The inner circle should now be silent. The outer circle may now assess the inner circle's response, praising good points and adding suggestions or extending other points.

SUBJECT VOCABULARY

symbolic where a person, object or event is used by a writer to convey a meaning other than its literal meaning

juxtaposition putting two very different things close together in order to encourage comparison between them

KEY POINT

Use appropriate literary devices to engage your reader in feeling a sense of the place you have chosen.

▲ Golding sets his story on a remote Pacific island.

ACTIVITY 3 | **A01** | **A02** | **SKILLS** CRITICAL THINKING, ANALYSIS, INTERPRETATION

▼ **THINKING ABOUT FIGURATIVE LANGUAGE IN PROSE**

1 Annotate the extract from *Lord of the Flies*, considering the following two questions.
  ▶ How is the island described? How is the setting outside the island described? Do you think these places might be **symbolic**?
  ▶ How does the way in which this contrast is set up make the reader feel about the novel?
2 Make a Socratic circle and discuss the following question as a class.
  ▶ The island is described as 'torn everywhere' by uprooted trees and shadowed by the 'darkness of the forest'. Does Golding's **juxtaposition** of this with the beautiful 'white surf' and 'coral lagoon' around it forewarn the reader of the events about to unfold?

ACTIVITY 4 | **A04** | **A05** | **SKILLS** CREATIVITY, INNOVATION

▼ **A SENSE OF PLACE**

Write a short descriptive passage that gives a sense of place. You are not allowed to name the place, or say where it is. Concentrate on using language to describe it indirectly. Swap passages with a partner. Can you guess the place that your partner has described?

LEARNING OBJECTIVES

This lesson will help you to:
- understand and analyse how writers introduce characters
- develop fictional characters in your writing
- understand how writers develop and use setting and atmosphere.

CREATING CHARACTER, ATMOSPHERE AND EMOTION

Creating characters is not an easy job. Good writers carefully reveal aspects of a character's personality through a combination of description, behaviour and dialogue.

ACTIVITY 1 — AO4 AO5 — SKILLS: CREATIVITY, INNOVATION

▼ **WHAT'S IN YOUR POCKET?**

The best way to approach character is to put yourself in someone else's shoes or, in this case, pocket!

Create an imaginary character. Think of a few details about them such as their name, age and job. Now imagine which objects they might carry in their pocket or bag. Write down or draw at least three of these and put them into an envelope. You have now created your character's 'pocket' or 'bag'.

Swap envelopes with a partner. Remove the items from your partner's envelope, one item at a time. Try to imagine what kind of person would own these items. Share your ideas with your partner.

Write a short paragraph about the character that your partner created, using some of the items in their 'pocket' to develop the character.

▲ The things that you always carry around with you can reveal your character.

INTRODUCING A CHARACTER

It is often said that first impressions are the most important, and this is often true of fictional characters. The following extract from Christopher Isherwood's novel *Goodbye to Berlin* introduces the memorable and quirky character Sally Bowles.

▼ **FROM *GOODBYE TO BERLIN* BY CHRISTOPHER ISHERWOOD**

A few minutes later, Sally herself arrived.

"Am I terribly late, Fritz darling?"

"Only half of an hour, I suppose", Fritz drawled, beaming with proprietary pleasure. "May I introduce Mr Isherwood – Miss Bowles? Mr Isherwood is commonly known as Chris."

"I'm not," I said. "Fritz is about the only person who's ever called me Chris in my life."

Sally laughed. She was dressed in black silk, with a small cape over her shoulders and a little cap like a page-boy's stuck jauntily on one side of her head:

PAPER 2 | **READING SKILLS: FICTION TEXTS** | 217

KEY POINT
The introduction of a new fictional character is a key moment. The language you choose lays the foundations for filling out the character later.

> "Do you mind if I use your telephone, sweet?"
>
> "Sure. Go right ahead." Fritz caught my eye. "Come into the other room, Chris. I want to show you something." He was evidently longing to hear my first impressions of Sally, his new acquisition.
>
> "For heaven's sake, don't leave me alone with this man!" she exclaimed. "Or he'll seduce me down the telephone. He's most terribly passionate."
>
> As she dialed the number, I noticed that her finger-nails were painted emerald green, a colour unfortunately chosen, for it called attention to her hands, which were much stained by cigarette-smoking and as dirty as a little girl's. She was dark enough to be Fritz's sister. Her face was long and thin, powdered dead white. She had very large brown eyes which should have been darker, to match her hair and the pencil she used for her eyebrows.
>
> "Hilloo," she cooed, pursing her brilliant cherry lips as though she were going to kiss the mouthpiece: "Ist das Du, mein Liebling?" Her mouth opened in a fatuously sweet smile. Fritz and I sat watching her, like a performance at the theatre.

ACTIVITY 2 | **AO2** | **SKILLS** CREATIVITY, ANALYSIS, INTERPRETATION

▼ BUILDING A SENSE OF CHARACTER

Read the extract from *Goodbye to Berlin*. How does Isherwood build up a vivid sense of character in this extract? Consider his use of colour, the use of direct speech and any desciptions using adjectives and adverbs. Write at least two Point-Evidence-Explain paragraphs about this.

ACTIVITY 3 | **AO4** | **AO5** | **SKILLS** ADAPTIVE LEARNING, CREATIVITY, INNOVATION

▼ CHARACTER DEVELOPMENT

Using the techniques that you have considered, write your own short, vivid character description that begins with the description of your character's shoes. You could choose to develop your character based on the character created in Activity 1 or start with a new idea.

CONSIDERING CHARACTER

Consider the following prompts to help extend your understanding of characters. You can apply this to the Anthology texts.

- **How they appear to others**: What kinds of words are used to describe their features, build and clothing? What does the writer want to suggest to the reader about the character's behaviour, attitude or interests?
- **What they do**: What can the reader guess about the characters from their actions and behaviour?
- **What they say**: Does the writer use direct speech? What does this tell you about what the character thinks, feels or is likely to do?

- **How they say it**: How does the writer make the character speak? Are they always talking about the same thing? Do they have a particular way of talking, e.g. dialect, tone? What is the writer saying about their background, feelings or interests?
- **What other characters say or think about them**: How are you made to see them through other people's eyes? Do other characters like or dislike them, admire or despise them, trust or distrust them? Do you believe what others say about them?

ACTIVITY 4 — A01 A02

SKILLS: CRITICAL THINKING, ANALYSIS, REASONING, INTERPRETATION

▼ CHARACTERS IN POETRY

Character is not unique to prose; poems often present readers with strong and well-drawn characters. Read 'Dulce et Decorum Est' by Wilfred Owen and answer the following questions.

1. Why do the poem's characters remain nameless?
2. How is description of the gassed man used to build up a strong visual image of him?
3. What do the final two verses (lines 15–28) tell you about the narrator's relationship with death?
4. How does the poem make you feel about the narrator?
5. Why do you think Owen wrote this poem?

KEY POINT

Understanding character is a critical part of analysing a text. Authors can convey meaning through characters' words and actions and how they interact with each other. Characters can also be used to show how a writer feels about a bigger theme or issue.

▼ 'DULCE ET DECORUM EST' BY WILFRED OWEN

Bent double, like old beggars under sacks,
Knock-kneed, coughing like hags, we cursed through sludge,
Till on the haunting flares we turned our backs,
And towards our distant rest began to trudge.
Men marched asleep. Many had lost their boots,   5
But limped on, blood-shod. All went lame; all blind;
Drunk with fatigue; deaf even to the hoots
Of gas-shells dropping softly behind.

Gas! GAS! Quick, boys!—An ecstasy of fumbling
Fitting the clumsy helmets just in time,   10
But someone still was yelling out and stumbling
And flound'ring like a man in fire or lime.—
Dim through the misty panes and thick green light,
As under a green sea, I saw him drowning.

▲ Owen had deep empathy for his war comrades.

> In all my dreams before my helpless sight,   15
> He plunges at me, guttering, choking, drowning.
>
> If in some smothering dreams, you too could pace
> Behind the wagon that we flung him in,
> And watch the white eyes writhing in his face,
> His hanging face, like a devil's sick of sin;   20
> If you could hear, at every jolt, the blood
> Come gargling from the froth-corrupted lungs,
> Obscene as cancer, bitter as the cud
> Of vile, incurable sores on innocent tongues,—
> My friend, you would not tell with such high zest   25
> To children ardent for some desperate glory,
> The old Lie: *Dulce et decorum est*
> *Pro patria mori.*

SETTING AND ATMOSPHERE

SUBJECT VOCABULARY

setting the place where something is or where something happens, and the general environment

atmosphere the feeling that an event or place gives you

KEY POINT

The setting and the atmosphere it evokes are important devices used by a writer in order to influence readers. Careful choice of language is important in conveying this.

The **setting** of a text can tell you a lot about the text and helps to create **atmosphere**. If a novel is set entirely in one room, it can evoke a tense, claustrophobic feeling. A poem featuring open countryside under clear skies could suggest feelings of freedom and opportunity.

CONSIDERING SETTING AND ATMOSPHERE

When approaching a new text, identify the setting and atmosphere more closely by considering the questions below. Does the writer:

- establish the sense of place, weather, time?
- create a particular atmosphere? For example, is it tense or mysterious?
- give details of the setting? How does this link with the atmosphere created?
- choose specific vocabulary to create mood? Can you find examples of nouns, adjectives, verbs which do this?
- use images or stage instructions to create effects? Are these linked to a subject or theme?
- link setting and mood to the action or characters' feelings? For example, is a sad scene set in a rainy, windy, open space?

ACTIVITY 5   **AO2**   **SKILLS** CRITICAL THINKING, ANALYSIS, REASONING, INTERPRETATION

▼ SETTING

Look at the questions in the list above. Answer them in response to one of the fiction texts in the Anthology.

LEARNING OBJECTIVES

This lesson will help you to:
- select and interpret information, ideas and perspectives
- comment on the language used.

SUBJECT VOCABULARY

first person written from the perspective of one person – that is, using 'I'; this differs from the second person, which directly addresses the reader ('you'), and the third person ('he', 'she' and 'it')

third person using the third person – that is, 'he', 'she' and 'it'; this differs from the first person ('I') and the second person, which directly addresses the reader ('you')

narrator a character that tells the story in a novel, play, poem or film

CONSIDERING NARRATIVE VOICE

DID YOU KNOW?

Second-person narration speaks directly to the reader, usually referring to them as 'you'. This technique is not used very often but can make the reader feel part of the story as it invites involvement or agreement with the narrator.

NARRATIVE VOICE

When considering a text, it is important to study and discuss the techniques and features of narratives, including style, plot, character, theme, viewpoint, tone and mood. A useful starting point is to consider the 'voice' which is used to tell the story. Is the story written in the **first person** ('I'), or **third person** (written from an external perspective separate from the characters)?

ACTIVITY 1 — AO1 — SKILLS: CRITICAL THINKING, REASONING

▼ **FIRST- AND THIRD-PERSON NARRATION:**

Whether a text is narrated in the first person or in the third person can have an impact on how a reader feels about the text. For example, a first-person narrative is more personal and a third-person narrative is more detached. Draw up a list of other differences between them.

When thinking about the narrative voice, consider these questions.
- Does the writer tell the story from a narrator's point of view?
- Does the writer give the reader several different points of view?
- What tone is used? For example, is it urgent, anxious, relaxed, excited?
- Do you get a sense of the narrator as a character? What details of their lives are suggested?
- Is the narrator writing the story about themselves?
- Can the reader trust the narrator? Are there any clues that you should not believe everything that they say?
- Is a setting and time period established? What kinds of words are used for this?

▼ **FROM *THE SALT ROAD* BY JANE JOHNSON**

When I was a child, I had a wigwam in our back garden: a circle of thin yellow cotton draped over a bamboo pole and pegged to the lawn. Every time my parents argued, that was where I went. I would lie on my stomach with my fingers in my ears and stare so hard at the red animals printed on its bright decorative border that after a while they began to dance and run, until I wasn't in the garden any more but out on the plains, wearing a fringed deerskin tunic and feathers in my hair, just like the braves in the films I watched every Saturday morning in the cinema down the road.

Even at an early age I found it preferable to be outside in my little tent rather than inside the house. The tent was my space. It was as large as

PAPER 2 | **READING SKILLS: FICTION TEXTS** | 221

grandeur Grandness.

Georgian British style of architecture during the period 1714–1811.

archaeologists Scientists who study the past by looking at historical objects and sites.

unbiddable Will not be told what to do.

oddly attenuated Strangely long and thin.

mannequins Models or dummies.

KEY POINT

The narrative voice in a text is another key part of a text. The tone can help set the mood and atmosphere and the choice of first- or third-person narration can help shape how events are reported.

my imagination, which was infinite. But the house, for all its grandeur and Georgian spaciousness, felt small and suffocating. It was stuffed with things, as well as with my mother and father's bitterness. They were both archaeologists, my parents: lovers of the past, they had surrounded themselves with boxes of yellowed papers, ancient artefacts, dusty objects; the fragile, friable husks of lost civilizations. I never understood why they decided to have me: even the quietest baby, the most house-trained toddler, the most studious child, would have disrupted the artificial, museum-like calm they had wrapped around themselves. In that house they lived separated from the rest of the world, in a bubble in which dust motes floated silently like the fake snow in a snow-globe. I was not the child to complement such a life, being a wild little creature, loud and messy and unbiddable. I liked to play rough games with the boys instead of engaging in the sedate, codified exchanges of the other girls. I had dolls, but more often than not I beheaded or scalped them, or buried them in the garden and forgot where they were. I had no interest in making fashionable outfits for the oddly attenuated pink plastic mannequins with their insectile torsos and brassy hair that the other girls so worshipped and adorned.

ACTIVITY 2 | **AO1** | **SKILLS** CRITICAL THINKING

▼ ANALYSING A NARRATIVE VOICE

Re-read the extract from *The Salt Road* by Jane Johnson. Highlight any information the reader is given about the narrator in the passage. Then construct a P-E-E paragraph to answer the following question.

▶ What sense of the narrator's home life is suggested in this passage?

▲ Narrative voices can be used to direct focus and attention.

LEARNING OBJECTIVES

This lesson will help you to:
- understand how writers organise their work for effect.

STRUCTURE

Writers often use a variety of interesting structural devices to arrange their prose or poems. In the exam, you need to be able to write about how the Anthology texts are organised, considering how structure contributes to your understanding and interpretation of the text.

ANALYSING STRUCTURE

The simplest way to tell a story is in linear fashion, starting at the beginning and going on until you reach the end. When commenting on the structure of narrative, consider the following questions.

BEGINNINGS
- **Is a setting or time period established?** What kinds of words are used for this?
- **Is a character (or characters) introduced?** Who are they? What do you learn about them?
- **Is a theme suggested?** What effect does this have on the reader?
- **Is there a narrator?** Do they speak in a commentary (first or third person)? What is their tone of voice like? For example, is it urgent, anxious, relaxed, excited…?
- **Is dialogue used?** What effect does it have on the reader? For example, is it entertaining, tense, fast-moving, thoughtful?
- **Is there a prevailing tense (past or present)?** What effect does this have?

MIDDLES
- **Is a problem introduced?** How?
- **Are all the characters behaving the same way that they did at the beginning?** Which ones have changed?
- **Has the setting changed?** How does it fit in with the plot? Does it give added interest?
- **Are there clear links with earlier parts of the story or poem?** What are they? Are they shown through words or actions?
- **Does the writer suggest what is to come?** How?

ENDINGS
- **Does the story or poem come to a definite end?** Does the writer leave the reader to guess what happens?
- **Does the book end as you expected?** Or is it a surprise, or even a shock, ending?
- **Does the end echo the opening?** Does it return to the same theme, setting, characters, for example?
- **Is there a moral or message?** Have the characters learned a lesson? Does the author want to tell the reader something?

HINT

When analysing the structure of a text as a whole, consider the following questions.
- Is the structure linear or does it involve **time-shifts**?
- What narrative links are used to suggest a movement in time?
- Is there a contrast in the tone and mood between two parts of a text when time moves?
- How much is revealed about the characters at any one time? What do you learn about the characters when time moves?

SUBJECT VOCABULARY

narrative the story or plot
time-shift moving between different periods of time

PAPER 2 — READING SKILLS: FICTION TEXTS

DID YOU KNOW?
Some writers create interesting effects by handling time in a more fluid way and not relying on a simple beginning-middle-end structure. By using the technique of time-shift, also known as **prolepsis**, narrative can work in a non-linear way. This allows the reader to make connections between widely separated events. **Flashbacks** to the past can change the reader's interpretation of events and shifts forward can give you a glimpse of the future of the narrative.

SUBJECT VOCABULARY
prolepsis suggestions of things that will happen, before they do
flashback when the narrator of a story jumps out of the present in order to describe an event which happened in the past; often flashbacks are in the form of the memories of characters in the present

KEY POINT:
How a text is structured can influence your understanding of a text and your reaction to it. How and when information is revealed is important to both the plot and character development.

ACTIVITY 1 — A01
SKILLS: ADAPTIVE LEARNING, CREATIVITY, TEAMWORK

▼ CONSTRUCTING A NARRATIVE

Working in pairs, cut up the first part of any story into short phrases, place them in an envelope and swap them with another group.

Arrange the contents of your envelope into whatever order makes the most sense. Discuss this with your partner and explain your thinking. Try rearranging the story using different structures to produce different effects.

▼ FROM *MRS DALLOWAY* BY VIRGINIA WOOLF

Mrs Dalloway said she would buy the flowers herself. For Lucy had her work cut out for her. The doors would be taken off their hinges; Rumplemayer's men were coming. And then, thought Clarissa Dalloway, what a morning – fresh as if issued to children on a beach.

What a lark! What a plunge! For so it had always seemed to her when, with a squeak of the hinges, which she could hear now, whe had burst open the French windows and plunged at Bourton into the open air. How fresh, how calm, stiller than a wave; the kiss of a wave; chill and sharp and yet (for a girl of eighteen as she then was) solemn, feeling as she did, standing there at the open window, that something awful was about to happen; looking at the flowers, at the trees with the smoke winding off them and the rooks rising, falling; standing and – was that it? – "I prefer men to cauliflowers" – was that it? He must have said it at breakfast one morning when she had gone out on to the terrace – Peter Walsh. He would be back from India one of these days, June or July, she forgot which, for his letters were awfully dull; it was his sayings one remembered; his eyes, his pocket-knife, his smile, his grumpiness and, when millions of things had utterly vanished – how strange it was! – a few sayings like this about cabbages.

ACTIVITY 2 — A01
SKILLS: CRITICAL THINKING, ANALYSIS, INTERPRETATION

▼ ANALYSING STRUCTURE

Mrs Dalloway is a novel with an unusual structure. The technique used in which the thoughts and feelings that are running through the mind of a character are described is known as stream of consciousness. You can see from this piece how structure and narrative voice are linked.

Re-read the opening of the novel and answer the following questions.
- What is this passage about?
- How does the author show you what Mrs Dalloway is thinking?
- How do you feel about Mrs Dalloway at the end of the passage? Why?

STRUCTURE IN PROSE

'NIGHT' BY ALICE MUNRO

Alice Munro (1931–) is a famous Canadian short story writer. She has won numerous literary awards, including the Nobel Prize in Literature in 2013. She is an innovative writer who made changes to the short story as a genre. Chief among these is the way she uses time shifts and moves the narrative forwards and backwards. Character development and how they are coping with life at different stages is often more important than plot in her stories.

ACTIVITY 3 — A01, A02 — **SKILLS:** CRITICAL THINKING, ANALYSIS, INTERPRETATION

▼ ANALYSING STRUCTURE

Consider the structure of Alice Munro's short story 'Night'. Using the series of questions on beginnings, middles and ends on page 222, comment on the story. In particular, think about the ending.

ACTIVITY 4 — A04, A05 — **SKILLS:** ADAPTIVE LEARNING, CREATIVITY, INNOVATION

▼ AN ALTERNATIVE ENDING

Like many writers, Alice Munro often makes revisions to her stories before they are published. Can you write an alternative ending to 'Night', considering the structural techniques that you have learned about in this chapter?

STRUCTURE IN POETRY

Structure is important when analysing poetry too. You should think about the following:

- organisation of the stanzas
- line length
- punctuation
- rhyme
- rhythm.

Consider how these might lend themselves to create different effects.

'OUT, OUT—' BY ROBERT FROST

Robert Frost (1874–1963) was a popular and critically respected American poet. His poetry often tackles complicated themes about American people and society through the rural settings of New England where he spent most of his life. His work is also influenced by the grief and loss he suffered in his personal life. He won four Pulitzer Prizes for Poetry.

GENERAL VOCABULARY

New England an area in the north-east of the United States of America

PAPER 2 READING SKILLS: FICTION TEXTS

▲ American poet Robert Frost

GENERAL VOCABULARY

conversational informal, as though spoken in conversation with someone else

KEY POINT

Think how structure in poetry might lend itself to different effects. Focus on the stanzas, line length, rhyme and rhythm.

SUBJECT VOCABULARY

retrospective written in the past tense; looking back at events that have already occurred

ACTIVITY 5 | A02 | SKILLS ▸ CRITICAL THINKING

▼ **LOOKING OUT FOR STRUCTURE**

Read 'Out, Out—' (pages 232–233). Make a note of anything that you notice about the structure of the poem. Consider the points in the bullet list on page 224.

'Out, Out—' consists of a single stanza. It is written in 'blank verse', with five stresses to a line, which is known formally as 'iambic pentameter' and which is often used to replicate a **conversational** tone. It also lacks a formal rhyme scheme. This form suits the conversational tone. The poem is realistic, shocking and dramatic, so consider how the construction of the poem helps to achieve these effects.

The importance of the unusual title is something to be discussed. Particularly, the dash after the repeated word 'out' in the title indicates an unfinished statement.

ACTIVITY 6 | A02 | SKILLS ▸ CRITICAL THINKING, ANALYSIS, INTERPRETATION

▼ **WRITING ABOUT STRUCTURE IN POETRY**

Re-read 'Out, Out—' and look out for the points that have just been discussed. Then write your own P-E-E paragraph about structure in the poem.

ACTIVITY 7 | A02 | SKILLS ▸ CRITICAL THINKING, ANALYSIS, REASONING, INTERPRETATION

▼ **ANTHOLOGY TEXTS**

Review the fiction texts in the Anthology. Which ones are **retrospective** or use time-shifts? Write a P-E-E paragraph about the narrative structure, considering the following points.

- What narrative links are used to suggest a movement in time?
- How much is revealed about the characters? Using time-shift can give depth to a character, but can also be used to create a sense of mystery.
- Is there a strong contrast between the tone or mood of the paragraphs where time shifts? Is weather, setting or situation used to reinforce this sense of contrast?

LEARNING OBJECTIVES

This lesson will help you to:
- prepare for the Paper 2 exam.

PUTTING IT INTO PRACTICE

The question asked in Paper 2 Section A of the exam tests your reading and analytical skills. It is based on the fiction texts in the Anthology.

UNDERSTANDING THE EXAM CRITERIA

KEY POINT

Exam essays should be fully developed not just in terms of length but in ideas. It is important that you pick out the key terms from the question and evaluate the text, rather than just pointing out features. You need to think and write about the effect of the use of distinctive features in an analytical manner.

In order to succeed in answering this question in the exam you need to:
- show that you have understood what you have read by writing about the text in a way that shows that you've understood (you can do this by referring to the text and then commenting appropriately on what you've quoted)
- choose suitable lines from the text to comment upon in support of your points
- show that you understand the way in which language is used in texts and how writers use language and structure to create meaning.

WHAT YOU WILL BE ASKED TO DO

In the exam you will be asked to respond to **one** of the fiction Anthology texts. There is only one question in Section A of the exam and you must answer it. The question is worth 30 marks.

In this section, you will be presented with a passage from a text and asked to analyse it in the way you will need to do in the exam. This will allow you to practise the skills that you have learned. In the exam you will only be asked to answer about a text from the Anthology, so this activity is for illustrative purposes only.

▼ FROM *FRANKENSTEIN* BY MARY WOLLSTONECRAFT SHELLEY

It was on a dreary night of November that I beheld the accomplishment of my toils. With an anxiety that almost amounted to agony, I collected the instruments of life around me, that I might infuse a spark of being into the lifeless thing that lay at my feet. It was already one in the morning; the rain pattered dismally against the panes, and my candle was nearly burnt out, when, by the glimmer of the half-extinguished light, I saw the dull yellow eye of the creature open; it breathed hard, and a convulsive motion agitated its limbs.

How can I describe my emotions at this catastrophe, or how delineate the wretch whom with such infinite pains and care I had endeavoured to form? His limbs were in proportion, and I had selected his features as beautiful. Beautiful! Great God! His yellow skin scarcely covered the work of muscles and arteries beneath; his hair was of a lustrous black, and flowing; his teeth of a pearly whiteness; but these luxuriances only formed a more horrid contrast with his watery eyes, that seemed almost of the same colour as the dun-white sockets in which they were set, his shrivelled complexion and straight black lips.

PAPER 2 — READING SKILLS: FICTION TEXTS

> The different accidents of life are not so changeable as the feelings of human nature. I had worked hard for nearly two years, for the sole purpose of infusing life into an inanimate body. For this I had deprived myself of rest and health. I had desired it with an ardour that far exceeded moderation; but now that I had finished, the beauty of the dream vanished, and breathless horror and disgust filled my heart. Unable to endure the aspect of the being I had created, I rushed out of the room and continued a long time traversing my bedchamber, unable to compose my mind to sleep. At length lassitude succeeded to the tumult I had before endured, and I threw myself on the bed in my clothes, endeavouring to seek a few moments of forgetfulness. But it was in vain; I slept, indeed, but I was disturbed by the wildest dreams. I thought I saw Elizabeth, in the bloom of health, walking in the streets of Ingolstadt. Delighted and surprised, I embraced her, but as I imprinted the first kiss on her lips, they became livid with the hue of death; her features appeared to change, and I thought that I held the corpse of my dead mother in my arms; a shroud enveloped her form, and I saw the grave-worms crawling in the folds of the flannel. I started from my sleep with horror; a cold dew covered my forehead, my teeth chattered, and every limb became convulsed; when, by the dim and yellow light of the moon, as it forced its way through the window shutters, I beheld the wretch— the miserable monster whom I had created.

EXAM-STYLE QUESTION

AO1
AO2

SKILLS CRITICAL THINKING, ANALYSIS, REASONING, INTERPRETATION

Read the extract from *Frankenstein*.

How does the author convey the narrator's emotions?

In your answer, you should write about:
- the imagery
- the setting and sense of place
- the use of language.

You should support your answer with close reference to the passage, including **brief** quotations.

(30 marks)

HINT

Use this paragraph to get you started.

> immediately creates connotations of darkness and unease **This demonstrates a good understanding of the effects of the writer's language choices.**
>
> The use of emotive descriptions acts to explore both the states emotional state of the narrator, whilst also offering an underlying suggestion towards his state of mind **Emotive language is a good feature to discuss, but could this be expressed more clearly and succinctly?**
>
> This is complimented by the use of short, sharp sentences and questions to convey both excitement and further nerves. **Sentence structure is another good feature to discuss; can you find evidence from the text for this?**

> The author conveys the narrator's emotions in a wide range of ways, utilising a number of literary techniques to explore the mixture of emotions present. The setting, 'a dreary night of November' where 'the rain pattered dismally against the panes' **immediately creates connotations of darkness and unease**, reflecting both the reader and narrator. **The use of emotive descriptions acts to explore both the states emotional state of the narrator, whilst also offering an underlying suggestion towards his state of mind;** 'an anxiety that almost amounted to agony' clearly suggests apprehension but by suggesting it almost amounts to physical pain adds an additional layer to the notion. **This is complimented by the use of short, sharp sentences and questions to convey both excitement and further nerves.**

The student shows a good understanding of the writer's language choices, such as description of setting, and sentence structures. Expression is generally clear, formal and sophisticated.

'DISABLED' WILFRED OWEN

BACKGROUND AND CONTEXT
Wilfred Owen is the best known of the English poets who wrote about their experiences of the First World War (1914–1918). These experiences had deep effects on the writers, and cost many of them their lives. Owen was strongly influenced by another officer and poet called Siegfried Sassoon. They met at Craiglockhart Hospital where they had both been sent to recover from shell-shock. Owen twice said that his theme was 'war and the pity of war'. Having returned to his regiment after his time in hospital, he died in battle in November 1918, just seven days before the armistice brought the war to an end on 11th November 1918.

Wilfred Owen in 1916

▲ Owen said his writing was about 'war and the pity of war'.

BEFORE YOU START READING
1 You can find out more about Wilfred Owen and his poetry from reference books or on the internet. You could read some more of his poems, which will help you to understand his attitudes to war and how he wrote about it.
2 How would you feel about living with a physical disability such as the loss of a limb? What attitudes to people with disabilities do you find in your society?
3 What can you find out about the kinds of injuries that soldiers suffered in the First World War and the way in which they were treated when they returned from the front?

▼ 'DISABLED' BY WILFRED OWEN

He sat in a wheeled chair, waiting for dark,
And shivered in his ghastly suit of grey,
Legless, sewn short at elbow. Through the park
Voices of boys rang saddening like a hymn,
Voices of play and pleasure after day,   5
Till gathering sleep had mothered them from him.

About this time Town used to swing so gay
When glow-lamps budded in the light blue trees,
And girls glanced lovelier as the air grew dim –
In the old times, before he threw away his knees.   10
Now he will never feel again how slim

Girls' waists are, or how warm their subtle hands;
All of them touch him like some queer disease.

There was an artist silly for his face,
For it was younger than his youth, last year.   15
Now, he is old; his back will never brace;
He's lost his colour very far from here,
Poured it down shell-holes till the veins ran dry,
And half his lifetime lapsed in the hot race,
And leap of purple spurted from his thigh.   20

One time he liked a blood-smear down his leg,
After the matches, carried shoulder-high.
It was after football, when he'd drunk a peg,
He thought he'd better join. – He wonders why.
Someone had said he'd look a god in kilts,   25
That's why; and maybe, too, to please his Meg;
Aye, that was it, to please the giddy jilts
He asked to join. He didn't have to beg;

Smiling they wrote his lie: aged nineteen years.
Germans he scarcely thought of; all their guilt,   30
And Austria's, did not move him. And no fears
Of Fear came yet. He thought of jewelled hilts
For daggers in plaid socks; of smart salutes;
And care of arms; and leave; and pay arrears;
Esprit de corps; and hints for young recruits.   35
And soon, he was drafted out with drums and cheers.

Some cheered him home, but not as crowds cheer Goal.
Only a solemn man who brought him fruits
Thanked him; and then enquired about his soul.

Now, he will spend a few sick years in institutes,   40

Esprit de corps French expression meaning a feeling of pride.

And do what things the rules consider wise,

And take whatever pity they may dole.

Tonight he noticed how the women's eyes

Passed from him to the strong men that were whole.

How cold and late it is! Why don't they come   45

And put him into bed? Why don't they come?

UNDERSTANDING THE TEXT

Owen's wounded soldier, who has lost his legs and his arms, sits in a wheelchair in hospital listening to the shouts of boys playing at sunset. He is reminded of the excitement of former early evenings in town before he joined up; 'before he threw away his knees'.

Copy and complete the table, which contains some key phrases that show the soldier's present situation and his memories. Write a comment on each.

KEY POINT

This is a text that blends the past and present to powerful effect. Analyse how Owen achieves this.

▼ PHRASE	▼ COMMENT
'waiting for dark'	The soldier does not have anything positive to look forward to – only the arrival of the end of the day.
'sewn short at elbow'	The sleeves of his suit have had to be cut short because of the loss of his arms.
'Town used to swing so gay'	The evening had been a time for happiness and parties in town.
'glow-lamps budded in the light blue trees'	
'his back will never brace'	
'Poured it down shell-holes'	
'lapsed in the hot race'	
'He thought of jewelled hilts / For daggers in plaid socks'	
'soon, he was drafted out with drums and cheers'	
'not as crowds cheer Goal'	
'do what things the rules consider wise'	

EXPLORING LANGUAGE

Owen chose his words carefully to help you understand the mind of the soldier. Copy and complete the following table, making explanatory comments on the examples from the poem.

▼ EXAMPLE	▼ EXPLANATION
'he liked a blood-smear down his leg'	A slight injury or graze from playing football was something he could feel proud of, a type of 'war wound'.
'look a god in kilts'	
'to please the giddy jilts'	
'he noticed how the women's eyes / Passed from him'	He realises that girls look away from him in horror or embarrassment and turn their attention to healthy, able-bodied men.
'How cold and late it is!'	
'Why don't they come… Why don't they come?'	The repeated rhetorical question shows how much he wishes to get away from the sights and thoughts that have been troubling him (end of day / end of life).

There are also some striking phrases that convey Owen's powerful ideas. Copy and complete the following table, adding your own comments to show why you find the language effective in the examples listed and adding more examples of your own.

▼ EXAMPLE	▼ EXPLANATION
'saddening like a hymn'	Even the happy cries of children sound sad to him, like a mournful hymn in church.
'girls glanced lovelier'	
'touch him like some queer disease'	
'*Thanked* him; and then enquired about his soul'	
'spend a few sick years in institutes'	

ACTIVITY 1 — AO4, AO5 — SKILLS: CRITICAL THINKING, ANALYSIS, INTERPRETATION, ADAPTIVE LEARNING, CREATIVITY

▼ WRITING TASK

Write an article in which you describe the lives of the wounded soldiers who are being cared for in an institution.

EXAM-STYLE QUESTION

AO1
AO2
SKILLS: CRITICAL THINKING, ANALYSIS, REASONING, INTERPRETATION

How successfully does the writer compare the ideas of sport and war in 'Disabled'?

In your answer, you should write about:
- the effects of war
- the present and past attitudes of the disabled soldier
- the writer's imagery and use of colour
- the use of contrast
- the writer's use of words, phrases and techniques.

You should support your answer with close reference to the passage, including **brief** quotations.

(30 marks)

'OUT, OUT—' ROBERT FROST

BACKGROUND
Robert Frost (1874–1963) was one of the major American poets of the 20th century. His poetry is based mainly on the life and scenery of rural New England. 'Out, Out –' was published in the collection *Mountain Interval* in 1916.

The setting of this poem is a farm. The scenery around the farm is beautiful. Life is too hard for it to be enjoyed fully by the family, even by the young son, who has to work all day cutting up wood with a buzz saw. It is believed that Frost based the poem on a real incident that he read about in a newspaper.

▲ Frost's poetry draws upon life in rural New England, USA.

BEFORE YOU START READING
1 You can find out more about Robert Frost and his poetry from reference books or on the internet. You could read some more of his poems, which will help you to understand the sort of subjects that he wrote about. These include 'Stopping by Woods on a Snowy Evening', 'Mending Wall', and 'Meeting and Passing'.
2 Think about the way a newspaper would describe this tragic event in comparison with how the poet presents the incident.

▼ 'OUT, OUT—' BY ROBERT FROST

The buzz saw snarled and rattled in the yard
And made dust and dropped stove-length sticks of wood,
Sweet-scented stuff when the breeze drew across it.
And from there those that lifted eyes could count
Five mountain ranges one behind the other　　　　　　　　5
Under the sunset far into Vermont.
And the saw snarled and rattled, snarled and rattled,
As it ran light, or had to bear a load.
And nothing happened: day was all but done.
Call it a day, I wish they might have said　　　　　　　　10
To please the boy by giving him the half hour
That a boy counts so much when saved from work.
His sister stood beside them in her apron
To tell them 'Supper.' At the word, the saw,
As if to prove saws knew what supper meant,　　　　　　　15

Leaped out at the boy's hand, or seemed to leap–
He must have given the hand. However it was,
Neither refused the meeting. But the hand!
The boy's first outcry was a rueful laugh,
As he swung toward them holding up the hand,   20
Half in appeal, but half as if to keep
The life from spilling. Then the boy saw all–
Since he was old enough to know, big boy
Doing a man's work, though a child at heart–
He saw all spoiled. "Don't let him cut my hand off–   25
The doctor, when he comes. Don't let him, sister!"
So. But the hand was gone already.
The doctor put him in the dark of ether.
He lay and puffed his lips out with his breath.
And then–the watcher at his pulse took fright.   30
No one believed. They listened at his heart.
Little–less–nothing!–and that ended it.
No more to build on there. And they, since they
Were not the one dead, turned to their affairs.

ether An anaesthetic gas used in the 19th and early 20th century.

UNDERSTANDING THE TEXT

The title of the poem is from Shakespeare's *Macbeth*, Act V Scene IV, where Macbeth learns of the death of Lady Macbeth, his wife.

▼ FROM *MACBETH* BY WILLIAM SHAKESPEARE

She should have died hereafter;
There would have been a time for such a word.
To-morrow, and to-morrow, and to-morrow,
Creeps in this petty pace from day to day,   5
To the last syllable of recorded time;
And all our yesterdays have lighted fools
The way to dusty death. Out, out, brief candle!
Life's but a walking shadow, a poor player,
That struts and frets his hour upon the stage,   10
And then is heard no more. It is a tale
Told by an idiot, full of sound and fury,
Signifying nothing.

▲ Word choice in poetry is often used to create vivid impressions; in this case, 'stove-length sticks of wood'.

Think about the way in which Frost makes use of the quotation from *Macbeth* and in particular why the reference to death as life's 'brief candle' going out might apply particularly to the situation that Frost describes in the poem.

Frost generally uses straightforward vocabulary, but 'Out, Out—' contains some difficult phrases. These are listed in the following table. Copy and complete the table with explanations of these difficult phrases to develop your understanding of the poem.

▼ LANGUAGE	▼ EXPLANATION
'stove-length sticks of wood'	Logs the right size to put in a wood-burning stove.
'As it ran light'	When it ran freely because it was not cutting anything difficult.
'As if to prove saws knew what supper meant'	
'Neither refused the meeting'	
'put him in the dark of ether'	
'the watcher at his pulse took fright'	
'No more to build on there'	

EXPLORING LANGUAGE

Word choice in poetry is often used to create vivid impressions. Frost uses a wide range of techniques to create striking images, build atmosphere and engage the reader. By analysing the language features used, it is possible to explore Frost's writing style and appreciate the ways in which he adds depth to the narrative within the poem. Copy and complete the following table, finding examples of each of the techniques and saying what you think the effect is.

▼ LANGUAGE TECHNIQUE	▼ EXAMPLE	▼ EFFECT
Personification	'The buzz saw snarled and rattled'	Makes the machine seem like a savage beast.
Onomatopoeia		
Alliteration		
Oxymoron		
Direct speech		
Repetition		
Short sentence		
Idiom		
Pathos		
Dissonance		
Colloquialism		

| PAPER 2 | TEXT ANTHOLOGY: FICTION | 235 |

KEY POINT

The language of this poem articulates ideas indirectly. Draw out how the substance of the poem is the 'unsaid'.

ACTIVITY 1 — A01 — SKILLS: CRITICAL THINKING, ANALYSIS, INTERPRETATION

▼ READING BETWEEN THE LINES

Although the boy is shown to be part of a family, he also seems quite isolated in the poem, and there is little sympathy for the rest of the family's attitudes. What does the poem's language show you about:
- the boy's sister
- the relationships within the family
- the family's reactions to the boy's tragic early death?

Copy and complete the table with examples of language referring to the above points, explaining what each example shows you.

▼ LANGUAGE REFERRING TO FAMILY	▼ WHAT DOES THIS SHOW?

ACTIVITY 2 — A01 — SKILLS: TEAMWORK, EMPATHY

▼ EXPLAINING THE ACCIDENT

Work with a partner, imagining that one of you is a police officer and that the other is a member of the family who actually saw the accident, describing the event to the police officer. In your roles, conduct an interview to investigate the circumstances of the accident.

ACTIVITY 3 — A04 — A05 — SKILLS: CRITICAL THINKING, ANALYSIS, INTERPRETATION, ADAPTIVE LEARNING, CREATIVITY

▼ WRITING TASK

Write an article on the dangers to children of undertaking adult work, persuading people to adhere to health and safety advice.

EXAM-STYLE QUESTION

A01

A02

SKILLS: CRITICAL THINKING, ANALYSIS, REASONING, INTERPRETATION

How does the writer create a sense of horror in 'Out, Out—'?

In your answer, you should write about:
- the way in which the chainsaw is presented
- the way in which the seriousness of the situation is gradually revealed
- the poet's use of words, phrases and techniques.

You should support your answer with close reference to the passage, including **brief** quotations. **(30 marks)**

'AN UNKNOWN GIRL'
MONIZA ALVI

BACKGROUND
Moniza Alvi was born in Lahore, Pakistan. She has a Pakistani father and an English mother. Her father moved the family to England when she was very young, and she did not go back to Pakistan until after her first book of poems had been published. She worked for several years as a teacher in London and is now a freelance writer and tutor.

▲ Henna being used for body decoration

BEFORE YOU START READING

1 You can find out more about Moniza Alvi and her poetry from reference books or on the internet. You could read some more of her poems, such as 'Presents from my Aunts', which will help you to understand her attitudes toward her Pakistani heritage.

2 Think about what Moniza Alvi says about her background and its links to her poetry:

> 'Presents from My Aunts' … was one of the first poems I wrote. When I wrote this poem, I hadn't actually been back to Pakistan. The girl in the poem would be me at about 13. The clothes seem to stick to her in an uncomfortable way, a bit like a kind of false skin and she thinks things aren't straightforward for her.'

I found it was important to write the Pakistan poems because I was getting in touch with my background. And maybe there's a bit of a message behind the poems about something I went through, that I want to maybe open a few doors if possible.

3 Talk to someone who has moved to another country. Ask them about how they feel about where they come from. Read about other people's experiences of moving from one country to another.

4 If you or your family have moved from one country to another, think about your feelings about the original country. If you have not, talk to someone you know who has moved from one country to another and ask them about how they feel about the place that their family came from, or read about other people's experiences.

▼ 'AN UNKNOWN GIRL' BY MONIZA ALVI

bazaar A marketplace.

hennaing A method of applying a temporary tattoo using a strong reddish-brown dye (henna).

In the evening bazaar
studded with neon
an unknown girl
is hennaing my hand.
She squeezes a wet brown line   5
from a nozzle.
She is icing my hand,
which she steadies with hers
on her satin-peach knee.
In the evening bazaar   10
for a few rupees
an unknown girl
is hennaing my hand.
As a little air catches

kameez A loose-fitting tunic.

my shadow-stitched kameez   15
a peacock spreads its lines
across my palm.
Colours leave the street
float up in balloons.
Dummies in shop-fronts   20
tilt and stare
with their Western perms.

Miss India The national winner in a Miss World beauty contest.

Banners for Miss India 1993,

for curtain cloth

and sofa cloth 25

canopy me.

I have new brown veins.

In the evening bazaar

very deftly

an unknown girl 30

is hennaing my hand.

I am clinging

to these firm peacock lines

like people who cling

to the sides of a train. 35

Now the furious streets

are hushed.

I'll scrape off

the dry brown lines

before I sleep, 40

reveal soft as a snail trail

the amber bird beneath.

It will fade in a week.

When India appears and reappears

I'll lean across a country 45

with my hands outstretched

longing for the unknown girl

in the neon bazaar.

UNDERSTANDING THE TEXT

This poem describes the poet's visit to India and the time she had her hand hennaed by a girl in the bazaar. It was an experience she never forgot.

The poem makes many connections between western and eastern culture. The 'unknown girl' seems to stand for the true spirit of India, which has now been influenced heavily by aspects of western culture (often called 'westernisation'). India is seen as colourful and beautiful and this is reflected in the decoration of the henna pattern, with its complicated peacock design.

PAPER 2 — TEXT ANTHOLOGY: FICTION

KEY POINT

The poem draws on the tension in India between western and eastern culture.

The poem has a number of themes:

- cultural identity
- a sense of belonging
- feelings of loss
- the known and the unknown
- the importance of people's appearance
- the contrast between east and west.

Copy and complete the following table, finding examples from the poem that relate to its themes and adding your thoughts about how the selected example illustrates the theme.

▼ THEME	▼ EXAMPLE	▼ COMMENT
Cultural identity	'I'll lean across a country'	She feels the pull of India and her Asian heritage even when back in England.
A sense of belonging		
Feelings of loss		
The known and the unknown		
The importance of people's appearance		
The contrast between east and west		

The language that Alvi uses is mostly quite straightforward, but the poem includes some words that may be less familiar. Copy and complete the following table, giving the meaning of the words or phrases that are listed.

▼ TEXT	▼ MEANING
'bazaar'	A market place.
'icing my hand'	
'their Western perms'	
'canopy me'	
'I have new brown veins'	
'amber bird'	

EXPLORING LANGUAGE

Alvi chooses her words to convey the atmosphere and colourful scenes in India and also to illustrate some westernised elements of Indian society. Copy and complete the following table, writing a comment on each example and explain what the language suggests to you.

▼ EXAMPLE	▼ EXPLANATION
'studded with neon'	This is a traditional market scene, but the market is lit up by a large number of electric lights.
'on her satin-peach knee'	
'my shadow-stitched kameez'	
'a peacock spreads its lines'	
'Dummies … tilt and stare / with their Western perms'	
'Banners for Miss India 1993'	
'like people who cling / to the sides of a train'	
'the furious streets / are hushed'	

▲ Modern India is much influenced by western culture.

ACTIVITY 1 — A04 — SKILLS: INTELLECTUAL INTEREST, SELF-PRESENTATION

▼ REPORTING ON ANOTHER CULTURE

Imagine you are a television reporter who is sent to another country to report for a travel programme. Research your chosen destination and prepare a short talk about your impressions.

ACTIVITY 2 — A04 — A05 — SKILLS: CRITICAL THINKING, ANALYSIS, INTERPRETATION, ADAPTIVE LEARNING, CREATIVITY

▼ WRITING TASK

Write an article entitled either 'Why I like make-up', or 'Make-up: a waste of time and money'.

EXAM-STYLE QUESTION

A01

A02

SKILLS: CRITICAL THINKING, ANALYSIS, REASONING, INTERPRETATION

How successfully does the writer of 'An Unknown Girl' present her feelings about the country she has visited?

In your answer, you should write about:
- the images of the country
- the way she feels about having her hand painted
- the writer's use of words, phrases and techniques.

You should support your answer with close reference to the passage, including **brief** quotations.

(30 marks)

'THE BRIGHT LIGHTS OF SARAJEVO'
TONY HARRISON

BACKGROUND AND CONTEXT

Tony Harrison was born in Leeds, Yorkshire, in 1937 and is a leading poet and translator. He has often written about social issues and sometimes about international issues. He wrote 'The Bright Lights of Sarajevo' when a national British newspaper sent him to write about Bosnia, a country in **the Balkans**, in September 1995.

The Bosnian War took place between 1992 and 1995. It was a bitter conflict between parts of the former **Yugoslavia**, which broke out along old national and cultural boundaries at the beginning of the 1990s. The main division was between Bosnia and Serbia, but the political situation was very complex. The war was motivated by ethnic prejudice and Muslims in the region suffered horrific **ethnic cleansing**.

The poem is set in Sarajevo, capital city of Bosnia, during the **siege** mounted by Serb forces which lasted the entire duration of the war. Thousands of people died in the city during the siege.

GENERAL VOCABULARY

the Balkans a group of countries in south-eastern Europe
Yugoslavia a country which separated into several smaller countries in the early 1990s
ethnic cleansing the action of forcing people to leave an area or country or killing them because of their ethnic or religious identity
siege a situation in which an army or the police surround a place and try to gain control of it or force someone to come out of it

BEFORE YOU START READING

1. The siege of Sarajevo is the longest siege of a capital city in modern history. Using the internet, do some research into the series of conflicts that broke apart Yugoslavia.
2. One event that captured the attention of the international media and people worldwide was the gunning down of a young couple commonly referred to as 'the Romeo and Juliet of Sarajevo'. Find out about them.
3. Think about how you would feel if your daily routines became restricted and it became too dangerous to even go out to buy a loaf of bread. How would you cope?

▲ 'match-lit flare test'

'THE BRIGHT LIGHTS OF SARAJEVO' BY TONY HARRISON

After the hours that Sarajevans pass
queuing with empty canisters of gas
to get the refills they wheel home in prams,
or queuing for the precious meagre grams
of bread they're rationed to each day, 5
and often dodging snipers on the way,
or struggling up sometimes eleven flights
of stairs with water, then you'd think the nights
of Sarajevo would be totally devoid
of people walking streets Serb shells destroyed, 10
but tonight in Sarajevo that's just not the case–
The young go walking at a stroller's pace,
black shapes impossible to mark
as Muslim, Serb or Croat in such dark,
in unlit streets you can't distinguish who 15
calls bread *hjleb* or *hleb* or calls it *kruh*.
All takes the evening air with a stroller's stride,
no torches guide them, but they don't collide
except as one of the flirtatious ploys
when a girl's dark shape is fancied by a boy's. 20
Then the tender radar of the tone of voice
shows by its signals she approves his choice.
Then match or lighter to a cigarette
to check in her eyes if he's made progress yet.

And I see a pair who've certainly progressed 25
beyond the tone of voice and match-lit flare test
and he's about, I think, to take her hand
and lead her away from where they stand

1992 On 27th May 1992, a breadline in Sarajevo was attacked with mortar fire, killing many people.

Pleiades An open star cluster of the constellation Taurus, also known as Seven Sisters. In Greek mythology, they were the daughters of Atlas who became stars.

AID flour-sacks Humanitarian aid is provided to conflict sites by international organisations. There is irony here in the fact that the sack is used to create barricades that protect civilians from mortar and sniper fire.

>   on two shell scars, where, in 1992
>   Serb mortars massacred the breadshop queue   30
>   and blood-dunked crusts of shredded bread
>   lay on this pavement with the broken dead.
>   And at their feet in holes made by the mortar
>   that caused the massacre, now full of water
>   from the rain that's poured down half the day,   35
>   though now even the smallest clouds have cleared away,
>   leaving the Sarajevo star-filled evening sky
>   ideally bright and clear for bomber's eye,
>   in those two rain-full shell-holes the boy sees
>   fragments of the splintered Pleiades,   40
>   sprinkled on those death-deep, death-dark wells
>   splashed on the pavement by Serb mortar shells.
>
>   The dark boy-shape leads dark girl-shape away
>   to share one coffee in a candlelit café
>   until the curfew, and he holds her hand   45
>   behind AID flour-sacks refilled with sand.

UNDERSTANDING THE TEXT

KEY POINT

The poet is writing about a complex conflict and it is a great challenge to capture its multiple facets in poetry, but it is also a situation with great literary potential.

The poem is about the devastation and disruption caused by war and the resilience of the human spirit in the face of this. The poem highlights the difficulties faced by the citizens of Sarajevo and contrasts this with young couples whose relationships are slowly progressing in a city that seems to symbolise death. Harrison also uses references to the couples' surroundings to show that, while life will continue in harsh environments, the reality of the situation is inescapable. He also explores the roots of the conflict, by showing that ethnic divides disappear in the shadows of the night.

THEMES

▶ **What are the main themes of the poem?**

The table on page 244 shows some of the themes. Complete the table by finding examples from the text and adding your ideas, explaining how the example illustrates the theme. One quotation illustrating the theme of 'war' has been added for you as an example.

▼ THEME	▼ EXAMPLE	▼ COMMENT
War	'and often dodging snipers on the way'	Shows that, even while doing an ordinary task, there is a real risk of being killed. This highlights the reality of living in a war zone.
Deprivation		
Love		

SETTING AND EVENTS

▶ Think about the setting and the events of the poem. What can you say about the setting and the events? Do they seem unusual to you?

To help you understand what is happening, choose some of the poet's observations and explain what they can tell you about Sarajevo and its people when the poem was written. One example has been done for you using the following table.

▼ HARRISON'S OBSERVATION	▼ WHAT THIS TELLS YOU ABOUT THE CITY AND PEOPLE
'to get the refills they wheel home in prams'	Shows how the Sarajevans improvise to cope with the situation.

The poem describes some unlikely-sounding events: at night, in bomb-damaged Sarajevo, young people from different ethnic groups move around the city and boys meet girls, despite the danger and darkness. However, it also hints at more violent events.

The poem also shows the **paradoxes** of the time – for example, how ethnic conflict disappears at night; how romance can burst into life in terrible conditions; how gentle feelings can exist in the very place where people had been killed by shells earlier in the war.

SUBJECT VOCABULARY

paradox a situation (or piece of writing) which contains strongly contrasting elements or meanings

PAPER 2 — TEXT ANTHOLOGY: FICTION — 245

EXPLORING LANGUAGE

GENERAL VOCABULARY

conversational informal, as though spoken in conversation with someone else
predominate have the most importance or influence, or to be most easily noticed

KEY POINT

Visual imagery is common in literature; however, a writer can deploy other kinds of imagery, all of which evoke the human senses to draw in the reader.

STYLE

The language of the poem is mostly straightforward and even quite conversational.

▶ Find two or three examples of this style of language.
▶ What do you think is the effect of this style? Does it make the poem more realistic? Does it seem more accessible to you?

IMAGES

The images that the writer creates in this poem are not only visual. In fact, although visual imagery predominates this text, there are many other types of images used as well. Copy and complete the following table with examples of different types of imagery and their effect.

▼ TYPE OF IMAGE	▼ EXAMPLE	▼ EFFECT
Visual (sight)		
Auditory (sound)	'tender radar of the tone of voice'	The image of radar is taken from the language of warfare. This makes it appropriate for the situation and also creates irony. The emotion expressed is in direct contrast to the horror of war.
Tactile (touch)		

LIGHT AND DARKNESS

Reference to light and darkness are important in this poem and a variety of nouns as well as adjectives are used to show this. Copy and complete the following table with examples and explain their effect. One has been done for you.

▼ NOUN	▼ EFFECT	▼ ADJECTIVE	▼ EFFECT
'match'	A source of light; being small it resembles the fading signs of life in Sarajevo.		

RHYME

A technique often seen in poetry is the use of rhyme. Different rhyme schemes can have different effects.

▶ What is the rhyme scheme of the poem? What effect does this have on you, the reader? Why do you think the writer chose such a simple rhyme scheme?

SUBJECT VOCABULARY

rhyme scheme the rhyming pattern used in a poem

SUBJECT VOCABULARY

contrast where tow objects, people or ideas are placed next to each other to highlight their differences

CONTRAST

Throughout the poem, Harrison conveys the **contrast** between the activities of ordinary Sarajevans and the strange and difficult conditions in which they live. He does this by presenting everyday activities alongside evidence of the violence of war.

Some of the techniques used in the language to express this contrast are:

- associations – that is, hinting at a setting, a situation or feelings by using related words and phrases
- contrasting word chains, such as lists of peaceful activities followed by contrasting vocabulary suggesting violence and war.

Copy and complete the following table with examples of contrasting language and its effect.

▼ LINES	▼ CONTRASTING WORDS OR PHRASES	▼ EFFECT OF THE CONTRAST
4-6	'queuing for the …grams of bread / often dodging snipers on the way'	Queueing is an everyday activity, but the idea of being shot at becoming part of the routine is shocking.
10-12	'streets Serb shells destroyed / walking at a stroller's pace'	

ACTIVITY 1 — AO4 AO5

SKILLS: PROBLEM SOLVING, CREATIVITY, INNOVATION, INTELLECTUAL INTEREST

▼ **WRITING TASKS**

1. Research the story of Vedran Smailovic, a cellist in the Sarajevo Philharmonic Orchestra.
2. Write a story that focuses on an act that shows courage or celebrates life.
3. Do some more research on daily life during the Bosnian War, then write a piece called 'Romance under Siege' about trying to establish a relationship during wartime conditions.

EXAM-STYLE QUESTIONS

AO1

AO2

SKILLS: CRITICAL THINKING, ANALYSIS, REASONING, INTERPRETATION

How does the writer successfully convey the horror of war and the ability of human beings to rise above it? In your answer, you should write about:

- the ideas about war conveyed in the poem
- the way the writer uses images and contrast
- the writer's use of words, phrases and techniques.

You should support your answer with close reference to the passage, including **brief** quotations.

(30 marks)

PAPER 2 — TEXT ANTHOLOGY: FICTION

HINT:
Remember that the word 'how' means that you are expected to discuss methods or techniques used by the writer to create certain effects. To improve your answers, you need to be able to comment in some detail about particular words and phrases, explaining the impact on the reader or how you think the poet intends the reader to react. It is better to write about a few techniques and quotations in detail than to try to fit in a lot of points without explaining them properly.

How does the writer present the difficult and dangerous conditions in Sarajevo in 'The Bright Lights of Sarajevo'? In your answer, you should write about:

- the description of the physical environment
- the way people are behaving
- the writer's use of language and techniques.

You should support your answer with close reference to the passage, including **brief** quotations.

(30 marks)

ACTIVITY 2 — AO3

SKILLS: CRITICAL THINKING, ANALYSIS, INTERPRETATION, DECISION MAKING

▼ **FINDING SIMILARITIES AND DIFFERENCES**

'Corpse' is a poem taken from *Sarajevo Blues*, a collection written by Semezdin Mehmedinovic, who lived in Sarajevo during the siege. Written by a citizen rather than an observer, this poem has similarities to as well as differences from 'The Bright Lights of Sarajevo' in terms of ideas and language. Think about these similarities and differences and write them down in the table that follows. You can look at techniques such as rhyme scheme, as well as the themes and ideas.

▼ **'CORPSE' BY SEMEZDIN MEHMEDINOVIC**

We slowed down at the bridge
to watch some dogs tear a
corpse apart by the river
and then we went on

nothing in me has changed   5

I heard the crunch of snow under tires
like teeth biting into an apple
and felt the wild desire to laugh
at you
because you call this place hell   10
and you flee from here convinced
that death outside Sarajevo does not exist

TEXT ANTHOLOGY: FICTION

▲ Bosnian cellist Vedran Smailovic

▼ SIMILARITIES	▼ DIFFERENCES
Both poems give details from daily life, such as 'crunch of snow under the tires', 'empty canisters of gas'.	The titles. 'Bright Lights…' has apparently positive connotations but 'Corpse' creates an immediately negative impression.

WRITING A SUCCESSFUL ANSWER

▶ How does the writer use contrast to convey his message in the poem?

Below are two examples of opening paragraphs that respond to this question. Which do you think is better? Annotate the samples with your observations, referring to the wording of AO2 (see page 209) as you do so. What improvements would you make to both answers?

EXAMPLE STUDENT ANSWER A

'The Bright Lights of Sarajevo' is a poem by Tony Harrison that is set in the background of the Bosnian war. This war went on for many years and resulted in lots of causalities. The writer wants to show that he is against war and uses contrast for this purpose. The biggest contrast he uses is colour. He describes the city in detail as well.

EXAMPLE STUDENT ANSWER B

Set against the Bosnian war, this poem delivers a strong message about the devastation caused by war and the way people are able to rise above it. For this purpose he mainly uses contrast as a technique. Firstly, he creates the world of Sarajevo by day and by night. This helps the reader to visualise the contrasting times of day.

'STILL I RISE'
MAYA ANGELOU

BACKGROUND
Maya Angelou was an American poet, writer, singer, composer, actor, director, lecturer and civil rights activist. Her illustrious career, which spanned six decades, won her both fame and critical acclaim as well as numerous awards and honorary degrees. Her work centres on such themes as racism, family, women and identity, and she is an important figure in the black literary tradition.

She has written seven autobiographies, which include *I Know Why the Caged Bird Sings* and *A Song Flung up to Heaven*. Her candid discussion of her life and background as well as the range of her artistic talent and expression has made her an inspiration to many.

BEFORE YOU START READING
1 Read about slavery in the United States of America.
2 Everyone wants to be treated fairly and become angry if treated unfairly. But are you always fair to other people? Talk about situations where you might have behaved unfairly.
3 Percy Bysshe Shelley (1792–1822) was a major Romantic poet who wrote that 'poets are the unacknowledged legislators of the world'. Throughout history, poetry has been used as a medium of protest and a call to social change. Do some research to find examples of poetry of protest. You could also look at the work of modern-day rap and hip hop artists, and at the way in which pop music has become a medium through which social and political issues are addressed.

▼ 'STILL I RISE' BY MAYA ANGELOU

You may write me down in history
With your bitter, twisted lies,
You may trod me in the very dirt
But still, like dust, I'll rise.

Does my sassiness upset you? 5
Why are you beset with gloom?
'Cause I walk like I've got oil wells
Pumping in my living room.

Just like moons and like suns,
With the certainty of tides, 10
Just like hopes springing high,
Still I'll rise.

Did you want to see me broken?
Bowed head and lowered eyes?
Shoulders falling down like teardrops, 15
Weakened by my soulful cries?

---

sassiness Lively spiritedness, sometimes considered cheeky.

oil wells In the 19th and early 20th century the discovery of oil and the rapid growth of the petroleum industry made oil an integral part of the US economy and a symbol of wealth.

▲ The oil industry grew rapidly in the US in the 19th and early 20th century.

haughtiness Being arrogantly superior.

gold mines The discovery of gold in California in 1848 and the period of panning and mining for gold that followed is a significant period in American history.

huts A reference to slave accommodation on plantations.

> Does my haughtiness offend you?
> Don't you take it awful hard
> 'Cause I laugh like I've got gold mines
> Diggin' in my own backyard. 20
>
> You may shoot me with your words,
> You may cut me with your eyes,
> You may kill me with your hatefulness,
> But still, like air, I'll rise.
>
> Does my sexiness upset you? 25
> Does it come as a surprise
> That I dance like I've got diamonds
> At the meeting of my thighs?
>
> Out of the huts of history's shame
> I rise 30
> Up from a past that's rooted in pain
> I rise
> I'm a black ocean, leaping and wide,
> Welling and swelling I bear in the tide.
>
> Leaving behind nights of terror and fear 35
> I rise
> Into a daybreak that's wondrously clear
> I rise
> Bringing the gifts that my ancestors gave,
> I am the dream and the hope of the slave. 40
> I rise
> I rise
> I rise.

UNDERSTANDING THE TEXT

'Still I Rise' is a powerful challenge aimed at the people who have oppressed the speaker and her community. Instead of expressing simple anger at the unfairness of one group oppressing another, she challenges the very foundations of oppression by asserting her pride in who she is. She is proud of herself and her people and implies that this pride is rooted in the strength and resilience of her people. The similes she uses, of oil wells and diamonds, assert that the wealth of her innate qualities more than equals the pride brought by material wealth.

The speaker's spirit is compared with a force of nature through the use of vocabulary relating to the natural world. The range of vocabulary varies from dust, usually seen as worthless but is overpowering when it rises like a storm, to moons and suns, sources of light and life with many positive connotations.

The poem has several themes:
- racism
- oppression
- pride in oneself and one's background
- feminism
- beauty
- independence.

KEY POINT

The poet uses similes to signify resistance to oppression and the indomitable power of the human spirit.

PAPER 2 — TEXT ANTHOLOGY: FICTION — 251

Copy and complete the following table, finding examples from the poem that relate to these themes and adding your thoughts about how the language illustrates each theme.

▼ THEME	▼ EXAMPLE	▼ COMMENT
Racism		
Oppression		
Pride in oneself and one's background	'Bringing the gifts that my ancestors gave'	The speaker sees her background as a source of pride rather than as a disadvantage. The word 'gifts' shows everything she inherited in a positive light.
Feminism		
Beauty		
Independence		

EXPLORING LANGUAGE

Look carefully at the quotations in the following table and identify the technique that they demonstrate. Then copy and complete the table, explaining the effect of each example and adding other examples of your own.

KEY POINT

Practising your ability to recognise writer's techniques will enhance your ability to assess how the writer is working and therefore sharpen your critical skills.

▼ TECHNIQUE	▼ EXAMPLE	▼ EFFECT
	'like dust'	
Colloquial speech	'Don't you take it awful hard'	The poet uses colloquial American language to highlight her sense of amusement at the lack of confidence her oppressors feel when they are directly challenged.
	'history's shame'	
	'I rise / I rise / I rise'	

Direct address is a technique that dominates this poem. The poem is both personal and political in nature and it intends that the audience will listen and respond to the speaker's rhetoric. Both the speaker and the audience who is addressed are clearly defined by the language used.

Copy and complete the following table with examples that define the characteristics of speaker and audience.

▼ SPEAKER

▼ EXAMPLE	▼ CHARACTERISTIC EXPLAINED
'Does my sexiness upset you?'	The speaker is someone who has confidence in her femininity.

▼ AUDIENCE

▼ EXAMPLE	▼ CHARACTERISTIC EXPLAINED
'You may write me down in history / With your bitter, twisted lies'	The audience is accused of being manipulative and dishonest, legitimising racial oppression through the way in which history is written.

ACTIVITY 1 — **AO2** — **SKILLS** CRITICAL THINKING, ANALYSIS, INTERPRETATION

▼ USING STRUCTURE

Angelou uses structure to effectively convey the idea that both the speaker and her people will continue to rise in spite of discrimination and oppression.

First, write down the rhyme scheme of the poem. Do you think that Angelou's choice of rhyme scheme is important? Does the rhyme scheme change at any point? What is the effect of this change?

▼ RHYME SCHEME	▼ COMMENT

| PAPER 2 | TEXT ANTHOLOGY: FICTION | 253 |

▲ Award-winning American writer Maya Angelou

Now look at each verse and comment on its purpose and how it contributes to the overall structure.

▼ VERSE	▼ PURPOSE AND STRUCTURE
1	Offers a direct challenge to the audience and establishes the theme. The construction, 'You may…', lists the different types of injustice that the speaker has had to face, while the emphatic statement, 'I'll rise', suggests that she will overcome these injustices. It is a structural feature that will be repeated in the poem.
2	Questions the audience. It establishes the overall structural feature of questioning followed by an assertion of strength and superiority.
3	
4	
5	
6	
7	
8	'I rise' is given in separate lines to …
9	

ACTIVITY 2 — A01 — A04 — SKILLS: INTERPERSONAL SKILLS, NEGOTIATION

▼ FREEDOM AS A RIGHT OR A DUTY

Many people believe that the right to be free is one of the most important rights that human beings have, and some feel that it is everyone's duty to ensure that every person in the world is free. Do you agree? Discuss your reasons why or why not.

ACTIVITY 3 — A04 A05

SKILLS: CRITICAL THINKING, ANALYSIS, INTERPRETATION, ADAPTIVE LEARNING, CREATIVITY

▼ WRITING TASK

Write an essay on the topic, 'By the Colour of My Skin', exploring your ideas of self and how important or unimportant appearance is to you and others.

ACTIVITY 4 — A01

SKILLS: CRITICAL THINKING, CREATIVITY, INNOVATION

▼ REACTIONS TO OPPRESSION

Times of oppression often cause people to react in creative and innovative ways. Harriet Tubman was an African-American abolitionist who, after escaping from slavery herself, helped to rescue groups of enslaved men and women. The route used for these escapes was known as the Underground Railroad, and the safe houses and helpers on the way were referred to as 'stations' and 'conductors'. The journeys that Tubman and other 'conductors' undertook were difficult and dangerous and it was necessary for Tubman to communicate using code. It is thought that spirituals were used to give instructions to those waiting to escape.

Match the purposes (a–d) with the song lyrics.

a Communicates that the singer is planning to escape.
b When a slave hears this song he knows that he must be ready to escape.
c This is a set of directions.
d This song indicates that it is safe for the escaping slaves to meet the conductor.

GENERAL VOCABULARY

abolitionist someone who wants to end a system or law such as slavery
spirituals religious songs associated with African-American Christians living in the southern United States of America

☐
Steal away, steal away!

Steal away to Jesus!
Steal away, steal away home!
I ain't got long to stay here!

☐
Hail, oh hail, ye happy spirits,
Death no more shall make you fear,
Grief nor sorrow, pain nor anguish,
Shall no more distress you there.

☐
Wade in the water, wade in the water children.

Wade in the water. God's gonna trouble the water.
Who are those children all dressed in red?
God's gonna trouble the water.
Must be the ones that Moses led.
God's gonna trouble the water.

Who are those children all dressed in white?
God's gonna trouble the water.
Must be the ones of the Israelites.
God's gonna trouble the water.

☐
Swing low, sweet chariot,
Coming for to carry me home,
Swing low, sweet chariot,
Coming for to carry me home.

I looked over Jordan and what did I see
Coming for to carry me home,
A band of angels coming after me,
Coming for to carry me home.

PAPER 2 | TEXT ANTHOLOGY: FICTION | 255

Now write some simple rhyming verses of your own that have hidden meanings. These meanings could be messages or even directions. Copy and complete the following table, writing the verse in the first column and the hidden meaning in the second one. You may wish to work in pairs for this task.

KEY POINT

Writing with hidden meaning requires you to use all your resources of literary imagery and symbolism.

▼ VERSE	▼ MEANING

EXAM-STYLE QUESTION

SKILLS: CRITICAL THINKING, ANALYSIS, REASONING, INTERPRETATION

A01
A02

How does the poet pose a challenge to and triumph over her oppressors?
In your answer, you should write about:
- the ideas about racism and oppression conveyed in the poem
- the way the poet uses comparison and images
- the poet's use of words, phrases and techniques.

You should support your answer with close reference to the passage, including **brief** quotations.

(30 marks)

'THE STORY OF AN HOUR' KATE CHOPIN

BACKGROUND AND CONTEXT

Katherine O'Flaherty, known by her married name Chopin, was an American author of short stories and novels. She is best known for her collection of short stories, *The Awakening*, published in 1899.

The roles of men and women were very traditionally defined in the 19th century, and this was common in 19th century writing. However, Chopin's stories were daring rather than traditional and often portrayed women as trapped and unhappy in their marriages. As a result, she was criticised and her books were even banned from libraries. She is now known as an important early feminist writer and admired for her honest depictions of women's lives.

'The Story of an Hour' was first published in *Vogue* in 1894 and is one of her most popular stories. It tells the story of a woman's reaction to being told that her husband has died in an accident.

▲ Kate Chopin, writing in the late 19th century, was a pioneer of feminist literature.

KEY POINT

Kate Chopin's short stories are notable for their honest portrayal of women's lives in the period.

BEFORE YOU START READING

1. Feminism means supporting women's rights and the equality of the sexes. You can find out more about the history of feminism from reference books or on the internet. You might like to research the following questions.
   - What law in the UK gave women the right to have their own earnings and property for the first time?
   - When were women first allowed to graduate from Oxford University?
   - When were women first allowed to vote in UK parliamentary elections?

2. Kate Chopin's short stories are widely available online and in print. You could read more of her short stories, such as 'Reflections', 'Desiree's Baby' or 'The Storm', which will help you to understand her attitudes towards being a woman in the 19th century. You might like to explore some short stories written by other female authors of the time: Charlotte Perkins Gilman's 'Turned' (1911) presents similarly unconventional female characters for the period.

3. *Five Stories of an Hour* presents five dramatisations of the story; each one keeps the brevity of the story, but reads between the lines in a different way. Watch this online and to compare these interpretations with one other and with your own reading of the story and the characters.

▼ 'THE STORY OF AN HOUR' BY KATE CHOPIN

Knowing that Mrs. Mallard was afflicted with a heart trouble, great care was taken to break to her as gently as possible the news of her husband's death.

It was her sister Josephine who told her, in broken sentences; veiled hints that revealed in half concealing. Her husband's friend Richards was there, too,

'... the tops of trees that were all aquiver with the new spring life.'

near her. It was he who had been in the newspaper office when intelligence of the railroad disaster was received, with Brently Mallard's name leading the list of "killed." He had only taken the time to assure himself of its truth by a second telegram, and had hastened to forestall any less careful, less tender friend in bearing the sad message.

She did not hear the story as many women have heard the same, with a paralyzed inability to accept its significance. She wept at once, with sudden, wild abandonment, in her sister's arms. When the storm of grief had spent itself she went away to her room alone. She would have no one follow her.

There stood, facing the open window, a comfortable, roomy armchair. Into this she sank, pressed down by a physical exhaustion that haunted her body and seemed to reach into her soul.

She could see in the open square before her house the tops of trees that were all aquiver with the new spring life. The delicious breath of rain was in the air. In the street below a peddler was crying his wares. The notes of a distant song which some one was singing reached her faintly, and countless sparrows were twittering in the eaves.

There were patches of blue sky showing here and there through the clouds that had met and piled one above the other in the west facing her window.

She sat with her head thrown back upon the cushion of the chair, quite motionless, except when a sob came up into her throat and shook her, as a child who has cried itself to sleep continues to sob in its dreams.

She was young, with a fair, calm face, whose lines bespoke repression and even a certain strength. But now there was a dull stare in her eyes, whose gaze was fixed away off yonder on one of those patches of blue sky. It was not a glance of reflection, but rather indicated a suspension of intelligent thought.

There was something coming to her and she was waiting for it, fearfully. What was it? She did not know; it was too subtle and elusive to name. But she felt it, creeping out of the sky, reaching toward her through the sounds, the scents, the color that filled the air.

Now her bosom rose and fell tumultuously. She was beginning to recognize this thing that was approaching to possess her, and she was striving to beat it back with her will—as powerless as her two white slender hands would have been. When she abandoned herself a little whispered word escaped her slightly parted lips. She said it over and over under her breath: "free, free, free!" The vacant stare and the look of terror that had followed it went from her eyes. They stayed keen and bright. Her pulses beat fast, and the coursing blood warmed and relaxed every inch of her body.

She did not stop to ask if it were or were not a monstrous joy that held her. A clear and exalted perception enabled her to dismiss the suggestion as trivial. She knew that she would weep again when she saw the kind, tender hands folded in death; the face that had never looked save with love upon her, fixed and gray and dead. But she saw beyond that bitter moment a long procession of years to come that would belong to her absolutely. And she opened and spread her arms out to them in welcome.

There would be no one to live for during those coming years; she would live for herself. There would be no powerful will bending hers in that blind persistence with which men and women believe they have a right to impose a private will upon a fellow-creature. A kind intention or a cruel intention made the act seem no less a crime as she looked upon it in that brief moment of illumination.

And yet she had loved him—sometimes. Often she had not. What did it matter! What could love, the unsolved mystery, count for in the face of this possession of self-assertion which she suddenly recognized as the strongest impulse of her being!

"Free! Body and soul free!" she kept whispering.

Josephine was kneeling before the closed door with her lips to the keyhole, imploring for admission. "Louise, open the door! I beg; open the door—you will make yourself ill. What are you doing, Louise? For heaven's sake open the door."

"Go away. I am not making myself ill." No; she was drinking in a very elixir of life through that open window.

Her fancy was running riot along those days ahead of her. Spring days, and summer days, and all sorts of days that would be her own. She breathed a quick prayer that life might be long. It was only yesterday she had thought with a shudder that life might be long.

She arose at length and opened the door to her sister's importunities. There was a feverish triumph in her eyes, and she carried herself unwittingly like a goddess of Victory. She clasped her sister's waist, and together they descended the stairs. Richards stood waiting for them at the bottom.

Some one was opening the front door with a latchkey. It was Brently Mallard who entered, a little travel-stained, composedly carrying his grip-sack and umbrella. He had been far from the scene of the accident, and did not even know there had been one. He stood amazed at Josephine's piercing cry; at Richards' quick motion to screen him from the view of his wife.

But Richards was too late.

When the doctors came they said she had died of heart disease—of the joy that kills.

UNDERSTANDING THE TEXT

'The Story of an Hour' is about a woman, Mrs Mallard, who has a heart condition which means that she should not become over-excited. She is told, and briefly believes, that her husband has been killed in a train accident. The story documents the mix of the intense emotions, confusion and sense of freedom that she feels upon hearing this news.

The story describes the **epiphany** that Mrs Mallard experiences as she considers her husband's 'death'. She comes to the realisation that, although she sometimes loved her husband, that she is free and happier without him. She looks forward to her future, rather than worrying about it as she had before.

The reader learns that her name is Louise: she has her own identity and is known by her own, rather than married, name because she is free. She opens the door to her sister Josephine with a sparkle in her eye and a new sense of self. They descend the staircase together. Someone opens the door. It is her husband, Brently Mallard, unharmed and unaware of the transformation that has occurred with his absence. You hear a scream from Josephine and see the attempt to conceal the living dead from the view of the heart patient. But it is too late and Mrs. Mallard's heart stops.

GENERAL VOCABULARY

epiphany a moment of sudden and great understanding or realisation

EXPLORING LANGUAGE

Mrs Mallard's appearance, status and feelings are described in detail over the course of the story. Copy and complete the following table, considering her thoughts and finding evidence to support you.

▼ DESCRIPTION	▼ WHAT IT TELLS YOU ABOUT MRS MALLARD
'Knowing that Mrs. Mallard had a heart condition, great care was taken to break to her as gently as possible about her husband's death.'	
'she was young, with a fair, calm face, whose lines bespoke repression'	
	She feels trapped by her marriage.
	She feels freed by her husband's death.

ACTIVITY 1 — **AO2** — **SKILLS** CRITICAL THINKING, ANALYSIS, INTERPRETATION

▼ NARRATIVE TECHNIQUES

When reading texts like this, it is important to consider the way in which the author has used narrative techniques to create meaning. Look at the following table of narrative techniques and definitions, then find more examples from the text for each one.

▼ NARRATIVE TECHNIQUE	▼ DEFINITION	▼ EXAMPLE	▼ EXPLANATION
Pathetic fallacy	Giving human emotions to nature	'delicious breath of rain'	The language here shows the happiness she feels at being free. The description of the sky shows patches of blue between white clouds; birds are singing and the air is fresh and fertile.
Oxymoron	A contradiction in terms	'a monstrous joy'	This demonstrates the conflict of emotions and emphasises the extent to which the actual emotion (joy) differs from the expected and 'appropriate' emotion, sorrow.
Symbolism	The use of symbols to represent ideas or qualities	'she was drinking in the very elixir of life through that open window'	The open window represents the liberation and freedom Mrs Mallard feels from her stifling and repressive marriage.

KEY POINT

Your knowledge of narrative technique will inform your assessment of the meaning made in texts.

EXAM-STYLE QUESTION

AO1

AO2

SKILLS CRITICAL THINKING, ANALYSIS, REASONING, INTERPRETATION

How does the writer create feelings of freedom and liberation in 'The Story of an Hour'?

In your answer, you should write about:
- the narrator's reaction to the news
- the effect of setting
- the use of language.

You should support your answer with close reference to the passage, including **brief** quotations.

(30 marks)

'THE NECKLACE' GUY DE MAUPASSANT

BACKGROUND AND CONTEXT

This story is translated from French. It was written by Guy de Maupassant, who lived from 1850 to 1893 and was famous for his short stories. It is set against the background of 19th century Paris in France, where society was divided into strict social classes. Monsieur and Madame Loisel (the main characters) are not poor, but neither are they rich. They depend on the little money Monsieur Loisel earns from his minor job with the government.

BEFORE YOU START READING

1 Find out more about Guy de Maupassant. There are many websites giving information about him. His short stories are also available online, such as 'Vendetta' and 'Boule de Suif'.
2 Think of a time when you made a mistake that had serious consequences. Who or what was to blame? What lessons did you draw from the experience?

▼ 'THE NECKLACE' BY GUY DE MAUPASSANT

She was one of those pretty, delightful girls who, apparently by some error of Fate, get themselves born the daughters of very minor civil servants. She had no dowry, no expectations, no means of meeting some rich, important man who would understand, love, and marry her. So she went along with a proposal made by a junior clerk in the Ministry of Education.

She dressed simply, being unable to afford anything better, but she was every whit as unhappy as any daughter of good family who has come down in the world. Women have neither rank nor class, and their beauty, grace, and charm do service for birthright and connections. Natural guile, instinctive elegance, and adaptability are what determines their place in the hierarchy, and a girl of no birth to speak of may easily be the equal of any society lady.

She was unhappy all the time, for she felt that she was intended for a life of refinement and luxury. She was made unhappy by the run-down apartment they lived in, the peeling walls, the battered chairs, and the ugly curtains. Now all this, which any other woman of her station might never even have noticed, was torture to her and made her very angry. The spectacle of the young Breton peasant girl who did the household chores stirred sad regrets and impossible fancies. She dreamed of silent antechambers hung with oriental tapestries, lit by tall, bronze candelabras, and of two tall footmen in liveried breeches asleep in the huge armchairs, dozing in the heavy heat of a stove. She dreamed of great drawing-rooms dressed with old silk, filled with fine furniture which showed off trinkets beyond price, and of pretty little parlours, filled with perfumes and just made for intimate talk at five in the afternoon with one's closest friends who would be the most famous and sought-after men of the day whose attentions were much coveted and desired by all women.

▲ Maupassant's favourite themes include the countryside and daily life, but also pessimism, despair, madness and death.

hierarchy A strict order of importance.

Breton Someone from Britanny, an area of north-western France.

liveried Part of a uniform, usually a servant's uniform.

trinket A small decorative object.

When she sat down to dinner at the round table spread with a three-day-old cloth, facing her husband who always lifted the lid of the soup-tureen and declared delightedly: 'Ah! Stew! Splendid! There's nothing I like better than a nice stew…', she dreamed of elegant dinners, gleaming silverware, and tapestries which peopled the walls with mythical characters and strange birds in enchanted forests; she dreamed of exquisite dishes served on fabulous china plates, of pretty compliments whispered into willing ears and received with Sphinx-like smiles over the pink flesh of a trout or the wings of a hazel hen.

She had no fine dresses, no jewellery, nothing. And that was all she cared about; she felt that God had made her for such things. She would have given anything to be popular, envied, attractive, and in demand.

She had a friend who was rich, a friend from her convent days, on whom she never called now, for she was always so unhappy afterwards. Sometimes, for days on end, she would weep tears of sorrow, regret, despair, and anguish.

One evening her husband came home looking highly pleased with himself. In his hand he brandished a large envelope.

'Look,' he said, 'I've got something for you.'

She tore the paper flap eagerly and extracted a printed card bearing these words:

> 'The Minister of Education and Madame Georges Ramponneau request the pleasure of the company of Monsieur and Madame Loisel at the Ministry Buildings on the evening of 18 January.'

Instead of being delighted as her husband had hoped, she tossed the invitation peevishly onto the table and muttered: 'What earthly use is that to me?'

'But, darling, I thought you'd be happy. You never go anywhere and it's an opportunity, a splendid opportunity! I had the dickens of a job getting hold of an invite. Everybody's after them; they're very much in demand and not many are handed out to us clerks. You'll be able to see all the big nobs there.'

She looked at him irritably and said shortly: 'And what am I supposed to wear if I do go?'

He had not thought of that. He blustered: 'What about the dress you wear for the theatre? It looks all right to me…' The words died in his throat. He was totally disconcerted and dismayed by the sight of his wife who had begun to cry. Two large tears rolled slowly out of the corners of her eyes and down towards the sides of her mouth.

'What's up?' he stammered. 'What's the matter?'

Making a supreme effort, she controlled her sorrows and, wiping her damp cheeks, replied quite calmly: 'Nothing. It's just that I haven't got anything to wear and consequently I shan't be going to any reception. Give the invite to one of your colleagues with a wife who is better off for clothes than I am.'

He was devastated. He went on: 'Oh come on, Mathilde. Look, what could it cost to get something suitable that would do for other occasions, something fairly simple?'

She thought for a few moments, working out her sums but also wondering

---

Sphinx-like Mysterious and difficult to interpret.

Monsieur and Madame Loisel Mr and Mrs Loisel.

peevishly Irritably, crossly.

big nobs Wealthy people of high social status.

francs The former currency of France before the introduction of the euro.

posy A small bunch of flowers.

how much she could decently ask for without drawing an immediate refusal and pained protests from her husband who was careful with his money. Finally, after some hesitation, she said: 'I can't say precisely, but I daresay I could get by on four hundred francs.'

He turned slightly pale, for he had been setting aside just that amount to buy a gun and finance hunting trips the following summer in the flat landscape around Nanterre with a few friends who went shooting larks there on Sundays. But he said: 'Very well. I'll give you your four hundred francs. But do try and get a decent dress.'

The day of the reception drew near and Madame Loisel appeared sad, worried, anxious. Yet all her clothes were ready. One evening her husband said: 'What's up? You haven't half been acting funny these last few days.'

She replied: 'It vexes me that I haven't got a single piece of jewellery, not one stone, that I can put on. I'll look like a church mouse. I'd almost as soon not go to the reception.'

'Wear a posy,' he said. 'It's all the rage this year. You could get two or three magnificent roses for ten francs.'

She was not convinced. 'No. There's nothing so humiliating as to look poor when you're with women who are rich.'

But her husband exclaimed: 'You aren't half silly! Look, go and see your friend, Madame Forestier, and ask her to lend you some jewellery. You know her well enough for that.'

She gave a delighted cry: 'You're right! I never thought of that!'

The next day she called on her friend and told her all about her problem. Madame Forestier went over to a mirror-fronted wardrobe, took out a large casket, brought it over, unlocked it, and said to Madame Loisel: 'Choose whatever you like.'

Venetian From Venice, in Italy.

At first she saw bracelets, then a rope of pearls and a Venetian cross made of gold and diamonds admirably fashioned. She tried on the necklaces in the mirror, and could hardly bear to take them off and give them back. She kept asking: 'Have you got anything else?'

'Yes, of course. Just look. I can't say what sort of thing you'll like best.'

All of a sudden, in a black satinwood case, she found a magnificent diamond necklace, and her heart began to beat with immoderate desire. Her hands shook as she picked it up. She fastened it around her throat over her high-necked dress and sat looking at herself in rapture. Then, diffidently, apprehensively, she asked: 'Can you lend me this? Nothing else. Just this.'

'But of course.'

She threw her arms around her friend, kissed her extravagantly, and then ran home, taking her treasure with her.

The day of the reception arrived. Madame Loisel was a success. She was the prettiest woman there, elegant, graceful, radiant, and wonderfully happy. All the men looked at her, enquired who she was, and asked to be introduced. All the cabinet secretaries and under-secretaries wanted to waltz with her. She was even noticed by the Minister himself.

homage Respect.

Seine The river that runs through Paris.

hackney cab An early form of taxi.

'... her heart began to beat with immoderate desire'

She danced ecstatically, wildly, intoxicated with pleasure, giving no thought to anything else, swept along on her victorious beauty and glorious success, and floating on a cloud of happiness composed of the homage, admiration, and desire she evoked and the kind of complete and utter triumph which is so sweet to a woman's heart.

She left at about four in the morning. Since midnight her husband had been dozing in a small, empty side-room with three other men whose wives were having an enjoyable time.

He helped her on with her coat which he had fetched when it was time to go, a modest, everyday coat, a commonplace coat violently at odds with the elegance of her dress. It brought her down to earth, and she would have preferred to slip away quietly and avoid being noticed by the other women who were being arrayed in rich furs. But Loisel grabbed her by the arm: 'Wait a sec. You'll catch cold outside. I'll go and get a cab.'

But she refused to listen and ran quickly down the stairs. When they were outside in the street, there was no cab in sight. They began looking for one, hailing all the cabbies they saw driving by in the distance.

They walked down to the Seine in desperation, shivering with cold. There, on the embankment, they at last found one of those aged nocturnal hackney cabs which only emerge in Paris after dusk, as if ashamed to parade their poverty in the full light of day. It bore them back to their front door in the rue des Martyrs, and they walked sadly up to their apartment. For her it was all over, while he was thinking that he would have to be at the Ministry at ten.

Standing in front of the mirror, she took off the coat she had been wearing over her shoulders, to get a last look at herself in all her glory. Suddenly she gave a cry. The necklace was no longer round her throat!

Her husband, who was already half undressed, asked: 'What's up?'

She turned to him in a panic: 'I... I... Madame Forestier's necklace... I haven't got it!'

He straightened up as if thunderstruck: 'What?... But... You can't have lost it!'

They looked in the pleats of her dress, in the folds of her coat, and in her pockets. They looked everywhere. They did not find it.

'Are you sure you still had it when you left the ballroom?' he asked.

'Yes, I remember fingering it in the entrance hall.'

'But if you'd lost it in the street, we'd have heard it fall. So it must be in the cab.'

'That's right. That's probably it. Did you get his number?'

'No. Did you happen to notice it?'

'No.'

They looked at each other in dismay. Finally Loisel got dressed again. 'I'm going to go back the way we came,' he said, 'to see if I can find it.' He went out. She remained as she was, still wearing her evening gown, not having the strength to go to bed, sitting disconsolately on a chair by the empty grate, her mind a blank.

Her husband returned at about seven o'clock. He had found nothing.

He went to the police station, called at newspaper offices where he advertised a reward, toured the cab companies, and tried anywhere where the faintest of hopes led him. She waited for him all day long in the same distracted condition, thinking of the appalling catastrophe which had befallen them.

Loisel came back that evening, hollow-cheeked and very pale. He had not come up with anything.

'Look,' he said, 'you'll have to write to your friend and say you broke the catch on her necklace and you are getting it repaired. That'll give us time to work out what we'll have to do.'

She wrote to his dictation.

A week later they had lost all hope.

Loisel, who had aged five years, said: 'We'll have to start thinking about replacing the necklace.'

The next day they took the case in which it had come and called on the jeweller whose name was inside. He looked through his order book.

'It wasn't me that sold the actual necklace. I only supplied the case.'

After this, they trailed round jeweller's shops, looking for a necklace just like the other one, trying to remember it, and both ill with worry and anxiety.

In a shop in the Palais Royal they found a diamond collar which they thought was identical to the one they were looking for. It cost forty thousand francs. The jeweller was prepared to let them have it for thirty-six.

They asked him not to sell it for three days. And they got him to agree to take it back for thirty-four thousand if the one that had been lost turned up before the end of February.

Loisel had eighteen thousand francs which his father had left him. He would have to borrow the rest.

He borrowed the money, a thousand francs here, five hundred there, sometimes a hundred and as little as sixty. He signed notes, agreed to pay exorbitant rates of interest, resorted to usurers and the whole tribe of moneylenders. He mortgaged the rest of his life, signed papers without knowing if he would ever be able to honour his commitments, and then, sick with worry about the future, the grim poverty which stood ready to pounce, and the prospect of all the physical privation and mental torture ahead, he went round to the jeweller's to get the new necklace with the thirty-six thousand francs which he put on the counter.

When Madame Loisel took it round, Madame Forestier said in a huff: 'You ought really to have brought it back sooner. I might have needed it.'

She did not open the case, as her friend had feared she might. If she had noticed the substitution, what would she have thought? What would she have said? Would she not have concluded she was a thief?

▲ Shops in Palais Royale, Paris

Then began for Madame Loisel the grindingly horrible life of the very poor. But quickly and heroically, she resigned herself to what she could not alter: their appalling debt would have to be repaid. She was determined to pay. They dismissed the maid. They moved out of their apartment and rented an attic room.

She became used to heavy domestic work and all kinds of ghastly kitchen chores. She washed dishes, wearing down her pink nails on the greasy pots and saucepans. She washed the dirty sheets, shirts, and floorcloths by hand and hung them up to dry on a line; each morning she took the rubbish down to the street and carried the water up, pausing for breath on each landing. And, dressed like any working-class woman, she shopped at the fruiterer's, the grocer's, and the butcher's, with a basket over her arm, haggling, frequently abused and always counting every penny.

Each month they had to settle some accounts, renew others, and bargain for time.

Her husband worked in the evenings doing accounts for a shopkeeper and quite frequently sat up into the early hours doing copying work at five sous a page.

sous Coins of very small value.

They lived like this for ten years.

By the time ten years had gone by, they had repaid everything, with not a penny outstanding, in spite of the extortionate conditions and including the accumulated interest.

Madame Loisel looked old now. She had turned into the battling, hard, uncouth housewife who rules working-class homes. Her hair was untidy, her skirts were askew, and her hands were red. She spoke in a gruff voice and scrubbed floors on her hands and knees. But sometimes, when her husband had gone to the office, she would sit by the window and think of that evening long ago when she had been so beautiful and so admired.

What might not have happened had she not lost the necklace? Who could tell? Who could possibly tell? Life is so strange, so fickle! How little is needed to make or break us!

One Sunday, needing a break from her heavy working week, she went out for a stroll on the Champs-Elysées. Suddenly she caught sight of a woman pushing a child in a pram. It was Madame Forestier, still young, still beautiful, and still attractive.

Champs-Elysées A famous street in Paris.

Madame Loisel felt apprehensive. Should she speak to her? Yes, why not? Now that she had paid in full, she would tell her everything. Why not? She went up to her.

'Hello, Jeanne.'

The friend did not recognize her and was taken aback at being addressed so familiarly by a common woman in the street. She stammered: 'But... I'm sorry... I don't know... There's some mistake.'

'No mistake. I'm Madame Loisel.'

Her friend gave a cry: 'But my poor Mathilde, how you've changed!'

'Yes, I've been through some hard times since I saw you, very hard times. And it was all on your account.'

'On my account? Whatever do you mean?'

'Do you remember that diamond necklace you lent me to go to the reception at the Ministry?'

'Yes. What about it?'

'Well I lost it.'

'Lost it? But you returned it to me.'

'No, I returned another one just like it. And we've been paying for it these past ten years. You know, it wasn't easy for us. We had nothing… But it's over and done with now, and I'm glad.'

Madame Forestier stopped. 'You mean you bought a diamond necklace to replace mine?'

'Yes. And you never noticed the difference, did you? They were exactly alike.' And she smiled a proud, innocent smile.

Madame Forestier looked very upset and, taking both her hands in hers, said:

'Oh, my poor Mathilde! But it was only an imitation necklace. It couldn't have been worth much more than five hundred francs!…'

UNDERSTANDING THE TEXT

The story has a lot in common with the fairytale 'Cinderella', but the outcome is completely different. Everything hinges on the surprise ending, but the effectiveness of this depends on the events which lead up to it and, in particular, on the characters involved. Of these, Madame Loisel is the most important and the most controversial. You will need to understand her character well in order to answer exam questions.

In the first few sentences of the story, you learn that Madame Loisel is young and attractive, and, whilst not rich, she is certainly not poor. Why then, is she 'unhappy all the time'? Copy and complete the table, making a list of the reasons you can find for her unhappiness, using the first section (up to 'tears of sorrow, regret, despair, and anguish').

▼ REASON	▼ SUPPORTING QUOTATION	▼ EFFECT
Her background and family were very ordinary.	'She is one of those who get themselves born the daughters of very minor civil servants.'	She has no possibility of marrying a rich or important man.
She has charm and beauty but is relatively poor.		She feels degraded and undervalued.
She feels she is a victim of the strict order of society.		

PAPER 2 — TEXT ANTHOLOGY: FICTION

KEY POINT

Maupassant's moral world is not simple. The reader is drawn into making judgements but immediately has them challenged by another point of view.

Most readers blame Madame Loisel for what happens, though some sympathise with her. You need to decide what your own view is. Read through the story and note all the occasions when you consider her to be a victim, and all those when you think she is responsible for her own problems. Remember to find a quotation to support each of your points.

Copy and complete the following table, balancing out the arguments for and against and adding some points of your own. Find quotations to support each of your own points. You will probably have more points in one column than the other.

▼ MADAME LOISEL	
▼ **POINTS IN HER FAVOUR**	▼ **POINTS AGAINST HER**
She deserves more than society offers her – her birth is an 'error of Fate.'	She is vain and frivolous – she had no fine dresses and no jewellery, and that was all she cared about.
Her husband is rather boring and too 'careful with his money'.	She is ungrateful to a thoughtful husband.
Her suffering is not related to what she did; it is unfair that she loses all her beauty whereas Madame Forestier remains 'still young, still beautiful'.	She is the victim of her own pride; she could have simply told her friend the truth but did not want to lose face.
Her hard work at the end makes her admirable – 'quickly and heroically, she resigned herself to what she could not alter'.	Yes, she does make up for her mistake – but this does not mean she did not deserve what happened to her.

▶ Having considered all the evidence, what is your overall opinion of Madame Loisel and how Maupassant has presented her?

The other characters are not so developed, although Monsieur Loisel is the most important. Here are two candidates' views of him. With which do you agree and why?

EXAMPLE STUDENT ANSWER A

Monsieur Loisel is a loving husband, who is presented by the writer as both generous and indulgent. He goes to great lengths to get the invitation to the occasion and even sleeps in a separate room while his wife enjoys the dancing. When faced with the problems caused by the loss of the necklace, he works hard with his wife to pay for the new necklace. He never criticises her. He is her victim.

EXAMPLE STUDENT ANSWER B

Monsieur Loisel is only a junior clerk without any kind of ambition. He loves his wife but has no real understanding of her or what her hopes must be; he is out of his depth with her. At the end he is as stubbornly proud as his wife and, instead of suggesting that she simply tells the truth, he accepts their joint fate. They are equally responsible for what happens.

Madame Forestier, Madame Loisel's friend, is not written about in detail. While she shows some kindness by loaning the necklace, she doesn't tell Madame Loisel that it is an imitation and is quite sharp when it is returned late. At the end of the story, is she really sympathetic or is she mocking Madame Loisel? Ironically, she is exactly the kind of woman that Madame Loisel, at the start of the story, had hoped to be.

EXPLORING LANGUAGE

Because this is a translation, you are not commenting directly on the writer's use of language. However, some points about language can be made.

- Look for contrasts, such as that between the rich and sophisticated language used to describe Madame Loisel's dreams and her experiences at the party ('She danced ecstatically, wildly, intoxicated with pleasure…') compared with the blunter and more direct language used to emphasise the extent of her poverty after the necklace is lost ('Her hair was untidy … her hands were red').
- Dialogue is used to illustrate character, such as the homeliness of her husband: 'Ah! Stew! Splendid! There's nothing I like better…'. It is also used to create drama. For example, look at the exchange between Madame Loisel and Madame Forestier at the very end.

Find some more examples to illustrate these points.

ACTIVITY 1 — **A01** — SKILLS: COLLABORATION, REASONING, INTERPRETATION, NEGOTIATION

▼ THEMES OF 'THE NECKLACE'

In a small group or pairs, consider the following ideas about the themes of 'The Necklace'.

> 'The story is about fate and its unfairness and uncertainty.'
>
> 'The story shows us that honesty is always the best policy.'
>
> 'The story is about vanity and shows that pride comes before a fall.'
>
> 'The story is about social class and the problems of being born into a poor family.'

Discuss these views with your partner or your group, answering the following questions.

- ▶ Which of these statements do you think is the most accurate description of 'The Necklace'? Is the story about anything else?
- ▶ Some readers say that, in 'The Necklace', Maupassant is making fun of his characters and that he hates women. Do you agree?

ACTIVITY 2 — **A04** **A05** — SKILLS: CRITICAL THINKING, ANALYSIS, INTERPRETATION, ADAPTIVE LEARNING, CREATIVITY

▼ WRITING TASK

In the story, Mathilde seems to be trapped by society. To what extent do you think women in today's world are trapped by society? Write an essay explaining your views on this subject.

EXAM-STYLE QUESTION

A01

A02

SKILLS: CRITICAL THINKING, ANALYSIS, REASONING, INTERPRETATION

How does the writer try to make the character of Madame Loisel interesting for the reader in 'The Necklace'?

In your answer, you should write about:

- the way she is presented up to the loss of the necklace
- her relationship with her husband up to the loss of the necklace
- the changes after the loss of the necklace
- the use of language.

You should support your answer with close reference to the passage, including **brief** quotations.

(30 marks)

'SIGNIFICANT CIGARETTES' (FROM *THE ROAD HOME*) ROSE TREMAIN

BACKGROUND AND CONTEXT

Rose Tremain is an established and very successful English novelist who seeks out the strange, the unfamiliar and the near-unknowable as subjects for her fiction. 'Significant Cigarettes' is an extract from her novel, *The Road Home*. It tells the story of a journey of a desperately poor man called Lev. He travels from Eastern Europe to London, where he hopes to make a better life for himself. Before Lev left his own country, his wife had died. In order to make the journey he has to leave his young daughter behind.

The arrival in Britain of large numbers of migrants who want to find work has caused concern and anger among some people. In 'Significant Cigarettes', Tremain shows the reader something of what it is like to be poor, homeless and desperate.

▲ Novelist Rose Tremain has said that she aims to attain a 'new clarity' through her books for both herself and her readers.

BEFORE YOU START READING

1. What do you think might be difficult about welcoming strangers into your home?
2. How would you try to help a child who was suddenly left in your care by a parent who was fleeing abroad? What considerations would be the most important?
3. Have you ever explored or visited a place that was totally unfamiliar to you? What did you find? What did you learn?

▼ 'SIGNIFICANT CIGARETTES' BY ROSE TREMAIN

On the coach, Lev chose a seat near the back and he sat huddled against the window, staring out at the land he was leaving: at the fields of sunflowers scorched by the dry wind, at the pig farms, at the quarries and rivers and at the wild garlic growing green at the edge of the road.

Lev wore a leather jacket and jeans and a leather cap pulled low over his eyes and his handsome face was grey-toned from his smoking and in his hands he clutched an old red cotton handkerchief and a dented pack of Russian cigarettes. He would soon be forty-three.

After some miles, as the sun came up, Lev took out a cigarette and stuck it between his lips, and the woman sitting next to him, a plump, contained person with moles like splashes of mud on her face, said quickly: 'I'm sorry, but there is no smoking allowed on this bus.'

Lev knew this, had known it in advance, had tried to prepare himself mentally for the long agony of it. But even an unlit cigarette was a companion – something to hold on to, something that had promise in it – and all he could be bothered to do now was to nod, just to show the woman that he'd heard what she'd said, reassure her that he wasn't going to cause trouble; because there they would have to sit for fifty hours or more, side by side with their separate aches and dreams, like a married couple. They would hear each other's snores and sighs, smell the food and drink each had brought with them, note the degree to which each was fearful or unafraid, make short forays into conversation. And then later, when they finally arrived in London, they would probably separate with barely a word or a look, walk out into a rainy morning, each alone and beginning a new life. And Lev thought how all of this was odd but necessary and already told him things about the world he was travelling to, a world in which he would break his back working – if only that work could be found. He would hold himself apart from other people, find corners and shadows in which to sit and smoke, demonstrate that he didn't need to belong, that his heart remained in his own country.

There were two coach-drivers. These men would take turns to drive and to sleep. There was an on-board lavatory, so the only stops the bus would make would be for gas. At gas stations, the passengers would be able to clamber off, walk a few paces, see wild flowers on a verge, soiled paper among bushes, sun or rain on the road. They might stretch up their arms, put on dark glasses against the onrush of nature's light, look for a clover leaf, smoke and stare at the cars rushing by. Then they would be herded back onto the coach, resume their old attitudes, arm themselves for the next hundred miles, for the stink of another industrial zone, or the sudden gleam of a lake, for rain and sunset and the approach of darkness on silent marshes. There would be times when the journey would seem to have no end.

Sleeping upright was not something Lev was practised in. The old seemed to be able to do it, but forty-two was not yet old. Lev's father, Stefan, sometimes used to sleep upright, in summer, on a hard wooden chair in his lunch break at the Baryn sawmill, with the hot sun falling onto the slices of sausage wrapped in paper on his knee and onto his flask of tea. Both Stefan and Lev could sleep lying down on a mound of hay or on the mossy carpet of a forest. Often, Lev had slept on a rag rug beside his daughter's bed, when she was ill or afraid. And when his wife, Marina, was dying, he'd lain for five nights on an area of linoleum flooring no wider than his outstretched arm, between Marina's hospital bed and a curtain patterned with pink and purple daisies, and sleep had come and gone in a mystifying kind of way, painting strange pictures in Lev's brain that had never completely vanished.

Towards evening, after two stops for gas, the mole-flecked woman unwrapped a hard-boiled egg. She peeled it silently. The smell of the egg reminded Lev of the sulphur springs at Jor, where he'd taken Marina, just in case nature could cure what man had given up for lost. Marina had immersed her body obediently in the scummy water, lain there looking at a female stork returning to its high nest, and said to Lev: 'If only we were storks.'

'Why d'you say that?' Lev had asked.

'Because you never see a stork dying. It's as though they didn't die.'

If only we were storks.

On the woman's knee a clean cotton napkin was spread and her white hands smoothed it and she unwrapped rye bread and a twist of salt.

'My name is Lev,' said Lev.

'My name is Lydia,' said the woman. And they shook hands, Lev's hand holding the scrunched-up kerchief, and Lydia's hand rough with salt and smelling of egg, and then Lev asked: 'What are you planning to do in England?' and Lydia said: 'I have some interviews in London for jobs as a translator.'

'That sounds promising.'

'I hope so. I was a teacher of English at School 237 in Yarbl, so my language is very colloquial.'

Lev looked at Lydia. It wasn't difficult to imagine her standing in front of a class and writing words on a blackboard. He said: 'I wonder why you're leaving our country when you had a good job at School 237 in Yarbl?'

'Well,' said Lydia. 'I became very tired of the view from my window. Every day, summer and winter, I looked out at the school yard and the high fence and the apartment block beyond, and I began to imagine I would die seeing these things, and I didn't want this. I expect you understand what I mean?'

Lev took off his leather cap and ran his fingers through his thick grey hair. He saw Lydia turn to him for a moment and look very seriously into his eyes.

He said: 'Yes, I understand.'

Then there was a silence, while Lydia ate her hard-boiled egg. She chewed very quietly. When she'd finished the egg, Lev said: 'My English isn't too bad. I took some classes in Baryn, but my teacher told me my pronunciation wasn't very good. May I say some words and you can tell me if I'm pronouncing them correctly?'

'Yes, of course,' said Lydia.

Lev said: 'Lovely. Sorry. I am legal. How much please. Thank you. May you help me.'

'May I help you,' corrected Lydia. 'May I help you,' repeated Lev.

'Go on,' said Lydia.

'Stork,' said Lev. 'Stork's nest. Rain. I am lost. I wish for an interpreter. Bee-and-bee.'

'Be-and-be?' said Lydia. 'No, no. You mean "to be, or not to be".'

'No,' said Lev. 'Bee-and-bee. Family hotel, quite cheap.'

'Oh, yes, I know. B & B.'

Lev could now see that darkness was falling outside the window and he thought how, in his village, darkness had always arrived in precisely the same way, from the same direction, above the same trees, whether early or late, whether in summer, winter or spring, for the whole of his life. This darkness – particular to that place, Auror – was how, in Lev's heart, darkness would always fall. And so he told Lydia that he came from Auror, had worked in the Baryn sawmill until it closed two years ago, and since then he'd found no work at all and his family – his mother, his five-year-old daughter and he – had lived off the money his mother made selling jewellery manufactured from tin.

'Oh,' said Lydia. 'I think that's very resourceful, to make jewellery from tin.'

'Sure,' said Lev. 'But it isn't enough.'

Tucked into his boot was a small flask of vodka. He extracted the flask and took a long swig. Lydia kept eating her rye bread. Lev wiped his mouth with the red handkerchief and saw his face reflected in the coach window. He looked away. Since the death of Marina, he didn't like to catch sight of his own reflection, because what he always saw in it was his own guilt at still being alive.

'Why did the sawmill at Baryn close?' asked Lydia.

'They ran out of trees,' said Lev.

'Very bad,' said Lydia. 'What other work can you do?'

Lev drank again. Someone had told him that in England vodka was too expensive to drink.

Immigrants made their own alcohol from potatoes and tap water, and when Lev thought about these industrious immigrants, he imagined them sitting by a coal fire in a tall house, talking and laughing, with rain falling outside the window and red buses going past and a television flickering in a corner of the room. He sighed and said: 'I will do any work at all. My daughter Maya needs clothes, shoes, books, toys, everything. England is my hope.'

Towards ten o'clock, red blankets were given out to the coach passengers, some of whom were already sleeping. Lydia put away the remnants of her meal, covered her body with the blanket and switched on a fierce little light above her under the baggage rack and began reading a faded old paperback, printed in English. Lev saw that the title of her book was The Power and the Glory. His longing for a cigarette had grown steadily since he'd drunk the vodka and now it was acute. He could feel the yearning in his lungs and in his blood, and his hands grew fidgety and he felt a tremor in his legs. How long before the next gas stop? It could be four or five hours. Everyone on the bus would be asleep by then, except him and one of the two drivers. Only they would keep a lonely, exhausting vigil, the driver's body tensed to the moods and alarms of the dark, unravelling road; his own aching for the comfort of nicotine or oblivion – and getting neither.

He envied Lydia, immersed in her English book. Lev knew he had to distract himself with something.... In desperation, he took from his wallet a brand new British twenty-pound note and reached up and switched on his own little reading light and began to examine the note. On one side, the frumpy Queen, E II R, with her diadem, her face grey on a purple ground, and on the other, a man, some personage from the past, with a dark drooping moustache and an angel blowing a trumpet above him and all the angel's radiance falling on him in vertical lines. 'The British venerate their history,' Lev had been told in his English class, 'chiefly because they have never been subjected to Occupation. Only intermittently do they see that some of their past deeds were not good.'

The indicated lifespan of the man on the note was 1857–1934. He looked like a banker, but what had he done to be on a twenty-pound note in the twenty-first century? Lev stared at his determined jaw, squinted at his name written out in a scrawl beneath the wing collar, but couldn't read it. He thought that this was a person who would never have known any other system of being alive but Capitalism. He would have heard the names Hitler and Stalin, but not been afraid – would have had no need to be afraid of anything except a little loss of capital in what Americans called the Crash, when men in New York had jumped out of windows and off roofs. He would have died safely in his bed before London was bombed to ruins, before Europe was torn apart. Right to the end of his days, the angel's radiance had probably shone on this man's brow and on his fusty clothes, because it was known across the world: the English were lucky. Well, thought Lev, I'm going to their country now and I'm going to make them share it with me: their infernal luck. I've left Auror and that leaving of my home was hard and bitter, but my time is coming.

▲ 'I'm going to their country now and I'm going to make them share it with me: their infernal luck ...'

UNDERSTANDING THE TEXT

KEY POINT

It is important to realise that this is a scene from the early part of a novel, not a text designed to stand alone.

'Significant Cigarettes' is an extract from a novel. This means that you should not simply read it as an account of events but as a piece of writing designed to draw you in to the novel's characters and themes. In this piece you learn about Lev and Lydia and the things that concern them, themes which may be important in the novel from which this extract is taken.

The author provides a contrast between two characters who are travelling side by side, for some days, on a bus. You are told about their lives back home and their reasons for travelling, and you are provided with an insight into their expectations of life when they arrive in London. This information encourages you to imagine how they will cope at their journey's end.

Copy and complete the following table, identifying as many themes from the passage as you can and add examples of each from the text.

▼ THEME	▼ EXAMPLE FROM THE TEXT
Departure and leaving things behind	'huddled against the window, staring out at the land he was leaving'
Travelling companions	
Never-ending travel	
Desperation	
England and the English	

EXPLORING LANGUAGE

The writer arranges the text to help you explore important aspects of the story. Events on the journey lead you through Lev's thoughts, providing an apparently natural opportunity to hear about the life he has left behind and what he imagines life will be like once he reaches London. When he sees that it is getting dark outside, he is reminded of the way in which night falls in his village, and these memories give the reader an insight into Lev's background.

There is a contrast too between the confident speech of Lydia and Lev's requests for help with the English language.

The words and phrases used by a writer affect the way in which you see and understand things. For example, Lydia speaks first: 'I'm sorry, but there is no smoking allowed on this bus.' She apologises for speaking to him – 'I'm sorry' – then adds words which suggest that she feels that she should point out the ban on smoking. This is different from 'No smoking on the bus' or 'Don't think you're going to smoke next to me.' Later, Lev's craving for a cigarette grows and a number of the symptoms are shown in striking words and phrases ('his hands grew fidgety'), and a succession of sentences ending with a much longer sentence that reflect his growing urge to smoke. The cigarettes provide a symbol, a reminder of what Lev desperately wants to do, but may not do on the bus. This inability to act is contrasted with Lydia's confident use of English when she makes clear that smoking is not permitted.

What things trouble Lev during his journey? Copy and complete the following table, listing them and finding evidence in the text to back them up.

▼ WHAT TROUBLES LEV?	▼ EVIDENCE
Leaving his home country	'staring out at the land he was leaving'

ACTIVITY 1 — A01 — SKILLS: INTERPERSONAL SKILLS, NEGOTIATION

▼ FUNCTION OF THE EXTRACT WITHIN THE NOVEL

Discuss the effect that Lydia has on Lev. Why do you think that their meeting and travelling together is important in this extract and perhaps in the novel as a whole?

ACTIVITY 2 — A04 — A05 — SKILLS: ADAPTIVE LEARNING, CREATIVITY, INNOVATION

▼ WRITING TASKS

1. Write the sort of article that Lev might write to a newspaper or magazine back in his home country, in which he advises people there who might be considering coming to Britain to find work.
2. Write about a strange journey with an unusual companion.

EXAM-STYLE QUESTIONS

A01

A02

SKILLS: CRITICAL THINKING, ANALYSIS, REASONING, INTERPRETATION

How does the writer create feelings of nostalgia in 'Significant Cigarettes'?
In your answer, you should write about:
- the dialogue between characters
- Lev's memories and thoughts
- the use of language.

You should support your answer with close reference to the passage, including **brief** quotations. **(30 marks)**

How does the writer bring out Lev's uncertainty in 'Significant Cigarettes'? In your answer, you should write about:
- the dialogue between Lev and Lydia
- Lydia's confidence
- the setting, the transition between home and a new country.

You should support your answer with close reference to the passage, including **brief** quotations. **(30 marks)**

| PAPER 2 | TEXT ANTHOLOGY: FICTION |

'WHISTLE AND I'LL COME TO YOU' (FROM *THE WOMAN IN BLACK*)
SUSAN HILL

BACKGROUND AND CONTEXT
Susan Hill is an English writer of literary novels, ghost stories, children's books, detective novels and memoirs. She has won the Whitbread, Somerset Maugham and John Llewellyn Rhys awards and has been shortlisted for the Booker Prize. She is known for writing in the Gothic style with its distinctive creation of suspense through a description of background and atmosphere.
The Woman in Black is probably the most well-known of her ghost stories written in this tradition and its stage production is the second longest running play in London's West End.

The novel is the story of Arthur Kipps and is narrated in the first person. It recounts his experiences in the town of Crythin Gifford when he was a young junior solicitor. The story centres around Eel Marsh House, where unexplained noises are heard and the ghostly figure of the Woman in Black is sighted. Kipps later learns that this is the ghost of Jennet Humfrye, a woman whose son died in an accident on the marshes, and that her appearance foretells the death of a child. Kipps's involvement in events at Eel Marsh House ultimately lead to the deaths of his wife and child.

▲ English writer Susan Hill

GENERAL VOCABULARY
Booker Prize prestigious British award given for outstanding literary works in English
London's West End an area of London where a number of good quality professional theatres are located

BEFORE YOU START READING
1. Read about the Gothic novel and find out about some of its more famous examples, such as Horace Walpole's *The Castle of Otranto* and Ann Radcliffe's *The Mysteries of Udolpho*.
2. There are several movie adaptations of *The Woman in Black*. Try to watch one as a class, paying particular attention to the way in which the story's background is shown and how an atmosphere of eeriness and suspense is created.
3. Do you believe in ghosts and the supernatural? Talk about some of the ghost stories you know from the folklore of your country and culture. What are their common features? Are they similar or different to the typical stories of the Gothic tradition?

▼ 'WHISTLE AND I'LL COME TO YOU' BY SUSAN HILL

During the night the wind rose. As I had lain reading I had become aware of the stronger gusts that blew every so often against the casements. But when I awoke abruptly in the early hours it had increased greatly in force. The house felt like a ship at sea, battered by the gale that came roaring across the

casements Windows that are set on hinges and open like doors.

marsh An area of low-lying land that generally remains flooded all year round.

nook and cranny An idiom pair that means every possible place.

nostalgically Thinking about a pleasure from the past.

banshee In Irish folklore, a female spirit whose wailing warns of an impending death.

anguish Severe mental or physical suffering.

▲ Susan Hill's ghost stories are distinctive for their creation of suspense.

conjecture An opinion formed on the basis of incomplete information.

Mrs. Drablow Owner of Eel Marsh House; it was to sort out the legal matters arising from her death that the narrator had come to Crythin Gifford.

retainer A person attached or owing service to a household; a servant.

open marsh. Windows were rattling everywhere and there was the sound of moaning down all the chimneys of the house and whistling through every nook and cranny.

At first I was alarmed. Then, as I lay still, gathering my wits, I reflected on how long Eel Marsh House had stood here, steady as a lighthouse, quite alone and exposed, bearing the brunt of winter after winter of gales and driving rain and sleet and spray. It was unlikely to blow away tonight. And then, those memories of childhood began to be stirred again and I dwelt nostalgically upon all those nights when I had lain in the warm and snug safety of my bed in the nursery at the top of our family house in Sussex, hearing the wind rage round like a lion, howling at the doors and beating upon the windows but powerless to reach me. I lay back and slipped into that pleasant, trance-like state somewhere between sleeping and waking, recalling the past and all its emotions and impressions vividly, until I felt I was a small boy again.

Then from somewhere, out of that howling darkness, a cry came to my ears, catapulting me back into the present and banishing all tranquility.

I listened hard. Nothing. The tumult of the wind, like a banshee, and the banging and rattling of the window in its old, ill-fitting frame. Then yes, again, a cry, that familiar cry of desperation and anguish, a cry for help from a child somewhere out on the marsh.

There was no child. I knew that. How could there be? Yet how could I lie here and ignore even the crying of some long dead ghost?

'Rest in peace,' I thought, but this poor one did not, could not.

After a few moments I got up. I would go down into the kitchen and make myself a drink, stir up the fire a little and sit beside it trying, trying to shut out that calling voice for which I could do nothing, and no one had been able to do anything for… how many years?

As I went out onto the landing, Spider the dog following me at once, two things happened together. I had the impression of someone who had just that very second before gone past me on their way from the top of the stairs to one of the other rooms, and, as a tremendous blast of wind hit the house so that it all but seemed to rock at the impact, the lights went out. I had not bothered to pick up my torch from the bedside table and now I stood in the pitch blackness, unsure for a moment of my bearings.

And the person who had gone by, and who was now in this house with me? I had seen no one, felt nothing. There had been no movement, no brush of a sleeve against mine, no disturbance of the air, I had not even heard a foot step. I had simply the absolutely certain sense of someone just having passed close to me and gone away down the corridor. Down the short narrow corridor that led to the nursery whose door had been so firmly locked and then, inexplicably, opened.

For a moment, I actually began to conjecture that there was indeed someone – another human being – living here in this house, a person who hid themselves away in that mysterious nursery and came out at night to fetch food and drink and to take the air. Perhaps it was the woman in black? Had Mrs Drablow harboured some reclusive old sister or retainer, had she left behind her a mad friend that no one had known about? My brain span all manner of wild, incoherent fantasies as I tried desperately to provide a

Samuel Daily A prosperous landowner that Kipps had met on the train to Crythin Gifford.

> rational explanation for the presence I had been so aware of. But then they ceased. There was no living occupant of Eel Marsh House other than myself and Samuel Daily's dog. Whatever was about, whoever I had seen, and heard rocking, and who had passed me by just now, whoever had opened the locked door was not 'real'. No. But what was 'real'? At that moment I began to doubt my own reality.
>
> The first thing I must have was a light and I groped my way back across to my bed, reached over it and got my hand to the torch at last, took a step back, stumbled over the dog who was at my heels and dropped the torch. It went spinning away across the floor and fell somewhere by the window with a crash and the faint sound of breaking glass. I cursed but managed by crawling about on my hands and knees, to find it again and to press the switch. No light came on. The torch had broken.
>
> For a moment I was as near to weeping tears of despair and fear, frustration and tension, as I had ever been since my childhood. But instead of crying I drummed my fists upon the floorboards, in a burst of violent rage, until they throbbed.
>
> It was Spider who brought me to my sense by scratching a little at my arm and then by licking the hand I stretched out to her. We sat on the floor together and I hugged her warm body to me, glad of her, thoroughly ashamed of myself, calmer and relieved, while the wind boomed and roared without, and again and again I heard that child's terrible cry borne on the gusts towards me.

UNDERSTANDING THE TEXT

'Whistle and I'll Come to You' is the title of the tenth chapter of *The Woman in Black*. This extract describes a night at Eel Marsh House and the ghostly happenings that worry the narrator. The text communicates the thoughts and feelings of the narrator as they shift from contemplating the harsh weather and reminiscing over his childhood, to extreme fear as he hears the wailing of the child and begins to strongly feel the presence of some being in the house.

The atmosphere of the house is effectively conveyed not only through the vivid description, but also from the way that Arthur Kipps is ready to believe that there may even be a person hiding there. The willingness of the narrator to believe in the supernatural creates a similar reaction in the reader making the extract all the more powerful and evocative.

Some of the themes in this extract are:

- isolation
- the supernatural
- fear
- a sense of the past.

KEY POINT

Think about these themes in the passage and any others you can draw out. Analyse how they work together to create the atmosphere.

Copy and complete the following table, finding examples from the text which relate to the extract's themes and commenting on the way in which these examples illustrate the theme.

▼ THEME	▼ EXAMPLE	▼ COMMENT
Isolation	'…quite alone and exposed, bearing the brunt of winter after winter of gales…'	The house itself is isolated. The word 'exposed' creates a sense of vulnerability that is enhanced by the fact that the house has had to survive the harsh elements. Ironically the narrator is trying to convince himself that the house is as 'steady as a lighthouse'.
The supernatural		
Fear		
A sense of the past		

The Woman in Black has many, though not all, of the features of the Gothic novel. The following table lists some of these features. Copy and complete the table, commenting on whether each element is present or not. If it is present, find evidence from the text to support your claim. If the feature is not present or has been changed to some extent, explain why.

▼ FEATURE	▼ PRESENT OR ABSENT	▼ EVIDENCE OR EXPLANATION
Set in a castle		
An atmosphere of mystery and suspense		
An ancient prophecy		
Supernatural or mysterious events		
High emotion		
Women in distress		
A woman threatened by a tyrannical male	Absent	The extract makes no reference to a female character being threatened. You only learn of Mrs Drablow, who owned the house.
Vocabulary associated with the Gothic and relating to mystery, fear, terror and darkness		

EXPLORING LANGUAGE

Hill uses a variety of techniques to build atmosphere and to convey the text's themes. Copy and complete the following table with examples of each technique, providing an explanation of its use. You may be able to spot more techniques than the ones which are mentioned.

▼ TECHNIQUE	▼ EXAMPLES	▼ COMMENT
Similes	1 2 3	
Pairs of words	1 'desperation and anguish' 2 3	This not only describes the pain contained in the cry but also hints at the terror that the narrator feels.
Questions	1 'But what was "real"?' 2 3	Connected to the theme of the supernatural, this question shows the doubt in the narrator's mind and contributes to an atmosphere of fear and uncertainty.
Powerful adjectives	1 'howling darkness' 2 3	
Short or incomplete sentences	1 2 3	
Images	1 2 3	

> **KEY POINT**
>
> An understanding of English grammar will better enable you to understand what the writer is trying to achieve.

Sometimes, writers use participle phrases as a technique. These can be present participle phrases (beginning with verbs ending in '-ing', such as 'running', 'thinking' and so on) or past participle phrases (beginning with verbs that have '-ed' endings, such as 'presented', 'created' or irregular ones such as 'driven').

In the sentence beginning, 'I lay back and slipped into that pleasant, trance-like state…', recalling the past is an action that happens while the narrator is lying back in bed. This participle phrase enables the reader to understand why the narrator felt like he was a child again.

In the same way, the sentence beginning, 'We sat on the floor together and I hugged her warm body to me…' shows the reader the narrator's mental state. His physical action of hugging the dog makes the reader think of relief; it is the past participle phrase 'ashamed of myself' that indicates there is a sense of shame as well.

The technique is often used to give more information about happenings. This adds detail to a text and gives variety to sentence structure as well.

Make a list of some of the present participle phrases you can find in the text.
1 'howling at the doors'
2 _____
3 _____
4 _____
5 _____

ACTIVITY 1 — A01 — SKILLS: CRITICAL THINKING

▼ STRUCTURE AS A TECHNIQUE

Structure is an effective technique in all types of writing and can be used to create tension and suspense in ghost stories. In this extract, suspense is built throughout to reach a climax, where the narrator drums his fists against the floor, and then to a sense of resolution, where he calms down.

Copy and complete the following table, listing the events and commenting on how each adds to the build-up of suspense.

▼ EVENTS	▼ COMMENT
Reads a book and then goes to sleep	Creates a sense of the ordinary, even though the weather is harsh. The sense of inner calm suggested here makes the change that occurs later more effective by contrast.
Wakes suddenly	Brings a change. The fact that he woke suddenly hints that something might be wrong.
The force of the wind has increased	
Hears a cry	

ACTIVITY 2 — A01 — A04 — SKILLS: INNOVATION, COMMUNICATION, TEAMWORK, INTERPERSONAL SKILLS

▼ URBAN LEGENDS

'Urban legends' are modern day folklore that consist of largely fictional stories that have supernatural and/or frightening elements.

1 Discuss why it is important to be able to distinguish between fact and fiction in the many stories you hear and read every day. Try to include examples of hoaxes with which you are familiar. For example, you may have heard of the Loch Ness Monster, a creature said to live in a lake in the Scottish Highlands. Someone claimed to have photographed the Monster in 1934, but the photograph was proved a hoax in the 1990s.

2 An urban legend that comes from the USA is that of the Candy Lady. It is a connected to the history of Clara Crane, a woman who is said to have lived in a small town in Texas around the turn of the 20th century. The story goes that her daughter died in an accident which Clara blamed on her husband. She then murdered him by giving

▲ The Loch Ness Monster is a modern Scottish legend.

poisoned sweets. Some years later, there were reports of children in the town finding candy on their window sills in the morning, and legend suggests that the children started disappearing. People blamed these disappearances on The Candy Lady.

In groups, prepare and present a short play about this urban legend. You could take on the roles of the adults and children of the Texan town and enact the disappearance of a child.

ACTIVITY 3 — A04 A05

SKILLS: CRITICAL THINKING, ANALYSIS, INTERPRETATION, ADAPTIVE LEARNING, CREATIVITY

▼ INFLUENCE OF CHILDHOOD

1 Read the extract below, in which Susan Hill describes the influence that her birthplace and childhood have had on her writing.

> I was born beside the North Sea, in Scarborough, Yorkshire one bitterly cold winter during WWII, when the snow was deep and the waves were crashing onto the cliffs not far away.
>
> How much do we carry with us of our birth – the when and the where? I certainly carry with me all the stories I was told about that day, that winter. But Scarborough, where I lived and rarely left until I was 16, is not the mere background but the whole setting of all my childhood memories. So many of my novels and short stories feature it, though always in disguise – feature the sea, and seaside places. Growing up in an unusual place gives a writer a big advantage because the imagination is stimulated and intrigued by everything in and about it from the beginning.

Write a blog entry about a childhood experience or place that is very memorable or which has had a strong influence on you.

2 Write a short story entitled 'The Deepest Shadow'.

KEY POINT

Your early childhood experiences inevitably have an influence on your outlook on life and so will influence your writing.

GENERAL VOCABULARY

Holy Inquisition a part of the Roman Catholic Church who sought to combat heresy from the 12th century onwards

Ann Radcliffe's novel, *The Italian*, is the story of a nobleman called Vivaldi and his attempt to marry Elena, a beautiful orphan. With many obstacles to the proposed marriage, Vivaldi has to contend with mysterious monks, ghostly figures and the Holy Inquisition. The following extract shows the way in which Radcliffe creates the eerie atmosphere of a chamber in a ruined fortress where Vivaldi and his servant Paulo are trapped for the night.

▼ FROM *THE ITALIAN* (1797) BY ANN RADCLIFFE

Vivaldi again examined the walls, and as unsuccessfully as before; but in one corner of the vault lay an object, which seemed to tell the fate of one who had been confined here, and to hint his own: it was a garment covered with blood. Vivaldi and his servant discovered it at the same instant; and a dreadful foreboding of their own destiny fixed them, for some moments, to the spot. Vivaldi first recovered himself, when instead of yielding to despondency, all his faculties were aroused to devise some means for escaping; but Paulo's hopes seemed buried beneath the dreadful vestments upon which he still gazed. 'Ah, my Signor!' said he, at length, in a faltering accent, 'who shall dare to raise that garment? What if it should conceal the mangled body whose blood has stained it!'

> Vivaldi, shudderingly, turned to look on it again.
>
> 'It moves!' exclaimed Paulo; 'I see it move!' as he said which, he started to the opposite side of the chamber. Vivaldi stepped a few paces back, and as quickly returned; when, determined to know the event at once, he raised the garment upon the point of his sword, and perceived, beneath, other remains of dress, heaped high together, while even the floor below was stained with gore.

Below is a student's answer to the question: 'How is suspense created in the extract from *The Italian*?'

> The extract from *The Italian* creates suspense through a range of techniques. First and foremost, it tells us that the character was looking for a way out 'unsuccessfully'. So we know he must be sort of really scared because he can't find a way out. Then the writer gets us to focus on something really frightening – a bloody garment. This really brings suspense because now we are thinking, what can this be. Also the word 'bloody' gives a good visual image and creates danger and suspense.

ACTIVITY 4 — AO2 — SKILLS: REASONING

▼ STRENGTHS AND WEAKNESSES

Copy and complete the following table, listing the good and bad points of the student's answer above, then write an answer of your own.

▼ POSITIVES	▼ NEGATIVES
Points out specific techniques, such as visual imagery.	Points are not developed. They are mentioned but the effect of each technique is not explained in detail.
Shows some evidence of structuring the answer with the phrase, 'First and foremost'.	

▲ *The Woman in Black* is considered part of the Gothic novel tradition.

EXAM-STYLE QUESTION

AO1 **AO2**

SKILLS: CRITICAL THINKING, ANALYSIS, REASONING, INTERPRETATION

How does the writer of 'Whistle and I'll Come to You' create an atmosphere of fear and suspense?

In your answer, you should write about:
- the setting and the weather
- the narrator's thoughts and feelings
- the use of language.

You should support your answer with close reference to the passage, including **brief** quotations.

(30 marks)

'NIGHT'
ALICE MUNRO

BACKGROUND AND CONTEXT

Alice Munro is a Canadian writer and Nobel Prize winner. She is best known for the changes that she introduced to the modern short story, particularly the way in which she moves the narrative between the past and the present. She has published several collections of short stories, including *Dance of the Happy Shades* (1968) and *Open Secrets* (1994).

Her stories are often set in Huron County, Ontario, where she was born in 1931. *Night* appeared in the collection *Dear Life*, published in 2012 as the second of four stories in the section titled 'Finale'. Munro herself called these 'not quite stories' in view of the fact that they are autobiographical writings with fictional elements.

▲ Canadian short story writer Alice Munro won the Nobel Prize in Literature in 2013.

KEY POINT
You can draw upon your own experiences in your writing but you can also be creative with that experience, changing events to explore what might have happened.

BEFORE YOU START READING

1. You may have siblings. Quite often, relationships with siblings are complicated, especially between teenagers. Discuss the advantages and disadvantages of having siblings.
2. Good physical health is something that people often take for granted. How would you feel if you were ill, not just for a few days, but for an extended period of time?
3. Read about Huron County, Ontario in Canada. What was life like in rural Canada in the 1940s and 1950s?

You can find the text of 'Night' in the Edexcel International GCSE English Anthology, pages 46-51, freely available on the Pearson Edexcel website.

UNDERSTANDING THE TEXT

KEY POINT
'Night' blends elements of the autobiography and short story genres. It narrates events but a present reflection upon on those events.

According to the writer, 'Night' is part of a 'separate unit, one that is autobiographical in feeling, though not, sometimes, entirely so in fact'. This means that, though it is a short story, it is not the same as others in the genre. It borrows heavily from the writer's own childhood experiences. The story, narrated from an adult's point of view, in the first person, is both a narration of events unfolding and a present reflection on those past events.

'Night' shows you the interior world of the narrator. Her thoughts about her illness and its effects, her conflicted feelings about her sister and general reflections about her family and background, are all a part of the narrative. At the same time, the reader is shown a glimpse of life in rural Canada in the 1950s and gains an understanding of the family relationships that have a significant impact on the narrator.

▶ Alice Munro was inspired by her native Huron County, Ontario in Canada.

Some of the themes in this extract are:

- family relationships
- the impact of prolonged illness
- fear for one's mental health
- reflecting on the past.

Look at the examples from the text that illustrate these themes in the following table. Match each example with one of the themes listed above and comment on their effect.

▼ THEME	▼ EXAMPLE	▼ COMMENT
	'I must not even think of it but I did think of it.'	
	'I knew now that he had not heard me getting up and walking around on just this one night.'	
	'I don't remember, at any rate having to tackle any of the jobs that piled up for me in later summers, when I fought quite willingly to maintain the decency of our house.'	
	'so that I could spend part of the time wandering about like a visitor'	This shows that she was allowed to be freer than she would have otherwise been, because of her illness. It hints at the idleness that would have contributed to the narrator's sense of unease.

AUTOBIOGRAPHY OR FICTION

The autobiographical and fictional elements of this short story are very cleverly intertwined, so it is difficult for the reader to judge where the autobiography ends and the storytelling begins. This is partly what makes the story both entertaining and effective. However, there are certain sections where the reader feels that one aspect is stronger than the other.

Two such extracts are given in the following table. Complete the table by adding more points to the 'Explanation' column. The first point has been included for you.

▼ ASPECT	▼ EXTRACT	▼ EXPLANATION
Fictional element is strong	'One night – I can't say whether it could be the twentieth or the twelfth or only the eighth or the ninth that I had got up and walked – I got a sense, too late for me to change my pace, that there was somebody around the corner. There was somebody waiting there and I could do nothing but walk right on'	Is important for plot development
Autobiographical element is strong	'I have thought that he was maybe in his better work clothes because he had a morning appointment to go to the bank, to learn, not to his surprise, that there was no extension to his loan. He had worked as hard as he could but the market was not going to turn around and he had to find a new way of supporting us and paying off what we owed at the same time. Or he may have found out that there was a name for my mother's shakiness and that it was not going to stop. Or that he was in love with an impossible woman.'	Strong sense of family history

PAPER 2 — TEXT ANTHOLOGY: FICTION — 285

EXPLORING LANGUAGE

Munro uses a range of techniques to convey her themes and to build an effective narrative. Copy and complete the following table with examples of each technique, providing an explanation of its use. You may be able to find more techniques than the ones which have been listed, so if you do you should add them to the list.

▼ TECHNIQUE	▼ EXAMPLES	▼ COMMENT
Contrast	1 2 3	
Repetition	1 'I must not even think… The thought…' 2 3	
Conversational tone that communicates directly with the reader	1 2 3	
Descriptive detail	1 2 3	
Short or incomplete sentences	1 'Think again.' 2 3	This highlights the narrator's changing perceptions about herself.

NARRATIVE AND SPEECH

In fictional narratives, speech is used to convey character, break up the narration and move the plot forward. Speech in narratives can come in many forms. Usually, dialogue is written as direct or indirect speech.

In **direct speech**, the words are written as they were spoken between quotation marks. For example:

'I felt very weak after the surgery,' Elena said.

In **indirect speech**, what was said is reported by the narrative voice. For example:

Elena said that she felt weak after the surgery.

KEY POINT

A writer will have reasons for deciding to use either direct or indirect speech. What difference do you think it makes?

ACTIVITY 1 — A01 — SKILLS ANALYSIS

▼ **DIRECT AND INDIRECT SPEECH**

Although 'Night' is a first-person narrative that primarily focuses on the narrator's thoughts and feelings, it uses speech as well. The text has both direct and indirect speech as well as direct speech written without quotation marks.

Copy and complete the following table with examples of each type of speech and explain its use or effect.

TYPE	EXAMPLE	EFFECT
Indirect speech		
Direct speech		
Direct speech without quotation marks		

Short stories have to have a tight structure in order to convey a complete story in relatively few words. This structure can be split into five different sections:

- exposition
- rising action
- climax
- falling action
- resolution.

The plot diagram below illustrates this common structural pattern. Copy and fill in the boxes below with an event or reference from 'Night' that corresponds with the different stages of the plot of a short story.

SUBJECT VOCABULARY

exposition a thorough introductory description

CLIMAX
RISING ACTION
FALLING ACTIONS
EXPOSITION
RESOLUTION

ACTIVITY 2 — AO4 — SKILLS: COLLABORATION, EMPATHY, NEGOTIATION

▼ **THINKING ABOUT ADVICE**

In groups, discuss the kind of advice you would give someone who is recovering from a long illness. Talk about different aspects such as taking care of their health, building up strength and stamina as well as ways to occupy their time.

PAPER 2 — TEXT ANTHOLOGY: FICTION

ACTIVITY 3 — AO4 AO5
SKILLS: CRITICAL THINKING, ANALYSIS, INTERPRETATION, ADAPTIVE LEARNING, CREATIVITY

▼ WRITING TASK

Write a short story that begins with the words, 'I had been alone for many days…'. Try to follow the structure of the short story in the diagram that you filled out.

ACTIVITY 4 — AO4
SKILLS: PROBLEM SOLVING, REASONING

▼ WRITING A SUCCESSFUL ANSWER

Look at the following thought cloud that could be used to plan an answer to the question, 'How is the narrator's fear and anxiety conveyed in 'Night'? Complete the thought cloud and number the points in the order in which you think they should appear in an answer. Find an example for each point and write a comment explaining why the example illustrates the point.

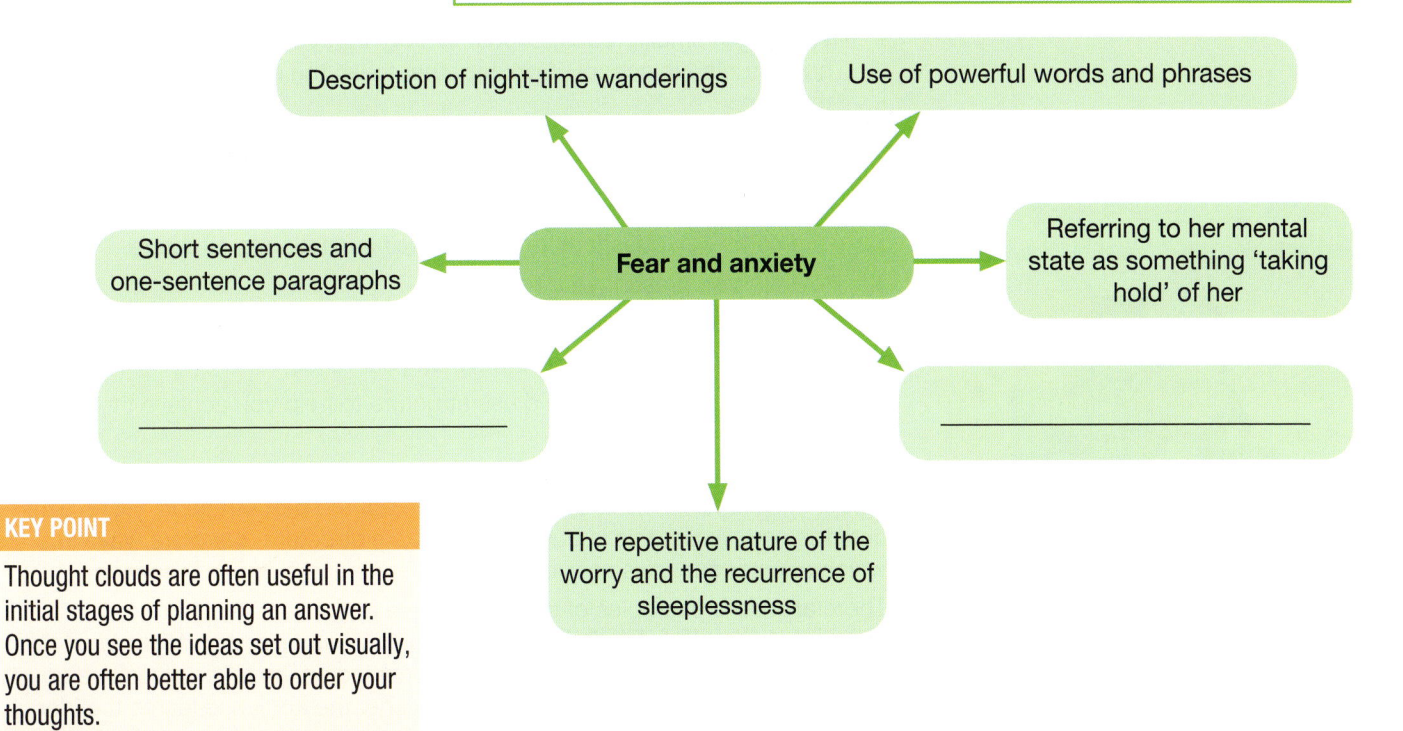

Fear and anxiety
- Description of night-time wanderings
- Use of powerful words and phrases
- Short sentences and one-sentence paragraphs
- Referring to her mental state as something 'taking hold' of her
- The repetitive nature of the worry and the recurrence of sleeplessness
- _____
- _____

KEY POINT
Thought clouds are often useful in the initial stages of planning an answer. Once you see the ideas set out visually, you are often better able to order your thoughts.

EXAM-STYLE QUESTION
AO1 AO2
SKILLS: CRITICAL THINKING, ANALYSIS, REASONING, INTERPRETATION

How does the writer of 'Night' show the varied mental states of the narrator?

In your answer you should write about:
- the background and situation
- the narrator's thoughts and feelings
- the use of language.

You should support your answer with close reference to the passage, including **brief** quotations.

(30 marks)

LEARNING OBJECTIVES

This lesson will help you to:
- understand how to follow your imagination in a way that will allow you to create a story for a reader to enjoy.

AN INTRODUCTION TO IMAGINATIVE WRITING

You can source ideas for your writing from stories you have already heard or read, or from events about which you know something. You may know or imagine a character to use in your story, whose actions and feelings you can convey to your reader.

PLOT

The plot consists of the main events of a story. You can develop a plot by listing the events that you think will take place in your story. These events, and the order in which they occur, may well change as you write and develop your characters and setting.

ACTIVITY 1 — A01 — SKILLS: CRITICAL THINKING, TEAMWORK

▼ **WORKING ON A PLOT**

Working in small groups, choose a story that you all know or that you have studied in school. Work together to list the main narrative points of the story.

STRUCTURE

Here are some key questions to ask yourself in relation to structure.
- How will you present your narrative?
- Will the end come at the end, or will you arrange things differently?
- What effect would you like to have on your reader?
- How do you think you could use structure to help you achieve the desired effect?

Works of crime fiction often follow a particular structure that is common to the genre, in which a crime is detailed early on but the perpetrator is not revealed until the end. Whilst this is quite a predictable structure, there are ways in which a writer can utilise structure to challenge and surprise the reader.

There are many examples of stories that use unconventional or non-chronological structures. For example, Emlyn Williams's play, *Night Must Fall*, concerns the actions of a murderer. The opening scene takes place in a court where the murderer is convicted. In this scene, the audience learns the identity of one victim, but not that of the second. The next scene is set before the second murder, and the audience has to follow the character that they know to be the killer through scenes with other characters, wondering who his second victim will be. The effect would be very different if both victims' identities were revealed in the opening scene.

▲ Emlyn Williams's *Night Must Fall* is a psychological thriller partly set in a courtroom.

PAPER 2 — IMAGINATIVE WRITING

ACTIVITY 2 — AO1
SKILLS: CRITICAL THINKING, PROBLEM SOLVING, ADAPTIVE LEARNING

▼ THINKING ABOUT STRUCTURE

Choose a story that you know well. It could be a film, book, a short story or even a fairytale.

1. Write down the way in which the story is structured. Do events run in chronological order or are they arranged differently?
2. Write down the key moments in the plot and try re-organising them into a different structure. What effect do you think this would have on the story and the reader's experience?

NARRATION

Who is telling your story? Is it told by an all-knowing narrator who knows the characters' thoughts, or is it told by one of the characters, whose knowledge and understanding of events is limited? Is it even narrated by someone unknown, who watches events without being involved.

ACTIVITY 3 — AO4 AO5
SKILLS: ADAPTIVE LEARNING, CREATIVITY, INNOVATION

▼ CHOOSING A NARRATOR

Working in pairs, write two versions of the first three or four sentences of a story entitled 'Runaway'. The first version should be told from the writer's point of view, while the second version should be told from the point of view of the first character that you introduce.

CHARACTER

HINT
Look back at the activities on pages 216–219 for more on creating characters.

How much do you need to know about your characters? How will this information be conveyed to the reader? Will you introduce the character upfront, so that the reader knows a lot about this character early on in the narrative, or will the reader slowly get to know the character as the story unfolds?

KEY POINT
With practice, you will develop a feel for imaginative writing. At first, you will have to consider the aspects of your writing separately, such as character, plot, structure and narration, but as you continue to practise you should find yourself considering these things automatically as you write. However, you should always remember to check what you have written.

ACTIVITY 4 — AO4 AO5
SKILLS: ADAPTIVE LEARNING, CREATIVITY, INNOVATION

▼ WRITING CHARACTER

Working on your own, write an introduction to a character at the start of a story entitled 'Not yet my friend, not yet'. You must decide whether to reveal things about this character immediately and whether you want to hint at events that will happen later. Write no more than 100 words. When you have finished, exchange your piece with someone else. Read your partner's character introduction, then write a continuation of the story and character development, following on from the first part that your partner has written.

LEARNING OBJECTIVES

This lesson will help you to:
- develop the confidence to consider ideas
- plan ways of handling ideas
- present ideas appropriately.

GENERATING IDEAS

Any exercise or exam question that requires you to write imaginatively will give you some sort of starter, even if it is simply a title. This is your starting point from which you will have to produce further ideas, develop them and turn them into an effective narrative that is written clearly and accurately.

GENERATING IDEAS FOR DIFFERENT PURPOSES

You may be asked to write in order to **explore**, to **imagine** or to **entertain**. Before you start trying to generate ideas, you should consider your purpose and what is expected.

- **To explore**: Think about a subject, considering its importance, especially if the question involves a particular reader or audience. What is important or significant about the subject? What do other people think about the subject? How do you react to thinking about it?

- **To imagine**: If you are asked to imagine something, the natural response is to write a narrative. Everyone is familiar with stories, whether imagined or real, and this makes telling a story a more comfortable option for many students in an exam. Remember that good story telling requires the same planning and organising as any other kind of writing.

- **To entertain**: This requires similar skills to story telling with the difference being that, in order to entertain, your story will have to amuse the reader and hold their attention. You will not be able to claim that a story is funny; you will have to tell it in a way that makes your reader smile or laugh.

Now you will need to consider possibilities, sources and other things with which you may be familiar or unfamiliar. It might help to ask yourself the question: 'What if…?'. There may be characters from stories that you know or from real life that you could adapt and manipulate or change to suit your purpose. It can be fun to realise that, in fiction, you can make your characters do things that people might not do in real life.

ACTIVITY 1 — A01 — SKILLS: CREATIVITY, COOPERATION

▼ ADAPTING STORIES AND CHARACTERS

In pairs, make a list of stories known to you that you could adapt for your own story telling. Make a note of interesting characters and situations that might form the basis of a good story.

▲ There are many world-famous characters in literature that you could use in your own writing, such as Sherlock Holmes.

Sharing initial thoughts and asking quick-fire questions of one another are techniques often used to help generate ideas. When people have to respond rapidly to questions, they are sometimes surprised how easily new ideas will appear. Sometimes there can be a chain reaction and a flood of unexpected ideas will result. The important thing is to engage with the exchange of ideas and opinions. Doing something different or unusual often triggers the discovery of new ideas.

ACTIVITY 2 — AO4 — SKILLS: CREATIVITY, TEAMWORK

▼ WHAT IF…?

In groups, try asking the question, 'What if…?' about people and situations with which you are familiar. Write down a list of key words that would provide you with the beginning of a story plan.

When you are required to write imaginatively, you may choose to use a familiar format, story elements or genre. For example, you could choose to write a fairytale, a horror story, a science fiction story about space travel, a historical story set in a particular time period, a detective story or an adventure story.

ACTIVITY 3 — AO4 — AO5 — SKILLS: ADAPTIVE LEARNING, CREATIVITY

▼ INTRODUCING DIFFERENT GENRES

In pairs, choose four of the types of story listed above that are familiar to you and list the main features of each type. Then decide what you would want to include in the first paragraph of each type of story. Finally, working on your own, write four introductory paragraphs, one for each story type.

> **KEY POINT**
>
> Consider the topic of your imaginative writing and plan carefully what you think you want to write before you start. However, once you have planned and started to write, do not be reluctant to change direction rather than continue with an idea that has lost its appeal.

LEARNING OBJECTIVES

This lesson will help you to:
- understand how to create a plot that suits your purpose in writing.

PLOT

When you are planning your story's plot, you should always consider the questions: 'What is happening?' and 'Why is it happening?'

The importance of these questions is that they make you think about what you want to present in your narrative and how that helps your purpose. You might produce a wonderful dramatic passage or a moving description but, unless it serves the purpose for which you are writing, you will not be successful. Examiners will notice this and will expect to find a sense of connected purpose as they read your work.

FIRST STEPS OF PLOTTING

Before you plot anything, you will need a clear sense of your purpose in writing. Even a simple sentence will guide you through the planning process.

ACTIVITY 1 — **AO1** — SKILLS: CRITICAL THINKING, INTERPRETATION

▼ **IDENTIFYING PURPOSE**

Working in pairs, list twelve stories that you know. They could be books, television programmes, films and so on. For each story, write one sentence to summarise the writer's purpose. In each case, ask yourselves what you think the writer was trying to achieve.

Sometimes a writer will set out their reasons for writing a particular book. For example, Charles Dickens introduced the purpose of his first novel, *The Pickwick Papers*, with just one sentence:

> The author's object in this work was to place before the reader a constant succession of characters and incidents; to paint them in as vivid colours as he could command; and to render them, at the same time, life-like and amusing.

KEY POINT

The plot is a key step in planning imaginative writing. Once it has been established, you can start to apply details, remembering that further ideas may come to you as you plan and write and that you should be ready to respond to these ideas. Ideas can come from thinking about and developing the events and characters in your plan, so make use of these ideas where possible.

ACTIVITY 2 — **AO4** — SKILLS: CREATIVITY, TEAMWORK

▼ **STARTING TO CREATE A PLOT**

1. In pairs, follow Dickens's idea for a succession of characters and amusing incidents by listing people you know. For each of these people, try to imagine an amusing incident in which they might easily become involved. Make brief notes on the incident.
2. Still working in pairs, list the really important events that you want to include in your narrative, then write one sentence for each of these points, saying why they are important for readers following your story.

PAPER 2   IMAGINATIVE WRITING   293

DEVELOPING PLOT

Once you have established a clear sense of purpose for your writing, you can start to develop your plot further. Utilising the simple sentences and initial ideas you have used to outline your plot, you can start to expand these to create a more detailed outline of the narrative you wish to tell.

There are many ways in which you can develop ideas. Try using some of the following techniques.

- Using a photograph or an image, try applying your story idea to the subject matter or situation shown in the photograph. This can help you generate a chain of events, setting or story.
- Consider an alternative perspective from different characters to offer a differing view or approach to your idea.
- Establish a start, middle and end of your story. Once these key components have been created, use your ideas to connect them together and develop them further.
- Consider the type of plot you wish to use. Many writers experiment with time, perspective or twists to keep the reader engaged.

▲ What ideas for a plot does this photograph give you?

ACTIVITY 3 | A04 | SKILLS: ADAPTIVE LEARNING, CREATIVITY

▼ **ADAPTING PLOTS**

Using your list of plot points from Activity 2, make the following changes and note how each change alters the plot:
- Use a different narrative perspective.
- Present the plot in a different order.
- Add a shocking twist at the end.

LEARNING OBJECTIVES

This lesson will help you to:
- understand how to order important items in a narrative and link them in the most effective way.

STRUCTURE

The structure of a piece of writing involves both the order and the manner in which components of a narrative are assembled. Ordering the components is one thing, but deciding how they will fit together within the story is another. Each of the components will have to fit somehow with the component that precedes it and the component that follows. For example, will any two components be closely linked so that you move quickly from a physical description of a character to an explanation of that character's history or an account of some of the things done by that character?

These are the kinds of decisions that you will have to make as you plan and write.

BEGINNINGS AND ENDINGS

Beginnings and endings provide the support for the rest of the narrative in much the same way as two book-ends hold up a row of books. They are both important. The introduction sets the narrative in motion and establishes the tone or mood of the piece: is it relaxed or tense, detailed or in a hurry to move on? The conclusion provides the author's final word. Is it a happy one? Is the writer anxious to finish? Is the fate of major characters something that the writer is pleased with? Would the writer want to return to this topic, or to this character?

Look at the opening of Graham Greene's *Brighton Rock* and think about what this opening tells you about the rest of the story.

▼ FROM *BRIGHTON ROCK* BY GRAHAM GREENE

Hale knew they meant to murder him before he had been in Brighton three hours. With his inky fingers and his bitten nails, his manner cynical and nervous, anybody could tell he didn't belong – belong to the early summer sun, the cool Whitsun wind off the sea, the holiday crowd.

Whitsun A date in the Christian calendar, seven weeks after Easter.

▲ A scene from the film adaptation of Graham Greene's *Brighton Rock*.

This is the opening of a psychological drama where a desperate man, all alone, is filled with the terror of knowing that someone wants to murder him. This is the first, shocking thing that the reader is told about him. Immediately, Greene goes on to describe him in way that confirms what he has just told the reader: that this man no longer belongs to life (that is, to the sun, the wind or the crowds of holiday-makers).

ACTIVITY 1 | **A04** | **A05** | **SKILLS** ADAPTIVE LEARNING, CREATIVITY, INNOVATION

▼ IDENTIFYING PURPOSE

In pairs, create a list of points that make up the plot of a story. Write the opening sentences of this story, so that a character and his or her situation are introduced quickly and suddenly, so that the reader will be shocked. Now write a second opening to the same story. This time, link the two ideas more slowly, to give your reader more time to fully understand events. How does this change in structure affect the impact on the reader?

Now look at the end of an equally famous novel. In *Nineteen Eighty-Four*, George Orwell tells the story of a dystopian world where the population is under the complete control and supervision of a powerful and mysterious government Party, headed by Big Brother. The narrative follows Winston Smith as he seeks to rebel against Big Brother and the Party. His rebellion is short-lived however as he is captured and brainwashed to conform and love the Party.

▼ FROM *NINETEEN EIGHTY-FOUR* BY GEORGE ORWELL

The voice from the telescreen was still pouring forth its tale of prisoners and booty and slaughter, but the shouting outside had died down a little. The waiters were turning back to their work. One of them approached with the gin bottle. Winston, sitting in a blissful dream, paid no attention as his glass was filled up. He was not running or cheering any longer. He was back in the Ministry of Love, with everything forgiven, his soul white as snow. He was in the public dock, confessing everything, implicating everybody. He was walking down the white-tiled corridor, with the feeling of walking in sunlight, and an armed guard at his back. The long-hoped-for bullet was entering his brain.

He gazed up at the enormous face. Forty years it had taken him to learn what kind of smile was hidden beneath the dark moustache. O cruel, needless misunderstanding! O stubborn, self-willed exile from the loving breast! Two gin scented tears trickled down the sides of his nose. But it was all right, everything was all right, the struggle was finished. He had won the victory over himself. He loved Big Brother.

KEY POINT

Try to structure your sentences, paragraphs and whole narratives while bearing in mind the likely responses of your readers as you link the points that you make.

This is an uncomfortable and powerful conclusion for a number of reasons. The sentences and information sound detached, emotionless and impersonal as things happen quickly and outside of Winston's control showing him to be broken and defeated. The use of the pronoun 'he' instead of his name distances Winston from the rebellious character that the reader has grown to know throughout the story.

This is a particularly effective conclusion as it acts to bring the narrative to an end in a manner that shocks the reader and, most importantly, inspires a range of further thoughts and questions.

PAPER 2 — IMAGINATIVE WRITING

LEARNING OBJECTIVES

This lesson will help you to:
- develop the skill of drawing the reader into the narrative so that they will appreciate being entertained.

NARRATION

A narrative has to lead the reader. If the reader does not like the narrative, it is very easy for them to stop reading.

Non-fiction writing involves a greater level of sharing the writer's purposes in writing, such as to inform someone who needs to know something or to discuss a topic in which the reader is interested. However, a fictional narrative is designed to entertain someone who can choose to stop reading if they are not enjoying the experience of reading. The narrator has to present something that will trigger a reader's interest and satisfaction.

Kenneth Grahame's *The Wind in the Willows* was written for children in 1908. Read the following extract from the beginning of the story, paying attention to the way in which Grahame seeks to engage the reader.

▼ **FROM *THE WIND IN THE WILLOWS* BY KENNETH GRAHAME**

> The Mole had been working very hard all the morning, spring-cleaning his little home. First with brooms, then with dusters; then on ladders with steps and chairs, with a brush and a pail of whitewash; till he had dust all over his black fur, and an aching back and weary arms. Spring was moving in the air above and in the earth below and around him, penetrating even his dark and lowly little house with its spirit of divine discontent and longing. It was small wonder, then, that he suddenly flung down his brush on the floor, said, 'Bother!' and, 'O blow!', and also, 'Hang spring-cleaning!' and bolted out of the house without even waiting to put on his coat.

▲ 'The Mole had been working very hard all the morning...'

ACTIVITY 1 — AO1 — SKILLS: CRITICAL ANALYSIS, ANALYSIS, INTERPRETATION

▼ **ENGAGING THE READER'S INTEREST**

In small groups, list the ways in which Grahame begins this narrative. These could include things such as the image of someone hard at work, the details of Mole's equipment, and so on. For each of these techniques used by Grahame to engage the reader's interest, explain in one sentence how you react to them.

ACTIVITY 2 — AO1 — SKILLS: CREATIVITY, TEAMWORK

▼ **BEGINNING A STORY**

In pairs, make a list of stories that you have enjoyed. They do not necessarily have to be stories from books or films. They could be stories that you have simply heard from other people. For each story, write down one sentence explaining how the story begins. Note whether the story starts by focusing on a character, by describing something like the setting, or by presenting some action. You may discover a way of starting a story that is new to you, so be prepared to learn new techniques.

FIRST- AND THIRD-PERSON NARRATIVES

The three paragraphs that follow are written in the first person. First person narratives provide a sense of immediacy as we listen to someone who was there and saw for themselves what actually happened and what was actually said.

> I first began to take notice of the family when I ran into the mother on the way to the shops. She smiled and reached out her arm to touch my shoulder then allowed her hand to rest for a moment on the lapel of my jacket.
>
> 'Will you thank your wife for me?' Over her shoulder I could see the two little ones. Margaret had taken them in when their cat had been run over and looked after them until their mother had returned from the vet.
>
> 'That's OK,' I said. 'They were no trouble.' I nodded towards her children, who were about to catch her up. 'We enjoyed looking after them.'

The next three paragraphs are written in the third person and are more detached, as if the writer is observing from a distance rather than being involved. This can give the impression that the writer is giving a more balanced or reliable view of things, and is not affected by the things that he or she writes about.

> There had been rumours about the disused mine for years. Tom and his friend had played around the entrance when they were small, but, understandably, when their parents had found out a fuss had been made and the owners were obliged to seal it up.
>
> Still the rumours had continued. As the boys grew older, and their circle of friendship had widened, they had encountered other boys from further afield who had also heard the rumours. At school and at home there had been hand tools that they had learnt to use: hammers, chisels, crowbars and spades. At school there had been adventure stories about children their own age.
>
> They met one morning at what had been the mine entrance, carrying tools borrowed from garden sheds and garages, tools belonging to parents who would not have agreed to lend them for this particular purpose.

What difference do you think could be made by choosing one of these two narrative styles? How might the impact on the reader change, depending on whether the story is narrated in the first or third person?

ACTIVITY 3 | AO4 | AO5 | SKILLS: ADAPTIVE LEARNING, CREATIVITY, INNOVATION

▼ CHOOSING BETWEEN FIRST AND THIRD PERSON

In pairs or on your own, write a different version of each of the two narratives that you have just read. For the first narrative, which is currently written in the first person, use the third person. You could start with the words, 'He first began to…' For the second narrative, use the first person, writing perhaps from the point of view of one of the boys involved or one of their parents.

KEY POINT

Remember that, as the writer of a narrative, you will have to decide the character of the narrator. Is it you, a character in the story, or someone who is detached from the story and treats events like a newspaper reporter?

LEARNING OBJECTIVES

This lesson will help you to:
- think about how to create and use characters in your writing.

CHARACTERS

Characters influence readers in several ways: through your direct awareness of what they think, do and say; through their influence on other characters; and through what the author tells you about them.

Characters are not just the people in a story. One of them may be the narrator of the story. They may be the people in the story, about whom readers learn from the author, in a third-person narrative. A character may never actually appear in a story, but they may still be of importance and the reader may learn about them from the narrator or from other characters.

ACTIVITY 1 — **A01** — **SKILLS** CRITICAL THINKING

▼ LEARNING ABOUT CHARACTERS

In pairs, read the following excerpts from pieces of imaginative writing and identify how you learn about each of the characters. Do you learn about them through their own thoughts and actions, through the narrator's descriptions and judgements, or through another character's eyes?

- He thought she was stunning. You could tell when he spoke about her and when he waited after school, when most of us boys had set off for the park. You could tell when we asked him about her. Most telling was the cruel moment when someone said that she had been running after one of the boys in the other class.

- I noticed them gradually, as they crawled out of the rotten woodwork onto the paving slabs. What use they were I could never tell and so, before they could reach the dog's bowl, I lifted my foot and ground them into the concrete. Mary wouldn't have liked it but then she was not there to see what I had done.

- He was the biggest rabbit in the litter. Since they had arrived in the straw, under the lamp, he had quickly learnt to barge his brothers and sisters to one side so that he always got the best feed. Now that they were weaned the others simply moved aside when he wanted a drink or the best spot in the warm straw bed.

◀ 'He was the biggest rabbit in the litter...'

ACTIVITY 2 — AO1 — SKILLS: CRITICAL THINKING

▼ QUESTIONS TO ASK ABOUT CHARACTERS

Try answering the following questions about each of the characters in Activity 1.
- Who are they?
- What are they?
- What are they doing?
- What are they trying to achieve?
- How do they interact with each other?

REVEALING CHARACTER

An author has to decide whether characters should be revealed by someone such as the narrator, who passes on what they know or feel about them, or by the characters themselves, so that readers can see the characters in action and make up their own minds about them.

Sometimes the reader needs to know something about a character that the character would be reluctant to reveal themselves. Then the author, or another character, might need to tell the reader.

> She was far too modest to tell anyone about her bravery, how she had forced her way into the burning house to rescue her neighbours' children. When she forgot to put on her gloves you could see the scars.

Sometimes the reader is better convinced when they can see an event for themselves, rather than being told about it.

> She put down the phone and rushed outside. She looked over to the other neighbours' houses but there were no lights to be seen. Somehow she found the strength to force open the door and make her way in. Moments later she emerged with a small child whom she laid carefully on the grass, away from the house. By now a red glow showed itself from all the upstairs windows and smoke was streaming from the door. From some distance away came the sound of a siren. The girl paused, took a deep breath and turned back into the smoke.

ACTIVITY 3 — AO4 — AO5 — SKILLS: CREATIVITY, INNOVATION

▼ INTRODUCING CHARACTERS

Working on your own, write an opening section for a story containing introductions to two characters. One character should be introduced by the narrator or another character, whereas the second character should introduce themselves.

KEY POINT

You learn about characters by what they say and do, by the reactions of other characters and by what you are told by the author.

LEARNING OBJECTIVES

This lesson will help you to:
- use speech to reveal character.

MONOLOGUES AND DIALOGUES

Monologues represent the thoughts or speech of a single person or character, whereas dialogues are exchanges between more than one person or character. These serve different purposes in imaginative writing: monologues can be more fluid, like your thoughts, whereas dialogues can portray arguments, love or perhaps progress towards a resolution of some question.

The following extracts are taken from Susan Hill's novel, *I'm the King of the Castle*. When Edmund Hooper is about 11 years old, his father tells him that another boy is coming to live in their house, along with his mother who is to be their housekeeper. Edmund's mother had died a few years before. The story continues.

> Hooper began to mould plasticine between his hands, for another layer to the geological model, standing as a board beside the window. He thought of the boy called Kingshaw, who was coming.
>
> 'It is my house,' he thought, 'it is private, I got here first. Nobody should come here.'

Hooper's words here form a **monologue**. They are private words, whether spoken or thought. Through them Hooper reveals his determination that no one should share the house with him. No one else can know about these thoughts and the author has given the reader a private view, as it were, into the boy's jealous determination.

Soon the boys are left together.

> He walked round the table, towards the window. Kingshaw stepped back as he came.
>
> 'Scaredy!'
>
> 'No.'
>
> 'When my father dies,' Hooper said, 'this house will belong to me. I shall be master. It'll all be mine.'
>
> 'That's nothing. It's only an old house.'

Here the story moves on with a **dialogue**, and the reader can see the very beginning of the bullying and rivalry that will result in a death. This failure of the boys to cooperate can easily be presented in a natural situation such as this one, more so than using someone's private thoughts.

SUBJECT VOCABULARY

monologue the speech or thoughts of one person alone

dialogue the speech between two or more people involved in a conversation

▲ Monologues can be used to create the complexity of individual character.

ACTIVITY 1 — A04 A05 — SKILLS: ADAPTIVE LEARNING, CREATIVITY, INNOVATION, TEAMWORK

▼ USING MONOLOGUES

In pairs, briefly introduce four characters using monologues. Your characters will find themselves:

- alone at night, unable to sleep
- in a crowd
- with someone who refuses to speak to them
- in a situation of your own choice.

Speech and private thoughts provide a writer with useful tools for introducing characters. What people say and think when they are alone, or when they think that they are alone, can be very revealing about their character. Satirical magazines such as *Private Eye* make good use of this technique. One early novel in the English language, *Pamela* by Samuel Richardson, uses thoughts from a private diary to reveal important information.

ACTIVITY 2 — A04 A05 — SKILLS: ADAPTIVE LEARNING, CREATIVITY, INNOVATION, TEAMWORK

▼ USING DIALOGUE

In pairs, briefly introduce four characters or groups of characters through dialogue. Your characters will find themselves in the following situations.

- A home owner confronting a stranger in his or her back garden.
- A group of friends trying to persuade a bouncer or security guard to let them into a night club.
- A group of magistrates questioning someone who is on trial or who is giving evidence.
- A teacher asking a student why their homework has not been done.

ACTIVITY 3 — A04 A05 — SKILLS: ADAPTIVE LEARNING, CREATIVITY, INNOVATION

▼ USING PRIVATE THOUGHTS

In pairs or on your own, use a character's private thoughts or words that have been overheard to introduce one or more of the characters. Try not to tell your reader what you think of your character or characters. Instead, try to show what they are, using their words. You could use the following words as a starting point.

> They couldn't believe their luck. There, on the table in front of them, was the diary. It had been left open and there on the first pages were some of the words they had hoped to find.

KEY POINT

You are affected by what people say. In your writing, help your reader to sense what characters' words suggest about their personality

DESCRIPTIVE WRITING

LEARNING OBJECTIVES

This lesson will help you to:
- use your senses to guide your descriptive writing.

Descriptions can be written for their own sake or to accompany narratives, instructions, explanations and argument. They rely on an engagement of your senses and your imagination.

USING THE SENSES

It is through your five senses that you know the world around you. The more that you can engage your reader's senses, the more effective your writing will be.

Were you woken by an alarm clock or by the sound of a parent's voice this morning? Was the first thing that you saw a bright light shining in your face? Was the first thing you felt someone pulling back the blankets? Did you smell toast? Was the first thing you tasted toothpaste, some fruit juice or a boiled egg?

▲ Are your senses acute or dull in the morning?

ACTIVITY 1 — AO4 AO5 — SKILLS: CREATIVITY

▼ **USING YOUR SENSES**

Working on your own, try to remember and list the first things that you heard, saw, felt, smelt and tasted after waking up this morning. Use this list as the basis of a description of the first half hour of your day.

SHOW, NOT TELL

Sometimes, you can describe things more convincingly by 'showing' the reader rather than telling them.

ACTIVITY 2 — AO2 — SKILLS: ANALYSIS, COLLABORATION

▼ **SHOWING OR TELLING?**

In pairs, consider which of these pairs of sentences you find more convincing:

1. **A:** He removed his coat from a hook behind the door.
   B: He lifted one arm and eased his coat from the hook behind the door.
2. **A:** On the horizon a car appeared.
   B: From the horizon something hurried towards them along the road.
3. **A:** They heard the squeal of angry brakes and were thrown forward against the opposite seats.
   B: The driver applied the brakes suddenly.
4. **A:** The engine died.
   B: For no reason he could think of, the engine stopped.

PAPER 2 — IMAGINATIVE WRITING

ACTIVITY 3 — A02
SKILLS: CRITICAL THINKING, ANALYSIS

▼ CREATING EFFECT

In pairs, identify the words and phrases that are used to create effective description in the following passage adapted from *The War of the Worlds*. In H.G. Wells's story of an invasion by creatures from Mars, there is a description of one of their spaceships that serves to enhance the drama of its discovery. When the novel was dramatised and broadcast like live news on American radio, it caused widespread panic as listeners thought they were listening to a news bulletin.

▼ FROM *THE WAR OF THE WORLDS* BY H.G. WELLS

The Thing itself lay almost entirely buried in sand, amidst the scattered splinters of a fir tree it had shivered to fragments in its descent.

The uncovered part had the appearance of a huge cylinder, caked over and its outline softened by a thick scaly dun-coloured incrustation. It had a diameter of about thirty metres. He approached the mass, surprised at the size and more so at the shape, since most meteorites are rounded more or less completely. It was, however, still so hot from its flight through the air as to forbid his near approach. A stirring noise within its cylinder he ascribed to the unequal cooling of its surface; for at that time it had not occurred to him that it might be hollow.

Suddenly he noticed with a start that some of the grey clinker, the ashy incrustation that covered the meteorite, was falling off the circular edge of the end. It was dropping off in flakes and raining down upon the sand. A large piece suddenly came off and fell with a sharp noise that brought his heart into his mouth.

And then he perceived that, very slowly, the circular top of the cylinder was rotating on its body. It was such a gradual movement that he discovered it only through noticing that a black mark that had been near him five minutes ago was now at the other side of the circumference. Even then he scarcely understood what this indicated, until he heard a muffled grating sound and saw the black mark jerk forward an inch or so. Then the thing came upon him in a flash. The cylinder was artificial – hollow – with an end that screwed out! Something within the cylinder was unscrewing the top!

KEY POINT
An imaginative choice of words can enhance a description. For example, what is the difference in effect between 'the cat *sat* on the mat' and 'the cat *sprawled* on the mat'?

ACTIVITY 4 — A01 A04 A05
SKILLS: ANALYSIS, ADAPTIVE LEARNING, CREATIVITY, INNOVATION

▼ IDENTIFYING DESCRIPTION

1. In pairs, list the verbs and verbal adjectives that help to convey the descriptive elements in the extract from *The War of the Worlds*. There are 20. Then list the 17 ordinary adjectives that Wells uses.
2. Use the lists in order to write your own description of 'The Thing'.

LEARNING OBJECTIVES

This lesson will help you to:
- choose appropriate words
- feel empowered to make good choices when selecting vocabulary for effect.

VOCABULARY FOR EFFECT

Sometimes you may say that you are 'trying to find the right word'. Sometimes it is not until you stumble across the right word, by chance perhaps, that you will realise that you have found it.

CHOOSING THE RIGHT WORD

This sense of 'the right word' is a strong one and, just as we can realise this when you are writing or speaking, so you can appreciate it when you listen to someone else or read what they have to say.

Read the two versions of the same account that follows.

EXTRACT A

Before a visit to the dentist when I was about fourteen, I liked ice cream. Then I had a tooth removed, under a general anaesthetic.

Soon I was dreaming that I was eating an ice cream. The ice cream tasted of tomatoes. I had never liked tomatoes. For six months afterwards I didn't fancy ice cream until I made myself buy one and found that it tasted all right.

EXTRACT B

Before a visit to the dentist when I was about fourteen, I was unable to resist ice cream. Then I had a tooth removed, under a general anaesthetic.

Soon I was dreaming that I was eating an ice cream. Unfortunately the ice cream tasted of fried tomatoes and, worse still, smelled of fried tomatoes. I had never liked tomatoes, in fact I loathed them. For six months afterwards I was unable to face ice cream until I forced myself to buy one and discovered, much to my relief, that it tasted of ice cream.

▲ 'The ice cream tasted of tomatoes...'

ACTIVITY 1 — AO2 — SKILLS: INNOVATION

▼ THE EFFECTS OF DIFFERENT WORDS

In pairs, list the words that have been changed between Extract A and Extract B, starting with *liked* (in Extract A) and *was unable to resist* (in Extract B). Then, for each change, write one sentence explaining the effect of the change.

ACTIVITY 2 — AO4 — AO5 — SKILLS: CREATIVITY, INNOVATION

▼ CHOOSING THE PERFECT WORD

Working on your own, describe in one paragraph something that has surprised you. It could be a particular sight or scene or an event that you have witnessed. Try to use some *mots justes*. Exchange your description with someone else and try to identify your partner's *mots justes*.

SUBJECT VOCABULARY

mots justes a French phrase, meaning words that are apt, or just right

PAPER 2 — IMAGINATIVE WRITING

CREATING IMAGES

Writers often use images, or things that can be seen or visualised, as reminders of concepts or events, as a narrative progresses. In this way, associations between things allow the writer to provide quick links or reminders for the reader which nevertheless do not impede the story.

Read the following piece of imaginative writing.

> They were not used to lighting their own bonfires, but one of them had smuggled a box of matches out of the house. Ignoring precautions, they enjoyed seeing the flames leap, from the first match to the paper stuffed under the brush wood, then flare up through the heavier branches until the flames roared skywards over the wood and waste material that had been piled high.
>
> When a stiff breeze suddenly blew amongst them they watched horrified as the flames licked across to the garden shed which held their toys. Within minutes the roof was a blanket of flame and the toys had gone for ever.

Here, a box of matches becomes an image of danger and fear, a reminder in the characters' adult lives of something that can go badly wrong and cause danger and destruction.

ACTIVITY 3 | A04 | A05 | SKILLS: CREATIVITY, INNOVATION

▼ USING IMAGES TO CONVEY MEANING

Working on your own, choose one of the following objects and write a paragraph in which you turn it into an image of something important:

- a pen
- a pair of shoes
- a memory stick.

HINTING, SUGGESTING, UNDERSTATING

Consider the following instructions or comments.

- 'Keep an eye on him.'
- 'Your homework is dreadful.'

How do you think you would respond to these instructions or statements? Do you think you would respond differently if they were re-phrased as follows?

- 'Just try to keep an eye on him.'
- 'Your homework is rather disappointing.'

In the second list, the writer is trying to reduce or soften the impact of their words. The first instruction becomes a suggestion that perhaps you should keep an eye on someone. The second comment is amended so that, rather than sounding angry, the teacher is trying to make you regret letting them down.

KEY POINT

You readily use subtle forms of words when you speak to other people. With a little thought you can be just as flexible when writing.

ACTIVITY 4 | A04 | A05 | SKILLS: ADAPTIVE LEARNING, CREATIVITY, INNOVATION

▼ USING SUBTLE LANGUAGE

Working on your own, extend each of the six instructions or comments that you have just read so that they make it clear what is going on. You could follow the pattern of the example sentence below.

> I don't think this is going to work; the glue has already set.

Try to use subtle words and phrases to do so, so that you suggest what is going on rather than stating it.

LEARNING OBJECTIVES

This lesson will help you to:
- create effects in imaginative writing through the way in which sentences are organised.

SENTENCES FOR EFFECT

Sentences have various ways of being organised: short, compound or complex. All these types produce different effects.

SENTENCE TYPES

doing wheelies Balancing a bicycle on its rear wheel while riding it.

dog collar An informal description of the white collar worn by the clergy of some Christian churches.

▲ A mountain biker demonstrating a wheelie

HINT

Look back at previous sections about the effect of different sentences on pages 22–23, 38–39 and 198–199.

In her novel, *The Risk of Darkness*, Susan Hill describes a young woman priest walking home. At the time of the novel's setting, the sight of a woman priest was a novelty in England.

> A boy bounced past her on a bicycle doing wheelies over the cobbles. Jane smiled at him. He did not respond but when he had gone by, turned and stared over his shoulder. She was used to it. Here she was, a girl, wearing jeans, and a dog collar. People were still surprised.

The first sentence is a simple one containing only one main verb. It is also quite loose, as the main verb is found at the start of the sentence. This sentence could be stopped after just five words and it would still make sense. What do you think is achieved by including the rest of the sentence?

▶ In pairs, find the other two places in the extract where a sentence could be stopped early. What effect does the writer achieve by building up the sentences in this way?

ACTIVITY 1 | AO1 | SKILLS: ANALYSIS, CREATIVITY

▼ **DEVELOPING SENTENCES**

Decide how you could develop the following sentences. Write down the purpose for extending each one, then add to it.
- The door opened.
- They could see the dog.
- The streets were always the same.

What sort of sentences have you produced? Are they loose, periodic or balanced? Are they simple, compound or complex?

Look again at the paragraph from *The Risk of Darkness*. The third and fifth sentences grow in a similar way to the first sentence, but what about the other sentences? They are all simple, periodic sentences, but are related to the more complicated sentences that they follow. Look again at the third sentence.

> He did not respond but when he had gone by, turned and stared over his shoulder.

Here there is much detail added to the basic sentence and the boy's reaction to Jane is made clear. Her reaction is conveyed in only five words.

> She was used to it.

| PAPER 2 | IMAGINATIVE WRITING | 307 |

ACTIVITY 2 — A01 — SKILLS: ANALYSIS

▼ THE EFFECT OF DIFFERENT SENTENCE TYPES

In pairs, decide the effect of revealing Jane's reaction in this simple sentence without further detail. What effect is achieved in the sixth sentence?

OTHER WAYS OF ORGANISING SENTENCES

You have seen the way in which strong effects can be created when sentences of different types are carefully placed together. Now you are going to look at other ways of organising sentences. Read the following piece of imaginative writing.

> It was icy, bitter cold. The washing hung frozen on the lines and icicles reached down from gutters that were filled with water that could no longer flow, held in place by unbelievably low temperatures. He looked for his gloves. He had left them to one side, by the door, but the space on the shelf was empty now and only the marks which he had brushed in the dust remained to remind him that his memory was not playing tricks.

Instead of showing a reaction to something, as with the short sentences in Hill's paragraph from *The Risk of Darkness*, these long, complex sentences develop the ideas in the short sentences that they follow. Of course, the pairs of sentences here also develop a wider idea – the drama of this character and the bitter cold he faces.

ACTIVITY 3 — A04 — A05 — SKILLS: CREATIVITY, INNOVATION

▼ DEVELOPING AN IDEA USING SENTENCE TYPES

Working alone, decide on an idea that you would like to develop in one paragraph. Write down that idea in one sentence and then start. If you are writing on paper use only every third line to give yourself room to try out words and make improvements to what you have written as you make progress. Your paragraph should be a minimum of four sentences.

ACTIVITY 4 — A04 — A05 — SKILLS: CREATIVITY, INNOVATION, COLLABORATION

▼ USING DIFFERENT SENTENCE PATTERNS

In pairs or in groups, try to develop an idea using different patterns of sentences, investigating what might serve your purposes and focusing on what you were aiming to achieve at the outset.

Remember, you have to decide your purpose before you start to write, because you must bear it in mind while you are writing.

KEY POINT

While you are writing, be prepared to stop occasionally and ask yourself whether the words you have written will achieve your purpose or purposes.

PAPER 2 — IMAGINATIVE WRITING

LEARNING OBJECTIVES

This lesson will help you to:
- take greater control over your writing
- think about the use of the senses when writing
- make clear what you want to say about characters, actions and locations.

PUTTING IT INTO PRACTICE

In the exam, you will need to demonstrate the following points in your imaginative writing.
- Ideas that are communicated effectively and imaginatively. This is what you will have to plan before you start.
- Writing that is clear and accurate. This is what you will have to check after you finish.

EXAM-STYLE QUESTION

A04

A05

SKILLS CRITICAL THINKING, ANALYSIS, ADAPTIVE LEARNING, CREATIVITY, INNOVATION

Write about a time when you, or someone you know, had an unexpected experience. Your response could be real or imagined. **(30 marks)**

Now read the example student answer and the commentary that follows.

The condition is called fly-strike. A long, detailed description is followed by a short sentence to vary pace.

we sent the dogs round in wide sweeping paths The vocabulary is fairly straight forward, but chosen precisely to create a vivid image.

Below us, to our left, we could hear the sea crashing into the rocks at the foot of the cliffs. Suddenly, from ahead of us, came the blare of a fog horn. Adding these sensory details makes the scene feel more real and also creates suspense.

Ahead of us the dogs were barking furiously now and we stepped forwards to see what was troubling them The description of the clouds, and then the dogs barking 'furiously', increases tension.

Suddenly, the fog had surrounded us; damp and chill, it had been blown up behind us as the breeze had lifted. Use of a semicolon to link together descriptions of the fog is very effective.

It was a warm summer's day and we set off from the farmyard to round up some sheep. Early in the summer all the sheep were rounded up so that they could be dipped, pushed one at a time through a long narrow bath that contained an insecticide that would protect them from flies that would burrow into their flesh and lay their eggs in the wounds that they had created. **The condition is called fly-strike.** The sheep we were looking for had spread themselves over the moor and across to an open area of land between the road and the sea. With us we had two sheep dogs. Once we had crossed the road **we sent the dogs round in wide sweeping paths** to move the sheep together into a flock that we could move across the road and back to the farm.

Ahead of us we could see the dogs, their heads up as they looked from side to side for sheep that were standing still as if wondering whether to move or not. They moved on, and left us to follow, pushing the flock up towards the road. Then, as the ground sloped more steeply away beneath our feet, we could see them no longer. **Below us, to our left, we could hear the sea crashing into the rocks at the foot of the cliffs. Suddenly, from ahead of us, came the blare of a fog horn.**

We hadn't noticed the clouds that had come up behind us. They had yet to blot out the sun and we were more aware of the growing flock to our right that was moving slowly towards the road. **Ahead of us the dogs were barking furiously now and we stepped forwards to see what was troubling them.** Again the fog horn blared, this time almost above us.

Suddenly, the fog had surrounded us; damp and chill, it had been blown up behind us as the breeze had lifted. We could see nothing of dogs or sheep, but we could hear them and the rocks that were directly below us. To one side we leant on the round wall of the tower that housed the fog horn, built into the cliff. Around us sheep and dogs continued to move carefully, but we two-legged creatures were far less stable on the cliff face and so we waited until the breeze dropped and the fog slid away off the cliff and moved slowly, back down to the water.

This is a highly effective piece of imaginative writing. A vivid scene is created through precise use of vocabulary, which shows it's not always necessary to use lots of figurative language to describe effectively. The atmosphere becomes increasingly tense, showing the student has a good grasp of how to structure a piece of writing. There is a good balance of longer, more detailed sentences and short sentences for effect.

| PAPER 2 | IMAGINATIVE WRITING | 309 |

COMMENTARY

This is an explanation of how this sample answer was written. Try following this process in your own imaginative writing.

PLANNING THE PLOT

The planning of this piece is focused on the fog surrounding the two characters who were caught unawares. The rounding up of the sheep provides a context, a background or explanation as to why the characters were on the sloping cliffs where fog was more of a danger, a sense of drama that could be used to a lesser or greater extent by the writer.

As the gathering of the sheep proceeds, the task becomes a distraction for the characters as they watch the sheep, rather than the weather behind them. As the drama develops you can feel the slope of the cliffs, see the dogs disappear from sight, somewhere ahead, then you hear the waves and the sudden burst of the fog horn. The reader's senses are used to create the drama.

CHECKING

This is where you must read the passage aloud or, under exam conditions, imagine the sound of a voice reading it aloud. This is the most effective way of checking your writing. If the punctuation is poor, you will find yourself unable to read the passage fluently, and if there are lapses in the grammar then the sense of the writing will not be clear. If this happens, ask yourself, 'What is the subject of this sentence?' and 'What am I told about the subject?'. These questions should help you to clarify the sentence.

EXAM-STYLE QUESTIONS

AO4

AO5

SKILLS CRITICAL THINKING, ANALYSIS, ADAPTIVE LEARNING, CREATIVITY

Write a story with the title, 'Left Behind'. Your response could be real or imagined. **(30 marks)**

Allow yourself 45 minutes to respond to this question with a piece that is 300–400 words in length.

Exchange your finished piece with a partner, then read each other's work and exchange comments. Try to suggest ways of improving each other's work rather than simply finding faults.

KEY POINT

Engaging your audience is crucial. Remember that good imaginative writing usually involves something that the author wants to say. If the author wants something to be read, the reader must be given a reason to start and encouragement to keep reading.

▲ The reader's senses are used to create the drama.

CALIFORNIA
US
66

OLD
66
1926
←   →

PAPER 3: POETRY AND PROSE TEXTS AND IMAGINATIVE WRITING

Assessment Objective 1

Read and understand a variety of texts, selecting and interpreting information, ideas and perspectives

Assessment Objective 2

Understand and analyse how writers use linguistic and structural devices to achieve their effects

This chapter focuses on Paper 3: Poetry and Prose Texts and Imaginative Writing of the English Language A course. Working through these lessons and activities will help you develop the reading and writing skills that you will need for the Paper 3 coursework.

Paper 3 is worth 40% of the total marks for the course and is split into two sections:
- Assignment A: Poetry and prose texts
- Assignment B: Imaginative writing.

In assignment A of your coursework, you will need to be able to meet Assessment Objectives AO1 and AO2.

In assignment B of your coursework, you will need to be able to meet Assessment Objectives AO4 and AO5.

Assessment Objective 4

Communicate effectively and imaginatively, adapting form, tone and register of writing for specific purposes and audiences

Assessment Objective 5

Write clearly, using a range of vocabulary and sentence structures, with appropriate paragraphing and accurate spelling, grammar and punctuation

In Paper 3, the assessment objectives are worth the following amounts.
AO1 – 8%
AO2 – 12%
AO4 – 12%
AO5 – 8%

COURSEWORK OVERVIEW

These two pages give those taking this option a general idea of the coursework requirements. They are followed by a section on Assignment A and another on Assignment B. The coursework option (also called Paper 3), provides an alternative to examination Paper 2 and covers the same content in different ways. It has advantages and disadvantages.

The two coursework tasks for Paper 3 are as follows:

- Assignment A on Poetry and prose texts
- Assignment B on Imaginative writing.

UNDERSTANDING THE COURSEWORK OPTION

The written coursework that you will complete for Paper 3 is worth **40%** of your total English Language course (the same as Paper 2). You have to submit **two** assignments, (known as units). One will be based on Section B of the Pearson Edexcel Anthology, which will be assessed for your **reading** skills. The other will be a piece of personal imaginative writing, which is entirely your own work and which will be assessed for your **writing** skills.

You must work under the guidance of your teacher, who is authorised to assess your coursework and who has to authenticate it, but your coursework is something that you are in charge of. It is vital that you do not copy or borrow writing from elsewhere and then pretend it is your own, and you will be required to sign a form stating that the work is your own.

COURSEWORK TASKS FOR PAPER 3

Assignment A

Poetry and prose texts: study and analyse selections from a range of fictional poetry and prose texts, taken from Section B of the Pearson Edexcel Anthology.

In practice, this piece could focus on no more than two texts (but it must be on more than one).

Assignment B

Imaginative writing: explore and develop imaginative writing skills.

The emphasis of this assignment is very much on your own ideas and ways of expressing yourself.

ADVANTAGES AND DISADVANTAGES OF COURSEWORK

Coursework has many advantages.

- You have more time to plan, think about and improve your assignments.
- Work does not have to be completed under controlled conditions.
- You have more freedom to choose what to write about and what to submit.
- Your coursework folder is solid evidence of what you can do in your own time and to the best of your abilities.

However, there are disadvantages too.

- Coursework may take up too much of your time. The two assignments together are worth 40% of the GCSE, whereas the exam is worth 60%, so you must prioritise your exam preparation over your coursework.
- You may be tempted to take short-cuts. If you cheat and get found out, the penalties can be very severe. Teachers and moderators are very good at detecting plagiarism so it is simply not worth the risk. Furthermore, cheating will not help you to develop your writing skills.

WORD COUNT

There is no definite requirement regarding the length of coursework pieces, except that they should be as long as they need to be. Most students' coursework units are between 450 and 1000 words; the board advises that each assignment should be between 450 and 600 words in length, but there is no penalty for exceeding this recommendation. However, the commentary part of Assignment A should be no more than 200 words.

The best guide is to think about your chosen purpose and or audience. If your unit fits both of these requirements, then it will be the right length.

SUBJECT VOCABULARY

plagiarism taking someone else's work and passing it off as your own

PAPER 3 — COURSEWORK OVERVIEW

SUBMITTING ASSIGNMENTS

AUTHENTICITY

Near the end of the course, you will be asked to sign a Coursework Authentication to confirm that you produced your coursework independently. Teachers are always warned to look out for signs of plagiarism or excessive assistance from others. You should therefore work independently, although it is a good idea to show others what you have written and ask for verbal feedback. If you are unsure, ask your teacher what level of feedback is appropriate.

PRESENTATION OF THE COURSEWORK

Each piece of coursework should contain your name, the date on which the work was completed, the mark awarded and a brief teacher comment justifying the mark. This comment should be based on the assessment criteria for the mark range awarded.

Coursework pieces may be handwritten or word-processed.

STANDARDISATION OF COURSEWORK

Towards the end of the course, Pearson Edexcel will request a sample of coursework to be sent to a Pearson Edexcel-appointed coursework moderator. The moderator will either confirm the marks awarded by the teachers in your centre or will adjust marks accordingly. English departments always standardise the marking by sharing out work from each class amongst all the teachers in the department, so that the marking of the Pearson year group is consistent.

USING PREVIOUS CHAPTERS

ASSESSMENT OBJECTIVES FOR PAPER THREE

Reading (Assignment A):

AO1 Read and understand a variety of texts, selecting and interpreting information, ideas and perspectives

AO2 Understand and analyse how writers use linguistic and structural devices to achieve their effects

Writing (Assignment B):

AO4 Communicate effectively and imaginatively, adapting form, tone and register of writing for specific purposes and audiences

AO5 Write clearly, using a range of vocabulary and sentence structures, with appropriate paragraphing and accurate spelling, grammar and punctuation

HINT

Note that AO3 (relating to comparison) is not relevant to the coursework at all.

The assessment objectives for the coursework and for Papers 1 and 2 are the same. This means that the Paper 2 chapter on the fiction Anthology texts (pages 208–287) will give you plenty of activities and information that can be used to help you with Assignment A. For example, if your assignment is to compare two Anthology texts in some way, you should work your way carefully through the activities on those texts, as they will give you ideas and quotations to use in your coursework.

Likewise, for Assignment B, all the activities for Paper 2 Section B: Imaginative writing (pages 288–309) will be very helpful for your coursework. There are sections on generating ideas, plotting, characterisation, description, using monologues and dialogues, structure and so on, which will help you to create a good story. The fiction stories in the Anthology may also help to give you inspiration. Look at the way that they use technique and structure and handle character, situation, mood and theme.

Writing to **explore**, **imagine** and **entertain** also gives you a wide range of options, including stories, descriptions and magazine or newspaper articles. If you decide to write an article, consult the information about articles in the section on transactional writing (pages 188–190). However, remember that the purpose of the coursework is not to argue or explain but to explore or entertain.

People often write best when they can draw on their own experiences, such as a powerful memory or an eventful day. You could write to explore your feelings and thoughts, or you could use these experiences as part of an entertaining account or story. Your approach to this assignment can be light-hearted or deeply serious, and you can submit imaginative responses to any of the Anthology texts.

LEARNING OBJECTIVES

This lesson will help you to:
- understand how to approach Assignment A (reading skills).

ASSIGNMENT A: POETRY AND PROSE TEXTS

The first assignment is an analytical answer to a question on at least two of the texts in the Poetry and prose texts section of the Anthology. Your teacher will set the task but you can be involved in choosing which texts to write about.

Assignment A will be in two parts.
- Part 1 will be a response to the set assignment and will be marked out of 24 marks, with 6 marks for AO1 and 18 marks for AO2.
- Part 2 will be a short commentary explaining why you chose the texts that you discussed in the assignment. It is worth 6 marks for AO1. This is one of the reasons why you should choose the texts yourself.

This means that this assignment is worth a total of 30 marks, which corresponds to 20% of the International GCSE in English Language.

WORD COUNT

You should aim to write roughly 500–600 words for Part 1 and about 200 words for Part 2, the commentary. You will not be penalised for writing more for Part 1, but you will not be given more marks because you have written more. You must keep it short, since your response to Part 2 is only worth 6 marks.

ANTHOLOGY POETRY AND PROSE TEXTS

For Assignment A, you will write about texts from Section B of the Anthology.
- 'Disabled' by Wilfred Owen.
- 'Out, Out—' by Robert Frost.
- 'An Unknown Girl' by Moniza Alvi.
- 'The Bright Lights of Sarajevo' by Tony Harrison.
- 'Still I Rise' by Maya Angelou.
- 'The Story of An Hour' by Kate Chopin.
- 'The Necklace' by Guy de Maupassant.
- 'Significant Cigarettes' (from *The Road Home*) by Rose Tremain.
- 'Whistle and I'll Come to You' (from *The Woman in Black*) by Susan Hill.
- 'Night' by Alice Munro.

THE QUESTION

The assignment could be a detailed analysis of the language in two texts, or it could focus on a theme that two texts have in common. The following questions are good examples.

▶ **Discuss how the writers use language to present the situation and characters in 'Night' and 'The Bright Lights of Sarajevo'.**

▶ **Consider any two texts about aspects of growing up. How do they approach their subject matter?**

▲ Make detailed notes on your chosen texts, as this will ensure that you have read them thoroughly.

TIPS ON THE READING ASSIGNMENT

HINT

Remember that teachers and moderators are human beings and that they will respond to genuine engagement (that is, when students are doing their best to think for themselves). They will be less impressed by responses that show little individuality.

USING ACTIVITIES FROM PREVIOUS CHAPTERS

▶ **Choose two poems. How do they use language to focus on a significant moment or incident?**

All assignments for this unit must address the Assessment Objectives for reading. In simple terms, this means that you must:

- show that you have read your chosen texts thoroughly and understand them well enough to develop an interpretation
- show how language is used to achieve effects.

For this assignment, you must **not** submit:

- work based on Section A of the Anthology
- imaginative or empathetic responses to Section B texts (although these could be submitted for Assignment B).

1. 'Analyse, not summarise' is a useful motto to bear in mind. It is assumed that you could summarise the texts if you were asked to do so, but nobody is asking you to summarise. Instead, analyse what you have read.

2. Try to develop your own opinion on texts and think for yourself. Do not rely only on teacher notes. To access the higher grade bands, you have to develop a thorough and perceptive understanding of language and structure.

3. A key feature of higher-grade work is that it explores 'how both language and structure are used by writers to achieve effects'. The word 'explore' implies that there is a value in trying to be fresh and individual in your approach. Make your points tentatively, considering different ideas and using phrases such as 'this could be seen as…', 'on the other hand this may be…', and 'another meaning of this might be…'. This kind of writing shows that you are thinking about the texts and responding to them. Although you may misunderstand a text, it is equally true that there is no 'right answer' – only good and less good answers.

4. You must write about the language of the texts and how this helps to convey meaning and fulfil the writer's purpose. Just as in the exams, it is always better to write in some detail about a few quotations, than to quote frequently but fail to comment in detail.

5. It is best to focus closely only on the texts that you have chosen, and not to bring in any other texts that you might think of.

6. You must back up all of your points with clearly relevant and well-explained evidence (think 'P-E-E'!).

Once you have chosen the two texts that you are going to write about, you need to work carefully through the pages on those texts that you will find in the chapter on Paper 2.

Once you have done this, work through the lesson, 'Putting it into practice', on page 227. On this page, you will find the following question.

Read the extract from *Frankenstein*. How does the author convey the narrator's emotions? In your answer, you should write about:

- the imagery
- the setting and sense of place
- the use of language.

You should support your answer with close reference to the passage, including brief quotations. **(30 marks)**

This is an exam-style question, but you could adapt it to suit the coursework, substituting your chosen texts and themes for *Frankenstein* and its themes. In the coursework you will only be asked to answer about a text from the Anthology so this activity is for illustrative purposes only.

For example, you could ask the following question.

PAPER 3 — ASSIGNMENT A: POETRY AND PROSE TEXTS

▶ Show how the writers present the relationship between the physical environment and the events and feelings shown in two poems or texts: 'An Unknown Girl' and 'The Bright Lights of Sarajevo'.

PLANNING AN ANSWER

Once you have decided on a question and chosen which texts you will write about, you should spend some time planning your answer.

You may find it useful to draw up some tables of points, quotations, evidence and their effects. You can then include these in your coursework essay.

For example, these tables refer to the question above. Copy and complete them to find more information which you would include if you were answering this question.

▲ In his depiction of Sarajevo and its inhabitants, Harrison brings out the contradictions of wartime.

▼ EVIDENCE: A DETAIL ABOUT THE CITY NOTICED BY HARRISON	▼ WHAT THIS TELLS YOU ABOUT THE ENVIRONMENT
'To get the refills they wheel home in prams'	Shows how the Sarajevans improvise with whatever they have to cope with the situation.

▼ EVIDENCE: CONTRASTING WORDS OR PHRASES	▼ COMMENT ON THE EFFECT OF THE CONTRAST
'Queuing for the… grams of bread / Often dodging snipers on the way'	Queuing is an everyday activity, but the idea of being shot at as part of the routine is shocking.

SAMPLE STUDENT ANSWER

Read through the following student answer to this question.

> 'The Bright Lights of Sarajevo' describes how, at night, in besieged and bomb-damaged Sarajevo, the poet is surprised to find young people from different ethnic groups strolling about in the darkness, and how boys meet girls despite the danger and darkness, whilst also hinting at the violent events of the siege.
>
> The poem shows us the paradoxes of wartime: how ethnic conflict is submerged at night; how romance can burst into life in a terrible and fearful environment; how tender or romantic feelings can exist in the same place where people were killed by shells earlier in the war.
>
> The language of the poem is mostly straightforward and even quite conversational. This helps to make the poem more realistic: it sounds spontaneous and is more accessible to us (especially perhaps to the first readers of the poem in *The Guardian*). Perhaps Harrison was trying to convey the sense that he was there, recording his on-the-spot impressions. Throughout the poem Harrison conveys the contrast between the activities of ordinary, peaceable Sarajevans and the strange and difficult conditions in which they live, with evidence of large-scale violence all around them. The contrast is expressed in the language. Sometimes one phrase has associations or suggests a feeling very different from those of another.

> As the poem goes on, we can see a group or chain of words associated with each other, which denote peaceful activities, but these contrast or clash with another chain of words associated with a wartime environment. The effect is to make us aware of how the people are doing their utmost to keep living in the midst of danger. You could say that the ideas of the poem are structured around this contrast.

THE COMMENTARY

In your commentary, you should aim to explain why you chose the two texts and talk about interpreting ideals and perspectives in relation to each text. To do this, you could adopt the following plan.

- **Explain why you chose the two texts:** It is important to show that you have thought about which texts to write about, rather than simply done what you were told to do. For example, you might say that you were interested in them because they both explored aspects of a theme in which you are interested. Mention that you have read the other texts in the Anthology and why these two were more interesting than the others.

- **Interpreting ideas and perspectives:** Say something about these in relation to each text about which you have written. For example, if you wrote about 'Still I Rise' by Maya Angelou, you might say that the poem is written from the perspective of an intelligent and passionate black American girl at a time when the social status of African-Americans was finally improving.

If you have worked through the relevant sections on the texts that you have chosen, and have understood how to create an effective and perceptive answer about your chosen texts, then you should now be ready to plan your own piece of coursework. Good luck!

> **KEY POINT**
>
> Write about the motivations that inspired you to choose the two texts. What do you find really stimulating in them?

ASSESSMENT GRIDS

		▼ ASSIGNMENT A: POETRY AND PROSE TEXTS
▼ LEVEL	▼ MARK	▼ A01 READ AND UNDERSTAND A VARIETY OF TEXTS, SELECTING AND INTERPRETING INFORMATION, IDEAS AND PERSPECTIVES (6 MARKS)
		▼ A02 UNDERSTAND AND ANALYSE HOW WRITERS USE LINGUISTIC AND STRUCTURAL DEVICES TO ACHIEVE THEIR EFFECTS (18 MARKS)
	0	No rewardable material.
Level 1	1–4	■ Basic understanding of the texts. ■ Selection and interpretation of information/ideas/perspectives is limited. ■ Little understanding of language and structure and how these are used by writers to achieve effects. ■ Identification of the language and/or structure used by writers to achieve effects. ■ The use of references is limited.

ASSIGNMENT A: POETRY AND PROSE TEXTS

Level	Mark	Criteria
Level 2	5–9	■ Some understanding of the texts. ■ Selection and interpretation of information/ideas/perspectives is valid, but not developed. ■ Some understanding of language and structure and how these are used by writers to achieve effects. ■ Some comment on the language and/or structure used by writers to achieve effects, including use of vocabulary. ■ The selection of references is valid, but not developed.
Level 3	10–14	■ Sound understanding of the texts. ■ Selection and interpretation of information/ideas/perspectives is appropriate and relevant to the points being made. ■ Clear understanding of language and structure and how these are used by writers to achieve effects. ■ Explanation of how both language and structure are used by writers to achieve effects, including use of vocabulary and sentence structure. ■ The selection of references is appropriate and relevant to the points being made.
Level 4	15–19	■ Sustained understanding of the texts. ■ Selection and interpretation of information/ideas/perspectives is appropriate, detailed and fully supports the points being made. ■ Thorough understanding of language and structure and how these are used to achieve effects. ■ Exploration of how both language and structure are used by writers to achieve effects, including use of vocabulary, sentence structure and other language features. ■ The selection of references is detailed, appropriate and fully supports the points being made.
Level 5	20–24	■ Perceptive understanding of the texts. ■ Selection and interpretation of information/ideas/perspectives is apt and is persuasive in clarifying the points being made. ■ Perceptive understanding of language and structure and how these are used by writers to achieve effects. ■ Analysis of both language and structure are used by writers to achieve effects, including use of vocabulary, sentence structure and other language features. ■ The selection of references is discriminating and clarifies the points being made.

▼ ASSIGNMENT A: COMMENTARY

▼ LEVEL	▼ MARK	▼ AO1 READ AND UNDERSTAND A VARIETY OF TEXTS, SELECTING AND INTERPRETING INFORMATION, IDEAS AND PERSPECTIVES (6 MARKS)
	0	No rewardable material.
Level 1	1–2	■ Explanation of the selection of the texts is limited.
Level 2	3–4	■ Explanation of the selection of the texts is appropriate and relevant.
Level 3	5–6	■ Explanation of the selection of texts is apt and persuasive.

LEARNING OBJECTIVES

This lesson will help you to:
- understand how to approach the imaginative writing element of your coursework.

ASSIGNMENT B: IMAGINATIVE WRITING

The second assignment is a piece of personal and imaginative writing. This will be based on a topic or topics that will be given to you by your teacher.

The purpose or purposes of your piece of writing should be any or all of the following: **to explore, to imagine, to entertain**. In this way, it is like the imaginative writing task set in Section B of Paper 2.

The assignment is worth the same amount as Assignment A, making it worth 20 per cent of the International GCSE in English Language.

Your teacher will set the question or choice of questions.

THE TOPIC

The topic could be suggested by a piece in the Anthology, such as the following question.

▶ **'Free from the chains.' Write an imaginative piece ending with these words.**

Alternatively, it could be an unrelated topic, perhaps relating to an image or concept such as the following suggestions.

▶ **The dream**
▶ **Anxious moments**
▶ **The shame of it**

ELEMENTS OF STORYTELLING

Turn to the Paper 2 chapter on imaginative writing (pages 288–309) and work through as many of the activities as you can, particularly the sections on plot, structure, vocabulary for effect and sentences for effect. This will focus your mind on narrative methods and techniques.

ACTIVITY 1 | AO4 | AO5

SKILLS: CRITICAL THINKING, ANALYSIS, ADAPTIVE LEARNING, CREATIVITY, INNOVATION

▼ **GOALS IN WRITING**

There are three vital goals. You have to demonstrate:
- how expressively and how appropriately you can write;
- how effectively you can structure your writing
- how accurately you can write in terms of spelling, punctuation and grammar.

Write a detailed plan for one of the suggested titles on this page and two good opening paragraphs in response to your chosen title.

KEY POINT

Your goal should be to create expressive, well structured and grammatically accurate writing with good spelling and punctuation.

TIPS ON THE WRITING ASSIGNMENT

1 Write from your own perspective. Why set your story in a small town in another country, about which you know little, when there must be hundreds of stories near your home that are waiting to be told?
2 Remember that you don't have to be totally truthful, even when writing a story based on your own experience; you can imagine and pretend.
3 If you are aiming for the higher grades, you should consider presenting your work in a fresh or original way. You need to show skill in engaging and keeping your reader's interest.
4 Experiment with form. For example, try telling a story from different angles, from the points of view of different characters.
5 In stories, create characters as well as atmosphere and give them motives. Don't just focus on drama and violence: think of consequences.

Finally, remember:

- coursework takes careful thought and planning
- seek advice, but write as yourself in your own words
- use spell checkers carefully – it is allowed!

ACTIVITY 2 — A04 A05 — SKILLS: CRITICAL THINKING, ANALYSIS

▼ MARKING A RESPONSE

Before you start to plan your own story, here is an example of a piece written by an International GCSE candidate. Read it and then assess it using the mark scheme.

> 'Escape'
>
> The blade glinted in the light of the half-moon, hanging over the whispy dark clouds. Then a piercing beam from a spotlight, or was it headlights, shot through the darkness, lighting up trees, bushes and huge muddy puddles along the track through the woods. A shadowy figure ducked into the thick vegetation. He bent down and sawed at the padlock around a chain circling his leg, then, when it fell away onto the ground, he stood up, and went out into the cover of the night…
>
> His name was John O'Malley, leutenant – a sniper – the best in the regiment. During his escape from the prison camp in Germany, he had managed to keep his Lee-Enfield scope under his greatcoat. Just as he was preparing to move on swiftly, there was the roar of a vehecle. He ducked into the dark ditch, crouching in the dank greenery. Once the lorry was safely out of earshot he moved on through the trees, then descended down the frosty slopes to a village. If anyone had been watching as he flitted from tree to tree, he would have appeared like some woodland creature: but nobody was watching. The streets were deserted, no-one observed him as he slipped along them. Then he muttered to himself: 'Damn! Just my luck,' as he came in view of a checkpoint. There was nothing else he could do, so, sweating, he

> approached and handed his forged papers to the obnoxsious-looking guard. He scrutenised them with a bad-tempered expression on his face. Then he handed them back. The guard shouted something and the gate lifted. He bought a ticket, for he spoke good German, and boarded the train near the massive, snorting steam engine. For the first time he felt that he might really escape. He almost dared to relax a little, as he settled into a window seat. Then suddenly there was a sound of boots and someone shouting 'Halt! Halt!' as SS soldiers poured onto the train and issued abrupt commands. The exits were blocked, one of them asked for his papers, but was not satisfied with them. He shouted out some questions and ordered him off the train. John's heart sank, he was back to square one.
>
> He was shoved into the back of a van with a couple of dangerous-looking dogs and various bits of equipment. The door was locked. Drearily, he wondered what his chances were of escaping again on the way to the camp, or another, tougher camp. At least he was alive, and in one peice, he thought, it was something to be grateful for. At least the Germans did not exicute escaped prisoners. Not usually, in any case.
>
> There might be another chance, he told himself, he must stay alert…

Although this response is not perfect, it has many good points.

What marks for AO4 (out of 18) and AO5 (out of 12) do you think this should be given?

ASSIGNMENT B: IMAGINATIVE WRITING

LEVEL	MARK	AO4 COMMUNICATE EFFECTIVELY AND IMAGINATIVELY, ADAPTING FORM, TONE AND REGISTER OF WRITING FOR SPECIFIC PURPOSES AND AUDIENCES
	0	No rewardable material.
Level 1	1–3	■ Communication is at a basic level, and limited in clarity.
Level 2	4–7	■ Communicates in a broadly appropriate way.
Level 3	8–11	■ Communicates clearly.
Level 4	12–15	■ Communicates effectively. ■ A secure realisation of the writing task according to the writer's purpose and the expectations/requirements of the intended reader is shown. ■ Effective use of form, tone and register.
Level 5	16–18	■ Communication is perceptive and subtle with discriminating use of a full vocabulary.

ASSIGNMENT B: IMAGINATIVE WRITING

LEVEL	MARK	AO5 WRITE CLEARLY, USING A RANGE OF VOCABULARY AND SENTENCE STRUCTURES, WITH APPROPRIATE PARAGRAPHING AND ACCURATE SPELLING, GRAMMAR AND PUNCTUATION
	0	No rewardable material.
Level 1	1–2	■ Expresses information and ideas, with limited use of structural and grammatical features.
Level 2	3–4	■ Expresses and orders information and ideas; uses paragraphs and a range of structural and grammatical features.
Level 3	5–7	■ Develops and connects appropriate information and ideas; structural and grammatical features and paragraphing make the meaning clear.
Level 4	8–10	■ Manages information and ideas, with structural and grammatical features used cohesively and deliberately across the text. ■ Uses a wide, selective vocabulary with only occasional spelling errors. ■ Positions a range of punctuation for clarity, managing sentence structures for deliberate effect.
Level 5	11–12	■ Manipulates complex ideas, utilising a range of structural and grammatical features to support coherence and cohesion. ■ Uses extensive vocabulary strategically; rare spelling errors do not detract from overall meaning. ■ Punctuates writing with accuracy to aid emphasis and precision, using a range of sentence structures accurately and selectively to achieve particular effects.

ACTIVITY 3 — AO4 AO5 — SKILLS: ANALYSIS, REASONING, CREATIVITY

▼ THE STRUCTURE OF 'ESCAPE'

In pairs or individually, copy and complete the following table, dividing 'Escape' into five sections and writing a phrase to sum up the content of each section. You could begin by summarising the content of each paragraph, bearing in mind that a section may contain more than one paragraph.

▼ SECTION	▼ PARAGRAPH(S)	▼ SUMMARY OF CONTENT
1	1	Introduces the situation and character; describes setting.
2		
3		
4		
5		

Looking at the table, would you say that 'Escape' is a well-structured story?

If so, what are the things that make its planning or structure effective, given the limitation of the word count?

PLANNING STRUCTURE

KEY POINT

You can structure your writing around functions such as narrative, or dialogue. Not only does this maintain the reader's interest, it also provides a framework around which you can fill out the piece.

Another way to think about structure is to plan which types or functions of writing you are going to use.

Even though you may only write around 600 words, using several types or functions of writing will give your story a sense of variety, which will help to keep your reader interested.

These types or functions of writing are:

- description: many stories begin with brief scene-setting descriptions
- narrative: this tells you what happens and includes tiny actions and movements, such as 'he frowned', which are important in storytelling
- dialogue: speech often brings a story to life and conveys feelings very directly and convincingly
- thoughts and feelings: thoughts that are not included in the dialogue but are included when a character is thinking to themselves, which can help to give your characters more depth
- background information: it may be useful to tell the reader something about a character or place.

When you are planning, try to bring in several of these – it should help you to structure the piece. Even if you decide to have only one character, you may find that you can even use dialogue as it can be useful to have your character say something to themselves.

ACTIVITY 4 — AO4 AO5 — SKILLS: ADAPTIVE LEARNING, CREATIVITY, INNOVATION

▼ **USING TYPES OF WRITING TO PLAN STRUCTURE**

1. Using the following checklist, tick the functions of writing that you will probably use and write a short note on how you might use each one. You could concentrate on using one more than the others if you like. For example, your piece could be almost entirely description or dialogue: there are no exact rules, though some variety is surely a good idea.
   - ☐ Description
   - ☐ Narrative
   - ☐ Dialogue
   - ☐ Thoughts and feelings
   - ☐ Background information

2. Go back to 'Escape' and read it again. Find examples of each of the five functions of writing and label them. Notice how easily the writer slips from one function to another, so that the reader does not notice.

MAKING CHOICES ABOUT CONTENT AND GENRE

Answer the following questions about 'Escape'.

▶ Why is it probably best to base your story on one simple incident?

▶ Why is it best to have only one or two main characters?

▶ A lot of young people writing stories tend to include too many events and characters: why do you think this is?

BEGINNING, MIDDLE AND END

HINT

'Escape' has: one main character; two or three clear settings; a simple (though dramatic) situation; two incidents; a difficult problem; and an ending that was conclusive for the time being, though it left a cliffhanger. In other words, it contained more than enough for 400–500 words. Don't try to include too many characters or too many events – focus on one incident or one problem.

However long or short, all stories will have a beginning, a middle and an end. The beginning should preferably have a narrative hook that makes the reader want to read on (for example, in 'Escape', you probably wanted to know who the character was and what he was escaping from). The ending need not be a full conclusion, especially in a very short story, but it should give the reader some sense of resolution.

ACTIVITY 5 — **AO4** **AO5** — **SKILLS** CRITICAL THINKING, ANALYSIS, ADAPTIVE LEARNING, CREATIVITY, INNOVATION

▼ PLANNING YOUR STORY'S BEGINNING, MIDDLE AND END

Summarise how you think your story will begin, develop and end. When you finish writing your story, compare your original plan with the finished story. What has changed? What worked out as you expected?

What types of story have you found easiest, or perhaps most enjoyable, to write in the past? Choose two from the list below.

- Science fiction
- Fantasy
- War
- Romance
- Comedy
- Thriller
- Horror
- Realism.

Because the title that you will be given will normally be one or two very general words, it is likely that you will be able to relate the title to any genre. Imagine that the title that you have been given is 'The Decision'. Choose one of the two genres that you selected from the list and jot down some ideas for a story in that genre with that title. You could do this in a list or spider diagram. Include details about:

- the main character
- the setting
- the situation
- the central incident or event
- a problem to solve
- the ending.

◀ Your favourite film genres may inspire you to choose the genre of your writing: sci-fi, fantasy, romance?

ASSIGNMENT B: IMAGINATIVE WRITING

The following spider diagram is a plan for a simple realistic story entitled 'The Decision'.

- **Describe**: Setting near school – street
- **Characters**: Ant is quieter than others; one of the new members is seen in distance but they don't meet him – reactions to him?
- **Narrative**: Meets one or two friends – walks with them? later on his own thinks about problem
- **Situation**: 15-year-old boy; problem – is he going to go out with a group of friends, though he doesn't much like one or two new members, and he is worried that they will get them into trouble [how?]
- Decides at end to go with them, but might leave early – he tells best friend – reaction in **dialogue**
- Dialogue and thoughts or feelings

This example is based on a very simple situation that may be familiar to you. A lot of writers advise beginners to 'write about what you know', and this often makes sense. An idea such as this might be one in which you can draw on your own experience, and alter it as much as you like, and this will help you to make the writing vivid and believable. However, you can see that a title such as 'The Decision' could work in any genre at all.

CHARACTERISATION AND PERSPECTIVE

Part of the planning process will involve thinking about your main character. It is a good idea to tell the story from this character's point of view, as this will give the reader a strong sense of their personality. One of the things you should decide quite quickly is whether to tell the story in the first or third person. First-person narrative is best if you want the reader to see everything from your main character's point of view, whereas third-person narrative is best if you want the reader to understand everything via an all-knowing narrator.

Once you have chosen your narrative perspective, copy and complete the following table, filling it out with details about your main character.

Gender	
Age	
Ethnicity	
Where from originally?	
Living where (if different)?	
Outgoing/shy?	
Clever/average?	
Pleased about what in life?	
Upset about what in life?	
How do they dress?	
Social background?	
What objects would you associate with them (to do with work/hobbies/interests)?	
Problem in story?	

EXAM PREPARATION

SUCCESSFUL REVISION

Many books offer different suggestions and advice for revision. One thing is clear: not everything works for everyone. Each person has particular ways of revising and habits of working. Look at all the advice and try out the different suggestions. Decide clearly what the knowledge, skills and techniques you need to develop, consolidate or revisit.

PLAN YOUR LEARNING AND REVISION

HOW TO PLAN A SCHEDULE
- Draw up a table to show the days and weeks before the examination.
- Decide how much time to give to the subject in each week or day.
- Work out a timetable.
- Think about the need for variety and breaks.
- Make sure your schedule is building towards a 'peak' at the right time.

HOW TO IMPROVE
- Test yourself.
- Test a friend.
- Practise answering exam questions.
- Write answers to the time limits of questions in the actual exam.
- Check that you understand all texts, looking particularly at words, meaning, plot and character.
- Revise technical terms, using the glossary on pages 330–331.
- Make sure you can apply these terms properly, spell them properly, give examples, and explain how and why the techniques are used.

AIDS TO LEARNING
Write short, clear notes. Use aids such as:
- postcards
- diagrams
- flowcharts
- mnemonics (aids to memory, such as rhymes)
- computer programmes
- websites and apps.

GOOD PREPARATION
Good preparation is one of the main elements affecting how people perform in exams. This includes both attitude of mind and physical preparation.
- Check how long the exam lasts and use your time properly.
- Make sure you understand the specification and know what you have to do.

Don't be tempted to rush your initial reading. It is surprising how many exam candidates make basic mistakes because they did not read through the text in front of them properly.

EXAM PREPARATION

USING YOUR TIME EFFECTIVELY IN THE EXAMINATIONS

Note that the time allocation of 2 hours and 15 minutes for Paper 1 includes time to check instructions and read the paper carefully. Decide how much time you need to allocate to each question: the question paper gives suggestions. You should also aim to leave enough time for checking through at the end. An example of how to plan your time for each paper is given below.

PAPER 1: NON-FICTION TEXTS AND TRANSACTIONAL WRITING (COMPULSORY IN BOTH ROUTES)

▼ READING THE QUESTION PAPER	▼ SECTION A 80 MINUTES / 45 MARKS	▼ SECTION B 40 MINUTES / 45 MARKS	▼ FINAL CHECKING
5–10 minutes	Planning: 5 minutes Writing: 75 minutes	Planning: 5 minutes Writing: 25 minutes	5–10 minutes

Duration of exam: 135 minutes (2 hours 15 minutes) **Total marks: 90**

SPECIFICATION A: PAPER 2 (EXAM OPTION)

▼ READING THE QUESTION PAPER	▼ QUESTION 1 30 MARKS	▼ QUESTION 2 30 MARKS	▼ FINAL CHECKING
5–10 minutes	Planning: 5–10 minutes Writing: 30–35 minutes	Planning: 5–10 minutes Writing: 30–35 minutes	5–10 minutes

Duration of exam: 90 minutes (1 hour 30 minutes) **Total marks: 60**

CHECK YOUR WORK

Check that you are keeping to your planned timings. Keep thinking throughout about:
- relevance, presentation, accuracy and varied vocabulary.

If you manage to leave some checking time at the end:
- make sure you have answered all questions fully and appropriately
- correct any errors in spelling or punctuation (particularly that all sentences have full stops)
- Be certain make sure everything you have written can be read easily.

RELATIONSHIP OF ASSESSMENT OBJECTIVES TO UNITS

▼ UNIT NUMBER	▼ ASSESSMENT OBJECTIVE				
	AO1	AO2	AO3	AO4	AO5
PAPER 1	7%	8%	15%	18%	12%
PAPER 2 / PAPER 3	8%	12%	0%	12%	8%
TOTAL FOR INTERNATIONAL GCSE	15%	20%	15%	15%	20%

PLANNING YOUR ANSWERS

ANSWER THE QUESTION
Do **not** just write down everything you know: this is the most common mistake made by exam candidates. Planning consists of:
- reading the question carefully and deciding what the key words in it are
- deciding the main points you wish to make is, what the question is looking for and how you intend to tackle it
- making sure that the points you want to include are appropriately positioned and structured in the answer
- giving your answer a structure: introduction, main section(s) and conclusion
- choosing examples or quotations.

THINKING ABOUT THE QUESTION
Identifying the key words in the question can help to show:
- **what** the question is looking for
- **how** you intend to tackle it.

Key words and phrases in the question show what the examiner is expecting from an answer. For example:
- **'how does the writer'** is asking you to explain methods and techniques
- **'explain'** asks you to make clear to the examiner your understanding of the text and its methods
- **'analyse'** expects you to look in detail at the writing, its methods and techniques and its effects
- **'compare and contrast'** asks for an examination of similarities and differences in any relevant aspects (for example, themes, moods, forms and language).

KEY POINTS
Write down quickly, in note form, your immediate thoughts about the subject. You may find a diagram useful for this purpose. Do not write full sentences here, or you will waste too much time.

THE CONTENT OF THE ANSWER
The examiner **does** want to know what you think: your own, personal ideas and opinions. However, a series of unsupported statements that start with the words 'I think…' is not enough, since the examiner also needs to know that these ideas are based on your analysis of the texts, your understanding of the subject matter and other evidence.

DECIDING THE STRUCTURE: INTRODUCTION, MAIN SECTION(S) AND CONCLUSION
- **Introduction**: A clear, brief introductory paragraph can make a very good initial impression, showing the examiner that you are thinking about the actual question.
- **Main section(s)**: Decide how many paragraphs or sections you wish your answer to contain.
- **Conclusion**: This may be quite a brief paragraph. It should sum up clearly and logically the argument that has gone before. Above all, it should show the examiner that you have **answered the question**!

WRITING ANALYTICALLY
When writing analytically, whether for English Language or Literature, many students find it helpful to follow the acronym:
- **P** – Point
- **E** – Evidence
- **E** – Explain.

This may help to remind you to structure your paragraphs around a point, include quotations as evidence and then explain in some detail what it is about the quotations that validates your point.

A slightly more advanced approach is to add:

- L – Link.

This means that you should link your point to the previous and following points, giving your answer a tight and logical structure. Think P-E-E-L.

EVALUATIVE COMMENTS

When reading Section A answers that analyse aspects of a text, examiners will always give more credit for some detailed explanations of how the writer is using language, in which the student shows clearly that they have understood how language is working, than for 'technique-spotting'. In other words, you will get few marks for just saying that a writer uses short sentences and alliteration here and there; but if you can write a few lines on how a writer uses language effectively in just one sentence, you will write a better answer.

USING QUOTATIONS

When writing about texts, whether books, poems, articles or extracts, one of the most important techniques is to use quotations, where these are required and allowed. Quoting is a skill that has to be practised. Overuse of quotations is as significant a mistake as not using any at all. You should use quotations:

- to illustrate or give an example, for example, a simile or an instance of alliteration
- to explain why you believe something, to support an opinion or argument or to prove a point.

Quotations should be relevant, effective and short: a single word to a line or two at the most. Introduce quotations fluently into your sentence structure. Avoid writing things like, 'He says…'.

LESS CAN BE MORE

If you can, practise doing Section B type questions, but never rush them. Just as you should concentrate on explaining in some detail how a writer creates effects for Section A, so in Section B your aim should not be to show how much you can write, but to show that you can think as you write – think of ideas, paragraphing, sentence structure, vocabulary, persuasive or rhetorical techniques and so on. Try to write with care!

LAST-MINUTE REVISION

Think ahead. Revision the night or morning before an exam can be very useful, but generally only if you have done all of the work already. Last-minute revision should consist of looking at checklists, summative notes, mnemonics and any of your particular weaknesses. This can be very helpful, but make sure that you do not panic and make sure that you have done all of the actual work in the weeks before your exam.

ON THE DAY OF THE EXAM

Again, checklists and mnemonics can be useful to consult as you go into school, as might reading through a model answer or two. Always read the exam paper carefully all the way through, and look at the choices for Section B before you start Section A. Many experienced teachers would advise taking some 'mint-time' (that is, the time it would take a mint to dissolve in the mouth – and there is no reason why you should not take one just before you go into the exam room) to read and think and make some notes, before you begin the first question. This can have the effect of steadying the nerves as well as allowing you to think. (Not chewing gum, though!)

TIME WAITS FOR NO-ONE!

Your teacher may not make you practise answering exam questions against the clock, but you should do it anyway. It is invaluable practice for the real exam, which is always a race against time.

What is essential is that you divide your time up carefully in the exam: many students will find it harder to answer Section A with enough detail and accuracy than to complete a reasonable answer to Section B, so if you could allow more time for Section A, then aim to complete Section B in about 50 minutes. Remember that the Section A questions are marked against detailed mark schemes of what should be in the answers (your teacher can show you examples), whereas Section B questions are marked on more general guidelines. Also remember that your answer does not have to be a certain length, which means that you can gain good marks with a carefully written answer of 400 words.

Good luck!

GLOSSARY

adjective a word that describes a noun or pronoun

adverb a word that describes a verb or an adjective

alliteration the use of several words together that begin with the same sound or letter

anecdotal consisting of short stories based on someone's personal experience

atmosphere the feeling that an event or place gives you

broadsheet a newspaper printed on large sheets of paper, especially a serious newspaper

chronologically organised in linear time

clause a group of words that make up part of a sentence, built around a finite verb

clichés phrases that are used so often that they start to lose their impact

conjunction a word that joins parts of a sentence

connotation ideas linked to a word; ideas that have become associated with a word

contrast where two objects, people or ideas are placed next to each other to highlight their differences

denotation what something literally is or shows

determiner a word used before a noun in order to show which thing is being referred to

dialogue the speech between two or more people involved in a conversation

diction the writer's choice of words

direct address using second person pronouns 'you' or 'your'

direct speech words spoken by a character in a novel, play or poem

dynamic verb a verb that describes actions or events that are happening, e.g. 'I go'

emotive language language that produces an emotional reaction

explicit expressed in a way that is very clear and direct

exposition a thorough description

first person written from the perspective of one person – that is, using 'I'; this differs from the second person, which directly addresses the reader ('you'), and the third person ('he', 'she' and 'it')

flashback when the narrator of a story jumps out of the present in order to describe an event which happened in the past (often in the form of memories)

hyperbole exaggerating for effect

imperative verbs verbs that give an instruction or command

implicit suggested or understood without being stated directly

infer read between the lines

interjection a word used to express a strong feeling

ironic using words to convey a meaning that is completely opposite to their apparent meaning

juxtaposition putting two very different things close together in order to encourage comparison between them

litotes ironic understatement used to mean something by saying its opposite

memoir a form of autobiography

metaphor describing something by comparing it to an image which it resembles, in a way that says the object *is* the image

mnemonic a device used to aid memory – usually in the form of a saying or rhyme

modal auxiliary verb a verb that helps another to verb express a meaning, e.g. 'can', 'would', 'should'

monologue the speech or thoughts of one person alone

mots justes a French phrase, meaning words that are apt, or just right

narrative the story or plot

narrator a character that tells the story in a novel, play, poem or film

noun a word that represents a person, place, object or quality

objective based on facts, or making a decision that is based on facts rather than on your feelings or beliefs

onomatopoeia where a word sounds like the noise it makes

paradox a situation (or piece of writing) which contains strongly contrasting elements or meanings

periodic sentence a sentence that is not complete until the final word or clause

personal pronoun a word used instead of a noun, such as 'I', 'you' or 'they'

personification when something which is not human is made to sound human by attributing human qualities to it

persuasive able to make other people believe something or do what you ask

phonological relating to the sound structure of words

plagiarism taking someone else's work and passing it off as your own

premodified a noun with a description before it, e.g. 'the big blue car'

preposition a word that is used before a noun or pronoun to show time, place or direction

prolepsis suggestions of things that will happen, before they do

pronoun a word that is used instead of a noun

protagonist the main character

pun an amusing use of a word or phrase that has two meanings, or of words that have the same sound but different meanings

GLOSSARY

quotation marks punctuation marks used to indicate where you have quoted

quotations words from a text

referend the thing or idea to which a word refers

register the type or style of vocabulary used according to the situation

repetition saying the same thing more than once to highlight its importance

retrospective written in the past tense; looking back at events that have already occurred

rhetorical device using language in a certain way to achieve an effect

rhetorical question a question that you ask as a way of making a statement, without expecting an answer

rhyme scheme the rhyming pattern used in a poem

rule of three where three things are linked or something is repeated three times in order to emphasise them and ensure they are memorable

setting the place where something is or where something happens, and the general environment

simile a description that says that an object is *like* an image

stereotypes fixed and generalised ideas about particular types of people or groups

symbolic where a person, object or event is used by a writer to convey a meaning other than its literal meaning

synonym a word that shares the same meaning as another word; for example, 'quick' might be a synonym for 'fast'

syntax the way in which words and phrases are arranged into sentences

third person using the third person – that is, 'he', 'she' and 'it'; this differs from the first person ('I') and the second person, which directly addresses the reader ('you')

time-shift moving between different periods of time

topic sentence the first sentence in a paragraph, often used to explain the key idea

transactional non-fiction writing for a purpose: to inform, explain, review, argue, persuade or advise

travelogue a book that describes a travel experience

unbiased fair because not influenced by one's own or someone else's opinions

verb a word that describes actions

verbose excessively wordy or long-winded

INDEX

#
127 Hours (film) 117

A
Adichie, Chimamanda Ngozi: Danger of a Single Story, The 96–102
adjectives 16
adverbials (part of sentence) 21
adverbs 16
advisory writing 31, 89, 182–3
Alagiah, George: Passage to Africa, A 70–1, 103–7
Alvi, Moniza: Unknown Girl, An 236–40
anecdotal writing 100
Angelou, Maya: Still I rise 249–55
apostrophes 50
arguments 88–9, 180–1
articles 58, 71–4, 190
atmosphere 219
attitudes (in writing) 79
audience 82–3, 153, 176, 184–7
autobiographies 58, 59–60, 284

B
balanced sentences 38–9
Between a Rock and a Hard Place (Ralston) 117–18
    exploring language 120–1
    understanding the text 119–20
Beyond the Sky and Earth: A Journey into Bhutan (Zeppa) 95, 134–6
    exploring language 138–40
    understanding the text 137
bias 12, 58, 78
biographies 58, 59–60
blogs 58, 192–3
books, reference 76–7
Bowie, David 61
brackets 51, 53
Bright Lights of Sarajevo, The (Harrison) 241–2
    exploring language 245–6
    setting 244
    understanding the text 243–4
Brighton Rock (Greene) 294–5
Bryson, Bill: Walk in the Woods, A 6–7

C
capital letters 53
Capybara (review) 160–1
characters 216–19, 289, 298–9
Chinese Cinderella (Mah) 147–8, 167
    exploring language 151
    understanding the text 149–50
Chopin, Kate: Story of an Hour, The 256–9
Cider with Rosie (Lee) 90–1
clauses 20–1, 34
colons 51
commands 20, 87
commas 49, 53
comparison of texts 247–8, 281–2
    exam preparation 170–2
    techniques 162–7
complements (part of sentence) 21
complex sentences 21, 34–5, 87, 198
compound sentences 21, 34–5, 38, 87
conclusions 201
conjunctions 16, 21, 34
connotations 7, 18–19, 28–9, 195–6
Corpse (Mehemedinovic) 247–8
coursework 312–13

D
Danger of a Single Story, The (Adichie)
    exploring language 100
    structure 101–2
    understanding the text 99–100
dashes 51, 53
declarative sentences 20, 87
descriptive writing 31, 40, 302–3
determiners 16
dialogues 300–1
diaries 58, 65–8
Diary of a young girl, The (Frank) 65–6, 67–8
direct speech 285–6
Disabled (Owen) 228–9
    exploring language 230–1
    understanding the text 230
discursive writing 31, 40
Duffy, Carol Ann: Valentine 213
Dulce et Decorum est (Owen) 218–19

E
EDINGLY openers 22
editing 54–5
ellipses 51
emotive language 12, 13, 84, 195
Encyclopedia Britannica 76–7
entertaining writing 31
evaluating texts 10–15
evidence, selection 168–9
exclamation marks 48, 53
exclamations 20, 87
explanatory writing 177–8
explicit meaning 6–7, 162
Explorers, or Boys Messing About? (Morris) 113–14
    understanding the text 115–16
Explorer's Daughter, The (Herbert) 167
    exploring language 111–12
    understanding the text 111

F
facts 88–9
fiction writing
    exam preparation 226–7
    types 210–11
figurative language 212–15
first person 220, 297
flashbacks 223
form 188–9
Frank, Anne: Diary of a young girl, The 65–6, 67–8
Frankenstein (Shelley) 226–7

Frost, Robert: Out, Out– 224–5, 232–6
full stops 53

G

Game of Polo with a Headless Goat, A (Levine) 129–30
    exploring language 132–3
    structure 131–2
    understanding the text 131
Golding, William: Lord of the Flies 214–15
Goodbye to Berlin (Isherwood) 216–17
Grahame, Kenneth: Wind in the Willows, The 296
grammar 53
Greene, Graham: Brighton Rock 294–5

H

H is for Hawk (Macdonald)
    exploring language 144
    structure 145–6
    understanding the text 143–4
Harrison, Tony: Bright Lights of Sarajevo, The 241–8
Henri, Adrian: Love is… 213
Herbert, Kari: Explorer's Daughter, The 108–12
Hill, Susan
    I'm the King of the Castle 300
    Risk of Darkness, The 306
    Whistle and I'll come to you 275–82
How the Poor Die (Orwell) 158–60, 170
Hungry Cyclist, The (Kevill-Davies) 94–5
hyperbole 13

I

I have a dream (King) 63–4, 78
iambic pentameter 225
ideas 46–7
I'm the King of the Castle (Hill) 300
images 18
imaginative writing
    assignments 319–25
    exam preparation 308–9
    features 288–9
    purpose 290, 292
imperative sentences 20, 87
implicit meaning 6–7, 162
In the Empire of Genghis Khan (Stewart) 68–70, 71, 78
incomplete sentences 87
indirect speech 291–2
inferring 7, 19
informative writing 31, 40, 176–7
inspirational writing 31
interjections 16
interrogative sentences 20, 48, 87
intransitive verbs 21
ironic understatement 158, 197
ironic writing 31
Isherwood, Christopher: Goodbye to Berlin 216–17
Italian, The (Radcliffe) 281–2
It's so over: cool cyberkids abandon social networking sites (The Guardian) 10–11

J

Johnson, Jane: Salt Road, The 220–1
journals 58
juxtaposition 215

K

Kevill-Davies, Tom: The Hungry Cyclist 94–5
King, Martin Luther: I have a dream 63–4

L

language
    Beyond the Sky and Earth: A Journey into Bhutan (Zeppa) 139–40
    Bright Lights of Sarajevo, The (Harrison) 245–56
    Chinese Cinderella (Mah) 151
    Danger of a Single Story, The (Adichie) 100
    descriptors 87
    Disabled (Owen) 230–1
    effect of 30–1, 84–7
    Explorer's Daughter, The (Herbert) 111–12
    figurative 212–15
    Game of Polo with a Headless Goat, A (Levine) 132–3
    H is for Hawk (Macdonald) 144
    Necklace, The (Maupassant) 268
    Night (Munro) 285–7
    Out, Out - (Frost) 234–6
    Passage to Africa, A (Alagiah) 107
    Between a Rock and a Hard Place (Ralston) 120–1
    Significant Cigarettes (Tremain) 273–4
    spoken matter 55
    Still I rise (Angelou) 251–5
    Story of an Hour, The (Chopin) 258–9
    Unknown Girl, An (Alvi) 240
    use of 10, 12, 16–23, 79, 154–7
    Whistle and I'll come to you (Hill) 278–82
    Young and Dyslexic? You've got it going on (Zephaniah) 126–8
Lawrence, D.H. 66–7
Lee, Laurie: Cider with Rosie 90–1
letters 65–8, 191
Levine, Emma: Game of Polo with a Headless Goat 129–33
Lines written in Early Spring (Wordsworth) 210–11
literary devices 10, 155, 169
litotes 158, 197
loose sentences 38–9
Lord of the Flies (Golding) 214–15

Love is... (Henri) 213

M

MacArthur, Ellen: Taking on the World 59–60, 157–8
Macdonald, Helen: H is for Hawk 141–6
Maddox, Lucy: Myth of the Teenager 13–15
magazine articles 58, 71–4
Mah, Adeline Yen: Chinese Cinderella 147–51
Mandela, Nelson 61
Maupassant, Guy de: Necklace, The 260–8
Mehemedinovic, Semezdin: Corpse 247–8
memoirs 108
metaphors 212, 213
minor sentences 35
monologues 300–1
Morris, Steven: Explorers, or Boys Messing About? 113–16
Mrs. Dalloway (Woolf) 223
Munro, Alice: Night 224, 283–87
Myth of the Teenager (Maddox) 13–15

N

narrative voice 152, 220–1, 289, 296–7
narratives 44
Necklace, The (Maupassant) 260–5
    exploring language 268
    understanding the text 266–7
newspaper articles 58, 71–4, 190
Night (Munro) 224, 283–7
    exploring language 285–7
    understanding the text 283–4
Night Must Fall (Williams) 288
Nineteen Eighty-Four (Orwell) 295
non-fiction writing 58–9
    exam technique 94–5
    interpretation 152–73
    see also types of non-fiction writing e.g. autobiographies
nouns 16, 17

O

obituaries 58, 61–2
objects (part of sentence) 21
Of Mice and Men (Steinbeck) 9
openings 200–1
opinions 71–4, 88–9
Orwell, George
    How the Poor Die 158–60
    Nineteen Eighty-Four 295
Out, Out– (Frost) 224–5, 232
    exploring language 234–6
    understanding the text 233–4
Owen, Wilfred
    Disabled 228–31
    Dulce et Decorum est 218–19

P

paragraphs 8–9, 44–5, 90
Passage to Africa, A (Alagiah) 70–1, 84, 103–5, 170
    exploring language 107
    understanding the text 106
pathetic fallacy 214
patterns (in writing) 86
P-E-E see Point-Evidence-Explain (P-E-E)
periodic sentences 38–9
personal pronouns 13
personification 212, 214
perspective (in writing) 78–9
persuasive writing 31, 89, 100, 181–2, 196
planning in writing 202–3, 287
plot 288, 292–3
poetry
    analysing 210–11
    assignments 320–4
    characters in 218–19
    figurative language 212–14
    structure 224–5
Point-Evidence-Explain (P-E-E) 8–9, 93, 162, 169
predicates (part of sentence) 21
prepositions 16, 17
prolepsis 223
pronouns 13, 16

proof-reading 54–5
proper nouns 17
prose
    analysing 210
    assignments 318–8
    figurative language 214–15
    structure 224
punctuation 48–51, 53, 169, 199
purpose
    imaginative writing 290, 292
    sentences 40–1
    in writing 33, 80–3, 153

Q

question marks 48, 53
questions 20, 48, 87
quotations 168–9

R

Radcliffe, Ann: Italian, The 281–2
Ralston, Aron: Between a Rock and a Hard Place 117–21
readers, engaging with 84
reference works 76–7
referends 28
relative clauses 34–5
repetition 13, 195
reports 191–2
    news 58
retrospective writing 225
reviews 74–6, 160–1, 179, 190–1
rhetorical devices 10, 13, 64, 195
rhyme schemes 245
Risk of Darkness, The (Hill) 306
Road Home, The (Tremain) see Significant Cigarettes (Tremain)
rule of three 13

S

Salt Road, The (Johnson) 220–1
scanning 4–5
semi-colons 51
senses 26
sentences
    building 34–5
    effect of 22–3, 23, 38–9, 306–7

opening 36–7
purposes 40–1
structure 42, 48–51, 53, 87, 91, 156, 198–9
types 20–1, 22, 34–41
variance 39
setting 219
Bright Lights of Sarajevo, The (Harrison) 244
Shelley, Mary: Frankenstein 226–7
short sentences 199
short stories 286, 291
Shute, Nevil 46–7
Significant Cigarettes (Tremain) 269–72
exploring language 273–4
understanding the text 273
similes 212, 213
simple sentences 20–1, 87
Simpson, Joe: Touching the Void 155–6, 163–7
skimming 4–5
Slide Rule (Shute) 46
Social websites harm children's brains (Mail Online) 11–12
Socratic circle 215
speech 285–6
and character 300–1
parts of 16–17
speech marks 49
speeches 62–4
spelling 9, 52, 53
statements 20, 87
Steinbeck, John: Of Mice and Men 9
Stewart, Stanley: In the Empire of Genghis Khan 68–70, 71
Still I rise (Angelou) 249–50
exploring language 251–5
hidden meaning 254–5
structure 252–3
understanding the text 250–1
Story of an Hour, The (Chopin) 256–7
exploring language 258–9
understanding the text 258
structure
Danger of a Single Story, The (Adichie) 101–2

Game of Polo with a Headless Goat, A (Levine) 131–2
H is for Hawk (Macdonald) 145–6
imaginative writing 288–9, 294–5
poetry 224–5
prose 224
sentences 42, 48–51, 53, 87, 91, 156, 198–9
short stories 286
Still I rise (Angelou) 252–3
Whistle and I'll come to you (Hill) 280
of writing 9, 42–7, 90–1, 156, 222–5
subjects
part of sentence 21
unseen texts 152
subordinate clauses 21, 34–5
summarising 5, 9
suspense 22–3
symbolism 215
synonyms 7, 29, 93, 194
syntax 14

T

Taking on the world (MacArthur) 59–60, 157–8
TAP it 152–3
tense, unseen texts 152
third person 220, 297
This is just to say (Williams) 32–3
time shift 222, 223, 224
Touching the Void (Simpson) 155–6, 163–7
Town Like Alice, A (Shute) 46
transactional writing 31, 174–5
exam preparation 204–7
transitive verbs 21
travel writing 68–71, 129–33
Tremain, Rose: Significant Cigarettes 269–74

U

understanding the text
Beyond the Sky and Earth: A Journey into Bhutan (Zeppa) 137
Bright Lights of Sarajevo, The (Harrison) 243–4
Chinese Cinderella (Mah) 149–50
Danger of a Single Story, The (Adichie) 99–100
Disabled (Owen) 230
Explorers, or Boys Messing About? (Morris) 115–16
Explorer's Daughter, The (Herbert) 111
Game of Polo with a Headless Goat, A (Levine) 131
H is for Hawk (Macdonald) 143–4
Necklace, The (Maupassant) 266–7
Night (Munro) 283–4
Out, Out - (Frost) 233–4
Passage to Africa, A (Alagiah) 106
Between a Rock and a Hard Place (Ralston) 119–20
Significant Cigarettes (Tremain) 273
Still I rise (Angelou) 250–1
Story of an Hour, The (Chopin) 258
Unknown Girl, An (Alvi) 238–9
Whistle and I'll come to you (Hill) 277–8
Young and Dyslexic? You've got it going on (Zephaniah) 125–6
Unknown Girl, An (Alvi) 236–7
exploring language 240
understanding the text 238–9
unseen texts 92–3, 152–3
analysing 154–7
urban legends 280–1

V

Valentine (Duffy) 213
verbs 16, 17, 21
vocabulary 9, 28–9
choosing 26–7, 30–3, 304–5, 310–11

W

Walk in the Woods, A (Bryson) 6–7
War of the Worlds, The (Wells) 303
websites 76–7
Wells, H.G.: War of the Worlds, The 303
Whistle and I'll come to you (Hill) 275–6
    exploring language 278–82
    structure 280
    understanding the text 277–8
Williams, Emlyn: Night Must Fall 288
Williams, William Carlos: This is just to say 32–3
Wind in the Willows, The (Grahame) 296
wishes 87
Woman in Black, The (Hill) see Whistle and I'll come to you (Hill)

Woolf, Virginia: Mrs. Dalloway 223
words
    arrangement 31–3
    classes 16–17
    connotations of 19
    use of 155
Wordsworth, William: Lines written in Early Spring 210–11
writing
    for effect 31
    flow 46–7
    persuasive 13
    purpose of 33, 80–3, 153
    reviewing 53–5
    structure in 9, 42–7, 90–1, 156, 222–5

Y

Young and Dyslexic? You've got it going on (Zephaniah) 122–4
    exploring language 126–8
    understanding the text 125–6

Z

Zephaniah, Benjamin: Young and Dyslexic? You've got it going on 122–8
Zeppa, Jamie: Beyond the Sky and Earth: A Journey into Bhutan 134–40

NOTES

NOTES

NOTES

NOTES

NOTES

NOTES

NOTES

NOTES

Acknowledgements

The publisher would like to thank Rebecca Watkins for her contribution of additional material.

The author and publisher would like to thank the following individuals and organisations for permission to reproduce photographs:

(Key: b-bottom; c-centre; l-left; r-right; t-top)

123RF.com: 128, 282, 309, 324c, Anouk Stricher 112, Cathy Yeulet 196, foodandmore 8, Ilker Celik 47c, instinia 52l, Jan Gorzynik 55, Le Gal Michel 32, meinzahn 15; **Emma Gannon**: 192 (inset); **Fotolia.com**: Biletskiy Evgeniy 113, chelle129 18c, christianchan 202, cook_inspire 302, Coprid 13, Deyan Georgiev 212br, Focus Pocus LTD 300r, joda 276, jovannig 45, jsco 47t, Lijuan Guo 212tr, Lukas Gojda 212tl, Martin Valigursky 212bl, martinlisner 184, NH7 236, ping han 249, ramzi hachicho 263, shock 21, skaman306 138; **Pearson Education Ltd**: Gareth Boden 34, 180, Malcolm Harris 298, Cheuk-king Lo 140l, Tudor Photography 80t; **Shutterstock.com**: 2733991 219, 192 (main), Africa Studio 52r, Aleksey Stemmer 18b, Alessia Pierdomenico 61t, AND Inc. 37, Andre Coetzer 88, Andrey Bayda 310, Antonio Abrignani 264, brackish_nz 18t, Charlotte Purdy 53t, D. Kucharski K. Kucharska 296, Diana Taliun 273, Dragon Images 47b, Elena Yakusheva 85, Ermolaev Alexander 187, ffolas 241, francesco de marco 234, Galyna Andrushko 166, Gelpi JM 53b, iDigital Art 293, iofoto 324b, LesPalenik 283, LifePhotoStudio 191, Luciano Mortula 240, magicinfoto 174, Martin Christopher Parker 38, Matthew Connolly 215, Maxisport 41, Mikadun 153, Mikhail Pogosov 81, Morphart Creation 159, PCHT 29, Reddogs 315, Regien Paassen 117, Roberto Lusso 24, Sorbis 16, Stephen Coburn 288, Suzanne Tucker 105, Thorsten Rust 208, tourdottk 56, tsyhun 72, Vinterriket 23, Vladimir Krupenkin 2, wavebreakmedia 173, Zadiraka Evgenii 257; **Alamy Images**: AF archive 280, All Canada Photos 108, Andrew Fox 275, Aurora Photos 119, blickwinkel 142, Freddie Jones 300l, Granger, NYC 256, Janice and Nolan 94, LOOK Die Bildagentur 140r, louise murray 110, Reuters 132, ZUMA Press, Inc. 283; **Getty Images**: AFP 248, Alfred Gescheidt 290, Bob Thomas/Popperfoto 27, Caroline Purser 207, China Photos/Stringer 68, Christina Reichl 216, ColorBlind Images 42, Coneyl Jay 324t, Cultura RM Exclusive/Spark Photographic 221, Dave Hogan 61b, David Levenson 97, Dmitri Kessel 225, EPA 316, Eric Schaal 232, Fotosearch 228, Harry Borden 122, Hero Images 176, Jeff Overs 103, Jessica Antola 253, Lauren Nicole 199, Marcel Mochet 59, Matthieu Paley 130, mbbirdy 306, Meiko Arquillos 304, Rick Loomis 147, Staff 157, Stringer 62, Sturti 183, Time Life Pictures 260, Ulf Anderson 269, Ute Grabowsky 99, Zigy Kaluzny-Charles 6; **The Kobal Collection**: Brighton Rock (1947), FILM Copyright © 1947 294, Film Four/Pathe 169, **Topfoto**: The Granger Collection 33.

Inside front cover: **Shutterstock.com**: *Dmitry Lobanov*

All other images © Pearson Education Limited

We are grateful to the following for permission to reproduce copyright material:

Extract on pages 6-7, from A WALK IN THE WOODS: REDISCOVERING AMERICA ON THE APPALACHIAN TRAIL by Bill Bryson, copyright © 1997 by Bill Bryson. Used by permission of Broadway Books, and an imprint of the Crown Publishing Group, a division of Penguin Random House LLC. All rights reserved; Extract on page 10 from It's SO over: cool cyberkids abandon social networking sites, http://www.theguardian.com/media/2009/aug/06/young-abandon-social-networking-sites, The Guardian, Copyright Guardian News & Media Ltd 2016; Extract on pages 11-12 from David Derbyshire, Social websites harm children's brains, http://www.dailymail.co.uk/news/article-1153583/Social-web-sites-harm-childrens-brains-Chilling-warning-parents-neuroscientist.html, MailOnline.co.uk, Daily Mail, 2009; Extract on pages 14-15 from Lucy Maddox, Myth of the teenager, Does the stroppy adolescent exist?, http://www.prospectmagazine.co.uk/life/teenagers-adolescence-lucy-maddox, March 20, 2013; Extract on page 27 from Titanic Voices: 63 Survivors Tell Their Extraordinary Stories, 1e, Amberley Publishing (Holman, H. 2011; Poetry on page 32 'This is Just to Say' by William Carlos Williams, from THE COLLECTED POEMS: VOLUME I, 1909-1939, copyright ©1938 by New Directions Publishing Corp. Reprinted by permission of New Directions Publishing Corp, also copyrighted and reprinted here by kind permission of Carcanet Press Limited, Manchester, UK; Extract on pages 59-60 from Taking on the World, by Ellen MacArthur, Michael Joseph (MacArthur, E. 2002), the permission of United Agents LLP on behalf of Ellen MacArthur (Penguin Books 2003) Copyright © Ellen MacArthur, 2003; Extract on page 63 from Martin Luther King, I Have a Dream, Washington DC, in August 1963, Reprinted by arrangement with the Heirs to the Estate of Martin Luther King Jr., c/o Writers House as agent for the proprietor New York, NY.Copyright 1963 Dr. Martin Luther King, copyright renewed 1991 Coretta Scott King; Extract on page 65 Excerpt(s) from THE DIARY OF A YOUNG GIRL: THE DEFINITIVE EDITION by Anne Frank, edited by Otto H. Frank and Mirjam Pressler, translated by Susan Massotty, (Viking, 1997) copyright © The Anne Frank-Fonds, Basle, Switzerland, 1991. English translation copyright © Doubleday a division of Bantam Doubleday Dell Publishing Group Inc, a division of Random House LLC. Used by permission of Doubleday, an imprint of the Knopf Doubleday Publishing Group. All rights reserved. Extract on page 66-67 from The Faber Book Of Letters reprinted by permission of Pollinger Limited (www.pollingerltd.com) on behalf of Cambridge University Press and The Estate of Frieda Lawrence Ravagli; Extract on page 69 from Mongolia: Telegraph Travel Book Award 2001, The Telegraph (Stewart, S.), Edited extract from The Empire of Genghis Khan: A Journey Among Nomads, Copyright Telegraph Media Group Ltd 2016; Extract on pages 70-71 from A Passage to Africa, G. Alagiah, Little, Brown Book Group, reproduced by permission of the author c/o The Hanbury Agency Ltd, 53 Lambeth Walk, London SE11 6DX. Copyright © 2001 George Alagiah. All Rights Reserved; Extract on page 72 from Mike Elgan, Social Media Addiction Is A Bigger Problem Than You Think, Computer World (The YGS Group), used with permission of Computerworld Copyright© 2016. All rights reserved; Extract on page 73 adapted from an article published in The Guardian newspaper: Are humans definitely causing global warming?, Copyright Guardian News & Media Ltd 2016; Extract on page 75 from Mark Kermode, A Review Of Star Wars: Episode vii Copyright Guardian News & Media Ltd 2016; Extract on page 76 from Vladimir Slamecka, Information processing, Acquisition and recording of information in digital form, reprinted with permission from Encyclopædia Britannica, © 2016 by Encyclopædia Britannica, Inc.; Extract on page 77 from "rap". Encyclopaedia Britannica Online. Reprinted with permission from Encyclopædia Britannica, © 2016 by Encyclopædia Britannica, Inc.; Extract on pages 90-91 From Cider with Rosie by Laurie Lee and reprinted by permission of David R. Godine, Publisher, Inc. Copyright © 1980 by Laurie Lee and reproduced with permission of Curtis Brown Group Ltd, London on behalf of the Beneficiaries of the Estate of Laurie Lee and Copyright © 1959 [Laurie Lee/1050]; Extract on pages 94-95 from The Hungry Cyclist, reprinted by permission of Harper Collins Publishers Ltd, Kevill-Davies, T.; Extract on pages 96-98 from 'The Danger of a Single Story' by Chimamanda Ngozi Adichie. Copyright © Chimamanda Ngozi Adichie 2009, used by permission of The Wylie Agency (UK) Limited.; Extract on pages 104-105 from A Passage to Africa, G. Alagiah, Little, Brown Book Group, reproduced by permission of the author c/o The Hanbury Agency Ltd, 53 Lambeth Walk, London SE11 6DX. Copyright © 2001 George Alagiah. All Rights Reserved.; Extract on pages 109-110 from The Explorer's Daughter, Penguin (Harbert, K), by permission of Aitken Alexander Associates Ltd; Extract on pages 114-115 adapted from Steven Morris, Explorers, Or Boys Messing About? Either Way, Taxpayer Gets Rescue Bill, January 28, 2003 The Guardian newspaper. Copyright Guardian

News & Media Ltd 2016; Extract on pages 118-119 from BETWEEN A ROCK AND A HARD PLACE by Aron Ralston. Copyright 2004 Aron Ralston. Reprinted with the permission of Atria, a division of Simon & Schuster, Inc. All rights reserved; Poetry on page 122 from Benjamin Zephaniah, Poem: White Comedy, permission of United Artists on behalf of Benjamin Zephaniah; Extract on pages 123-125 from Benjamin Zephaniah, Young And Dyslexic? You've Got It Going On, permission of United Artists on behalf of Benjamin Zephaniah; Extract on pages 129-131 from A Game Of Polo With A Headless Goat, by Emma Levine. Andre Deutsch/Carlton Books; Extract on pages 134-136 excerpted from 'Beyond the Sky and the Earth: A Journey into Bhutan by Jamie Zeppa. Copyright 1999 Jamie Zeppa. Used by permission of Riverhead, an imprint of Penguin Publishing Group, a division of Penguin Random House LLC. Reprinted by permission of Doubleday Canada, a division of Penguin Random House Canada Limited, and by permission of The McDermid Agency Inc.; Extract on pages 141-143 from H IS FOR HAWK by Helen Macdonald copyright © 2014 by Helen Macdonald. Published by Jonathan Cape and reprinted by permission of The Random House Group Limited, used by permission of Grove/Atlantic, Inc. Any third party use of this material, outside of this publication, is prohibited. Extract on pages 147-149 from "Chapter 21: Playwriting Competition" from CHINESE CINDERELLA: THE TRUE STORY OF AN UNWANTED DAUGHTER by Adeline Yen Mah, (Penguin 1999) copyright © 1999 by Adeline Yen Mah. Used by permission of Delacorte Press, an imprint of Random House Children's Books, a division of and Penguin Random House LLC. All rights reserved. Extract on pages 158-160 from "How the Poor Die' from THE COLLECTED ESSAYS, JOURNALISM AND LETTERS OF GEORGE ORWELL, VOLUME I: An Age Like This. Copyright 1968 by Sonia Brownell Orwell and renewed 1996 by Mark Hamilton. Reprinted by permission of Houghton Mifflin Harcourt Publishing Company. All rights reserved, The Complete Works of George Orwell by George Orwell Published by Secker & Warburg and reprinted by permission of The Random House Group Limited; Excerpt from "How the Poor Die' from THE COLLECTED ESSAYS, JOURNALISM AND LETTERS OF GEORGE ORWELL, VOLUME I: An Age Like This. Copyright 1968 by Sonia Brownell Orwell and renewed 1996 by Mark Hamilton. Reprinted by permission of Houghton Mifflin Harcourt Publishing Company. All rights reserved; Extract on pages 163-164 From Touching The Void by Joe Simpson, excerpts from pp.72-78, copyright 1989 Joe Simpson. Published by Jonathan Cape. Reprinted by permission of Harper Collins Publishers and by permission of The Random House Group Limited.; Extract on page 185 from RSPCA, 2010, reproduced with permission of the RSPCA, 2016; Poetry on page 213 from 'Love Is' from The Mersey Sound by Adrian Henri. Published by Penguin, 1967. Copyright Adrian Henri. Reproduced by permission of the Estate of Adrian Henri c/o Rogers, Coleridge & White Ltd., 20 Powis Mews, London W11 1JN; Poetry on page 213, 'Valentine' from *Mean Time* by Carol Ann Duffy. Published by Anvil Press Poetry, 1993. Copyright © Carol Ann Duffy. Reproduced by permission of the author c/o Rogers, Coleridge & White Ltd., Powis Mews, London W11 1JN; Extract on page 215 from "The Sound of the Shell", from LORD OF THE FLIES by William Golding, copyright 1954, renewed © 1982 by William Gerald Golding. Used by permission of G. P. Putnam's Sons, an imprint of Penguin Publishing Group, a division of Penguin Random House LLC. Reproduced by permission of Faber and Faber Ltd; Extract on pages 216-217 from THE BERLIN STORIES, copyright ©1935 by Christopher Isherwood. Reprinted by permission of New Directions Publishing Corp & The Wylie Agency; Extract on pages 220-221 from 'The Salt Road' by Jane Johnson. Copyright 2010 Jane Johnson. (Penguin Books 2011) Reprinted by permission of Doubleday Canada, a division of Penguin Random House Canada Ltd. Baror International Inc.; Extract on page 223 from MRS DALLOWAY by Virginia Woolf. Copyright 1925 by Houghton Mifflin Harcourt Publishing Company, and renewed 1953 by Leonard Woolf. Reprinted by permission of Houghton Mifflin Harcourt Publishing Company. All rights reserved. The Society of Authors as the Literary Representative of the Estate of Virginia Woolf; Poetry on pages 237-238 from Moniza Alvi, "An Unknown Girl" Split World: Poems 1990-2005 (Bloodaxe Books, 2008), reproduced with permission of Bloodaxe Books. www.bloodaxebooks.com; Poetry on pages 242-243 from The Bright Lights of Sarajevo, Tony Harrison, 2013, Faber and Faber Ltd; Poetry on page 247 from Semezdin Mehmedinovic, "Corpse" from Sarajevo Blues. Copyright © 1995, 1998 by Semezdin Mehmedinovic. Reprinted with the permission of The Permissions Company, Inc., on behalf of City Lights Publishers, www.citylights.com; Poetry on pages 249-250 "Still I Rise" from AND STILL I RISE by Maya Angelou, copyright © 1978 by Maya Angelou. Little Brown Book Group, used by permission of Random House, an imprint and division of Penguin Random House LLC. All rights reserved; Extract on pages 260-266 from A DAY IN THE COUNTRY: AND OTHER STORIES translated by Coward (2009) 2996w from "The Necklace" pp.168-176. By permission of Oxford University Press; Extract on pages 269-273 from The Road Home, The Random House Group (Tremain, R.) pp. 1-6, 978-0099478461, From The Road Home by Rose Tremain. Copyright 2007 by Rose Tremain. Published by Jonathan Cape. Reprinted by permission of The Random House Group Limited. Used by permission of Little, Brown and Company. Extract on pages 275-277 from The Woman in Black by Susan Hill, published by Vintage Books © Susan Hill 1983. Reproduced by permission of Sheil Land Associates Ltd.

Select glossary terms have been taken from *The Longman Dictionary of Contemporary English Online*.